KU-435-142

THE LAW OF HUMAN RIGHTS

VOLUME 2

THE LAW OF HUMAN RIGHTS

by

Richard Clayton

Barrister, Devereux Chambers, London

Hugh Tomlinson

Barrister, Matrix Chambers, London

with

Carol George

Solicitor and Lecturer in International Economic Law, London School of Economics

and with the assistance of

Vina Shukla

Barrister, 4 Stone Buildings, London

UNIVERSITY PRESS

OXFORD
UNIVERSITY PRESS

Great Clarendon Street, Oxford OX2 6DP

Oxford University Press is a department of the University of Oxford.
It furthers the University's objective of excellence in research, scholarship,
and education by publishing worldwide in

Oxford New York

Athens Auckland Bangkok Bogotá Buenos Aires Calcutta
Cape Town Chennai Dar es Salaam Delhi Florence Hong Kong Istanbul
Karachi Kuala Lumpur Madrid Melbourne Mexico City Mumbai
Nairobi Paris São Paulo Shanghai Singapore Taipei Tokyo Toronto Warsaw

with associated companies in Berlin Ibadan

Oxford is a registered trade mark of Oxford University Press
in the UK and in certain other countries

Published in the United States
by Oxford University Press Inc., New York

First published 2000

British Library Cataloguing in Publication Data
Data available

Library of Congress Cataloging in Publication Data
Data available

ISBN 0–19–826223–X (set)

ISBN 0–19–924360–3 (Vol. 1)

ISBN 0–19–924361–1 (Vol. 2)

3 5 7 9 10 8 6 4 2

Typeset in Garamond by
Cambrian Typesetters, Frimley, Surrey

Printed in Great Britain
on acid-free paper by
The Bath Press, Bath

VOLUME 2—CONTENTS

Note on Materials vii

Table of Admissible United Kingdom Cases before the European Court of Human Rights xix

APPENDICES

United Kingdom Materials

A. Human Rights Act 1998 1
B. Rights Brought Home: The Human Rights Bill (1997) Cm 3782 23
C. Rules of Court and Practice Directions under the Human Rights Act 37
D. Practice Direction: Devolution Issues (and Crown Office applications in Wales) 43

European Materials

E. Convention for the Protection of Human Rights and Fundamental Freedoms, with Protocols 55
F. European Court of Human Rights: Rules of Court 77
G. European Social Charter 1961 107

United Nations Materials

H. Universal Declaration of Human Rights 1948 127
I. Convention Relating to the Status of Refugees 1951 131
J. International Convenant on Civil and Political Rights 1966 143
K. International Covenant on Economic, Social and Cultural Rights 1966 159
L. International Convention on the Elimination of All Forms of Racial Discrimination 1966 167
M. Convention on the Elimination of All Forms of Discrimination against Women 1979 177
N. Convention on the Rights of the Child 1989 185

Domestic Bills of Rights

O. Canadian Charter of Rights and Freedoms (Part I, Constitution Act 1982) 199
P. Constitution of India (Part III, Fundamental Rights, Arts 12–35) 205

Q. Irish Constitution (Chapter XII, Fundamental Rights, Arts 40–44) 215
R. New Zealand Bill of Rights Act 1990 219
S. Constitution of the Republic of South Africa 1996 (Chapter 2, Bill of Rights, ss 7–39) 225
T. Constitution of United States of America: Bill of Rights and Thirteenth to Fifteenth Amendments 235
U. Constitution of Zimbabwe (Chapter III, Declaration of Rights, ss 11–26) 239

Select Bibliography 255

NOTE ON MATERIALS

(1) Introduction

There is now a huge volume of international human rights treaties, conventions, resolutions and case law. Any full survey of this would now be of book length. In writing this book we have drawn primarily on English, European and Commonwealth materials. In this section we deal with the places where the primary materials and case law can be found and with the textbooks which we have found useful. We have not sought to be comprehensive and many useful sources have been omitted for reasons of space. We have also provided a guide to the increasing human rights resources available on the Internet. The speed of growth of this medium means that the information in this part of the Note is likely to be out of date very quickly.

(2) Treaties and conventions

A number of treaties, conventions and related documents on human rights can be found in the Appendix to this book. Fuller selections are contained in our *Human Rights Handbook*[1] in Ian Brownlie's, *Basic Documents on Human Rights*[2] and Rebecca Wallace's, *International Human Rights Law: Text and Materials*.[3] More comprehensive collections of international and national human rights documents and materials can be found on the Internet.[4]

(3) Case law

European Convention Series

The jurisprudence of the Convention is found in the Official Reports. *Series A* contains the official report of all the judgments of the European Court of Human Rights up to 1995, along with the Commission Report on merits. *Series B* contains the pleadings and documents submitted by the parties. Cases up to November 1995 are referred to by an 'A Series number'. From 1996 onwards, the Court's Judgments have been reported in *Reports of Judgments and Decisions* ('RJD').

---

1 R Clayton, H Tomlinson, and V Shukla, *Human Rights Handbook* (Hart Publishing, 2000).
2 3rd edn, Clarendon Press, 1992.
3 Sweet & Maxwell, 1997.
4 See Section 5 of this Note, 'Web sites', below.

The Commission's admissibility decisions before 1975 were published in a series known as *Collection of Decisions* ('Coll').[5] Early decisions are also reported in the *Yearbook of European Convention on Human Rights* ('YB'). From 1975 onwards, Commission decisions are to be found in the Decisions and Reports ('DR'). This contains selected admissibility decisions, reports of friendly settlements and decisions of the Committee of Ministers. There are consolidated index volumes.[6]

For the English lawyer, the most easily available source of case law is the *European Human Rights Reports* ('EHRR') published by Sweet & Maxwell. The first volume was published in 1979–1980 and contained all 36 cases decided by the Court up to that date. There are at present 28 volumes including until recently, most substantive cases in the Court and a selection of Commission cases which, in recent years, have been in separate sections at the back of each volume. There is a time delay of about 12 months between a judgment being given and its inclusion in the EHRR. Each volume has an index of the Court cases reported to date. There is, however, no comparable index for Commission materials in the EHRR.

General human rights series

The most useful general series is the *Law Reports of the Commonwealth* ('LRC') which began publication in 1985 and is now published by Butterworths. The series initially comprised separate volumes for Commercial, Criminal and Constitutional/Administrative cases. From 1993 there have been three or four volumes published annually covering all types of cases. This series is a valuable resource for Commonwealth case law and contains many of the important cases from Australia, Canada, India, New Zealand and South Africa as well as from Caribbean jurisdictions, Africa and Asia. There is an index volume covering the period 1980–1997 and annual indices thereafter.

The series is partially complemented by *Butterworths Human Rights Cases* ('BHRC') which have been published by Butterworths since 1997. Volume 7 was published in Spring 2000. These volumes include cases from all round the world and are a convenient source of important recent judgments from Canada and the United States. The reports also include a few leading European Court of Human Rights cases which are reported more quickly than in the EHRR. The wide range of the series means, however, that it is highly selective. There is, at present, no comprehensive index.

[5] This was roneoed and is now out of print.

[6] 1–20, 21–40, 41–60, 61–75, 76–83.

Individual country series

United Kingdom

Two new series of human rights reports devoted to the United Kingdom commenced publication in Spring 2000: *Human Rights Law Reports—UK Cases* published by Sweet & Maxwell and *UK Human Rights Reports* published by Jordans. These will provide full text reports of English and Scottish cases on human rights issues. The *Crown Office Digest* ('COD') will have enhanced coverage of human rights cases after October 2000. It will provide digests of the large number of cases which are likely to be dealt with in the Crown Office List.

Other jurisdictions

In relation to other individual jurisdictions, reference can be made to the official law reports such as the *Supreme Court Reports* ('SCR') in Canada, the *Commonwealth Law Reports* ('CLR') in Australia and the *New Zealand Law Reports* ('NZLR'). Three specific series of reports dealing with human rights and constitutional issues should also be mentioned:

> *The Canadian Charter of Rights: Annotated*[7] is a five volume looseleaf providing short digests of almost all Canadian Charter cases.
>
> *Human Rights Reports of New Zealand* ('HRNZ'),[8] four volumes of which have been published to date. This provides a comprehensive set of well indexed and headnoted reports on New Zealand Bill of Rights Act issues.
>
> *Butterworths Constitutional Law Reports* ('BCLR')[9] provides full text reports of the decisions of the Southern African Courts[10] on constitutional issues. It is published in monthly parts and is also available on CD-ROM.

(4) Textbooks

European Convention on Human Rights

The practitioner is well served by textbooks dealing with the Strasbourg jurisprudence under the European Convention on Human Rights. Many of the books have been written or co-written by Judges of the Court, members of the Commission or of the Secretariat. Two recent books stand out. The comprehensive textbook, *The Law of the European Convention on Human Rights*[11] by Harris, O'Boyle and Warbrick is unfailingly accurate and thought provoking. The

[7] Canada Law Book.
[8] Brookers.
[9] Butterworths South Africa.
[10] South Africa, Lesotho, Namibia and Zimbabwe.
[11] Butterworths, 1995, a new edition is due in 2000.

perspective of the Dutch authors of van Dijk and van Hoof's *Theory and Practice of the European Convention on Human Rights*[12] is slightly different but the book is no less thorough. Both books are indispensable for the consideration of any difficult Convention issue and recent writers on the subject have been indebted to them. *The European System for the Protection of Human Rights*[13] edited by Macdonald, Matscher and Petzold contains essays on every aspect of the Convention by what is perhaps the most distinguished and experienced body of commentators ever assembled in this area.

The recent editions of three pioneering textbooks also repay study:

> *The Application of the European Convention on Human Rights*[14] by Fawcett was published more than a decade ago but remains stimulating.
>
> *Human Rights in Europe: A Study of the European Convention on Human Rights* by Robertson and Merrills[15] was first published in 1963 by an author of unrivalled knowledge of the background to the Convention and provides valuable insights into its history.
>
> *The European Convention on Human Rights* by Jacobs and White[16] was first published in 1975 and is a careful summary of the principal strands in the Court's case law.

Mention should also be made of three other recent books devoted to the Convention:

> *A Practitioner's Guide to the European Convention on Human Rights*[17] by Karen Reid, a member of the Secretariat of the former Commission of Human Rights, summarises the Convention case law under a number of 'problem areas' which is particularly useful for practitioners. It also contains Tables of Court decisions on just satisfaction.
>
> *European Human Rights: Taking a Case under the Convention*[18] by Luke Clements, Nuala Mole and Alan Simmons is an exhaustive practical guide to bringing a claim in Strasbourg along with precedents. It is essential reading for anyone bringing such a claim for the first time.
>
> *La Convention Europééne des Droits de L'Homme*, edited by Louis-Edmond Pettiti, Emmanuel Decaix and Pierre-Henri Imbert[19] is a full article-by-article

[12] 3rd edn, Kluwer Law, 1998.
[13] Nijhoff, 1993.
[14] 2nd edn, Clarendon Press, 1987.
[15] 3rd edn, Manchester University Press, 1993.
[16] 2nd edn, Clarendon Press, 1996.
[17] Sweet & Maxwell, 1998.
[18] 2nd edn, Sweet & Maxwell, 1999.
[19] 2nd edn, Economica, 1999.

commentary on the Convention written by members of the Court and the Commission.

Finally, we draw attention to three useful casebooks:

The UK Before the European Court of Human Rights[20] edited by Sue Farran provides article-by-article extracts and commentary on the UK case law which helpfully puts the decisions in context.

Leading Cases of the European Court of Human Rights[21] is edited by R A Lawson and F G Schermers (who was a distinguished member of the Commission for 15 years). It contains 58 judgments of the Court of Human Rights with a penetrating commentary. It is the best place to begin for a person wishing to become familiar with Convention reasoning.

A Systematic Guide to the Case-Law of the European Court of Human Rights, Vols I–II (1960–1994) and Vol III (1995–1996)[22] by Peter Kempees contains extracts from judgments of the Court on the issues arising under each article of the Convention.

It should also be noted that very full discussions of the Convention case law are provided in several of the textbooks on the Human Rights Act which have been published over the past two years. These are dealt with in the next section.

Human Rights Act

A number of textbooks on the Human Rights Act have been published over the past two years. Some of these are general works dealing with the Act and the Convention but not with 'impact issues'. A number of others have sought to deal with the impact of the Act in specific areas of law and more generally.

In the first category, particular attention is drawn to five books:

The Human Rights Act 1998: Enforcing the European Convention in the Domestic Courts[23] by Jason Coppel was the first book to be published on the Act. It provides thorough coverage of the Act and the Convention and benefits from some useful cross-reference to the New Zealand case law.

Blackstone's Guide to the Human Rights Act 1998[24] by John Wadham and Helen Mountfield is the best short guide to the Act. The book includes copies of the relevant material, in particular, extracts from the Parliamentary Debates on the Human Rights Bill.

20 Blackstone Press, 1996.
21 Ars Aequi Libri, 1997.
22 Nijhoff, 1996 and 1998.
23 John Wiley & Sons, 1999.
24 Blackstone Press, 1999.

Human Rights Law and Practice[25] edited by Lord Lester and David Pannick with 13 specialist contributors is an authoritative and substantial work, providing a commentary on the Human Rights Act, an article-by-article commentary on the Convention and discussions of Scotland, Northern Ireland, Wales and International Codes.

European Human Rights Law[26] by Keir Starmer is a detailed treatment of the Act and the Convention. Convention principles are dealt with on a subject, rather than an article-by-article basis and the case law is set out with great clarity.

Human Rights: The 1998 Act and the European Convention[27] by Stephen Grosz, Jack Beatson and Peter Duffy provides thoughtful analysis of the Act and the Convention.

In the second category, books have been published in the following subject areas:

Criminal law: *Criminal Justice and the Human Rights Act 1998*[28] by Cheney, Dickson, Fitzpatrick and Uglow provides a helpful overview of the potential impact of the Act in this important area. *The Human Rights Act and the Criminal Justice and Regulatory Process*[29] edited by Beatson, Forsyth and Hare is based on papers given at a conference of the Cambridge Centre for Public Law in 1999 and contains some penetrating discussions on criminal law and practice and on regulation of financial services.

Family law: *Family Law and the Human Rights Act 1998*[30] by Swindells, Neaves, Kushner and Skilbeck provides a very useful discussion of the potential impact of the Act across the full range of family law issues along with a series of case summaries. *Rayden and Jackson on Divorce and Family Matters: The Human Rights Act 1998—A Special Bulletin for Family Lawyers*[31] by Horowitz, Kingscote and Nicholls also provides helpful guidance for family lawyers on the implications of the Act.

Local authority law: Supperstone, Goudie and Coppel, *Local Authorities and the Human Rights Act 1998*[32] deals with the potential impact of the Act across the whole range of local authority services.

Immigration and asylum law: *Immigration, Nationality and Asylum Under the*

[25] Butterworths, 1999.
[26] Legal Action Group, 1999.
[27] Sweet & Maxwell, 2000.
[28] Jordans, 1999.
[29] Hart Publishing, 1999.
[30] Family Law, 1999.
[31] Butterworths, 1999.
[32] Butterworths, 1999.

Human Rights Act 1998[33] edited by Blake and Fransman is a collection of papers given at a conference to consider the impact of the Act in this important area and provides a useful guide.

Five books have sought to deal with the potential impact of the Human Rights Act more generally:

The Impact of the Human Rights Bill on English Law[34] edited by Basil Markesinis contains the lectures given at a 1998 conference. It contains a number of important and incisive articles concerning the potential impact of the Act in different areas of law.

The Human Rights Act 1998: A Practitioners Guide[35] edited by Christopher Baker was an early and bold attempt to cover the Act and its impact across a wide range of areas including criminal justice, immigration and asylum, family, housing, planning, education, social security, employment and tax law.

The Human Rights Act 1998 What it Means[36] edited by Lammy Betten contains the proceedings of a conference on this topic held in 1998 at the Exeter Centre for European Legal Studies. It contains a number of contributions oriented to property and commercial issues.

The Civil Practitioners Guide to the Human Rights Act 1998[37] by Wendy Outhwaite and Marina Wheeler is a short and reflective book which covers a lot of ground.

The Essential Human Rights Act 1998, Wilberforce Chambers,[37a] is a stimulating examination of various topics including landlord and tenant, trusts, tax and financial services.

United Kingdom

Special mention should be made of a pioneering work which continues to be indispensable for anyone concerned with the law of human rights. *The Three Pillars of Liberty: Political Rights and Freedoms in the United Kingdom*[38] by Francesa Klug, Keir Starmer and Stuart Weir forms part of a project which seeks to audit the quality of democracy and political freedom in the United Kingdom. It seeks to carry out an audit of political rights and freedoms, comparing the United Kingdom to international human rights standards. It gives a wealth of materials on both domestic and international law and is an essential point of reference.

33 Butterworths, 1999.
34 Oxford University Press, 1998.
35 Sweet & Maxwell, 1998.
36 Kluwer Law, 1999.
37 Old Bailey Press, 1999.
37a Wilberforce Chambers, 2000.
38 Routledge, 1996.

As was mentioned in the Introduction[39] civil liberties and human rights have only recently become discrete areas of study and practice for English lawyers. Civil liberties has a slightly longer history. The *Halsbury's Laws* Volume on *Constitutional Law and Human Rights*,[40] is a necessary point of departure, providing a concise and reliable guide to the area, dealing with both domestic human rights law and with the Convention.

In addition, we draw attention to the following:

Civil Liberties: Cases and Materials[41] edited by Bailey, Harris and Jones is a rich collection providing insights into areas not covered by legal textbooks.

Civil Liberties and Human Rights in England and Wales[42] by David Feldman is a seminal work which consistently illuminates the areas discussed.

Civil Liberties[43] by Helen Fenwick was one of the first all embracing student textbooks in this field. It is valuable and thought provoking.

Outside the field of the Human Rights Act, the first and most important work on human rights in English law is Murray Hunt's *Using Human Rights Law in the English Courts*.[44] Its careful and nuanced analysis of the way in which domestic courts should approach international human rights law has not been superseded by the Act; and it will remain a vital first point of reference when considering the impact of unincorporated treaties and conventions.

United States

The literature on the Constitutional Law of the United States is immense. We have made use of four recent textbooks. Abraham and Perry's *Freedom and the Court: Civil Rights and Liberties in the United States*[45] deals with civil rights and liberties in the United States from the historian's perspective and is a useful introduction to the debates for the reader unfamiliar with US legal and political history. Antieau and Rich, *Modern Constitutional Law*[46] is a clear and comprehensive textbook dealing with the main issues. We have also found Nowak and Rotunda's *Constitutional Law*[47] to be of considerable assistance. Laurence Tribe's powerful and closely argued *American Constitutional Law*[48] grapples with many issues

[39] See para In.04ff.
[40] Vol 8(2), (4th edn Reissue, Butterworths, 1996), also published separately.
[41] 4th edn, Butterworths, 1995.
[42] Clarendon Press, 1993; 2nd edn due, 2001.
[43] 2nd edn, Cavendish Publishing, 1998.
[44] Hart Publishing, 1997.
[45] 7th edn, Oxford University Press, 1998.
[46] Vols 1 to 3 (2nd edn, West Group, 1997).
[47] 5th edn, West Group, 1995.
[48] 2nd edn, Foundation Press, 1988; Vol 1 of 3rd edn, Foundation Press, 1998.

which are likely to exercise the English courts in due course. The second volume of the Third Edition is eagerly awaited. Special mention should also be made of *The Constitutional Rights of Prisoners*[49] by Palmer and Palmer which provides comprehensive coverage of the Constitutional issues which arise in the prison system.

Other textbooks

Constitutional textbooks have been written in many Commonwealth jurisdictions. These almost always contain a discussion of the law of human rights. We would draw particular attention to the following:

Australia: The recent book by George Williams, *Human Rights Under the Australian Constitution*[50] is the first attempt to provide a comprehensive analysis of this topic in one of the few jurisdictions without a 'bill of rights'. Human rights are also dealt with in Peter Hanks, *Constitutional Law in Australia.*[51]

Canada: The most impressive work on the Canadian Charter remains Peter Hogg's, *Constitutional Law of Canada*[52] now in its Fourth Edition. In relation to the criminal law, Don Stuart's 1991 *Charter Justice in Canadian Criminal Law*[53] provides very useful material. The law of remedies is comprehensively covered in Kent Roach, *Constitutional Remedies in Canada.*[54]

Caribbean: Margaret Demerieux's book *Fundamental Rights in Commonwealth Caribbean Constitutions*[55] deserves to be better known. It deals carefully and insightfully with the different rights as they appear in the Convention influenced constitutions of Commonwealth Caribbean states.

India: The comprehensive work of H M Seervai, *Constitutional Law of India*[56] is engagingly eccentric but remains thought provoking in surprising places.

Ireland: The classic *The Irish Constitution*[57] is now in its third edition and is an invaluable source of material from the common law jurisdiction with the closest historical links with England and Wales.

New Zealand: The 1995 collection of essays, *Rights and Freedoms: The New Zealand Bill of Rights Act 1990 and the Human Rights Act 1993*[58] edited by

[49] 6th edn, Anderson Publishing, 1999.
[50] Oxford University Press, 1999.
[51] 2nd edn, Butterworths, 1996.
[52] 4th edn, Carswell, 1997.
[53] Carswell, 1991.
[54] Canada Law Book, 1999.
[55] Faculty of Law Library, University of West Indies, 1992.
[56] Vols 1 to 3, (4th edn, N M Tripathi, 1991–1996).
[57] 3rd edn by G Hogan and G Whyte, Butterworths, 1994.
[58] Brookers, 1995.

Huscroft and Rishworth provides a helpful introduction to the issues which have arisen in New Zealand.

South Africa: A team of 27 practitioner authors have produced the comprehensive looseleaf *Constitutional Law of South Africa*[59] which is a model for any textbook of its kind.

There are a number of books which deal with Human Rights from an international perspective. The first is a work which remains hugely important in this field, Paul Sieghart's seminal *The International Law of Human Rights*[60] which surveys the human rights treaties, conventions and case law in relation to each specific 'right'. The work of the Human Rights Committee in relation to eight Articles of the International Covenant on Civil and Political Rights is covered in McGoldrick's book on *The Human Rights Committee*,[61] and in a helpful series of essays in *The International Covenant on Civil and Political Rights and United Kingdom Law*[62] edited by David Harris and Sarah Joseph. The right to individual petition[63] is comprehensively covered in Ghandi's *The Human Rights Committee and the Right of Individual Communication: Law and Practice.*[64] Finally, the Project on International Courts and Tribunal's indispensable reference work, *Manual on International Courts and Tribunals*[65] has a section on international human rights bodies, covering the practical and procedural issues of making applications.

(5) **Web sites**

Several web sites provide free access to human rights cases from around the world. The most important of these for present purposes is the European Court of Human Rights Home Page (*www.echr.coe.int*). This provides access to the latest decisions of the European Court of Human Rights, on the day the judgments are given. The database includes all decisions of the Court and all decisions of the Commission and Committee of Ministers going back to the early 1980s. There is a powerful search engine, although it can sometimes be slow and it is best to conduct searches for titles of cases, application numbers or Articles rather than full word searches.

Only limited free access to full texts of judgments in the courts of England and Wales can be obtained at present. A full list of what is available is to be found on the extremely useful Lawonline: law on the internet in England and around the world (*www.lol.cc/welcome.htm*). However, the position is about to change

59 M Chaskalson, J Kentridge, J Klaaren, G Marcus, D Spitz, S Woolman (eds) (Juta, 1999).
60 Clarendon Press, 1983.
61 1996 updated edition, Clarendon Press.
62 Clarendon Press, 1995.
63 Which may soon be available to UK citizens.
64 Dartmouth, 1998.
65 P Sands, R Mackenzie and Y Shany (eds) (Butterworths, 2000).

following the creation of the Australian inspired British and Irish Legal Information Institute ('BAILII'). Its rapidly expanding website (*www.bailii.org*) contains full text reports from a number of English and Irish courts.

Access can be obtained to the full text of judgments from other jurisdictions as follows:

Australia: This is the best served country in the world, with both AUSTLII (*www.austlii.edu.au*) and Scaleplus (*www.scaleplus.law.gov.au*) providing access to a full database of High Court decisions, with a large amount of Federal and State material as well. There is a comprehensive search facility.

Canada: Decisions of the Supreme Court from 1989 are available on the Supreme Court of Canada web site (*www.lexam.umontreal.ca/csc-scc/en/index.html*). The site includes the volumes of the SCR from [1989] 1 SCR onwards and recent judgments, and is fully searchable.

India: Only a limited number of recent Supreme Court decisions are available on line (*www.supremecourtonline.com*).

New Zealand: A searchable database of Court of Appeal judgments from November 1995 can be found at the Brookers site (*www.brookers.co.nz*). Recent Court of Appeal judgments can also be found on AUSTLII (*www.austlii.edu.au/nz/cases/NZCA*).

Scotland: The decisions of the Scottish courts from September 1998 (*www.scotcourts.gov.uk/index1.htm*).

South Africa: Judgments of the Constitutional Court and related materials (*www.law.wits.ac.za/lawrepal.html*)

United States: The decisions of the US Supreme Court can be found in a number of places including FindLaw (*www.findlaw.com/casecode/supreme.html*) and on the Cornell University Supreme Court Collection site (*www.supct.law.cornell.edu/supct*). A good starting point for other US courts is the Cornell University Legal Information Institute site (*www.law.cornell.edu*).

A comprehensive collection of international human rights documents and materials can be found on the University of Minnesota Human Rights Library Website (*www1.umn.edu/humanrts*) which contains more than 6,000 documents in 26 categories including prevention of discrimination, women's rights, slavery, rights of prisoners and detainees, protection from torture, human rights in the administration of justice, rights of the child, freedom of association, employment and forced labour, marriage, education, freedom of information, refugees and freedom of movement and war crimes. Finally, many national constitutions can be found on the University of Wurzburg site dealing with International Constitutional Law (*www.uni-wuerzburg.de/law/index.html*).

TABLE OF ADMISSIBLE UNITED KINGDOM CASES BEFORE THE EUROPEAN COURT OF HUMAN RIGHTS TO 30 JUNE 2000

Date	Reference	Applicant	Articles	Summary	Court's Finding	Comments
21/02/75	A18 (1975) 1 EHRR 524	*Golder*	6(1), 8	Prisoner refused access to a solicitor to institute proceedings. Claim based on implied right of access to court.	Violation of 6(1) and 8	Finding of breach was sufficient compensation for non-pecuniary damage Res. No: (1976) 35 Action: Prison Rules Amended
07/12/76	A24 (1976) 1 EHRR 737	*Handyside*	10, 14, P1(1)	The applicant published *Little Red Schoolbook* and was convicted of an offence under the Obscene Publications Act 1959.	No violation of 10, 14, P1(1)	
18/01/78	A25 (1978) 2 EHRR 25	*Ireland*	3, 5	Interrogation techniques introduced in Northern Ireland in 1971 including 'hooding' of suspects.	Violation of 3 No violation of 5	Res. No: (1978) 35 Action: UK undertook not to use the techniques
25/04/78	A26 (1978) 2 EHRR 1	*Tyrer*	3	Use of birch on juvenile offenders in the Isle of Man.	Violation of 3	Res No: (1978) 39 Action: Executive Council gave undertaking to stop corporal punishment
26/05/79	A30 (1979) 2 EHRR 245	*Sunday Times*	10	Finding of contempt of court made against *Sunday Times* as a result of its reporting of ongoing Thalidomide litigation.	Violation of 10	Just satisfaction, costs and expenses award on 06/11/80, A38 Res No: DH(1981) 2 Action: Contempt of Court Act 1981
03/08/81	A44 (1981) 4 EHRR 38	*Young, James, and Webster*	11	Dismissal of workers for refusing to join a trade union closed shop.	Violation of 11	Just satisfaction judgment on 18/10/82, A55 Res No: DH(83) 2 Action: Mental Health (Amendment) Act

Date	Reference	Applicant	Articles	Summary	Court's Finding	Comments
22/10/81	A45 (1981) 4 EHRR 149	*Dudgeon*	8	Failure to decriminalise private homosexual acts in Northern Ireland.	Violation of 8	Just satisfaction judgment on 24/02/83, A59 Res No: DH(1983) 13 Action: Homesexual activity decriminalised
05/11/81	A46 (1981) 4 EHRR 188	*X*	5(1), 5(4)	Home Secretary's wide discretionary powers to decide whether or not mentally disordered offenders should be discharged from detention.	Violation of 5(4) No violation of 5(1)	Just satisfaction judgment on 18/10/82, A55 Action: Mental Health Tribunals established to review detention
25/02/82	A48 (1982) 4 EHRR 293	*Campbell and Cosans*	3, P1(2)	Parents of two children subject to corporal punishment in state schools complained it was contrary to their beliefs about how children should be educated.	Violation of P1(2) No violation of 3	Just satisfaction judgment on 22/03/83, A60 Res No: DH(1987) 9 Action: The Education (No 2) Act prohibited corporal punishment in state schools
25/03/83	A61 (1983) 5 EHRR 347	*Silver and Others*	6(1), 8, 13	Prisoners refused access to a solicitor, censorship of correspondence, 'prior ventilation' rule in relation to handling of complaints (internal settlement had to be sought first).	Violation of 6(1), 8, 13	Just satisfaction judgment on 24/10/83, A67 Res No: DH(1985) 15 Action: Prison Standing Orders amended 1982
28/06/84	A80 (1984) 7 EHRR 165	*Campbell and Fell*	6(1), 8, 13	Refusal of legal representation in prisoners' disciplinary proceedings, no privacy for solicitor's prison visit.	Violation of 6(1), 8, 13	Res. No: DH(1986) 7 Action: Regulations amended and procedure changed, incl. right to publicly funded legal representative

02/08/84	A82 (1984) 7 EHRR 14	*Malone*	8	Non statutory regime for telephone tapping in United Kingdom.	Violation of 8	Friendly settlement on 26/04/85, A95 Res No: DH(1986) 1 Action: Interception Of Communications Act 1985
28/05/85	A93 (1985) 7 EHRR 528	*Ashingdane*	5(4), 6	Failure to transport a mentally handicapped applicant from Broadmoor to a local psychiatric hospital due to industrial action. Immunity under the Mental Health Act 1959.	No violation of 5(4) or 6	
28/05/85	A94 (1985) 7 EHRR 471	*Abdulaziz, Cabales and Balkandali*	3, 8, 13, 14	Immigration rule preventing non-British husbands from joining their wives although wives could join husbands.	Violation of 8, 13, 14 No violation of 3	Res No: DH(1986) 2 Action: Immigration Rules amended so that both husbands and wives refused entry
21/02/86	A98 (1986) 8 EHRR 123	*James*	6,13,14, Prot 1, Art 1	Leasehold reform legislation requiring owners to sell freehold to tenants.	No violation	
08/07/86	A102 (1986) 8 EHRR 329	*Lithgow*	6(1), 13, 14, Prot 1, Art 1	Shareholders in a shipbuilding claimed that they had not received fair compensation following nationalisation.	No violation	
17/10/86	A106 (1986) 9 EHRR 56	*Rees*	8, 12	Refusal to alter the sex of a transsexual on the register of births. Prohibition against marriage of transsexuals.	No violation of 8 or 12	
24/11/86	A109 (1986) 11 EHRR 335	*Gillow*	6, 8, 14	Refusal by Guernsey authorities to allow applicants to occupy their house on the island because they no longer had a residence qualification.	Violation of Art 8 No violation of 6, 14	Just satisfaction judgment on 14/09/87, A124-C Res No: DH(1988) 2 Non-pecuniary damage £10,000

Date	Reference	Applicant	Articles	Summary	Court's Finding	Comments
02/03/87	A114 (1987) 10 EHRR 293	*Weeks*	5(1), 5(4)	Refusal of parole by Home Secretary to mentally disordered offenders serving life sentences.	Violation of 5(4) No violation of 5(1)	Just satisfaction judgment on 05/10/88, A145-A Res No: DH(1989) 18 CA jurispr.: unlikely to recur
02/03/87	A115 (1987) 10 EHRR 205	*Monnell and Morris*	5(1), 6, 14	On the refusal of application for leave to appeal in criminal cases court ordered that part of time spent in custody should not count towards the sentence. Application heard in private without oral hearing.	No violation	
08/07/87	A120 and A121 (1987) 10 EHRR 29, 74, 82, 87 95	*O,H,W,B,R*	6 and 8	Children taken into public care, parents denied contact and prevented from involvement in decisions. No right to independent review of the decisions.	Violation of 6(1), 8	Just satisfaction judgment on 09/06/88, A136-A-E Res No: DH(1990) 3/4/5/6 Action: New code of practice—Children Act 1989
27/04/88	A131 (1988) 10 EHRR 425	*Boyle and Rice*	8, 13	Restricting a prisoner's right to legal advice and reading of prisoner's letters.	Violation of 8 No violation of 13	Res No: DH(1988) 17 Action: UK undertook to apply rules properly in future
29/11/88	A145-B (1988) 11 EHRR 117	*Brogan and Others*	5(1), 5(3), 5(4), 5(5)	Detention for 7 days under the Prevention of Terrorism Act 1984.	Violation of 5(3), 5(5) No violation of 5(1), 5(4)	Just satisfaction judgment on 30/05/89, A152-B Res No: DH(1990) 23 Action: UK lodged derogation
30/03/89	A152 (1989) 12 EHRR 1	*Chappell*	8	Complaint concerning an Anton Piller Orders (now seizure orders).	No violation	
07/07/89	A161 (1989) 11 EHRR 439	*Soering*	3, 6, 13	Proposed extradition of a German national to USA on murder charges where he faced the death penalty.	Violation of 3 No violation of 6, 13	DH(1990) 8 Action: US Government undertook that S would not be subject to death penalty

07/07/89	A160 (1989) 12 EHRR 36	*Gaskin*	8, 10	Refusal to disclose social services files relating to applicant's time in local authority care.	Violation of 8 No violation of 10	Action: Legislation introduced
21/02/90	A172 (1990) 12 EHRR 355	*Powell and Rayner*	8, 13	Applicants living near Heathrow complained about excessive aircraft noise.	No violation of 8, 13	
28/03/90	A174 (1990) 12 EHRR 469	*Granger*	6	Refusal of legal aid in an appeal for appeal against conviction for perjury.	Violation of 6	Res No: DH(1991) 29 Action: Scottish legal aid system reformed
30/08/90	A182 (1990) 13 EHRR 157	*Fox, Campbell and Hartley*	5(1)	Detention under Northern Ireland (Emergency Powers)Act 1978 for periods of 30 to 44 hours.	Violation of 5(1)	Just satisfaction judgment on 27/03/91, A190-B Res No: DH(1991) 39 Action: Legislation amended
30/08/90	A183 (1990) 13 EHRR 596	*McCallum*	8	Denial of access to a solicitor and censorship of prisoner's correspondence.	Violation of 8	Res No: DH(1990) 38 Action: Prisons (Scotland) Standing Orders amended
27/09/90	A184 (1990) 13 EHRR 622	*Cossey*	8, 12	Refusal to alter the sex of a transsexual on the register of births. Prohibition against marriage between transsexuals.	No violation of 8, 12	
25/10/90	A190-A (1990) 13 EHRR 666	*Thynne, Wilson and Gunnell*	5(4)	Lawfulness of detention following release on licence.	Violation of 5(4)	Res No: DH(1992) 24 Action: Criminal Justice Act 1991 amended parole rules.
30/10/91	A215 (1991) 14 EHRR 248	*Vilvarajah and Others*	3, 13	Expulsion of Tamil refugees to Cyprus.	No violation of 3, 13	
26/11/91	A216 (1991) 14 EHRR 153	*Observer and Guardian*	10	Injunction preventing publication of extracts from *Spycatcher* in the press.	Violation of 10	Res No: DH(1992) 17 Compensation paid: £100,000
26/11/91	A217 (1991) 14 EHRR 229	*Sunday Times (2)*	10	Contempt proceedings arising out of *Spycatcher* which decided that the injunction against named newspapers bound other newspapers.	Violation of 10	Res No: DH(1992) 18 Compensation paid: £100,000

Date	Reference	Applicant	Articles	Summary	Court's Finding	Comments
25/03/92	A233 (1992) 15 EHRR 137	*Campbell*	8	Interference with prisoner's correspondence.	Violation of 8	Res No: DH(1993) 5 Action: Issued Circular detailing procedure to be followed.
29/10/92	A247-A (1992) 17 EHRR 238	*Y*	3, 8	Corporal punishment of a 15 year old pupil at a private school—applicant caned 4 times across clothed buttocks.	Friendly settlement	Res No: DH(1992) 63 Government agreed to pay £8,000 plus costs
16/12/92	A247-B (1992) 15 EHRR 417	*Edwards*	6	Non-disclosure of evidence to the defendant in a criminal trial. Evidence disclosed on appeal.	No violation of 6	
20/04/93	A258-A (1993) 17 EHRR 193	*Sibson*	11	After he resigned from trade union applicant required to move to another place of work or re-join the union.	No violation	
26/05/93	A258-B (1993) 17 EHRR 539	*Brannigan and McBride*	5(3)	Detention of applicants under the Prevention of Terrorism (Temporary Provisions) Act 1984 for 4 and 6 days respectively.	Violation of 5(3)	UK had a valid derogation
23/06/93	A258-C (1993) 17 EHRR 213	*Lamguindaz*	8	Deportation of a 19 year old Moroccan who had lived in the UK since the age of 7.	Friendly settlement	Res No: DH(1993) 55 Action: UK agreed to revoke deportation order, grant leave to remain, and pay costs.
28/06/93	A258-D (1993) 18 EHRR 119	*Colman*	10	Doctor complained about restrictions by the GMC on advertising by doctors.	Friendly settlement	Res No: DH(1993) 44 Action: GMC relaxed its restriction on advertising
26/10/93	A272 (1993) 18 EHRR 205	*Darnell*	6(1)	Delay in unfair dismissal proceedings of 9 years.	Violation of 6(1)	Res No: (1994) 33 Just satisfaction for non-pecuniary damage of £5,000

23/02/94	A282-A EHRR	*Stanford*	6(1)	Inability of the defendant to hear some of the evidence against him at his criminal trial.	No violation of 6(1)	
28/02/94	A282-B (1994) 19 EHRR 179	*Boyle*		Uncle unable to apply for contact with his 9 year old nephew who had been taken into care.	Friendly settlement	Res No: DH(1994) 65 Government agreed ex gratia payment of £15,000 plus costs
18/07/94	A294-A (1994) 19 EHRR 333	*Wynne*	5(4)	Review of the detention of a discretionary life prisoner who was also serving a mandatory life sentence.	No violation of 5(4)	
21/09/94	A294-B (1994) 18 EHRR 393	*Fayed*	6	Applicants were criticised in a DTI report. No effective challenge under English law. Denial of access to the courts.	No violation of 6	
28/10/94	A300-C (1994) 19 EHRR 97	*Maxwell*	6(3)	Refusal of legal aid for appeal against convictions.	Violation of 6(3)	Finding of breach was sufficient compensation for non-pecuniary damage Res No: DH (1996) 156 Action: Criminal Justice (Scotland) 1995 introduced new system of appeals.
28/10/94	A300-B (1994) 19 EHRR 246	*Boner*	6(3)	Refusal of legal aid for appeal against convictions.	Violation of 6(3)	Finding of breach was sufficient compensation for non-pecuniary damage Res No: DH(1996) 155
28/10/94	A300-A (1994) 19 EHRR 193	*Murray*	5(1), 8	Arrests under the Northern Ireland (Emergency Provision) Act 1978.	No violation of 5(1), 8	
09/02/95	A307-A (1995) 20EHRR 247	*Welch*	7	Imposition of retrospective confiscation order.	Violation of 7	Just satisfaction judgment on 26/02/96, Reports 1996-II Res No: DH(1997) 222

Date	Reference	Applicant	Articles	Summary	Court's Finding	Comments
24/02/95	A308 (1995) 20 EHRR 205	*McMichael*	6, 8	Denial of parental contact to child in care and refusal to disclose documents.	Violation of 6(1), 8	Res No: DH(1997) 508 Action: Children's Hearings (Scotland) Rules 1996 provided for disclosure of documents and information
05/05/95	A316 (1995) 20 EHRR 150	*Air Canada*	Protocol 1, Article 1, Article 6	Seizure of aircraft by Customs after drugs were found on board.	No violation of P 1(1) or 6	
13/07/95	A323 (1995) 20 EHRR 442	*Tolstoy*	6, 10	Size of libel damages awarded by juries. Security of costs of an appeal.	Violation of 10 No violation of 6	Res No: DH(1996) 20 Measures taken prior to judgement
27/09/95	A324 (1995) 21 EHRR 97	*McCann and Others*	2	Shooting of IRA members by SAS soldiers in Gibraltar.	Violation of 2	Res No: DH(1996) 102 Compensation paid: £38,700
22/11/95	A335-B and A335-C (1995) 21 EHRR 363	*SW and CR*	7(1)	Complaints were convicted of rape following removal of 'marital rape' exemption. Complaint about reporting provisions of Sexual Offenders Act 1997.	No violation of 7(1)	
22/11/95	A335-A (1995) 21 EHRR 342	*Bryan*	6(1)	Proceedings to challenge a planning enforcement notice involved the determination of civil rights. Impartiality of planning inspector was challenged.	No violation of 6(1)	
08/02/96	Reports 1996-I 30 (1996) 22 EHRR 29	*John Murray*	6(1)	Right to silence challenge on Northern Ireland legislation.	No violation of 6(1)	
21/02/96	Reports 1996-I 280; 252 (1996) 22 EHRR 1	*Singh and Hussain*	5(4)	Lawfulness of detention following sentences of detention at Her Majesty's Pleasure.	Violation of 5(4)	Res No: DH(1998) 149/150 Action: Crime (Sentences) Act 1997 amended parole rules

27/03/96	Reports 1996-II 483 (1996) 22 EHRR 123	*Goodwin*	10	Journalist refused to comply with an order under Contempt of Court Act to reveal a source.	Violation of 10	Res No: DH(1997) 507 Compensation paid: £37,595
10/06/96	Reports 1996-III 783 (1996) 22 EHRR 391	*Pullar*	6(1)	Jury bias as juror was an employee of key prosecution witness.	No violation of 6(1)	
10/06/96	Reports 1996-III 738 (1996) 22 EHRR 293	*Benham*	5(1), 6(1), 6(3)(c)	Refusal to award compensation after an order for imprisonment of applicant for failure to pay community charge was quashed by the Divisional Court.	No violation of 5(1) Violation of 6(1) and 6(3)(c)	
25/09/96	Reports 1996-IV 1271 (1996) 23 EHRR 101	*Buckley*	8	Refusal to grant applicant planning permission to keep caravans on her own land.	No violation of 8	
22/10/96	Reports 1996-IV 1485 (1996) 23 EHRR 213	*Stubbings and Others*	6(1), 8	Statute barred claim for personal injury damages for sexual abuse in childhood.	No violation of 6(1), 8	
15/11/96	Reports 1996-V 1831 (1996) 23 EHRR 413	*Chahal*	3, 5(1), 5(4), 13	Deportation and extradition of an individual where there is a 'real risk' of inhuman or degrading treatment takes priority over other considerations including national security.	Violation of 3, 5(4), 13 No violation of 5(1)	
25/11/96	Reports 1996-V 1937 (1996) 24 EHRR 1	*Wingrove*	10	Refusal to issue a film certificate on the grounds that it was blasphemous.	No violation of 10	
17/12/96	Reports 1996-VI 2044 (1996) 23 EHRR 313	*Saunders*	6(1)	Use of documents in criminal proceedings obtained under statutory powers of compulsion from DTI inquiry.	Violation of 6(1)	Res No: DH(2000) 27 Action: Youth Justice and Criminal Evidence Act 1999
19/02/97	Reports 1997-I 120 (1997) 24 EHRR 39	*Laskey, Jaggard and Brown*	8	Sado-masochists convicted of assault occasioning actual bodily harm.	No violation of 8	

Date	Reference	Applicant	Articles	Summary	Court's Finding	Comments
25/02/97	Reports 1997-I 296 (1997) 25 EHRR 577	*Gregory*	6(1)	Racial prejudice of jury. Jury sent a note to Judge when they were considering their verdicts informing the Judge that the 'Jury were showing racial overtones'.	No violation of 6(1)	
25/02/97	Reports 1997-I 263 (1997) 24 EHRR 221	*Findlay*	6(1)	Court martial not an independent and impartial tribunal.	Violation of 6(1)	
22/04/97	Reports 1997-II 619 (1997) 24 EHRR 143	*X, Y and Z*	8	Refusal to register a transsexual as father of a child.	No violation of 8	
02/05/97	Reports 1997-III 777 (1997) 24 EHRR 423	*D*	3	Removal from the UK to St. Kitts of a convicted drugs courier suffering from the advanced stages of AIDS related illness.	Violation of 3	Res No: DH(1998) 11 Action: Granted Applicant indefinite leave to remain in the UK to receive adequate medical treatment and palliative care.
25/06/97	Reports 1997-III 1004 (1997) 24 EHRR 523	*Halford*	8, 13	Telephone tapping, interception of office calls.	Violation of 8, 13	Res No: DH(1999) 725 Action: Published Consultation Paper (with proposed legislative changes)
23/09/97	Reports 1997-V 1842 (1997) 26 EHRR 527	*Robins*	6(1)	Delay of 4 years from date of judgment to resolution of costs proceedings.	Violation of 6(1)	Res No: DH(1998) 90 Action: Judgement circulated to Legal Aid Board and Department of Social Security
24/09/97	Reports 1997-V 1842	*Coyne*	6(1)	Independence and impartiality of court martial.	Violation of 6(1)	Res No: DH(1998) 12 Action: Armed Forces Act 1996 amended Court Martial practice and procedure

23/10/97	Reports 1997-VII 2325 (1997) 25 EHRR 127	*National & Provincial Building Society and Others*	6, Protocol 1, Article 1	Retrospective measures concerning the collection of income tax at source on investments in building societies.	No violation of 6, P1(1)	
24/10/97	Reports 1997- VII 2391 (1997) 27 EHRR 296	*Johnson*	5(1)	The applicant was to be discharged from the psychiatric hospital he had been detained in as he was no longer suffering a mental illness, but was not released as no suitable supervised accommodation could be found.	Violation of 5(1)	
19/02/98	Reports 1998-I 175 (1998) 26 EHRR 1	*Bowman*	10	The applicant was an anti-abortion campaigner prosecuted for her third party expenditure promoting a candidate in an election.	Violation of 10	
09/06/98	Reports 1998-III 1390 (1998) 27 EHRR 212	*LCB*	2, 3	Alleged that State's failure to monitor father's exposure to radiation during nuclear tests caused her leukaemia.	No violation	
09/06/98	Reports 1998-III 1334 (1998) 27 EHRR 1	*McGinley and Egan*	6(1), 8	Refusal to disclose documents concerning exposure of the applicants to radiation at Christmas Island.	No violation of 6(1), 8	Application for a Revision of the Judgment refused, 28/1/00
10/07/98	Reports 1998-IV 1633 (1998) 27 EHRR 249	*Tinnelly & Sons Ltd and Others*	6(1)	Use of ministerial certificates claiming public interest immunity in relation to complaint of discrimination in awarding public works contracts.	Violation of 6(1)	Res No: DH(2000) 49 Action: The Northern Ireland Act Tribunal Procedure Rules 1999 introduced.
30/07/98	Reports 1998-V 2011 (1998) 27 EHRR 163	*Sheffield and Horsham*	8, 12, 14	Refusal to alter the register of births of a transsexual. Prohibition against trannsexual marriage.	No violation of 8, 12 or 14	

Date	Reference	Applicant	Articles	Summary	Court's Finding	Comments
02/09/98	Reports 1998-VI 2356 (2000) 29 EHRR 1	*Ahmed and Others*	10, 11, P1(3)	Local government employees challenged restrictions placed on their political activities by the Local Government (Political Restrictions) Regulations 1990.	No violation of 10, 11 or P1(3)	
23/09/98	Reports 1998-VII 2774 (1998) 27 EHRR 493	*McLeod*	8	Police power to enter premises to prevent a breach of the peace.	Violation of 8	
23/09/98	Reports 1998-VII 2718 (1998) 28 EHRR 603	*Steel and Others*	5, 10	Protesters arrested for breach of the peace and refused to agree to be bound over.	Violation of 5 and 10	
23/09/98	Reports 1998-VI 2692 (1998) 27 EHRR 611	*A*	3	Corporal punishment on 9 year old by stepfather who was acquitted of assault. Complaint of failure by UK to take positive steps to protect child's Art 3 rights.	Violation of 3	
28/10/98	Reports 1998-VIII (1999) 29 EHRR 245	*Osman*	2, 6, 8	Failure by police to take proper measures to prevent a murder occurring. Police immunity for actions in negligence.	No violation of 2, 8 Violation of 6	Res No: DH(1999) 720 Action: Government circular issued
18/02/99	(1999) 28 EHRR 361	*Matthews*	P1(3)	The applicant was a British citizen resident in Gibraltar, whose attempts to register to vote in the European Parliament elections failed.	Violation of P 1(3)	
18/02/99	(2000) 29 EHRR 365	*Hood*	5(3), 6	Independence and impartiality of court martial.	Violation of 5(3) and 6	Res No: DH(2000) 82 Action: Investigation and Summary Dealing (Army) Regulations 1997 introduced

18/02/99	*The Times* 11 March 1999	*Cable and Others*	6(1)	Independence and impartiality of court martial.	Violation of 6(1)	Res No: DH(1999) 719 Action: Armed Forces Act 1996 amended the court martial practices and procedures
22/07/99	[1999] EHRLR 332	*Scarth*	6(1)	Denial of a public hearing in a county court arbitration.	Violation of 6(1)	Res No: DH(2000) 48 Action:Under the CPR, hearings, including those in small claims cases, are to be held in public
27/09/99	[1999] IRLR 734	*Smith and Grady*	8, 13	Investigation and dismissal of servicemen on the grounds of their homosexuality.	Violation of 8, 13	Just satisfaction judgment 25/7/00: Pecuniary damage: Smith £59,000; Grady £40,000 Non-pecuniary damage: £19,000 to each applicant
27/09/99	(1999) 7 BHRC 65	*Lustig-Prean and Beckett*	8	Investigation and dismissal of servicemen on the grounds of their homosexuality.	Violation of 8	Just satisfaction judgment 25/7/00: Pecuniary damage: Lustig-Prean: £98,875; Beckett £15,000 Non-pecuniary damage: £19,000 to each applicant
29/09/99	*The Times* 11 October 1999	*Smith and Ford*	6(1)	Independence and impartiality of court's martial.	Violation of 6(1)	Res No: DH(2000) 47 Action: Armed Forces Act 1996 amended the court martial practices and procedures
29/09/99	(2000) 29 EHRR 00	*Moore and Gordon*	6(1)	Independence and impartiality of court's martial.	Violation of 6(1)	Res No: DH(2000) 46 Action: Armed Forces Act 1996
12/10/99		*Perks and Others*	5(1), 6	Imprisonment for non-payment of community charge and refusal of legal aid.	No violation of 5(1) Violation of 6	

Date	Reference	Applicant	Articles	Summary	Court's Finding	Comments
09/11/99		*Crossland*	8, 14	The applicant complained that bereavement tax allowance was not available to husbands whose wives died, but was available to women whose husbands died.	Friendly settlement	Res No: DH(2000) 81 Action: UK indicated that legislation would be amended
25/11/99	*The Times* 1 December 1999	*Hashman and Harrup*	10	Binding over protesters to be of 'good behaviour'.	Violation of 10	
30/11/99	*The Times* 11 January 2000	*Faulkner*	6	Applicant who wished to bring claim for assault battery and false imprisonment complained of lack of a civil legal aid system in Guernsey.	Friendly settlement	Action: Government undertook to introduce a civil legal aid system in Guernsey
16/12/99	(2000) 7 BHRC 659	*T and V*	3, 6	Trial of two 11 year old boys in the Crown Court for murder and sentence of detention at Her Majesty's Pleasure.	No Violation of 3 Violation of 6	
8/2/00	(2000) 8 BHRC 56	*McGonnell*	6	Challenge to Guernsey bailiff who was personally involved in case in a legislative and judicial role.	Violation of 6	
8/2/00	*The Times* 29 February 2000	*Caballero*	5(3)	Automatic refusal of bail under s 25 Criminal Justice and Public Order Act 1994 because the applicant had a previous conviction.	Violation of 5(3)	UK did not contest
16/02/00	*The Times* 1 March 2000	*Jasper, Fitt*	6	Material subject to public interest immunity withheld from defence.	No violation of 6(1)	

16/02/00	*The Times* 1 March 2000	*Rowe and Davis*	6	Failure of prosecution to make an application to withhold material subject to public interest immunity.	Violation of 6	
14/03/00	*The Times* 17 March 2000	*Jordan*	5(3), 5(5)	Review of detention of suspect who was a soldier by commanding officer.	Violation of 5(3), 5(5)	UK did not contest
28/03/00	*The Times* 5 April 2000	*Curley*	5(4), 5(5)	Failure to review of prisoner detained at Her Majesty's Pleasure at the end of his tariff.	Violation of 5(4), 5(5)	
30/03/00		*J.T.*	8	The applicant objected to her 'nearest relative' appointed under s 26 Mental Health Act 1983 and complained that she could not change it during her detention in a psychiatric institution.	Friendly settlement	UK indicated that the legislation would be amended
25/04/00	*The Times* 20 May 2000	*Cornwell, Leary*	8, 14	The applicant complained about the fact that as a bereaved widower he was not entitled to widow's benefits.	Friendly settlement	UK indicated that the legislation would be amended
02/05/00	*The Times* 09 May 2000	*Condron*	6	Right to silence following advice from solicitor.	Violation of 6	
9/05/00		*Sander*	6	Racial prejudice of juror. Juror wrote a note to the Judge explaining that other jurors had made racist remarks. Note later retracted.	Violation of 6	
12/05/00	*The Times* 23 May 2000	*Khan*	8, 6, 13	Secret listening devices. Khan was convicted of drug dealing on the basis of evidence improperly obtained by a secret listening device, installed by the police.	Violation of 8, 13 No violation of 6	

Date	Reference	Applicant	Articles	Summary	Court's Finding	Comments
06/06/00	*The Times* 20 June 2000	*Magee*	6, 14	Right to silence in Northern Ireland. Refusal of access to a solicitor pursuant to 1988 Criminal Evidence (Northern Ireland) Order.	Violation of 6 No violation of 14	
06/06/00		*Downing*	5	Review of the detention of a prisoner serving a sentence of detention at her Majesty's Pleasure.	Friendly settlement	UK agreed to pay £500 non pecuniary damages plus costs
06/06/00	*Times* 20 June 2000	*Averill*	6	Right to silence in Northern Ireland and refusal of access to a solicitor.	Violation of 6	
20/06/00	*Times* 4 July 2000	*Foxley*	8	Interference with a bankrupt's correspondence with his legal advisers by his trustee in bankruptcy.	Violation of 8	

APPENDIX A

Human Rights Act 1998

1998 CHAPTER 42

ARRANGEMENT OF SECTIONS

Introduction

Section
1. The Convention rights
2. Interpretation of Convention rights

Legislation

3. Interpretation of legislation
4. Declaration of incompatibility
5. Right of Crown to intervene

Public authorities

6. Acts of public authorities
7. Proceedings
8. Judicial remedies
9. Judicial acts

Remedial action

10. Power to take remedial action

Other rights and proceedings

11. Safeguard for existing human rights
12. Freedom of expression
13. Freedom of thought, conscience and religion

Derogations and reservations

14. Derogations
15. Reservations
16. Period for which designated derogations have effect
17. Periodic review of designated reservations

Judges of the European Court of Human Rights

18. Appointment to European Court of Human Rights

Parliamentary procedure

19. Statements of compatibility

Supplemental

20. Orders etc. under this Act
21. Interpretation, etc.
22. Short title, commencement, application and extent

SCHEDULES

Schedule 1—The Articles
Part I—The Convention [Rights and Freedoms]
Part II—The First Protocol
Part III—The Sixth Protocol
Schedule 2—Remedial orders
Schedule 3—Derogation and reservation
Part I—Derogation
Part II—Reservation
Schedule 4—Judicial pensions*

An Act to give further effect to rights and freedoms guaranteed under the European Convention on Human Rights; to make provision with respect to holders of certain judicial offices who become judges of the European Court of Human Rights; and for connected purposes.

[9th November 1998]

BE IT ENACTED by the Queen's most Excellent Majesty, by and with the advice and consent of the Lords Spiritual and Temporal, and Commons, in this present Parliament assembled, and by the authority of the same, as follows:—

Introduction

The Convention rights

1.—(1) In this Act 'the Convention rights' means the rights and fundamental freedoms set out in—

(a) Articles 2 to 12 and 14 of the Convention,
(b) Articles 1 to 3 of the First Protocol, and
(c) Articles 1 and 2 of the Sixth Protocol,

as read with Articles 16 to 18 of the Convention.

(2) Those Articles are to have effect for the purposes of this Act subject to any designated derogation or reservation (as to which see sections 14 and 15).

(3) The Articles are set out in Schedule 1.

(4) The Secretary of State may by order make such amendments to this Act as he considers appropriate to reflect the effect, in relation to the United Kingdom, of a protocol.

(5) In subsection (4) 'protocol' means a protocol to the Convention—
(a) which the United Kingdom has ratified; or
(b) which the United Kingdom has signed with a view to ratification.

(6) No amendment may be made by an order under subsection (4) so as to come into force before the protocol concerned is in force in relation to the United Kingdom.

Interpretation of Convention rights

2.—(1) A court or tribunal determining a question which has arisen in connection with a Convention right must take into account any—

* Schedule 4 is not included.

(a) judgment, decision, declaration or advisory opinion of the European Court of Human Rights,
(b) opinion of the Commission given in a report adopted under Article 31 of the Convention,
(c) decision of the Commission in connection with Article 26 or 27(2) of the Convention, or
(d) decision of the Committee of Ministers taken under Article 46 of the Convention,

whenever made or given, so far as, in the opinion of the court or tribunal, it is relevant to the proceedings in which that question has arisen.

(2) Evidence of any judgment, decision, declaration or opinion of which account may have to be taken under this section is to be given in proceedings before any court or tribunal in such manner as may be provided by rules.

(3) In this section 'rules' means rules of court or, in the case of proceedings before a tribunal, rules made for the purposes of this section—
(a) by the Lord Chancellor or the Secretary of State, in relation to any proceedings outside Scotland;
(b) by the Secretary of State, in relation to proceedings in Scotland; or
(c) by a Northern Ireland department, in relation to proceedings before a tribunal in Northern Ireland—
(i) which deals with transferred matters; and
(ii) for which no rules made under paragraph (a) are in force.

Legislation

Interpretation of legislation

3.—(1) So far as it is possible to do so, primary legislation and subordinate legislation must be read and given effect in a way which is compatible with the Convention rights.

(2) This section—
(a) applies to primary legislation and subordinate legislation whenever enacted;
(b) does not affect the validity, continuing operation or enforcement of any incompatible primary legislation; and
(c) does not affect the validity, continuing operation or enforcement of any incompatible subordinate legislation if (disregarding any possibility of revocation) primary legislation prevents removal of the incompatibility.

Declaration of incompatibility

4.—(1) Subsection (2) applies in any proceedings in which a court determines whether a provision of primary legislation is compatible with a Convention right.

(2) If the court is satisfied that the provision is incompatible with a Convention right, it may make a declaration of that incompatibility.

(3) Subsection (4) applies in any proceedings in which a court determines whether a provision of subordinate legislation, made in the exercise of a power conferred by primary legislation, is compatible with a Convention right.

(4) If the court is satisfied—
(a) that the provision is incompatible with a Convention right, and
(b) that (disregarding any possibility of revocation) the primary legislation concerned prevents removal of the incompatibility,

it may make a declaration of that incompatibility.

(5) In this section 'court' means—
(a) the House of Lords;

(b) the Judicial Committee of the Privy Council;
(c) the Courts–Martial Appeal Court;
(d) in Scotland, the High Court of Justiciary sitting otherwise than as a trial court or the Court of Session;
(e) in England and Wales or Northern Ireland, the High Court or the Court of Appeal.

(6) A declaration under this section ('a declaration of incompatibility')—
(a) does not affect the validity, continuing operation or enforcement of the provision in respect of which it is given; and
(b) is not binding on the parties to the proceedings in which it is made.

Right of Crown to intervene

5.—(1) Where a court is considering whether to make a declaration of incompatibility, the Crown is entitled to notice in accordance with rules of court.

(2) In any case to which subsection (1) applies—
(a) a Minister of the Crown (or a person nominated by him),
(b) a member of the Scottish Executive,
(c) a Northern Ireland Minister,
(d) a Northern Ireland department,

is entitled, on giving notice in accordance with rules of court, to be joined as a party to the proceedings.

(3) Notice under subsection (2) may be given at any time during the proceedings.

(4) A person who has been made a party to criminal proceedings (other than in Scotland) as the result of a notice under subsection (2) may, with leave, appeal to the House of Lords against any declaration of incompatibility made in the proceedings.

(5) In subsection (4)—
'criminal proceedings' includes all proceedings before the Courts–Martial Appeal Court; and
'leave' means leave granted by the court making the declaration of incompatibility or by the House of Lords.

Public authorities

Acts of public authorities

6.—(1) It is unlawful for a public authority to act in a way which is incompatible with a Convention right.

(2) Subsection (1) does not apply to an act if—
(a) as the result of one or more provisions of primary legislation, the authority could not have acted differently; or
(b) in the case of one or more provisions of, or made under, primary legislation which cannot be read or given effect in a way which is compatible with the Convention rights, the authority was acting so as to give effect to or enforce those provisions.

(3) In this section 'public authority' includes—
(a) a court or tribunal, and
(b) any person certain of whose functions are functions of a public nature,

but does not include either House of Parliament or a person exercising functions in connection with proceedings in Parliament.

(4) In subsection (3) 'Parliament' does not include the House of Lords in its judicial capacity.

(5) In relation to a particular act, a person is not a public authority by virtue only of subsection (3)(b) if the nature of the act is private.

(6) 'An act' includes a failure to act but does not include a failure to—
(a) introduce in, or lay before, Parliament a proposal for legislation; or
(b) make any primary legislation or remedial order.

Proceedings

7.—(1) A person who claims that a public authority has acted (or proposes to act) in a way which is made unlawful by section 6(1) may—
(a) bring proceedings against the authority under this Act in the appropriate court or tribunal, or
(b) rely on the Convention right or rights concerned in any legal proceedings,

but only if he is (or would be) a victim of the unlawful act.

(2) In subsection (1)(a) 'appropriate court or tribunal' means such court or tribunal as may be determined in accordance with rules; and proceedings against an authority include a counterclaim or similar proceeding.

(3) If the proceedings are brought on an application for judicial review, the applicant is to be taken to have a sufficient interest in relation to the unlawful act only if he is, or would be, a victim of that act.

(4) If the proceedings are made by way of a petition for judicial review in Scotland, the applicant shall be taken to have title and interest to sue in relation to the unlawful act only if he is, or would be, a victim of that act.

(5) Proceedings under subsection (1)(a) must be brought before the end of—
(a) the period of one year beginning with the date on which the act complained of took place; or
(b) such longer period as the court or tribunal considers equitable having regard to all the circumstances,

but that is subject to any rule imposing a stricter time limit in relation to the procedure in question.

(6) In subsection (1)(b) 'legal proceedings' includes—
(a) proceedings brought by or at the instigation of a public authority; and
(b) an appeal against the decision of a court or tribunal.

(7) For the purposes of this section, a person is a victim of an unlawful act only if he would be a victim for the purposes of Article 34 of the Convention if proceedings were brought in the European Court of Human Rights in respect of that act.

(8) Nothing in this Act creates a criminal offence.

(9) In this section 'rules' means—
(a) in relation to proceedings before a court or tribunal outside Scotland, rules made by the Lord Chancellor or the Secretary of State for the purposes of this section or rules of court,
(b) in relation to proceedings before a court or tribunal in Scotland, rules made by the Secretary of State for those purposes,
(c) in relation to proceedings before a tribunal in Northern Ireland—
(i) which deals with transferred matters; and
(ii) for which no rules made under paragraph (a) are in force,

rules made by a Northern Ireland department for those purposes,

and includes provision made by order under section 1 of the Courts and Legal Services Act 1990.

(10) In making rules, regard must be had to section 9.

(11) The Minister who has power to make rules in relation to a particular tribunal may, to the extent he considers it necessary to ensure that the tribunal can provide an appropriate remedy in

relation to an act (or proposed act) of a public authority which is (or would be) unlawful as a result of section 6(1), by order add to—

(a) the relief or remedies which the tribunal may grant; or
(b) the grounds on which it may grant any of them.

(12) An order made under subsection (11) may contain such incidental, supplemental, consequential or transitional provision as the Minister making it considers appropriate.

(13) 'The Minister' includes the Northern Ireland department concerned.

Judicial remedies

8.—(1) In relation to any act (or proposed act) of a public authority which the court finds is (or would be) unlawful, it may grant such relief or remedy, or make such order, within its powers as it considers just and appropriate.

(2) But damages may be awarded only by a court which has power to award damages, or to order the payment of compensation, in civil proceedings.

(3) No award of damages is to be made unless, taking account of all the circumstances of the case, including—

(a) any other relief or remedy granted, or order made, in relation to the act in question (by that or any other court), and
(b) the consequences of any decision (of that or any other court) in respect of that act,

the court is satisfied that the award is necessary to afford just satisfaction to the person in whose favour it is made.

(4) In determining—

(a) whether to award damages, or
(b) the amount of an award,

the court must take into account the principles applied by the European Court of Human Rights in relation to the award of compensation under Article 41 of the Convention.

(5) A public authority against which damages are awarded is to be treated—

(a) in Scotland, for the purposes of section 3 of the Law Reform (Miscellaneous Provisions) (Scotland) Act 1940 as if the award were made in an action of damages in which the authority has been found liable in respect of loss or damage to the person to whom the award is made;
(b) for the purposes of the Civil Liability (Contribution) Act 1978 as liable in respect of damage suffered by the person to whom the award is made.

(6) In this section—

'court' includes a tribunal;
'damages' means damages for an unlawful act of a public authority; and
'unlawful' means unlawful under section 6(1).

Judicial acts

9.—(1) Proceedings under section 7(1)(a) in respect of a judicial act may be brought only—

(a) by exercising a right of appeal;
(b) on an application (in Scotland a petition) for judicial review; or
(c) in such other forum as may be prescribed by rules.

(2) That does not affect any rule of law which prevents a court from being the subject of judicial review.

(3) In proceedings under this Act in respect of a judicial act done in good faith, damages may not be awarded otherwise than to compensate a person to the extent required by Article 5(5) of the Convention.

(4) An award of damages permitted by subsection (3) is to be made against the Crown; but no award may be made unless the appropriate person, if not a party to the proceedings, is joined.

(5) In this section—

'appropriate person' means the Minister responsible for the court concerned, or a person or government department nominated by him;

'court' includes a tribunal;

'judge' includes a member of a tribunal, a justice of the peace and a clerk or other officer entitled to exercise the jurisdiction of a court;

'judicial act' means a judicial act of a court and includes an act done on the instructions, or on behalf, of a judge; and

'rules' has the same meaning as in section 7(9).

Remedial action

Power to take remedial action

10.—(1) This section applies if—

(a) a provision of legislation has been declared under section 4 to be incompatible with a Convention right and, if an appeal lies—

(i) all persons who may appeal have stated in writing that they do not intend to do so;

(ii) the time for bringing an appeal has expired and no appeal has been brought within that time; or

(iii) an appeal brought within that time has been determined or abandoned; or

(b) it appears to a Minister of the Crown or Her Majesty in Council that, having regard to a finding of the European Court of Human Rights made after the coming into force of this section in proceedings against the United Kingdom, a provision of legislation is incompatible with an obligation of the United Kingdom arising from the Convention.

(2) If a Minister of the Crown considers that there are compelling reasons for proceeding under this section, he may by order make such amendments to the legislation as he considers necessary to remove the incompatibility.

(3) If, in the case of subordinate legislation, a Minister of the Crown considers—

(a) that it is necessary to amend the primary legislation under which the subordinate legislation in question was made, in order to enable the incompatibility to be removed, and

(b) that there are compelling reasons for proceeding under this section,

he may by order make such amendments to the primary legislation as he considers necessary.

(4) This section also applies where the provision in question is in subordinate legislation and has been quashed, or declared invalid, by reason of incompatibility with a Convention right and the Minister proposes to proceed under paragraph 2(b) of Schedule 2.

(5) If the legislation is an Order in Council, the power conferred by subsection (2) or (3) is exercisable by Her Majesty in Council.

(6) In this section 'legislation' does not include a Measure of the Church Assembly or of the General Synod of the Church of England.

(7) Schedule 2 makes further provision about remedial orders.

Other rights and proceedings

Safeguard for existing human rights

11. A person's reliance on a Convention right does not restrict—

(a) any other right or freedom conferred on him by or under any law having effect in any part of the United Kingdom; or

(b) his right to make any claim or bring any proceedings which he could make or bring apart from sections 7 to 9.

Freedom of expression

12.—(1) This section applies if a court is considering whether to grant any relief which, if granted, might affect the exercise of the Convention right to freedom of expression.

(2) If the person against whom the application for relief is made ('the respondent') is neither present nor represented, no such relief is to be granted unless the court is satisfied—

(a) that the applicant has taken all practicable steps to notify the respondent; or
(b) that there are compelling reasons why the respondent should not be notified.

(3) No such relief is to be granted so as to restrain publication before trial unless the court is satisfied that the applicant is likely to establish that publication should not be allowed.

(4) The court must have particular regard to the importance of the Convention right to freedom of expression and, where the proceedings relate to material which the respondent claims, or which appears to the court, to be journalistic, literary or artistic material (or to conduct connected with such material), to—

(a) the extent to which—
(i) the material has, or is about to, become available to the public; or
(ii) it is, or would be, in the public interest for the material to be published;
(b) any relevant privacy code.

(5) In this section—
'court' includes a tribunal; and
'relief' includes any remedy or order (other than in criminal proceedings).

Freedom of thought, conscience and religion

13.—(1) If a court's determination of any question arising under this Act might affect the exercise by a religious organisation (itself or its members collectively) of the Convention right to freedom of thought, conscience and religion, it must have particular regard to the importance of that right.

(2) In this section 'court' includes a tribunal.

Derogations and reservations

Derogations

14.—(1) In this Act 'designated derogation' means—

(a) the United Kingdom's derogation from Article 5(3) of the Convention; and
(b) any derogation by the United Kingdom from an Article of the Convention, or of any protocol to the Convention, which is designated for the purposes of this Act in an order made by the Secretary of State.

(2) The derogation referred to in subsection (1)(a) is set out in Part I of Schedule 3.

(3) If a designated derogation is amended or replaced it ceases to be a designated derogation.

(4) But subsection (3) does not prevent the Secretary of State from exercising his power under subsection (1)(b) to make a fresh designation order in respect of the Article concerned.

(5) The Secretary of State must by order make such amendments to Schedule 3 as he considers appropriate to reflect—

(a) any designation order; or
(b) the effect of subsection (3).

(6) A designation order may be made in anticipation of the making by the United Kingdom of a proposed derogation.

Reservations

15.—(1) In this Act 'designated reservation' means—

(a) the United Kingdom's reservation to Article 2 of the First Protocol to the Convention; and

(b) any other reservation by the United Kingdom to an Article of the Convention, or of any protocol to the Convention, which is designated for the purposes of this Act in an order made by the Secretary of State.

(2) The text of the reservation referred to in subsection (1)(a) is set out in Part II of Schedule 3.

(3) If a designated reservation is withdrawn wholly or in part it ceases to be a designated reservation.

(4) But subsection (3) does not prevent the Secretary of State from exercising his power under subsection (1)(b) to make a fresh designation order in respect of the Article concerned.

(5) The Secretary of State must by order make such amendments to this Act as he considers appropriate to reflect—

(a) any designation order; or

(b) the effect of subsection (3).

Period for which designated derogations have effect

16.—(1) If it has not already been withdrawn by the United Kingdom, a designated derogation ceases to have effect for the purposes of this Act—

(a) in the case of the derogation referred to in section 14(1)(a), at the end of the period of five years beginning with the date on which section 1(2) came into force;

(b) in the case of any other derogation, at the end of the period of five years beginning with the date on which the order designating it was made.

(2) At any time before the period—

(a) fixed by subsection (1)(a) or (b), or

(b) extended by an order under this subsection,

comes to an end, the Secretary of State may by order extend it by a further period of five years.

(3) An order under section 14(1)(b) ceases to have effect at the end of the period for consideration, unless a resolution has been passed by each House approving the order.

(4) Subsection (3) does not affect—

(a) anything done in reliance on the order; or

(b) the power to make a fresh order under section 14(1)(b).

(5) In subsection (3) 'period for consideration' means the period of forty days beginning with the day on which the order was made.

(6) In calculating the period for consideration, no account is to be taken of any time during which—

(a) Parliament is dissolved or prorogued; or

(b) both Houses are adjourned for more than four days.

(7) If a designated derogation is withdrawn by the United Kingdom, the Secretary of State must by order make such amendments to this Act as he considers are required to reflect that withdrawal.

Periodic review of designated reservations

17.—(1) The appropriate Minister must review the designated reservation referred to in section 15(1)(a)—

(a) before the end of the period of five years beginning with the date on which section 1(2) came into force; and
(b) if that designation is still in force, before the end of the period of five years beginning with the date on which the last report relating to it was laid under subsection (3).

(2) The appropriate Minister must review each of the other designated reservations (if any)—
(a) before the end of the period of five years beginning with the date on which the order designating the reservation first came into force; and
(b) if the designation is still in force, before the end of the period of five years beginning with the date on which the last report relating to it was laid under subsection (3).

(3) The Minister conducting a review under this section must prepare a report on the result of the review and lay a copy of it before each House of Parliament.

Judges of the European Court of Human Rights

Appointment to European Court of Human Rights

18.—(1) In this section 'judicial office' means the office of—
(a) Lord Justice of Appeal, Justice of the High Court or Circuit judge, in England and Wales;
(b) judge of the Court of Session or sheriff, in Scotland;
(c) Lord Justice of Appeal, judge of the High Court or county court judge, in Northern Ireland.

(2) The holder of a judicial office may become a judge of the European Court of Human Rights ('the Court') without being required to relinquish his office.

(3) But he is not required to perform the duties of his judicial office while he is a judge of the Court.

(4) In respect of any period during which he is a judge of the Court—
(a) a Lord Justice of Appeal or Justice of the High Court is not to count as a judge of the relevant court for the purposes of section 2(1) or 4(1) of the Supreme Court Act 1981 (maximum number of judges) nor as a judge of the Supreme Court for the purposes of section 12(1) to (6) of that Act (salaries etc.);
(b) a judge of the Court of Session is not to count as a judge of that court for the purposes of section 1(1) of the Court of Session Act 1988 (maximum number of judges) or of section 9(1)(c) of the Administration of Justice Act 1973 ('the 1973 Act') (salaries etc.);
(c) a Lord Justice of Appeal or judge of the High Court in Northern Ireland is not to count as a judge of the relevant court for the purposes of section 2(1) or 3(1) of the Judicature (Northern Ireland) Act 1978 (maximum number of judges) nor as a judge of the Supreme Court of Northern Ireland for the purposes of section 9(1)(d) of the 1973 Act (salaries etc.);
(d) a Circuit judge is not to count as such for the purposes of section 18 of the Courts Act 1971 (salaries etc.);
(e) a sheriff is not to count as such for the purposes of section 14 of the Sheriff Courts (Scotland) Act 1907 (salaries etc.);
(f) a county court judge of Northern Ireland is not to count as such for the purposes of section 106 of the County Courts Act (Northern Ireland) 1959 (salaries etc.).

(5) If a sheriff principal is appointed a judge of the Court, section 11(1) of the Sheriff Courts (Scotland) Act 1971 (temporary appointment of sheriff principal) applies, while he holds that appointment, as if his office is vacant.

(6) Schedule 4 makes provision about judicial pensions in relation to the holder of a judicial office who serves as a judge of the Court.

(7) The Lord Chancellor or the Secretary of State may by order make such transitional provision (including, in particular, provision for a temporary increase in the maximum number of judges) as he considers appropriate in relation to any holder of a judicial office who has completed his service as a judge of the Court.

Parliamentary procedure

Statements of compatibility

19.—(1) A Minister of the Crown in charge of a Bill in either House of Parliament must, before Second Reading of the Bill—

(a) make a statement to the effect that in his view the provisions of the Bill are compatible with the Convention rights ('a statement of compatibility'); or

(b) make a statement to the effect that although he is unable to make a statement of compatibility the government nevertheless wishes the House to proceed with the Bill.

(2) The statement must be in writing and be published in such manner as the Minister making it considers appropriate.

Supplemental

Orders etc. under this Act

20.—(1) Any power of a Minister of the Crown to make an order under this Act is exercisable by statutory instrument.

(2) The power of the Lord Chancellor or the Secretary of State to make rules (other than rules of court) under section 2(3) or 7(9) is exercisable by statutory instrument.

(3) Any statutory instrument made under section 14, 15 or 16(7) must be laid before Parliament.

(4) No order may be made by the Lord Chancellor or the Secretary of State under section 1(4), 7(11) or 16(2) unless a draft of the order has been laid before, and approved by, each House of Parliament.

(5) Any statutory instrument made under section 18(7) or Schedule 4, or to which subsection (2) applies, shall be subject to annulment in pursuance of a resolution of either House of Parliament.

(6) The power of a Northern Ireland department to make—

(a) rules under section 2(3)(c) or 7(9)(c), or

(b) an order under section 7(11),

is exercisable by statutory rule for the purposes of the Statutory Rules (Northern Ireland) Order 1979.

(7) Any rules made under section 2(3)(c) or 7(9)(c) shall be subject to negative resolution; and section 41(6) of the Interpretation Act (Northern Ireland) 1954 (meaning of 'subject to negative resolution') shall apply as if the power to make the rules were conferred by an Act of the Northern Ireland Assembly.

(8) No order may be made by a Northern Ireland department under section 7(11) unless a draft of the order has been laid before, and approved by, the Northern Ireland Assembly.

Interpretation, etc.

21.—(1) In this Act—

'amend' includes repeal and apply (with or without modifications);

'the appropriate Minister' means the Minister of the Crown having charge of the appropriate authorised government department (within the meaning of the Crown Proceedings Act 1947);

'the Commission' means the European Commission of Human Rights;
'the Convention' means the Convention for the Protection of Human Rights and Fundamental Freedoms, agreed by the Council of Europe at Rome on 4th November 1950 as it has effect for the time being in relation to the United Kingdom;
'declaration of incompatibility' means a declaration under section 4;
'Minister of the Crown' has the same meaning as in the Ministers of the Crown Act 1975;
'Northern Ireland Minister' includes the First Minister and the deputy First Minister in Northern Ireland;
'primary legislation' means any—

(a) public general Act;
(b) local and personal Act;
(c) private Act;
(d) Measure of the Church Assembly;
(e) Measure of the General Synod of the Church of England;
(f) Order in Council—
  (i) made in exercise of Her Majesty's Royal Prerogative;
  (ii) made under section 38(1)(a) of the Northern Ireland Constitution Act 1973 or the corresponding provision of the Northern Ireland Act 1998; or
  (iii) amending an Act of a kind mentioned in paragraph (a), (b) or (c);

and includes an order or other instrument made under primary legislation (otherwise than by the National Assembly for Wales, a member of the Scottish Executive, a Northern Ireland Minister or a Northern Ireland department) to the extent to which it operates to bring one or more provisions of that legislation into force or amends any primary legislation;
'the First Protocol' means the protocol to the Convention agreed at Paris on 20th March 1952;
'the Sixth Protocol' means the protocol to the Convention agreed at Strasbourg on 28th April 1983;
'the Eleventh Protocol' means the protocol to the Convention (restructuring the control machinery established by the Convention) agreed at Strasbourg on 11th May 1994;
'remedial order' means an order under section 10;
'subordinate legislation' means any—

(a) Order in Council other than one—
  (i) made in exercise of Her Majesty's Royal Prerogative;
  (ii) made under section 38(1)(a) of the Northern Ireland Constitution Act 1973 or the corresponding provision of the Northern Ireland Act 1998; or
  (iii) amending an Act of a kind mentioned in the definition of primary legislation;
(b) Act of the Scottish Parliament;
(c) Act of the Parliament of Northern Ireland;
(d) Measure of the Assembly established under section 1 of the Northern Ireland Assembly Act 1973;
(e) Act of the Northern Ireland Assembly;
(f) order, rules, regulations, scheme, warrant, byelaw or other instrument made under primary legislation (except to the extent to which it operates to bring one or more provisions of that legislation into force or amends any primary legislation);
(g) order, rules, regulations, scheme, warrant, byelaw or other instrument made under legislation mentioned in paragraph (b), (c), (d) or (e) or made under an Order in Council applying only to Northern Ireland;
(h) order, rules, regulations, scheme, warrant, byelaw or other instrument made by a member of the Scottish Executive, a Northern Ireland Minister or a Northern Ireland department in exercise of prerogative or other executive functions of Her Majesty which are exercisable by such a person on behalf of Her Majesty;

'transferred matters' has the same meaning as in the Northern Ireland Act 1998; and
'tribunal' means any tribunal in which legal proceedings may be brought.

(2) The references in paragraphs (b) and (c) of section 2(1) to Articles are to Articles of the Convention as they had effect immediately before the coming into force of the Eleventh Protocol.

(3) The reference in paragraph (d) of section 2(1) to Article 46 includes a reference to Articles 32 and 54 of the Convention as they had effect immediately before the coming into force of the Eleventh Protocol.

(4) The references in section 2(1) to a report or decision of the Commission or a decision of the Committee of Ministers include references to a report or decision made as provided by paragraphs 3, 4 and 6 of Article 5 of the Eleventh Protocol (transitional provisions).

(5) Any liability under the Army Act 1955, the Air Force Act 1955 or the Naval Discipline Act 1957 to suffer death for an offence is replaced by a liability to imprisonment for life or any less punishment authorised by those Acts; and those Acts shall accordingly have effect with the necessary modifications.

Short title, commencement, application and extent

22.—(1) This Act may be cited as the Human Rights Act 1998.

(2) Sections 18, 20 and 21(5) and this section come into force on the passing of this Act.

(3) The other provisions of this Act come into force on such day as the Secretary of State may by order appoint; and different days may be appointed for different purposes.

(4) Paragraph (b) of subsection (1) of section 7 applies to proceedings brought by or at the instigation of a public authority whenever the act in question took place; but otherwise that subsection does not apply to an act taking place before the coming into force of that section.

(5) This Act binds the Crown.

(6) This Act extends to Northern Ireland.

(7) Section 21(5), so far as it relates to any provision contained in the Army Act 1955, the Air Force Act 1955 or the Naval Discipline Act 1957, extends to any place to which that provision extends.

SCHEDULES

Schedule 1
The Articles

Part I
The Convention*
Rights and Freedoms

Article 2
Right to Life

1. Everyone's right to life shall be protected by law. No one shall be deprived of his life intentionally save in the execution of a sentence of a court following his conviction of a crime for which this penalty is provided by law.

* The full text of the Convention and its Protocols are reproduced in Appendix E below.

2. Deprivation of life shall not be regarded as inflicted in contravention of this Article when it results from the use of force which is no more than absolutely necessary:
   (a) in defence of any person from unlawful violence;
   (b) in order to effect a lawful arrest or to prevent the escape of a person lawfully detained;
   (c) in action lawfully taken for the purpose of quelling a riot or insurrection.

Article 3
Prohibition of Torture

No one shall be subjected to torture or to inhuman or degrading treatment or punishment.

Article 4
Prohibition of Slavery and Forced Labour

1. No one shall be held in slavery or servitude.
2. No one shall be required to perform forced or compulsory labour.
3. For the purpose of this Article the term 'forced or compulsory labour' shall not include:
   (a) any work required to be done in the ordinary course of detention imposed according to the provisions of Article 5 of this Convention or during conditional release from such detention;
   (b) any service of a military character or, in case of conscientious objectors in countries where they are recognised, service exacted instead of compulsory military service;
   (c) any service exacted in case of an emergency or calamity threatening the life or well-being of the community;
   (d) any work or service which forms part of normal civic obligations.

Article 5
Right to Liberty and Security

1. Everyone has the right to liberty and security of person. No one shall be deprived of his liberty save in the following cases and in accordance with a procedure prescribed by law:
   (a) the lawful detention of a person after conviction by a competent court;
   (b) the lawful arrest or detention of a person for non-compliance with the lawful order of a court or in order to secure the fulfilment of any obligation prescribed by law;
   (c) the lawful arrest or detention of a person effected for the purpose of bringing him before the competent legal authority on reasonable suspicion of having committed an offence or when it is reasonably considered necessary to prevent his committing an offence or fleeing after having done so;
   (d) the detention of a minor by lawful order for the purpose of educational supervision or his lawful detention for the purpose of bringing him before the competent legal authority;
   (e) the lawful detention of persons for the prevention of the spreading of infectious diseases, of persons of unsound mind, alcoholics or drug addicts or vagrants;
   (f) the lawful arrest or detention of a person to prevent his effecting an unauthorised entry into the country or of a person against whom action is being taken with a view to deportation or extradition.
2. Everyone who is arrested shall be informed promptly, in a language which he understands, of the reasons for his arrest and of any charge against him.
3. Everyone arrested or detained in accordance with the provisions of paragraph 1(c) of this Article shall be brought promptly before a judge or other officer authorised by law to exercise

judicial power and shall be entitled to trial within a reasonable time or to release pending trial. Release may be conditioned by guarantees to appear for trial.

4. Everyone who is deprived of his liberty by arrest or detention shall be entitled to take proceedings by which the lawfulness of his detention shall be decided speedily by a court and his release ordered if the detention is not lawful.
5. Everyone who has been the victim of arrest or detention in contravention of the provisions of this Article shall have an enforceable right to compensation.

Article 6
Right to a Fair Trial

1. In the determination of his civil rights and obligations or of any criminal charge against him, everyone is entitled to a fair and public hearing within a reasonable time by an independent and impartial tribunal established by law. Judgment shall be pronounced publicly but the press and public may be excluded from all or part of the trial in the interest of morals, public order or national security in a democratic society, where the interests of juveniles or the protection of the private life of the parties so require, or to the extent strictly necessary in the opinion of the court in special circumstances where publicity would prejudice the interests of justice.
2. Everyone charged with a criminal offence shall be presumed innocent until proved guilty according to law.
3. Everyone charged with a criminal offence has the following minimum rights:
   (a) to be informed promptly, in a language which he understands and in detail, of the nature and cause of the accusation against him;
   (b) to have adequate time and facilities for the preparation of his defence;
   (c) to defend himself in person or through legal assistance of his own choosing or, if he has not sufficient means to pay for legal assistance, to be given it free when the interests of justice so require;
   (d) to examine or have examined witnesses against him and to obtain the attendance and examination of witnesses on his behalf under the same conditions as witnesses against him;
   (e) to have the free assistance of an interpreter if he cannot understand or speak the language used in court.

Article 7
No Punishment Withour Law

1. No one shall be held guilty of any criminal offence on account of any act or omission which did not constitute a criminal offence under national or international law at the time when it was committed. Nor shall a heavier penalty be imposed than the one that was applicable at the time the criminal offence was committed.
2. This Article shall not prejudice the trial and punishment of any person for any act or omission which, at the time when it was committed, was criminal according to the general principles of law recognised by civilised nations.

Article 8
Right to Respect for Private and Family Life

1. Everyone has the right to respect for his private and family life, his home and his correspondence.

2. There shall be no interference by a public authority with the exercise of this right except such as is in accordance with the law and is necessary in a democratic society in the interests of national security, public safety or the economic well-being of the country, for the prevention of disorder or crime, for the protection of health or morals, or for the protection of the rights and freedoms of others.

Article 9
Freedom of Thought, Conscience and Religion

1. Everyone has the right to freedom of thought, conscience and religion; this right includes freedom to change his religion or belief and freedom, either alone or in community with others and in public or private, to manifest his religion or belief, in worship, teaching, practice and observance.
2. Freedom to manifest one's religion or beliefs shall be subject only to such limitations as are prescribed by law and are necessary in a democratic society in the interests of public safety, for the protection of public order, health or morals, or for the protection of the rights and freedoms of others.

Article 10
Freedom of Expression

1. Everyone has the right to freedom of expression. This right shall include freedom to hold opinions and to receive and impart information and ideas without interference by public authority and regardless of frontiers. This Article shall not prevent States from requiring the licensing of broadcasting, television or cinema enterprises.
2. The exercise of these freedoms, since it carries with it duties and responsibilities, may be subject to such formalities, conditions, restrictions or penalties as are prescribed by law and are necessary in a democratic society, in the interests of national security, territorial integrity or public safety, for the prevention of disorder or crime, for the protection of health or morals, for the protection of the reputation or rights of others, for preventing the disclosure of information received in confidence, or for maintaining the authority and impartiality of the judiciary.

Article 11
Freedom of Assembly and Association

1. Everyone has the right to freedom of peaceful assembly and to freedom of association with others, including the right to form and to join trade unions for the protection of his interests.
2. No restrictions shall be placed on the exercise of these rights other than such as are prescribed by law and are necessary in a democratic society in the interests of national security or public safety, for the prevention of disorder or crime, for the protection of health or morals or for the protection of the rights and freedoms of others. This Article shall not prevent the imposition of lawful restrictions on the exercise of these rights by members of the armed forces, of the police or of the administration of the State.

Article 12
Right to Marry

Men and women of marriageable age have the right to marry and to found a family, according to the national laws governing the exercise of this right.

Article 14
Prohibition of Discrimination

The enjoyment of the rights and freedoms set forth in this Convention shall be secured without discrimination on any ground such as sex, race, colour, language, religion, political or other opinion, national or social origin, association with a national minority, property, birth or other status.

Article 16
Restrictions on Political Activity of Aliens

Nothing in Articles 10, 11 and 14 shall be regarded as preventing the High Contracting Parties from imposing restrictions on the political activity of aliens.

Article 17
Prohibition of Abuse of Rights

Nothing in this Convention may be interpreted as implying for any State, group or person any right to engage in any activity or perform any act aimed at the destruction of any of the rights and freedoms set forth herein or at their limitation to a greater extent than is provided for in the Convention.

Article 18
Limitation on Use of Restrictions on Rights

The restrictions permitted under this Convention to the said rights and freedoms shall not be applied for any purpose other than those for which they have been prescribed.

Part II
The First Protocol

Article 1
Protection of Property

Every natural or legal person is entitled to the peaceful enjoyment of his possessions. No one shall be deprived of his possessions except in the public interest and subject to the conditions provided for by law and by the general principles of international law.

The preceding provisions shall not, however, in any way impair the right of a State to enforce such laws as it deems necessary to control the use of property in accordance with the general interest or to secure the payment of taxes or other contributions or penalties.

Article 2
Right to Education

No person shall be denied the right to education. In the exercise of any functions which it assumes in relation to education and to teaching, the State shall respect the right of parents to ensure such education and teaching in conformity with their own religious and philosophical convictions.

Article 3
Right to Free Elections

The High Contracting Parties undertake to hold free elections at reasonable intervals by secret ballot, under conditions which will ensure the free expression of the opinion of the people in the choice of the legislature.

Part III
The Sixth Protocol

Article 1
Abolition of the Death Penalty

The death penalty shall be abolished. No one shall be condemned to such penalty or executed.

Article 2
Death Penalty in Time of War

A State may make provision in its law for the death penalty in respect of acts committed in time of war or of imminent threat of war; such penalty shall be applied only in the instances laid down in the law and in accordance with its provisions. The State shall communicate to the Secretary General of the Council of Europe the relevant provisions of that law.

Schedule 2
Remedial Orders

Orders

1.—(1) A remedial order may—

(a) contain such incidental, supplemental, consequential or transitional provision as the person making it considers appropriate;
(b) be made so as to have effect from a date earlier than that on which it is made;
(c) make provision for the delegation of specific functions;
(d) make different provision for different cases.

(2) The power conferred by sub-paragraph (1)(a) includes—

(a) power to amend primary legislation (including primary legislation other than that which contains the incompatible provision); and
(b) power to amend or revoke subordinate legislation (including subordinate legislation other than that which contains the incompatible provision).

(3) A remedial order may be made so as to have the same extent as the legislation which it affects.

(4) No person is to be guilty of an offence solely as a result of the retrospective effect of a remedial order.

Procedure

2. No remedial order may be made unless—

(a) a draft of the order has been approved by a resolution of each House of Parliament made after the end of the period of 60 days beginning with the day on which the draft was laid; or
(b) it is declared in the order that it appears to the person making it that, because of the urgency of the matter, it is necessary to make the order without a draft being so approved.

Orders laid in draft

3.—(1) No draft may be laid under paragraph 2(a) unless—
   (a) the person proposing to make the order has laid before Parliament a document which contains a draft of the proposed order and the required information; and
   (b) the period of 60 days, beginning with the day on which the document required by this sub-paragraph was laid, has ended.

(2) If representations have been made during that period, the draft laid under paragraph 2(a) must be accompanied by a statement containing—
   (a) a summary of the representations; and
   (b) if, as a result of the representations, the proposed order has been changed, details of the changes.

Urgent cases

4.—(1) If a remedial order ('the original order') is made without being approved in draft, the person making it must lay it before Parliament, accompanied by the required information, after it is made.

(2) If representations have been made during the period of 60 days beginning with the day on which the original order was made, the person making it must (after the end of that period) lay before Parliament a statement containing—
   (a) a summary of the representations; and
   (b) if, as a result of the representations, he considers it appropriate to make changes to the original order, details of the changes.

(3) If sub-paragraph (2)(b) applies, the person making the statement must—
   (a) make a further remedial order replacing the original order; and
   (b) lay the replacement order before Parliament.

(4) If, at the end of the period of 120 days beginning with the day on which the original order was made, a resolution has not been passed by each House approving the original or replacement order, the order ceases to have effect (but without that affecting anything previously done under either order or the power to make a fresh remedial order).

Definitions

5. In this Schedule—
   'representations' means representations about a remedial order (or proposed remedial order) made to the person making (or proposing to make) it and includes any relevant Parliamentary report or resolution; and
   'required information' means—
      (a) an explanation of the incompatibility which the order (or proposed order) seeks to remove, including particulars of the relevant declaration, finding or order; and
      (b) a statement of the reasons for proceeding under section 10 and for making an order in those terms.

Calculating periods

6. In calculating any period for the purposes of this Schedule, no account is to be taken of any time during which—
   (a) Parliament is dissolved or prorogued; or
   (b) both Houses are adjourned for more than four days.

Schedule 3
Derogation and Reservation

Part I
Derogation

The 1988 notification

The United Kingdom Permanent Representative to the Council of Europe presents his compliments to the Secretary General of the Council, and has the honour to convey the following information in order to ensure compliance with the obligations of Her Majesty's Government in the United Kingdom under Article 15(3) of the Convention for the Protection of Human Rights and Fundamental Freedoms signed at Rome on 4 November 1950.

There have been in the United Kingdom in recent years campaigns of organised terrorism connected with the affairs of Northern Ireland which have manifested themselves in activities which have included repeated murder, attempted murder, maiming, intimidation and violent civil disturbance and in bombing and fire raising which have resulted in death, injury and widespread destruction of property. As a result, a public emergency within the meaning of Article 15(1) of the Convention exists in the United Kingdom.

The Government found it necessary in 1974 to introduce and since then, in cases concerning persons reasonably suspected of involvement in terrorism connected with the affairs of Northern Ireland, or of certain offences under the legislation, who have been detained for 48 hours, to exercise powers enabling further detention without charge, for periods of up to five days, on the authority of the Secretary of State. These powers are at present to be found in Section 12 of the Prevention of Terrorism (Temporary Provisions) Act 1984, Article 9 of the Prevention of Terrorism (Supplemental Temporary Provisions) Order 1984 and Article 10 of the Prevention of Terrorism (Supplemental Temporary Provisions) (Northern Ireland) Order 1984.

Section 12 of the Prevention of Terrorism (Temporary Provisions) Act 1984 provides for a person whom a constable has arrested on reasonable grounds of suspecting him to be guilty of an offence under Section 1, 9 or 10 of the Act, or to be or to have been involved in terrorism connected with the affairs of Northern Ireland, to be detained in right of the arrest for up to 48 hours and thereafter, where the Secretary of State extends the detention period, for up to a further five days. Section 12 substantially re-enacted Section 12 of the Prevention of Terrorism (Temporary Provisions) Act 1976 which, in turn, substantially re-enacted Section 7 of the Prevention of Terrorism (Temporary Provisions) Act 1974.

Article 10 of the Prevention of Terrorism (Supplemental Temporary Provisions) (Northern Ireland) Order 1984 (SI 1984/417) and Article 9 of the Prevention of Terrorism (Supplemental Temporary Provisions) Order 1984 (SI 1984/418) were both made under Sections 13 and 14 of and Schedule 3 to the 1984 Act and substantially re-enacted powers of detention in Orders made under the 1974 and 1976 Acts. A person who is being examined under Article 4 of either Order on his arrival in, or on seeking to leave, Northern Ireland or Great Britain for the purpose of determining whether he is or has been involved in terrorism connected with the affairs of Northern Ireland, or whether there are grounds for suspecting that he has committed an offence under Section 9 of the 1984 Act, may be detained under Article 9 or 10, as appropriate, pending the conclusion of his examination. The period of this examination may exceed 12 hours if an examining officer has reasonable grounds for suspecting him to be or to have been involved in acts of terrorism connected with the affairs of Northern Ireland.

Where such a person is detained under the said Article 9 or 10 he may be detained for up to 48 hours on the authority of an examining officer and thereafter, where the Secretary of State extends the detention period, for up to a further five days.

In its judgment of 29 November 1988 in the Case of *Brogan and Others*, the European Court of Human Rights held that there had been a violation of Article 5(3) in respect of each of the applicants, all of whom had been detained under Section 12 of the 1984 Act. The Court held that even the shortest of the four periods of detention concerned, namely four days and six hours, fell outside the constraints as to time permitted by the first part of Article 5(3). In addition, the Court held that there had been a violation of Article 5(5) in the case of each applicant.

Following this judgment, the Secretary of State for the Home Department informed Parliament on 6 December 1988 that, against the background of the terrorist campaign, and the overriding need to bring terrorists to justice, the Government did not believe that the maximum period of detention should be reduced. He informed Parliament that the Government were examining the matter with a view to responding to the judgment. On 22 December 1988, the Secretary of State further informed Parliament that it remained the Government's wish, if it could be achieved, to find a judicial process under which extended detention might be reviewed and where appropriate authorised by a judge or other judicial officer. But a further period of reflection and consultation was necessary before the Government could bring forward a firm and final view.

Since the judgment of 29 November 1988 as well as previously, the Government have found it necessary to continue to exercise, in relation to terrorism connected with the affairs of Northern Ireland, the powers described above enabling further detention without charge for periods of up to 5 days, on the authority of the Secretary of State, to the extent strictly required by the exigencies of the situation to enable necessary enquiries and investigations properly to be completed in order to decide whether criminal proceedings should be instituted. To the extent that the exercise of these powers may be inconsistent with the obligations imposed by the Convention the Government has availed itself of the right of derogation conferred by Article 15(1) of the Convention and will continue to do so until further notice.

Dated 23 December 1988

The 1989 notification

The United Kingdom Permanent Representative to the Council of Europe presents his compliments to the Secretary General of the Council, and has the honour to convey the following information.

In his communication to the Secretary General of 23 December 1988, reference was made to the introduction and exercise of certain powers under section 12 of the Prevention of Terrorism (Temporary Provisions) Act 1984, Article 9 of the Prevention of Terrorism (Supplemental Temporary Provisions) Order 1984 and Article 10 of the Prevention of Terrorism (Supplemental Temporary Provisions) (Northern Ireland) Order 1984.

These provisions have been replaced by section 14 of and paragraph 6 of Schedule 5 to the Prevention of Terrorism (Temporary Provisions) Act 1989, which make comparable provision. They came into force on 22 March 1989. A copy of these provisions is enclosed.

The United Kingdom Permanent Representative avails himself of this opportunity to renew to the Secretary General the assurance of his highest consideration.

Dated 23 March 1989

Part II
Reservation

At the time of signing the present (First) Protocol, I declare that, in view of certain provisions of the Education Acts in the United Kingdom, the principle affirmed in the second sentence of Article 2 is accepted by the United Kingdom only so far as it is compatible with the provision of efficient instruction and training, and the avoidance of unreasonable public expenditure.

Dated 20 March 1952

Made by the United Kingdom Permanent Representative to the Council of Europe.

APPENDIX B

Rights Brought Home: The Human Rights Bill

CM 3782, 1 OCTOBER 1997

Contents

Preface by the Prime Minister
Introduction and Summary
Chapter 1: The case for change
Chapter 2: The Government's proposals for enforcing the Convention rights
Chapter 3: Improving compliance with the Convention rights
Chapter 4: Derogations, reservations and other protocols
[Annex: The Convention rights (relevant Articles of the European Convention on Human Rights and its First Protocol): not reproduced here]

PREFACE BY THE PRIME MINISTER

The Government is pledged to modernise British politics. We are committed to a comprehensive programme of constitutional reform. We believe it is right to increase individual rights, to decentralise power, to open up government and to reform Parliament.

The elements are well known:

— a Scottish Parliament and a Welsh Assembly giving the people of Scotland and Wales more control over their own affairs within the United Kingdom;
— new rights, based on bringing the European Convention on Human Rights into United Kingdom law;
— an elected Mayor and new strategic authority for London with more accountability in the regions of England;
— freedom of information;
— a referendum on the voting system for the House of Commons; and
— reform of the House of Lords.

This White Paper explains the proposals contained in the Human Rights Bill which we are introducing into Parliament. The Bill marks a major step forward in the achievement of our programme of reform. It will give people in the United Kingdom opportunities to enforce their rights under the European Convention in British courts rather than having to incur the cost and delay of taking a case to the European Human Rights Commission and Court in Strasbourg. It will enhance the awareness of human rights in our society. And it stands alongside our decision to put the promotion of human rights at the forefront of our foreign policy.

I warmly commend these proposals to Parliament and to the people of this counrty.

Introduction and Summary

The Government has a Manifesto commitment to introduce legislation to incorporate the European Convention on Human Rights into United Kingdom law. The Queen's Speech at the opening of the new Parliament announced that the Government would bring forward a Bill for this purpose in the current Session. We are now introducing the Human Rights Bill into Parliament. This White Paper explains what the Bill does, and why.

Before the General Election the Labour Party published a consultation document, *Bringing Rights Home*, setting out in some detail the case for incorporation, and its preliminary proposals for the way this should be done. A number of individuals and organisations responded helpfully with a range of comments on the paper, and have continued to make their knowledge and advice available to the Government. The Government's proposals for the Bill take full account of the responses to *Bringing Rights Home*. Any further comments in response to this White Paper or on the Bill should be sent to:

Human Rights Unit
Home Office
50 Queen Anne's Gate
London SW1H 9AT.

We may make any comments we receive publicly available. Respondents who would prefer their comments to be treated in confidence are invited to indicate this expressly.

Chapter 1 of this White Paper explains the content and status of the European Convention on Human Rights and why the Government considers it desirable to give people in this country easier access to their Convention rights.

The United Kingdom is bound in international law to observe the Convention, which it ratified in 1951, and is answerable for any violation. In some limited circumstances, the United Kingdom courts can already take the Convention into account in domestic proceedings. But public authorities in the United Kingdom are not required as a matter of domestic law to comply with the Convention and, generally speaking, there is no means of having the application of the Convention rights tested in the United Kingdom courts. The Government believes that these arrangements are no longer adequate, given the importance which it attaches to the maintenance of basic human rights in this country, and that the time has come to 'bring rights home'.

Chapter 2 explains the Government's proposals to make the Convention rights enforceable directly in this country. The Bill makes it unlawful for public authorities to act in a way which is incompatible with the Convention rights. This will make it possible for people to invoke their rights in any proceedings—criminal or civil—brought against them by a public authority, or in proceedings which they may bring against a public authority. The Government prefers a system in which Convention rights can be called upon as they arise, in normal court proceedings, rather than confining their consideration to some kind of constitutional court. Courts and tribunals will be able to award whatever remedy, within their normal powers, is appropriate in the circumstances.

Although the courts will not, under the proposals in the Bill, be able to set aside Acts of the United Kingdom Parliament, the Bill requires them to interpret legislation as far as possible in accordance with the Convention. If this is not possible, the higher courts will be able to issue a formal declaration to the effect that the legislative provisions in question are incompatible with the Convention rights. It will then be up to the Government and Parliament to put matters right. The Bill makes a 'fast-track' procedure available for the purpose of amending the law so as to bring it into conformity with the Convention.

Chapter 3 sets out the other measures which the Government intends to take to ensure that the Convention rights are taken more fully into account in the development of new policies and of legislation. It also suggests that Parliament should itself establish a new Human Rights Committee. Amongst the matters on which the Government would welcome advice from a Parliamentary Committee is the possible establishment of a Human Rights Commission, but for the time being the Government has concluded that a new Commission should not be set up by means of this Bill.

Chapter 4 reviews the position on the derogation and reservation which the United Kingdom currently has in place in respect of the Convention and its First Protocol. The Government has concluded that these must remain for the time being, but the Bill requires any derogation to be subject to periodic renewal by Parliament and reservations to be subject to periodic review.

Chapter 4 also reviews the position in respect of those Protocols to the Convention which guarantee other rights (Protocols 4, 6 and 7) and which the United Kingdom has not so far accepted. The Government does not propose that the United Kingdom should ratify at present Protocol 4 or Protocol 6, but it does propose to sign and ratify Protocol 7 once some existing legislation has been amended.

[The **Annex** sets out the text of the Convention rights themselves.[1]]

CHAPTER I
THE CASE FOR CHANGE

The European Convention on Human Rights

1.1 The European Convention for the Protection of Human Rights and Fundamental Freedoms is a treaty of the Council of Europe. This institution was established at the end of the Second World War, as part of the Allies' programme to reconstruct durable civilisation on the mainland of Europe. The Council was established before the European Union and, although many nations are members of both, the two bodies are quite separate.

1.2 The United Kingdom played a major part in drafting the Convention, and there was a broad agreement between the major political parties about the need for it (one of its draftsmen later became, as Lord Kilmuir, Lord Chancellor in the Conservative Administration from 1954 to 1962). The United Kingdom was among the first group of countries to sign the Convention. It was the very first country to ratify it, in March 1951. In 1966 the United Kingdom accepted that an individual person, and not merely another State, could bring a case against the United Kingdom in Strasbourg (the home of the European Commission of Human Rights and Court of Human Rights, which were established by the Convention). Successive administrations in the United Kingdom have maintained these arrangements.

1.3 The European Convention is not the only international human rights agreement to which the United Kingdom and other like-minded countries are party, but over the years it has become one of the premier agreements defining standards of behaviour across Europe. It was also for many years unique because of the system which it put in place for people from signatory countries to take complaints to Strasbourg and for those complaints to be judicially determined. These arrangements are by now well tried and tested. The rights and freedoms which are guaranteed under the Convention are ones with which the people of this country are plainly comfortable. They therefore afford an excellent basis for the Human Rights Bill which we are now introducing.

1.4 The constitutional arrangements in most continental European countries have meant that their acceptance of the Convention went hand in hand with its incorporation into their domestic law. In this country it was long believed that the rights and freedoms guaranteed by the Convention could be delivered under our common law. In the last two decades, however, there has been a growing awareness that it is not sufficient to rely on the common law and that incorporation is necessary.

1.5 The Liberal Democrat Peer, Lord Lester of Herne Hill QC, recently introduced two Bills on incorporation into the House of Lords (in 1994 and 1996). Before that, the then Conservative MP Sir Edward Gardner QC introduced a Private Member's Bill on incorporation into the House of Commons in 1987. At the time of introducing his Bill he commented on the language of the Articles in the Convention, saying: 'It is language which echoes right down the corridors of history. It goes deep into our history and as far back as Magna Carta.' (*Hansard*, 6 February 1987, col 1224). In preparing this White Paper the Government has paid close attention to earlier debates and proposals for incorporation.

[1] Not included here.

The Convention rights

1.6 The Convention contains Articles which guarantee a number of basic human rights. They deal with the right to life (Article 2); torture or inhuman or degrading treatment or punishment (Article 3); slavery and forced labour (Article 4); liberty and security of person (Article 5); fair trial (Article 6); retrospective criminal laws (Article 7); respect for private and family life, home and correspondence (Article 8); freedom of thought, conscience and religion (Article 9); freedom of expression (Article 10); freedom of peaceful assembly and freedom of association, including the right to join a trade union (Article 11); the right to marry and to found a family (Article 12); and discrimination in the enjoyment of these rights and freedoms (Article 14).

1.7 The United Kingdom is also a party to the First Protocol to the Convention, which guarantees the right to the peaceful enjoyment of possessions (Article 1), the right to education (Article 2) and the right to free elections (Article 3).

1.8 The rights in the Convention are set out in general terms, and they are subject in the Convention to a number of qualifications which are also of a general character. Some of these qualifications are set out in the substantive Articles themselves (see, for example, Article 10, concerning freedom of expression); others are set out in Articles 16 to 18 of the Convention. Sometimes too the rights guaranteed under the Convention need to be balanced against each other (for example, those guaranteed by Article 8 and Article 10).

Applications under the Convention

1.9 Anyone within the United Kingdom jurisdiction who is aggrieved by an action of the executive or by the effect of the existing law and who believes it is contrary to the European Convention can submit a petition to the European Commission of Human Rights. The Commission will first consider whether the petition is admissible. One of the conditions of admissibility is that the applicant must have gone through all the steps available to him or her at home for challenging the decision which he or she is complaining about. If the Commission decides that a complaint is admissible, and if a friendly settlement cannot be secured, it will send a confidential report to the Committee of Ministers of the Council of Europe, stating its opinion on whether there has been a violation. The matter may end there, with a decision by the Committee (which in practice always adopts the opinion of the Commission), or the case may be referred on to the European Court of Human Rights[1] for consideration. If the Court finds that there has been a violation it may itself 'afford just satisfaction' to the injured party by an award of damages or an award of costs and expenses. The court may also find that a formal finding of a violation is sufficient. There is no appeal from the Court.

Effect of a Court judgment

1.10 A finding by the European Court of Human Rights of a violation of a Convention right does not have the effect of automatically changing United Kingdom law and practice: that is a matter for the United Kingdom Government and Parliament. But the United Kingdom, like all other States who are parties to the Convention, has agreed to abide by the decisions of the Court or (where the case has not been referred to the Court) the Committee of Ministers. It follows that, in cases where a violation has been found, the State concerned must ensure that any deficiency in its internal laws is rectified so as to bring them into line with the Convention. The State is responsible for deciding what changes are needed, but it must satisfy the Committee of Ministers that the steps taken are sufficient. Successive United Kingdom administrations have accepted these obligations in full.

Relationship to current law in the United Kingdom

1.11 When the United Kingdom ratified the Convention the view was taken that the rights and freedoms which the Convention guarantees were already, in substance, fully protected in British law. It was not considered necessary to write the Convention itself into British law, or to introduce any new laws in the United Kingdom in order to be sure of being able to comply with the Convention.

[1] Protocol 11 to the Convention, which will come into force on 1 November 1998, will replace the existing part-time European Commission and Court of Human Rights with a single full-time Court.

1.12 From the point of view of the *international* obligation which the United Kingdom was undertaking when it signed and ratified the Convention, this was understandable. Moreover, the European Court of Human Rights explicitly confirmed that it was not a necessary part of proper observance of the Convention that it should be incorporated into the laws of the States concerned.

1.13 However, since its drafting nearly 50 years ago, almost all the States which are party to the European Convention on Human Rights have gradually incorporated it into their domestic law in one way or another. Ireland and Norway have not done so, but Ireland has a Bill of Rights which guarantees rights similar to those guaranteed by the Convention and Norway is also in the process of incorporating the Convention. Several other countries with which we have close links and which share the common law tradition, such as Canada and New Zealand, have provided similar protection for human rights in their own legal systems.

The case for incorporation

1.14 The effect of non-incorporation on the British people is a very practical one. The rights, originally developed with major help from the United Kingdom Government, are no longer actually seen as British rights. And enforcing them takes too long and costs too much. It takes on average five years to get an action into the European Court of Human Rights once all domestic remedies have been exhausted; and it costs an average of £30,000. Bringing these rights home will mean that the British people will be able to argue for their rights in the British courts—without this inordinate delay and cost. It will also mean that the rights will be brought much more fully into the jurisprudence of the courts throughout the United Kingdom, and their interpretation will thus be far more subtly and powerfully woven into our law. And there will be another distinct benefit. British judges will be enabled to make a distinctively British contribution to the development of the jurisprudence of human rights in Europe.

1.15 Moreover, in the Government's view, the approach which the United Kingdom has so far adopted towards the Convention does not sufficiently reflect its importance and has not stood the test of time.

1.16 The most obvious proof of this lies in the number of cases in which the European Commission and Court have found that there have been violations of the Convention rights in the United Kingdom. The causes vary. The Government recognises that interpretations of the rights guaranteed under the Convention have developed over the years, reflecting changes in society and attitudes. Sometimes United Kingdom laws have proved to be inherently at odds with the Convention rights. On other occasions, although the law has been satisfactory, something has been done which our courts have held to be lawful by United Kingdom standards but which breaches the Convention. In other cases again, there has simply been no framework within which the compatibility with the Convention rights of an executive act or decision can be tested in the British courts: these courts can of course review the exercise of executive discretion, but they can do so only on the basis of what is lawful or unlawful according to the law in the United Kingdom as it stands. It is plainly unsatisfactory that someone should be the victim of a breach of the Convention standards by the State yet cannot bring any case at all in the British courts, simply because British law does not recognise the right in the same terms as one contained in the Convention.

1.17 For individuals, and for those advising them, the road to Strasbourg is long and hard. Even when they get there, the Convention enforcement machinery is subject to long delays. This might be convenient for a government which was half-hearted about the Convention and the right of individuals to apply under it, since it postpones the moment at which changes in domestic law or practice must be made. But it is not in keeping with the importance which this Government attaches to the observance of basic human rights.

Bringing Rights Home

1.18 We therefore believe that the time has come to enable people to enforce their Convention rights against the State in the British courts, rather than having to incur the delays and expense which are involved in taking a case to the European Human Rights Commission and Court in Strasbourg and which may altogether deter some people from pursuing their rights. Enabling courts in the United Kingdom to rule on the application of the Convention will also help to influence the development of case law on the

Convention by the European Court of Human Rights on the basis of familiarity with our laws and customs and of sensitivity to practices and procedures in the United Kingdom. Our courts' decisions will provide the European Court with a useful source of information and reasoning for its own decisions. United Kingdom judges have a very high reputation internationally, but the fact that they do not deal in the same concepts as the European Court of Human Rights limits the extent to which their judgments can be drawn upon and followed. Enabling the Convention rights to be judged by British courts will also lead to closer scrutiny of the human rights implications of new legislation and new policies. If legislation is enacted which is incompatible with the Convention, a ruling by the domestic courts to that effect will be much more direct and immediate than a ruling from the European Court of Human Rights. The Government of the day, and Parliament, will want to minimise the risk of that happening.

1.19 Our aim is a straightforward one. It is to make more directly accessible the rights which the British people already enjoy under the Convention. In other words, to bring those rights home.

Chapter 2
The Government's Proposals for Enforcing the Convention Rights

2.1 The essential feature of the Human Rights Bill is that the United Kingdom will not be bound to give effect to the Convention rights merely as a matter of international law, but will also give them further effect directly in our domestic law. But there is more than one way of achieving this. This Chapter explains the choices which the Government has made for the Bill.

A new requirement on public authorities

2.2 Although the United Kingdom has an international obligation to comply with the Convention, there at present is no requirement in our domestic law on central and local government, or others exercising similar executive powers, to exercise those powers in a way which is compatible with the Convention. This Bill will change that by making it unlawful for public authorities to act in a way which is incompatible with the Convention rights. The definition of what constitutes a public authority is in wide terms. Examples of persons or organisations whose acts or omissions it is intended should be able to be challenged include central government (including executive agencies); local government; the police; immigration officers; prisons; courts and tribunals themselves; and, to the extent that they are exercising public functions, companies responsible for areas of activity which were previously within the public sector, such as the privatised utilities. The actions of Parliament, however, are excluded.

2.3 A person who is aggrieved by an act or omission on the part of a public authority which is incompatible with the Convention rights will be able to challenge the act or omission in the courts. The effects will be wide-ranging. They will extend both to legal actions which a public authority pursues against individuals (for example, where a criminal prosecution is brought or where an administrative decision is being enforced through legal proceedings) and to cases which individuals pursue against a public authority (for example, for judicial review of an executive decision). Convention points will normally be taken in the context of proceedings instituted against individuals or already open to them, but, if none is available, it will be possible for people to bring cases on Convention grounds alone. Individuals or organisations seeking judicial review of decisions by public authorities on Convention grounds will need to show that they have been directly affected, as they must if they take a case to Strasbourg.

2.4 It is our intention that people or organisations should be able to argue that their Convention rights have been infringed by a public authority in our courts at any level. This will enable the Convention rights to be applied from the outset against the facts and background of a particular case, and the people concerned to obtain their remedy at the earliest possible moment. We think this is preferable to allowing cases to run their ordinary course but then referring them to some kind of separate constitutional court which, like the European Court of Human Rights, would simply review cases which had already passed through the regular legal machinery. In considering Convention points, our courts will be required to take account of relevant decisions of the European Commission and Court of Human Rights (although these will not be binding).

2.5 The Convention is often described as a 'living instrument' because it is interpreted by the European Court in the light of present day conditions and therefore reflects changing social attitudes and the changes in the circumstances of society. In future our judges will be able to contribute to this dynamic and evolving interpretation of the Convention. In particular, our courts will be required to balance the protection of individuals' fundamental rights against the demands of the general interest of the community, particularly in relation to Articles 8-11 where a State may restrict the protected right to the extent that this is 'necessary in a democratic society'.

Remedies for a failure to comply with the Convention

2.6 A public authority which is found to have acted unlawfully by failing to comply with the Convention will not be exposed to criminal penalties. But the court or tribunal will be able to grant the injured person any remedy which is within its normal powers to grant and which it considers appropriate and just in the circumstances. What remedy is appropriate will of course depend both on the facts of the case and on a proper balance between the rights of the individual and the public interest. In some cases, the right course may be for the decision of the public authority in the particular case to be quashed. In other cases, the only appropriate remedy may be an award of damages. The Bill provides that, in considering an award of damages on Convention grounds, the courts are to take into account the principles applied by the European Court of Human Rights in awarding compensation, so that people will be able to receive compensation from a domestic court equivalent to what they would have received in Strasbourg.

Interpretation of legislation

2.7 The Bill provides for legislation—both Acts of Parliament and secondary legislation—to be interpreted so far as possible so as to be compatible with the Convention. This goes far beyond the present rule which enables the courts to take the Convention into account in resolving any ambiguity in a legislative provision. The courts will be required to interpret legislation so as to uphold the Convention rights unless the legislation itself is so clearly incompatible with the Convention that it is impossible to do so.

2.8 This 'rule of construction' is to apply to past as well as to future legislation. To the extent that it affects the meaning of a legislative provision, the courts will not be bound by previous interpretations. They will be able to build a new body of case law, taking into account the Convention rights.

A declaration of incompatibility with the Convention rights

2.9 If the courts decide in any case that it is impossible to interpret an Act of Parliament in a way which is compatible with the Convention, the Bill enables a formal declaration to be made that its provisions are incompatible with the Convention. A declaration of incompatibility will be an important statement to make, and the power to make it will be reserved to the higher courts. They will be able to make a declaration in any proceedings before them, whether the case originated with them (as, in the High Court, on judicial review of an executive act) or in considering an appeal from a lower court or tribunal. The Government will have the right to intervene in any proceedings where such a declaration is a possible outcome. A decision by the High Court or Court of Appeal, determining whether or not such a declaration should be made, will itself be appealable.

Effect of court decisions on legislation

2.10 A declaration that legislation is incompatible with the Convention rights will not of itself have the effect of changing the law, which will continue to apply. But it will almost certainly prompt the Government and Parliament to change the law.

2.11 The Government has considered very carefully whether it would be right for the Bill to go further, and give to courts in the United Kingdom the power to set aside an Act of Parliament which they believe is incompatible with the Convention rights. In considering this question, we have looked at a number of models. The Canadian Charter of Rights and Freedoms 1982 enables the courts to strike down any legislation which is inconsistent with the Charter, unless the legislation contains an explicit statement that it is to apply 'notwithstanding' the provisions of the Charter. But legislation which has been struck down may be re-enacted with a 'notwithstanding' clause. In New Zealand, on the other hand, although there was an earlier proposal for legislation on lines similar to the Canadian Charter, the human rights legislation which was eventually enacted after wide consultation took a different form. The New Zealand Bill of Rights Act 1990 is an 'interpretative' statute which requires past and future legislation to be interpreted consistently with the rights contained in the Act as far as possible but provides that legislation stands if that is impossible. In Hong Kong, a middle course was adopted. The Hong Kong Bill of Rights Ordinance 1991 distinguishes between legislation enacted before and after the Ordinance took effect: previous legislation is subordinated to the provisions of the Ordinance, but subsequent legislation takes precedence over it.

2.12 The Government has also considered the European Communities Act 1972 which provides for European law, in cases where that law has 'direct effect', to take precedence over domestic law. There is, however, an essential difference between European Community law and the European Convention on Human Rights, because it is a *requirement* of membership of the European Union that member States give priority to directly effective EC law in their own legal systems. There is no such requirement in the Convention.

2.13 The Government has reached the conclusion that courts should not have the power to set aside primary legislation, past or future, on the ground of incompatibility with the Convention. This conclusion arises from the importance which the Government attaches to Parliamentary sovereignty. In this context, Parliamentary sovereignty means that Parliament is competent to make any law on any matter of its choosing and no court may question the validity of any Act that it passes. In enacting legislation, Parliament is making decisions about important matters of public policy. The authority to make those decisions derives from a democratic mandate. Members of Parliament in the House of Commons possess such a mandate because they are elected, accountable and representative. To make provision in the Bill for the courts to set aside Acts of Parliament would confer on the judiciary a general power over the decisions of Parliament which under our present constitutional arrangements they do not possess, and would be likely on occasions to draw the judiciary into serious conflict with Parliament. There is no evidence to suggest that they desire this power, nor that the public wish them to have it. Certainly, this Government has no mandate for any such change.

2.14 It has been suggested that the courts should be able to uphold the rights in the Human Rights Bill in preference to any provisions of earlier legislation which are incompatible with those rights. This is on the basis that a later Act of Parliament takes precedence over an earlier Act if there is a conflict. But the Human Rights Bill is intended to provide a new basis for judicial interpretation of all legislation, not a basis for striking down any part of it.

2.15 The courts will, however, be able to strike down or set aside secondary legislation which is incompatible with the Convention, unless the terms of the parent statute make this impossible. The courts can already strike down or set aside secondary legislation when they consider it to be outside the powers conferred by the statute under which it is made, and it is right that they should be able to do so when it is incompatible with the Convention rights and could have been framed differently.

Entrenchment

2.16 On one view, human rights legislation is so important that it should be given added protection from subsequent amendment or repeal. The Constitution of the United States of America, for example, guarantees rights which can be amended or repealed only by securing qualified majorities in both the House of Representatives and the Senate, and among the States themselves. But an arrangement of this kind could not be reconciled with our own constitutional traditions, which allow any Act of Parliament to be amended or repealed by a subsequent Act of Parliament. We do not believe that it is necessary or would be desirable to attempt to devise such a special arrangement for this Bill.

Amending legislation

2.17 Although the Bill does not allow the courts to set aside Acts of Parliament, it will nevertheless have a profound impact on the way that legislation is interpreted and applied, and it will have the effect of putting the issues squarely to the Government and Parliament for further consideration. It is important to ensure that the Government and Parliament, for their part, can respond quickly. In the normal way, primary legislation can be amended only by further primary legislation, and this can take a long time. Given the volume of Government business, an early opportunity to legislate may not arise; and the process of legislating is itself protracted. Emergency legislation can be enacted very quickly indeed, but it is introduced only in the most exceptional circumstances.

2.18 The Bill provides for a fast-track procedure for changing legislation in response either to a declaration of incompatibility by our own higher courts or to a finding of a violation of the Convention in Strasbourg. The appropriate Government Minister will be able to amend the legislation by Order so as to make it compatible with the Convention. The Order will be subject to approval by both Houses of Parliament before taking effect, except where the need to amend the legislation is particularly urgent, when the Order will take effect immediately but will expire after a short period if not approved by Parliament.

2.19 There are already precedents for using secondary legislation to amend primary legislation in some circumstances, and we think the use of such a procedure is acceptable in this context and would be welcome as a means of improving the observance of human rights. Plainly the Minister would have to exercise this power only in relation to the provisions which contravene the Convention, together with any necessary consequential amendments. In other words, Ministers would not have carte blanche to amend unrelated parts of the Act in which the breach is discovered.

Scotland

2.20 In Scotland, the position with regard to Acts of the Westminster Parliament will be the same as in England and Wales. All courts will be required to interpret the legislation in a way which is compatible with the Convention so far as possible. If a provision is found to be incompatible with the Convention, the Court of Session or the High Court will be able to make a declarator to that effect, but this will not affect the validity or continuing operation of the provision.

2.21 The position will be different, however, in relation to Acts of the Scottish Parliament when it is established. The Government has decided that the Scottish Parliament will have no power to legislate in a way which is incompatible with the Convention; and similarly that the Scottish Executive will have no power to make subordinate legislation or to take executive action which is incompatible with the Convention. It will accordingly be possible to challenge such legislation and actions in the Scottish courts on the ground that the Scottish Parliament or Executive has incorrectly applied its powers. If the challenge is successful then the legislation or action would be held to be unlawful. As with other issues concerning the powers of the Scottish Parliament, there will be a procedure for inferior courts to refer such issues to the superior Scottish courts; and those courts in turn will be able to refer the matter to the Judicial Committee of the Privy Council. If such issues are decided by the superior Scottish courts, an appeal from their decision will be to the Judicial Committee. These arrangements are in line with the Government's general approach to devolution.

Wales

2.22 Similarly, the Welsh Assembly will not have power to make subordinate legislation or take executive action which is incompatible with the Convention. It will be possible to challenge such legislation and action in the courts, and for them to be quashed, on the ground that the Assembly has exceeded its powers.

Northern Ireland

2.23 Acts of the Westminster Parliament will be treated in the same way in Northern Ireland as in the rest of the United Kingdom. But Orders in Council and other related legislation will be treated as subordinate legislation. In other words, they will be struck down by the courts if they are incompatible with the

Convention. Most such legislation is a temporary means of enacting legislation which would otherwise be done by measures of a devolved Northern Ireland legislature.

Chapter 3
Improving Compliance with the Convention Rights

3.1 The enforcement of Convention rights will be a matter for the courts, whilst the Government and Parliament will have the different but equally important responsibility of revising legislation where necessary. But it is also highly desirable for the Government to ensure as far as possible that legislation which it places before Parliament in the normal way is compatible with the Convention rights, and for Parliament to ensure that the human rights implications of legislation are subject to proper consideration before the legislation is enacted.

Government legislation

3.2 The Human Rights Bill introduces a new procedure to make the human rights implications of proposed Government legislation more transparent. The responsible Minister will be required to provide a statement that in his or her view the proposed Bill is compatible with the Convention. The Government intends to include this statement alongside the Explanatory and Financial Memorandum which accompanies a Bill when it is introduced into each House of Parliament.

3.3 There may be occasions where such a statement cannot be provided, for example because it is essential to legislate on a particular issue but the policy in question requires a risk to be taken in relation to the Convention, or because the arguments in relation to the Convention issues raised are not clear-cut. In such cases, the Minister will indicate that he or she cannot provide a positive statement but that the Government nevertheless wishes Parliament to proceed to consider the Bill. Parliament would expect the Minister to explain his or her reasons during the normal course of the proceedings on the Bill. This will ensure that the human rights implications are debated at the earliest opportunity.

Consideration of draft legislation within Government

3.4 The new requirement to make a statement about the compliance of draft legislation with the Convention will have a significant and beneficial impact on the preparation of draft legislation within Government before its introduction into Parliament. It will ensure that all Ministers, their departments and officials are fully seized of the gravity of the Convention's obligations in respect of human rights. But we also intend to strengthen collective Government procedures so as to ensure that a proper assessment is made of the human rights implications when collective approval is sought for a new policy, as well as when any draft Bill is considered by Ministers. Revised guidance to Departments on these procedures will, like the existing guidance, be publicly available.

3.5 Some central co-ordination will also be extremely desirable in considering the approach to be taken to Convention points in criminal or civil proceedings, or in proceedings for judicial review, to which a Government department is a party. This is likely to require an inter-departmental group of lawyers and administrators meeting on a regular basis to ensure that a consistent approach is taken and to ensure that developments in case law are well understood by all those in Government who are involved in proceedings on Convention points. We do not, however, see any need to make a particular Minister responsible for promoting human rights across Government, or to set up a separate new Unit for this purpose. The responsibility for complying with human rights requirements rests on the Government as a whole.

A Parliamentary Committee on Human Rights

3.6 *Bringing Rights Home* suggested that 'Parliament itself should play a leading role in protecting the rights which are at the heart of a parliamentary democracy'. How this is achieved is a matter for Parliament to decide, but in the Government's view the best course would be to establish a new Parliamentary Committee with functions relating to human rights. This would not require legislation or any change in Parliamentary procedure. There could be a Joint Committee of both Houses of Parliament or each House could have its own Committee; or there could be a Committee which met jointly for some purposes and separately for others.

3.7 The new Committee might conduct enquiries on a range of human rights issues relating to the Convention, and produce reports so as to assist the Government and Parliament in deciding what action to take. It might also want to range more widely, and examine issues relating to the other international obligations of the United Kingdom such as proposals to accept new rights under other human rights treaties.

Should there be a Human Rights Commission?

3.8 *Bringing Rights Home* canvassed views on the establishment of a Human Rights Commission, and this possibility has received a good deal of attention. No commitment to establish a Commission was, however, made in the Manifesto on which the Government was elected. The Government's priority is implementation of its Manifesto commitment to give further effect to the Convention rights in domestic law so that people can enforce those rights in United Kingdom courts. Establishment of a new Human Rights Commission is not central to that objective and does not need to form part of the current Bill.

3.9 Moreover, the idea of setting up a new human rights body is not universally acclaimed. Some reservations have been expressed, particularly from the point of view of the impact on existing bodies concerned with particular aspects of human rights, such as the Commission for Racial Equality and the Equal Opportunities Commission, whose primary concern is to protect the rights for which they were established. A quinquennial review is currently being conducted of the Equal Opportunities Commission, and the Government has also decided to establish a new Disability Rights Commission.

3.10 The Government's conclusion is that, before a Human Rights Commission could be established by legislation, more consideration needs to be given to how it would work in relation to such bodies, and to the new arrangements to be established for Parliamentary and Government scrutiny of human rights issues. This is necessary not only for the purposes of framing the legislation but also to justify the additional public expenditure needed to establish and run a new Commission. A range of organisational issues need more detailed consideration before the legislative and financial case for a new Commission is made, and there needs to be a greater degree of consensus on an appropriate model among existing human rights bodies.

3.11 However, the Government has not closed its mind to the idea of a new Human Rights Commission at some stage in the future in the light of practical experience of the working of the new legislation. If Parliament establishes a Committee on Human Rights, one of its main tasks might be to conduct an inquiry into whether a Human Rights Commission is needed and how it should operate. The Government would want to give full weight to the Committee's report in considering whether to create a statutory Human Rights Commission in future.

3.12 It has been suggested that a new Commission might be funded from non-Government sources. The Government would not wish to deter a move towards a non-statutory, privately-financed body if its role was limited to functions such as public education and advice to individuals. However, a non-statutory body could not absorb any of the functions of the existing statutory bodies concerned with aspects of human rights.

Chapter 4
Derogations, Reservations and Other Protocols

Derogations

4.1 Article 15 of the Convention permits a State to derogate from certain Articles of the Convention in time of war or other public emergency threatening the life of the nation. The United Kingdom has one derogation in place, in respect of Article 5(3) of the Convention.

4.2 The derogation arose from a case in 1988 in which the European Court of Human Rights held that the detention of the applicants in the case before it under the Prevention of Terrorism (Temporary Provisions) Act 1984 for more than four days constituted a breach of Article 5(3) of the Convention, because they had not been brought promptly before a judicial authority. The Government of the day entered a derogation following the judgment in order to preserve the Secretary of State's power under the Act to extend the period of detention of persons suspected of terrorism connected with the affairs of Northern Ireland for a total of up to seven days. The validity of the derogation was subsequently upheld by the European Court of Human Rights in another case in 1993.

4.3 We are considering what change might be made to the arrangements under the prevention of terrorism legislation. Substituting judicial for executive authority for extensions, which would mean that the derogation could be withdrawn, would require primary legislation. In the meantime, however, the derogation remains necessary. The Bill sets out the text of the derogation, and Article 5(3) will have effect in domestic law for the time being subject to its terms.

4.4 Given our commitment to promoting human rights, however, we would not want the derogation to remain in place indefinitely without good reasons. Accordingly its effect in domestic law will be time-limited. If not withdrawn earlier, it will expire five years after the Bill comes into force unless both Houses of Parliament agree that it should be renewed, and similarly thereafter. The Bill contains similar provision in respect of any new derogation which may be entered in future.

Reservations

4.5 Article 64 of the Convention allows a state to enter a reservation when a law in force is not in conformity with a Convention provision. The United Kingdom is a party to the First Protocol to the Convention, but has a reservation in place in respect of Article 2 of the Protocol. Article 2 sets out two principles. The first states that no person shall be denied the right to education. The second is that, in exercising any functions in relation to education and teaching, the State shall respect the right of parents to ensure that such education and teaching is in conformity with their own religious and philosophical convictions. The reservation makes it clear that the United Kingdom accepts this second principle only so far as it is compatible with the provision of efficient instruction and training, and the avoidance of unreasonable public expenditure.

4.6 The reservation reflects the fundamental principle originally enacted in the Education Act 1944, and now contained in section 9 of the Education Act 1996, 'that pupils are to be educated in accordance with the wishes of their parents so far as that is compatible with the provision of efficient instruction and training and the avoidance of unreasonable public expenditure'. There is similar provision in Scottish legislation. The reservation does not affect the right to education in Article 2. Nor does it deny parents the right to have account taken of their religious or philosophical convictions. Its purpose is to recognise that in the provision of State-funded education a balance must be struck in some cases between the convictions of parents and what is educationally sound and affordable.

4.7 Having carefully considered this, the Government has concluded that the reservation should be kept in place. Its text is included in the Bill, and Article 2 of the First Protocol will have effect in domestic law subject to its terms.

4.8 Whilst derogations are permitted under the Convention only in times of war or other public emergency, and so are clearly temporary, there is no such limitation in respect of reservations. We do not therefore propose to make the effect of the reservation in domestic law subject to periodic renewal by Parliament, but the Bill requires the Secretary of State (the Secretary of State for Education and Employment) to review the reservation every five years and to lay a report before Parliament.

Other Protocols

4.9 Protocols 4, 6 and 7 guarantee a number of rights additional to those in the original Convention itself and its First Protocol. These further rights have been added largely to reflect the wider range of rights subsequently included under the International Covenant on Civil and Political Rights. There is no obligation upon States who are party to the original Convention to accept these additional Protocols, but the Government has taken the opportunity to review the position of the United Kingdom on Protocols 4, 6 and 7.

4.10 **Protocol** 4 contains a prohibition on the deprivation of liberty on grounds of inability to fulfil contractual obligations; a right to liberty of movement; a right to non-expulsion from the home State; a right of entry to the State of which a person is a national; and a prohibition on the collective expulsion of aliens.

These provisions largely reflect similar (but not identical) rights provided under the International Covenant on Civil and Political Rights. Protocol 4 was signed by the United Kingdom in 1963 but not subsequently ratified because of concerns about what is the exact extent of the obligation regarding a right of entry.

4.11 These are important rights, and we would like to see them given formal recognition in our law. But we also believe that existing laws in relation to different categories of British nationals must be maintained. It will be possible to ratify Protocol 4 only if the potential conflicts with our domestic laws can be resolved. This remains under consideration but we do not propose to ratify Protocol 4 at present.

4.12 **Protocol 6** requires the complete abolition of the death penalty other than in time of war or imminent threat of war. It does not permit any derogation or reservation. The Protocol largely parallels the Second Optional Protocol to the International Covenant on Civil and Political Rights, which the United Kingdom has not accepted.

4.13 The death penalty was abolished as a sentence for murder in 1965 following a free vote in the House of Commons. It remains as a penalty for treason, piracy with violence, and certain armed forces offences. No execution for these offences has taken place since 1946, when the war-time Nazi propagandist William Joyce (known as Lord Haw-Haw) was hanged at Wandsworth prison. The last recorded execution for piracy was in 1830. Thus there might appear to be little difficulty in our ratifying Protocol 6. This would, however, make it impossible for a United Kingdom Parliament to re-introduce the death penalty for murder, short of denouncing the European Convention. The view taken so far is that the issue is not one of basic constitutional principle but is a matter of judgement and conscience to be decided by Members of Parliament as they see fit. For these reasons, we do not propose to ratify Protocol 6 at present.

4.14 **Protocol** 7 contains a prohibition on the expulsion of aliens without a decision in accordance with the law or opportunities for review; a right to a review of conviction or sentence after criminal conviction; a right to compensation following a miscarriage of justice; a prohibition on double jeopardy in criminal cases; and a right to equality between spouses. These rights reflect similar rights protected under the International Covenant on Civil and Political Rights.

4.15 In general, the provisions of Protocol 7 reflect principles already inherent in our law. In view of concerns in some of these areas in recent years, the Government believes that it would be particularly helpful to give these important principles the same legal status as other rights in the Convention by ratifying and incorporating Protocol 7. There is, however, a difficulty with this because a few provisions of our domestic law, for example in relation to the property rights of spouses, could not be interpreted in a way which is compatible with Protocol 7. The Government intends to legislate to remove these inconsistencies, when a suitable opportunity occurs, and then to sign and ratify the Protocol.

4.16 The Secretary of State will be able to amend the Human Rights Act by Order so as to insert into it the rights contained in any Protocols to the Convention which the United Kingdom ratifies in future. The Order will be subject to approval by both Houses of Parliament. The Bill also enables any reservation to a Protocol to be added, but as with the existing reservation it will have to be reviewed every five years if not withdrawn earlier.

APPENDIX C

Rules of Court and Practice Directions under the Human Rights Act*

Civil Procedure Rules and Practice Directions

Section 2—citation of authorities

To be inserted in the first practice direction to CPR Part 39 (Hearings)

Citation of Human Rights Material

8.1 Section 2 of the Human Rights Act 1998 provides that a court or tribunal determining a question which has arisen in connection with a Convention right must take into account judgments, decisions, declarations and advisory opinions of the European Court of Human Rights, the Commission and the Committee of Ministers, so far as, in the opinion of the court or tribunal, they are relevant to the proceedings in which that question has arisen ('Strasbourg authorities').

8.2 This paragraph sets out the procedure where a party intends to cite a Strasbourg authority at a hearing.

(1) The Strasbourg authority to be cited should be from an authoritative and complete report that is readily available. The reports listed in paragraph 8.3 meet those criteria. Permission is required to cite from any other source.

(2) The party must give to the court and any other party a list of the Strasbourg authorities he intends to cite and copies of the reports or other sources from which they are to be cited not more than 7 days nor less than three days before the hearing.

8.3 The reports of Strasbourg authorities referred to in paragraph 8.2 are:

Copies of the complete original texts issued by the European Court and Commission either paper based or from the Court's judgment database (HUDOC), which is available on the Internet.

Judgments of the European Court of Human Rights, (published by Carl Heymanns Verlag KG).

Reports, Judgments and Decisions of the European Court of Human Rights, (published by Carl Heymanns Verlag KG).

Decisions of the European Commission of Human Rights, (published by Carl Heymanns Verlag KG).

Decisions and Reports of the European Commission of Human Rights volumes 1–96, (published by Carl Heymanns Verlag KG).

European Human Rights Reports (published by Sweet and Maxwell).

Human Rights Cases (published by Butterworths).

Full texts of Strasbourg authorities taken from the following electronic databases:

- *Case Law Service* (published byLawtel)
- *Eurolaw* (published by ILI)
- *JUSTIS* (published by Context Electronic Publishers)
- *Lexis-Nexis*
- *Westlaw UK*.

* At the time of writing, the government has chosen not to promulgate the rules until September 2000. Only drafts were available at the time of going to press.

Sections 4 and 5—declaration of incompatibility, joining a Minister

To be inserted in CPR Part 19 (Parties and Group Litigation)

Human Rights

19.5(1) Where at any time in any proceedings a court begins to consider whether to make a declaration of incompatibility in accordance with section 4 of the Human Rights Act 1998 it must give notice to the Crown.

(2) Where paragraph (1) applies a Minister, or other person permitted by the Human Rights Act 1998, shall be joined as a party on giving notice to the court.

(3) The court may not make a declaration of incompatibility until either—
(a) a Minister, or other person permitted by the Human Rights Act 1998, has been joined as a party, or
(b) 21 days after the date of the notice to the Crown, if earlier.

(A practice direction makes provision for these notices. Only courts specified in section 4 of the Human Rights Act 1998 can make a declaration of incompatibility.)

(4) Where in any proceedings a claim is made under section 7(1)(a) of the Human Rights Act 1998 in respect of a judicial act to which section 9(3) and (4) of that Act applies—
(a) that claim must be set out in the statement of case or the appeal notice; and
(b) the court must give notice to the Crown.

(5) Where paragraph (4) applies and the appropriate person does not apply to be joined as a party the court may join the appropriate person as a party to the proceedings, 21 days after service of the notice.

(A practice direction makes provision for these notices. It may make different provision for different situations. Section 9(4) of the Human Rights Act 1998 provides that an award of damages is to be made against the Crown but no award can be made unless the appropriate person is a party to the proceedings. The appropriate person is defined in section 9(5) of the Act.)

To be inserted in the practice direction to CPR Part 19 (Parties and Group Litigation)

Human Rights

6.1 The notice given under rule 19.5(1) shall be sent by the court to the person named in the list published by HM Treasury under section 17 of the Crown Proceedings Act 1947. The notice must contain—
(1) sufficient details to identify—
(a) the claim,
(b) the parties to the claim,
(c) the court, and
(d) the Convention rights under consideration and
(2) a statement of the issues which have led to the court considering making a declaration of incompatibility.

6.2 Unless the court orders otherwise, the Minister or other person permitted by the Human Rights Act 1998 to be joined as a party must, if he wishes to be joined, within 21 days of the date of the notice given by the court give notice of his intention to be joined as a party to the court and every other party. Where the Minister has nominated a person to be joined as a party the notice must be accompanied by the written nomination.

(Section 5(2)(a) of the Human Rights Act 1998 permits a person nominated by a Minister of the Crown to be joined as a party.)

6.3 The notice will be given in all cases including where the Crown, a Minister or a governmental body is already a party to the proceedings.

6.4(1) The procedure in paragraphs 6.1 and 6.2 also applies where a claim is made under sections 7(1)(a) and 9(3) of the Human Rights Act 1998 in respect of a judicial act. The notice must be given to the appropriate person. The appropriate person is the Lord Chancellor and the notice should be sent to the Treasury Solicitor on his behalf.

(2) The statement required by paragraph 6.1(2) shall give details of the judicial act which is the subject of the claim and of the court or tribunal which made it.

(Section 9(4) of the Human Rights Act 1998 provides that no award of damages may be made against the Crown as provided for in section 9(3) unless the appropriate party is joined in the proceedings. The appropriate person is the Minister responsible for the court concerned or a person or department nominated by him.)

Section 7—claims against a public authority which has acted or is to act contrary to section 6 (*for courts and tribunals see also section 9 below*)

To be inserted in the practice direction to CPR Part 16 (Statements of case)

Human Rights

9.3 A claimant who is bringing proceedings against a public authority under section 7(1)(a) of the Human Rights Act 1998

(1) must state that fact in the claim form; and
(2) must in the claim form or particulars of claim—
  (a) give details of the Convention right which its is alleged has been infringed and of the infringement, and
  (b) where the claim is founded on a finding of unlawfulness by another court or tribunal, give details of the finding.

(The practice direction to Part 19 provides for the Lord Chancellor to be joined as a party where the claim is in respect of a judicial act; see section 9(3)–(5) of the Human Rights Act 1998.)

To be inserted in the practice direction to CPR Part 52 (Appeals)

Human Rights

5.8 Where the appellant is adding a claim against a public authority under section 7(1)(a) of the Human Rights Act 1998 in the appeal must in the appeal notice—

(1) state that fact; and
(2) give details of—
  (a) the Convention right which its is alleged has been infringed and of the infringement, and
  (b) the finding of the court or tribunal, where there is a finding of unlawfulness by another court or tribunal, or
  (c) the judicial act and the court or tribunal which made it, where it is the act of that court or tribunal which is complained of as provided by section 9 of the Human Rights Act 1998.

(The practice direction to Part 19 provides for the Lord Chancellor to be joined as a party where the claim is in respect of a judicial act; see section 9(3)–(5) of the Human Rights Act 1998.)

Section 9—claims under section 7(1)(a) for judicial acts

To be inserted in CPR Part 30 (Transfer)

Human Rights

30.9 Any claim where the statement of case or a notice of appeal includes a claim under section 7(1)(a) and section 9(3) of the Human Rights Act 1998 in respect of a judicial act which would be heard in the county court may be transferred to the High Court.

To be inserted in the practice direction to CPR Part 30 (Transfer)

Human Rights

7.1 Where an issue arises in a claim or appeal relating to breach of a Convention right as a result of a judicial act under section 7(1)(a) and section 9(3) of the Human Rights Act 1998 which would be heard in the county court then that claim or appeal will be transferred to the Crown Office in the High Court.

To be inserted in CPR Part 33 (miscellaneous rules about evidence)

Human Rights

33.9(1) This rule applies where a claim is

(a) for a remedy under section 7 of the Human Rights Act 1998 in respect of a judicial act which is alleged to have infringed the claimants Article 5 Convention rights; and

(b) based on a finding by a Crown Court.

(2) The court hearing the claim may reconsider the evidence of the alleged infringement and the finding of the Crown Court.

To be inserted in the second practice direction to CPR Part 40 (judgments and orders)

14.4 On any application or appeal concerning—

(i) a committal order;

(ii) a refusal to grant habeas corpus or

(iii) a secure accommodation order made under section 25 of the Children Act 1989

the judgment or order must, if the court orders the release of the person, state whether or not the original order was made in circumstances which infringed that person's Convention rights.

Family Proceedings Rules and Practice Directions

Section 2—citation of authorities

To be included in the new family proceedings practice direction

Citation of Human Rights Material

1.1 Section 2 of the Human Rights Act 1998 provides that a court or tribunal determining a question which has arisen in connection with a Convention right must take into account judgments, decisions, declarations and advisory opinions of the European Court of Human Rights, the Commission and the Committee of Ministers, so far as, in the opinion of the court or tribunal, they are relevant to the proceedings in which that question has arisen ('Strasbourg authorities').

1.2 This paragraph sets out the procedure where a party intends to cite a Strasbourg authority at a hearing.

(1) The Strasbourg authority to be cited should be from an authoritative and complete report that is readily available. The reports listed in paragraph 1.3 meet those criteria. Permission is required to cite from any other source.

(2) The party must give to the court and any other party a list of the Strasbourg authorities he intends to cite and copies of the reports or other sources from which they are to be cited not more than 7 days nor less than three days before the hearing.

1.3 The reports of Strasbourg authorities referred to in paragraph 1.2 are:

Copies of the complete original texts issued by the European Court and Commission either paper based or from the Court's judgment database (HUDOC), which is available on the Internet.

Judgments of the European Court of Human Rights, (published by Carl Heymanns Verlag KG).

Reports, Judgments and Decisions of the European Court of Human Rights, (published by Carl Heymanns Verlag KG).

Decisions of the European Commission of Human Rights, (published by Carl Heymanns Verlag KG).

Decisions and Reports of the European Commission of Human Rights volumes 1–96, (published by Carl Heymanns Verlag KG).

European Human Rights Reports (published by Sweet and Maxwell).

Human Rights Cases (published by Butterworths).

Full texts of Strasbourg authorities taken from the following electronic databases:

- *Case Law Service* (published byLawtel)
- *Eurolaw* (published by ILI)
- *JUSTIS* (published by Context Electronic Publishers)
- *Lexis-Nexis*
- *Westlaw UK*.

Sections 4 and 5—declaration of incompatibility, joining a Minister

To be inserted after FPR rule 10.25

Human Rights Act 1998

10.26(1) Where at any time in any proceedings in the High Court the court begins to consider whether to make a declaration of incompatibility in accordance with section 4 of the Human Rights Act 1998 it must give notice to the Crown.

(2) Where paragraph (1) applies a Minister, or other person permitted by the Human Rights Act 1998, shall be joined as a party on giving notice to the court.

(3) The court may not make a declaration of incompatibility until either—

(a) a Minister, or other person permitted by the Human Rights Act 1998, has been joined as a party, or

(b) 21 days after the date of the notice to the Crown, if earlier.

(4) Where in any appeal a claim is made under section 7(1)(a) of the Human Rights Act 1998 in respect of a judicial act to which section 9(3) and (4) of that Act applies—

(c) that claim must be set out in the notice of appeal; and

(d) the court must give notice to the Crown.

(5) Where paragraph (4) applies and the appropriate person does not apply to be joined as a party the court may join the appropriate person as a party to the proceedings, 21 days after service of the notice.

To be included in the new family proceedings practice direction

Giving Notice to The Crown

2.1 The notice given under rule 10.26(1) shall be sent by the court to the person named in the list published by HM Treasury under section 17 of the Crown Proceedings Act 1947. The notice must contain—

(1) sufficient details to identify—

(e) the proceedings,

(f) the parties to the proceedings,

(g) the court, and

(h) the Convention rights under consideration and

(2) a statement of the issues which have led to the court considering making a declaration of incompatibility.

2.2 Unless the court orders otherwise, the Minister or other person permitted by the Human Rights Act 1998 to be joined as a party must, if he wishes to be joined, within 21 days of the date of the notice given by the court give notice of his intention to be joined as a party to the court and every other party. Where the Minister has nominated a person to be joined as a party the notice must be accompanied by the written nomination.

2.3 The notice will be given in all cases including where the Crown, a Minister or a governmental body is already a party to the proceedings.

2.4(1) The procedure in paragraphs 2.1 and 2.2 also applies where a claim is made under sections 7(1)(a) and 9(3) of the Human Rights Act 1998 in respect of a judicial act. The notice must be given to the appropriate person. The appropriate person is the Lord Chancellor and the notice should be sent to the Treasury Solicitor on his behalf.

(2) The statement required by paragraph 2.1(2) shall give details of the judicial act which is the subject of the claim and of the court which made it.

Section 7—claims against a public authority which has or is to act contrary to section 6 (*for courts or tribunals see also section 9 below*)

To be included in the new family proceedings practice direction

Claims in Respect of Judicial Acts

3.1 Where the appellant is adding in the appeal a claim under sections 7(1)(a) and 9(3) of the Human Rights Act 1998 in respect of a judicial act the appellant must in the appeal notice—

(3) state that fact; and

(4) give details of—

(a) the Convention right which it is alleged has been infringed and of the infringement, and

(b) the judicial act complained of and the court which made it.

Section 9—claims under section 7(1)(a) for judicial acts

To be inserted in FPR rule 10.10 (Orders for transfer of family proceedings)

(8) Any appeal where the notice of appeal includes a claim under section 7(1)(a) and section 9(3) of the Human Rights Act 1998 in respect of a judicial act which would be heard in the county court may be transferred to the High Court.

To be included in the new family proceedings practice direction

3.2 Where an issue arises in an appeal to which paragraph 3.1 applies, which would be heard in the county court, then that claim or appeal shall be transferred to the Crown Office in the High Court.

3.3 On any application or appeal concerning—

(i) a committal order;

(ii) a refusal to grant habeas corpus or

(iii) a secure accommodation order made under section 25 of the Children Act 1989

the judgment or order must, if the court orders the release of the person, state whether or not the original order was made in circumstances which infringed that person's Convention rights.

APPENDIX D

Practice Direction
Devolution Issues (and Crown Office applications in Wales)*

This Practice Direction applies to proceedings in England and Wales in the Court of Appeal (Civil and Criminal Divisions), the High Court, the Crown Court, the county courts and the magistrates' courts.

It is made:

(i) by the Lord Chief Justice as President of the Criminal Division of the Court of Appeal and President of the Queen's Bench Division of the High Court;
(ii) by the Master of the Rolls as President of the Court of Appeal (Civil Division);
(iii) by the President of the Family Division of the High Court;
(iv) by the Vice-Chancellor as Vice-President of the Chancery Division of the High Court; and
(v) by the Vice-Chancellor, on behalf of the Lord Chancellor, pursuant to *s 5 of the Civil Procedure Act 1997.*

30 June 1999

This Practice Direction is divided into 4 parts:

Part I Introduction
Part II Directions applicable to all proceedings
Part III Directions applicable to specific proceedings (paragraphs 14.2 and 14.3 deal with Crown Office applications in Wales)
Part IV Appeals

Part I
Introduction

Definitions

1. In this Practice Direction—

'the Assembly' means the National Assembly for Wales or Cynulliad Cenedlaethol Cymru
'the GWA' means the *Government of Wales Act 1998*
'the NIA' means the *Northern Ireland Act 1998*
'the SA' means the *Scotland Act 1998*
'the Acts' mean the GWA, the NIA and the SA
'the Judicial Committee' means the Judicial Committee of the Privy Council
'the CPR' means the *Civil Procedure Rules 1998*
'the FPR' means the *Family Proceedings Rules 1991*
'the FPC' means the *Family Proceedings Courts (Children Act 1989) Rules 1991*
'devolution issue' has the same meaning as in paragraph 1, schedule 8 to the GWA; paragraph 1, schedule 10 to the NIA; and paragraph 1, schedule 6 of the SA
'devolution issue notice' means a notice that a devolution issue has arisen in proceedings

* At the time of writing, the government has chosen not to promulgate the rules until September 2000. Only drafts were available at the time of going to press.

Scope

2.1 This Practice Direction supplements the provisions dealing with devolution issues in the Acts. It deals specifically with the position if a devolution issue arises under the GWA. If a devolution issue arises under the NIA or the SA the procedure laid down in this Practice Direction should be adapted as required.

2.2 This Practice Direction also deals with Crown Office applications in Wales (see paragraphs 14.2 and 14.3).

The devolution legislation

3.1 Schedule 8 to the GWA contains provisions dealing with devolution issues arising out of the GWA; schedule 10 to the NIA contains provisions dealing with devolution issues arising out of the NIA; and schedule 6 to the SA contains provisions dealing with devolution issues arising out of the SA.

3.2 Broadly a devolution issue will involve a question whether a devolved body has acted or proposes to act within its powers (which includes not acting incompatibly with Convention rights[1] and Community law[2] or has failed to comply with a duty imposed on it. Reference should be made to the Acts where 'devolution issue' is defined.

3.3(1) If a devolution issue under the GWA arises in proceedings, the court must order notice of it to be given to the Attorney General and the Assembly if they are not already a party. They have a right to take part as a party in the proceedings so far as they relate to a devolution issue, if they are not already a party (paragraph 5, schedule 8 to the GWA.) If they do take part, they may require the court to refer the devolution issue to the Judicial Committee (paragraph 30, schedule 8 to the GWA)[3]

(2) There are similar provisions in the NIA and the SA although the persons to be notified are different (paragraphs 13, 14, and 33, schedule 10 to the NIA; paragraphs 16, 17 and 33, schedule 6 to the SA).

3.4 Under all the Acts the court may refer a devolution issue to another court as follows:

(1) A magistrates' court may refer a devolution issue arising in civil or summary proceedings to the High Court (paragraphs 6 and 9, schedule 8 to the GWA; paragraphs 15 and 18, schedule 10 to the NIA; and paragraphs 18 and 21, schedule 6 to the SA).

(2) The Crown Court may refer a devolution issue arising in summary proceedings to the High Court and a devolution issue arising in proceedings on indictment to the Court of Appeal (paragraph 9, schedule 8 to the GWA; paragraph 18, schedule 10 to the NIA; paragraph 21, schedule 6 to the SA).

(3) A county court, the High Court (unless the devolution issue has been referred to the High Court)[4] and the Crown Court[5] may refer a devolution issue arising in civil proceedings to the Court of Appeal

---

[1] The rights and fundamental freedoms set out in—(a) *Articles 2 to 12 and 14 of the European Convention on Human Rights* (ECHR), (b) Articles 1 to 3 of the First Protocol (agreed at Paris on 20 March 1952), and (c) Articles 1 and 2 of the Sixth Protocol (agreed at Strasbourg on 11 May 1994), as read with Articles 16 and 18 of the ECHR (*Section 1 Human Rights Act 1998*; s 107(1) and (5) GWA; sections 6(2); 24(1) and 98(1) NIA; sections 29(2); 57(2) and 126(1) SA).

[2] All the rights, powers, liabilities, obligations and restrictions from time to time created or arising by or under the Community Treaties; and all the remedies and procedures from time to time provided for by or under the Community Treaties (sections 106(7) and 155(1), GWA; sections 6(2); 24(1) and 98(1), NIA; sections 29(2); 57(2) and 126(9) SA).

[3] If the Attorney General or the Assembly had become a party to the original proceedings but did not exercise their right to require the devolution issue to be referred to the Judicial Committee and the court decided the case, they would have the same rights of appeal as parties. These would not allow them to appeal a decision made in proceedings on indictment, although the Attorney General has a power under *section 36 of the Criminal Justice Act 1972* to refer a point of law to the Court of Appeal where the defendant has been acquitted in a trial on indictment.

Paragraph 31, schedule 8 to the GWA, allows the Attorney General and Assembly to refer to the Judicial Committee any devolution issue which is not the subject of proceedings. This power could possibly be used if a court reached a decision where they had not been parties and so had no rights of appeal but such a reference could not affect the decision of the court.

[4] If an appeal by way of case stated in criminal proceedings goes to the Divisional Court there appears to be no power for the Divisional Court to refer a devolution issue to the Court of Appeal.

[5] eg in appeals from a magistrates' court in a licensing matter.

(paragraph 7, schedule 8 to the GWA; paragraph 16, schedule 10 to the NIA; paragraph 19, schedule 6 to the SA).

(4) A tribunal from which there is no appeal must, and any other tribunal may, refer a devolution issue to the Court of Appeal (paragraph 8, schedule 8 to the GWA; paragraph 17, schedule 10 to the NIA; paragraph 20, schedule 6 to the SA).

(5) The Court of Appeal may refer a devolution issue to the Judicial Committee, unless the devolution issue was referred to it by another court (paragraph 10, schedule 8 to the GWA; paragraph 19, schedule 10 to the NIA; paragraph 22, schedule 6 to the SA).

(6) An appeal against the determination of a devolution issue by the High Court or the Court of Appeal on a reference lies to the Judicial Committee with the leave of the court concerned, or, failing such leave, with special leave of the Judicial Committee (paragraph 11, schedule 8 to the GWA; paragraph 20, schedule 10 to the NIA; paragraph 23, schedule 6 to the SA).

3.5 A court may take into account additional expense which the court considers that a party has incurred as a result of the participation of the Attorney General or the Assembly in deciding any question as to costs (paragraph 35, schedule 8 to the GWA).

Part II
Directions Applicable to All Proceedings

Scope

4. Paragraphs 5 to 13 apply to proceedings in England and Wales in the magistrates' courts, the county courts, the Crown Court, the High Court and the Court of Appeal (Civil and Criminal Division). Paragraph 10 also applies to the form and procedure for a reference to the Court of Appeal by a tribunal.

Raising the question as to whether a devolution issue arises

5.1 Where a party to any form of proceedings wishes to raise an issue which may be a devolution issue whether as a claim (or part of a claim) to enforce or establish a legal right or to seek a remedy or as a defence (or part of a defence), the provisions of this Practice Direction apply in addition to the rules of procedure applicable to the proceedings in which the issue arises.

5.2 A court may, of its own volition, require the question of whether a devolution issue arises to be considered, if the materials put before the court indicate such an issue may arise, even if the parties have not used the term 'devolution issue'.

Determination by a court of whether a devolution issue arises

6.1 The court may give such directions as it considers appropriate to obtain clarification or additional information to establish whether a devolution issue arises.

6.2 In determining whether a devolution issue arises the court, notwithstanding the contention of a party to the proceedings, may decide that a devolution issue shall **not** be taken to arise if the contention appears to the court to be frivolous or vexatious (paragraph 2 of schedule 8 to the GWA).

6.3 If the court determines that a devolution issue arises it must state what that devolution issue is clearly and concisely.

Notice of devolution issue to the Attorney General and the Assembly

7.1 If a court determines that a devolution issue arises in the proceedings, it must order a devolution issue notice substantially in the form numbered 'DI 1' in Annex 1 to be given to the Attorney General and the Assembly unless they are already a party to the proceedings (paragraph 5(1), schedule 8 to the GWA).

7.2 A court receiving a reference does not have to serve a devolution issue notice unless it determines that a devolution issue that was not identified by the court making the reference has arisen. In that case the court receiving the reference must serve a devolution issue notice which must:

(1) state what devolution issue has been referred to it;
(2) state what further devolution issue has arisen; and
(3) identify the referring court.

7.3 If the devolution issue has arisen in criminal proceedings, the devolution issue notice must state:
(1) whether the proceedings have been adjourned;
(2) whether the defendant is remanded in custody; and
(3) if the defendant has been remanded in custody and his trial has not commenced, when the custody time limit expires.[6]

7.4 If the devolution issue arises in an appeal, the devolution issue notice must:
(1) state that the devolution issue arises in an appeal;
(2) identify the court whose decision is being appealed; and
(3) state whether the devolution issue is raised for the first time on appeal; or, if it is not, state that the devolution issue was raised in the court whose decision is being appealed, what decision was reached by that court, and the date of the previous notice to the Attorney General and the Assembly.

7.5 The devolution issue notice will specify a date which will be 14 days, or such longer period as the court may direct (see below), after the date of the devolution issue notice as the date by which the Attorney General or the Assembly must notify the court that he or it wishes to take part as a party to the proceedings, so far as they relate to a devolution issue.

7.6 The court may, in exceptional circumstances, specify a date longer than 14 days after the date of the devolution issue notice as the date by which the Attorney General and the Assembly must notify the court that he or it wishes to take part as a party to the proceedings. The court may do this before the notice is given, or before or after the expiry of the period given in the notice.

7.7—(1) On the date of the devolution issue notice,
(a) the devolution issue notice for the Attorney General must be faxed to him by the court;[7] and
(b) the devolution issue notice for the Assembly must be faxed by the court to the Counsel General for the Assembly.

(2) On the same day as a fax is sent a copy of the devolution issue notice must be sent by the court by first class post to the Attorney General and the Counsel General for the Assembly.

7.8 The court may, on such terms as it considers appropriate, order such additional documents to be served (eg in civil proceedings, the claim form) or additional information to be supplied with the devolution issue notice.

7.9—(1) When a court orders a devolution notice issue to be given the court may make such further orders as it thinks fit in relation to any adjournment, stay, continuance of the proceedings, or interim measures, during the period within which the Attorney General and the Assembly have to notify the court if they intend to take part as a party to the proceedings.

(2) Before ordering an adjournment in criminal proceedings, the court will consider all material circumstances, including whether it would involve delay that might extend beyond the custody time limits if the defendant is remanded in custody and his trial has not commenced.

7.10 If neither the Attorney General nor the Assembly notify the court within the specified time that he or it wishes to take part as a party to the proceed—
(1) the proceedings should immediately continue on expiry of the period within which they had to notify the court; and

---

[6] Custody time limits are imposed by the Prosecution of Offences (Custody Time Limits) Regulations 1987 as amended.

[7] See Annex 2 for information about fax numbers and addresses.

(2) the court has no duty to inform them of the outcome of the proceedings apart from the duty to notify them if the court decides to refer the devolution issue to another court (see paragraph 10.3(5)).[8]

Adding the Attorney General or the Assembly to the proceedings and their right to require referral of a devolution issue to the Judicial Committee

8.1 If the Attorney General or the Assembly wishes to take part as a party to the proceedings so far as they relate to a devolution issue, he or it must send to the court and the other parties (and to each other if only one of them has become a party) a notice substantially in the form numbered 'DI 2' shown in Annex 1 within the time specified in the devolution issue notice.

8.2 On receipt of this form the court may give such consequential directions as it considers necessary.

8.3 If the Attorney General or the Assembly is a party to the proceedings, and either of them wishes to require the court to refer the devolution issue to the Judicial Committee, he or it must as soon as practicable send to the court and the other parties (and to each other if only one of them has become a party) a notice substantially in the form numbered 'DI 3' shown in Annex 1.

Determination by the court of whether or not to make a reference of a devolution issue if the Attorney General or the Assembly do not require a reference

9.1 If the court is not required to refer the devolution issue to the Judicial Committee, the court will decide whether it should refer the devolution issue to the relevant court as specified in paragraph 3.4.

9.2 Before deciding whether to make a reference the court may hold a directions hearing or give written directions as to the making of submissions on the question of whether to make a reference.

9.3 The court may make a decision on the basis of written submissions if its procedures permit this and it wishes to do so, or the court may have a hearing before making a decision.

9.4 In exercising its discretion as to whether to make a reference, the court will have regard to all relevant circumstances and in particular to:

(1) the importance of the devolution issue to the public in general;
(2) the importance of the devolution issue to the original parties to the proceedings;
(3) whether a decision on the reference of the devolution issue will be decisive of the matters in dispute between the parties;
(4) whether all the relevant findings of fact have been made (a devolution issue will not, unless there are exceptional circumstances, be suitable for a reference if it has to be referred on the basis of assumed facts);
(5) the delay that a reference would entail particularly in cases involving, children and Criminal cases (Including whether the reference is likely to involve delay that would extend beyond the expiry of the custody time limits if the defendant is remanded in custody and his trial has not commenced); and
(6) additional costs that a reference might involve.[9]

9.5 The court should state its reasons for making or declining to make a reference.

9.6 If the court decides not to refer the case, it will give directions for the future conduct of the action, which will include directions as to the participation of the Attorney General and the Assembly if they are parties.

---

[8] If there is an appeal, the appeal court will serve a devolution issue notice on the Attorney General and the Assembly (see paragraph 7.4).

[9] In criminal cases *section 16 of the Prosecution of Offences Act 1985* does not enable a court receiving a reference to make a defendant's costs order. If the defendant is subsequently acquitted by the court who made the reference that court can make a defendant's costs order. However it would not cover the costs of the reference as 'proceedings' is defined in section 21 as including proceedings in any court below but makes no mention of proceedings on a reference.

Form and procedure for references

10.1 If the court or tribunal is required by the Attorney General or the Assembly (in relation to any proceedings before the court to which he or it is a party) to refer the devolution issue to the Judicial Committee:

(1) the court or tribunal will make the reference as soon as practicable after receiving the notice from the Attorney General or the Assembly substantially in the form numbered 'DI 3' shown in Annex 1, and follow the procedure for references in the *Judicial Committee (Devolution Issues) Rules Order 1999*; and

(2) the court or tribunal may order the parties, or any of them, to draft the reference.

10.2 If the Court of Appeal decides to refer the devolution issue to the Judicial Committee:

(1) it will follow the procedure in the *Judicial Committee (Devolution Issues) Rules Order 1999*; and

(2) the court may order the parties, or any of them, to draft the reference.

10.3 If any other court or tribunal decides, or if a tribunal is required, to refer the devolution issue to another court:

(1) the reference must be substantially in the form numbered 'DI 4' shown in Annex 1 and must set out the following:

(a) the question referred;

(b) the addresses of the parties, except in the case of family proceedings, for which see paragraphs 15.2–4;

(c) a concise statement of the background of the matter including—

(i) the facts of the case, including, any relevant findings of fact by the referring court or lower courts; and

(ii) the main issues in the case and the contentions of the parties with regard to them;

(d) the relevant law, including the relevant provisions of the GWA;

(e) the reasons why an answer to the question is considered necessary for the purpose of disposing of the proceedings;

(2) all judgments already given in the proceedings will be annexed to the reference;

(3) the court may order the parties, or any of them, to draft the reference;

(4) the court or tribunal will transmit the reference to:

(a) the Civil Appeals Office Registry if the reference is to the Court of Appeal from a county court, the High Court or the Crown Court in civil proceedings, or from a tribunal;

(b) the Registrar of Criminal Appeals if the reference is to the Court of Appeal from the Crown Court in proceedings on indictment; and

(c) the Crown Office if the reference is to the High Court from a magistrates' court in civil or summary proceedings or from the Crown Court in summary proceedings.[10]

If the reference is transmitted to Cardiff an additional copy of the reference must be filed so that it can be retained by the Cardiff Office. The original reference will be forwarded to the Crown Office in London.

(5) at the same time as the reference is transmitted to the Crown Office a copy of the reference will be sent by first class post to:

(a) the parties;

(b) the Attorney General if he is not already a party; and

(c) the Assembly if it is not already a party;

(6) each person on whom a copy of the reference is served must within 21 days notify the court to which the reference is transmitted and the other persons on whom the reference is served whether they wish to be heard on the reference;

---

[10] See Annex 2 for the relevant addresses. It shows The Law Courts, Cathays Park, Cardiff, CF10 3PG and the Royal Courts of Justice, Strand, London WC2A 2LL as alternative addresses for transmitting documents to the Crown Office. If the order is transmitted to Cardiff, the additional copy will be forwarded by the Cardiff Office to the Crown Office in London.

(7) the court receiving the reference (either the Court of Appeal or the High Court) will give directions for the conduct of the reference, the lodging of cases or skeleton arguments; and transmit a copy of the determination on the reference to the referring court; and
(8) if there has been an appeal to the Judicial Committee against a decision of the High Court or the Court of Appeal on a reference, and a copy of the Judicial Committee's decision on that appeal has been sent to the High Court or Court of Appeal (as the case may be), that court will send a copy to the court which referred the devolution issue to it.

10.4 When a court receives notification of the decision on a reference, it will determine how to proceed with the remainder of the case.

Power of the court to deal with pending proceedings if a reference is made (whether by the Attorney General, the Assembly or the court)

11. If a reference is made the court will adjourn or stay the proceedings in which the devolution issue arose, unless it otherwise orders; and will make such further orders as it thinks fit in relation to any adjournment or stay.

The Welsh language

12.1 If any party wishes to put forward a contention in relation to a devolution issue that involves comparison of the Welsh and English texts of any Assembly subordinate legislation, that party must give notice to the court as soon as possible.

12.2 Upon receipt of the notification, the court will consider the appropriate means of determining the issue, including, if necessary, the appointment of a Welsh speaking judicial assessor to assist the court.

12.3 Parties to any proceedings in which the Welsh language may be used must also comply with the ***Practice Direction of 16 October 1998 (relating to proceedings in the Crown Court)*** and the ***Practice Direction of 26 April 1999 (relating to civil proceedings)***. These Practice Directions apply, as appropriate, to proceedings involving, a devolution issue in which the Welsh language may be used.

Crown Proceedings Act 1947 (Section 19)

13. Where the court has determined that a devolution issue arises, the Attorney General will give any necessary consent to:
(1) the proceedings being transferred to The Law Courts, Cathays Park, Cardiff, CF10 3PG, or to such other district registry as shall (exceptionally) be directed by the court; and
(2) to the trial taking place at Cardiff or at such other trial location as shall (exceptionally) be directed by the court.

Part III
Directions Applicable to Specific Proceedings

Judicial review proceedings; Crown Office applications in Wales

14.1 *RSC Order 53, schedule 1* to the *CPR* contains the procedure to be followed in applications for judicial review.

14.2 Notwithstanding Queen's Bench Practice Direction 23 and prescribed forms 86A and 86B[11] facilities will be available for applications for judicial review to be lodged at The Law Courts, Cathays

[11] Queen's Bench Practice Direction 23 2C(2) provides that wherever practicable proceedings should be commenced in London, although applications can be made outside London in cases of urgency. Prescribed forms 86A and 86B give the address for delivery of the forms as the Crown Office, Royal Courts of Justice, Strand, London, WC2A 2LL. It is hoped that these forms will be amended to give The Law Courts, Cathays Park, Cardiff, CF10 3PG as an alternative address for the Crown Office.

Park, Cardiff, CF10 3PG if the relief sought or the grounds of the application involve either or both of the following:

(1) a devolution issue arising out of the GWA;

(2) an issue concerning the Welsh Assembly, the Welsh executive, or any Welsh public body (including a Welsh local authority) even if it does not involve a devolution issue.

Such applications may continue to be lodged at the Crown Office in London, if the applicant prefers to do that.

14.3 If applications are lodged at Cardiff an additional copy of the application must be filed so that it can be retained by the Cardiff Office. The original application will be forwarded to the Crown Office in London.

14.4 If a party intends to raise a devolution issue, the application notice must (in addition to the matters listed in *RSC Order 53, rule 3(2)(a))*:

(1) specify that the applicant wishes to raise a devolution issue and identify the relevant provisions of the GWA; and

(2) contain a summary of the facts and circumstances and points of law on the basis of which it is alleged that a devolution issue arises in sufficient detail to enable the court to determine whether a devolution issue arises.

Family proceedings in the magistrates' courts, the county courts and the High Court

15.1 In any proceedings in which any question with respect to the upbringing of a child arises, the court shall have regard to the general principle that any delay in determining the question is likely to prejudice the welfare of the child.[12]

15.2 If the FPR apply, the court will comply with rule 10.21.[13]

15.3 If Part IV of the FPR applies, the court will comply with rule 4.23.[14]

15.4 If the FPC apply, the court will comply with Rules 23 and 33A.[15]

---

[12] Section 1(2), Children Act 1989

[13] Rule 10.21 states: (1) Subject to rule 2.3 [of the FPR] nothing in these rules shall be construed as requiring any party to reveal the address of their private residence (or that of any child) save by order of the court. (2) Where a party declines to reveal an address in reliance upon paragraph (1) above, he shall give notice of that address to the court in Form C8 and that address shall not be revealed to any person save by order of the court.

[14] Rule 4.23 states: (1) Notwithstanding any rule of court to the contrary, no document, other than a record of an order, held by the court and relating to proceedings to which [Part IV] applies shall be disclosed, other than to—(a) a party, (b) the legal representative of a party (c) the guardian ad litem, (d) the Legal Aid Board, or (e) a welfare officer, without the leave of the judge or the district judge. (2) Nothing in this rule shall prevent the notification by the court or the proper officer of a direction under section 37(1) to the authority concerned. (3) Nothing—in this rule shall prevent the disclosure of a document prepared by a guardian ad litem for the purpose of—(a) enabling a person to perform functions required by regulations made under section 41(7); (b) assisting a guardian ad litem or a reporting officer (within the meaning of *section 65(1)(b) of the Adoption Act 1976*) who is appointed under any enactment to perform his functions.

[15] Rule 23 states: (1) No document, other than a record of an order, held by the court and relating to relevant proceedings shall be disclosed, other than to—(a) a party, (b) the legal representative of a party, (c) the guardian ad litem, (d) the Legal Aid Board, or (c) a welfare officer, without leave of the justices' clerk or the court. (2) Nothing in this rule shall prevent the notification by the court or the justices' clerk of a direction under section 37(1) to the authority concerned. (3) Nothing in this rule shall prevent the disclosure of a document prepared by a guardian ad litem for the purpose of—(a) enabling a person to perform functions required by regulations made under section 41(7)—(b) assisting a guardian ad litem or a reporting officer (within the meaning of *section 65(1)(b) of the Adoption Act 1976*) who is appointed under any enactment to perform his functions.

Rule 33A states: (1) Nothing in these Rules shall be construed as requiring any party to reveal the address of their private residence (or that of any child) except by order of the court. (2) Where a party declines to reveal an address in reliance upon paragraph (1) he shall give notice of that address to the court in Form C8 and that address shall not be revealed to any person except by order of the court.

15.5 If the proceedings are listed in column (i) of Appendix 3 to the FPR or Schedule 2 to the FPC, a copy of any notice to be given to the parties must also be given to the persons set out in column (iv) of Appendix 3 or Schedule 2 as the case may be.

15.6 A party wishing to raise a devolution issue must, wherever possible, raise it (giving full particulars of the provisions relied on) in the application or answer or at the first directions hearing where appropriate.

15.7 If a party has not raised a devolution issue as above, the party must seek the permission of the court to raise it at a later stage.

15.8 Where a court has referred the devolution issue to another court and has received notification of the decision on the reference, the matter should so far as is practicable be placed before the same judge or magistrates who dealt with the case before the reference.

Civil proceedings in the county courts and the High Court

16.1 A party wishing to raise a devolution issue must specify in the claim form, or if he is a defendant, in the defence (or written evidence filed with the acknowledgement of service in a Part 8 claim) that the claim raises a devolution issue and the relevant provisions of the GWA.

16.2 The particulars of claim or defence if the devolution issue is raised by the defendant (or written evidence filed with the acknowledgement of service in a Part 8 claim) must contain the facts and circumstances and points of law on the basis of which it is alleged that a devolution issue arises in sufficient detail to enable the court to determine whether a devolution issue arises in the proceedings.

16.3 Whether or not the allocation rules apply, if a question is raised during the proceedings that might be a devolution issue, then a directions hearing must take place and the matter must be referred to a circuit judge (in county court actions) or a High Court judge (in High Court actions) for determination as to whether a devolution issue arises and for further directions.

16.4 If a party fails to specify in the appropriate document that a devolution issue arises but that party subsequently wishes to raise a devolution issue, that party must seek the permission of the court.

16.5 Where any party has specified that a devolution issue arises, no default judgment can be obtained.

Criminal proceedings in the Crown Court

17. If the defendant wishes to raise a devolution issue he should do so at the Plea and Directions Hearing.

Criminal and civil proceedings in the magistrates' courts

18.1—(1) Where a defendant, who has been charged or has had an information laid against him in respect of a criminal offence and has entered a plea of 'Not Guilty', wishes to raise a devolution issue he should, wherever possible, give full particulars of the provisions relied on by notice in writing.

(2) Where a party to a complaint, or applicant for a licence wishes to raise a devolution issue he should, wherever possible, give full particulars of the provisions relied on by notice in writing.

(3) Such notice should be given to the prosecution (and other party if any) and the court as soon as practicable after the 'Not Guilty' plea is entered or the complaint or application is made as the case may be.

18.2 Where proceedings are to be committed or transferred to the Crown Court by the magistrates, the question as to whether a devolution issue arises shall be a matter for the Crown Court.

Part IV
Appeals

Appeals to the Court of Appeal (Civil and Criminal Division)

19.1 This paragraph applies if a devolution issue is raised in any appeal to either the Civil or the Criminal Division of the Court of Appeal.

19.2 The devolution issue may already have been raised in the court whose decision is being appealed. The devolution issue may, however, be raised for the first time on appeal.

19.3 Where an application for permission to appeal is made, or an appeal is brought where permission is not needed, the appellant must specify in the application notice (or the notice of appeal or notice of motion as the case may be):

(1) that the appeal raises a devolution issue and the relevant provisions of the GWA;
(2) the facts and circumstances and points of law on the basis of which it is alleged that a devolution issue arises in sufficient detail to enable the court to determine whether a devolution issue arises; and to enable the court to determine whether the devolution arises.
(3) whether the devolution issue was considered in the court below, and, if so, provide details of the decision.

19.4 An appellant may not seek to raise a devolution issue without the permission of the court after he has filed an application notice; or a notice of appeal or notice of motion (if no application notice).

19.5 Where permission to appeal is sought and a party to the appeal wishes to raise a devolution issue which was not raised in the lower court, the court will determine if a devolution issue arises before deciding whether to grant leave to appeal.

Appeals to the Crown Court

20. A notice of appeal from a decision of the magistrates courts to the Crown Court must specify whether the devolution issue was considered in the court below and if so, provide details of the decision. If it was not so considered, the notice should specify:

(1) that the appeal raises a devolution issue and the relevant provisions of the GWA; and
(2) the facts and circumstances and points of law on the basis of which it is alleged that a devolution issue arises in sufficient detail to enable the court to determine whether a devolution issue arises.

Annex 1

DI 1

Devolution Issues

Notice of Devolution Issue to Attorney General and the National Assembly for Wales

[Name of Case]

Take notice that the above mentioned case has raised a devolution issue as defined by *Schedule 8 to the Government of Wales Act 1998*. Details of the devolution issue are given in the attached schedule.

This notice meets the notification requirements 4 under *paragraph 5(1) of Schedule 8 to the Government of Wales Act 1998*. You may take part as a party to these proceedings, so far as they relate to a devolution issue (paragraph 5(2) of Schedule 8). If you want to do this you must notify the court by completing the attached form, and returning it to the court at [address] by [date].

Dated

To: The Attorney General
The National Assembly for Wales
Other parties (where appropriate)

18/06/99

DI 2

Devolution Issues

Notice of intention of Attorney General or the National Assembly for Wales to become party to proceedings, so far as they relate to a devolution issue, under paragraph 5(2) Schedule 8 to the Government of Wales Act 1998

In the [name of court]

[case name 1]

Take notice that the [Attorney General] [the National Assembly for Wales] intends to take part as a party to proceedings so far as they relate to a devolution issue as permitted by *paragraph 5(2) of Schedule 8 to the Government of Wales Act 1998* in relation to the devolution issue raised by [ ] of which notice was received by the Attorney General] [Assembly] on [ ].

[The [ ] also gives notice that it [requires the matter to be referred to] [is still considering whether to require the matter to be referred to] the Judicial Committee of the Privy Council under paragraph 30 of Schedule 8 to the Government of Wales Act 1998.]

[Date]

On behalf of the [Attorney General National Assembly for Wales]

To: The clerk of the court at [ ]
The parties to the case
[Attorney General] [National Assembly for Wales]

18/06/99

DI 3
Devolution Issues

Notice by Attorney General or National Assembly for Wales that they require devolution issue to be referred to the Judicial Committee of the Privy Council

In the [court]

[case name]

The [Attorney General] [National Assembly for Wales] gives notice that the devolution issue, which has been raised in the above case and to which [he] [it] is a party, must be referred to the Judicial Committee of the Privy Council under *paragraph 30 of Schedule 8 to the Government of Wales Act 1998.*

[Date]

On behalf of the [Attorney General] [National Assembly for Wales]

To: The clerk of the court at [ ]
The parties to the case
[Attorney General] [National Assembly for Wales]

18/06/99

DI 4
Devolution Issues

Reference by the court or tribunal of devolution issue to [High Court] [Court of Appeal] [Judicial Committee of the Privy Council]

In the [court]

[case name]

It is ordered that the devolution issue(s) set out in the schedule be referred to the [High Court] [Court of Appeal] [Judicial Committee of the Privy Council] for determination in accordance with paragraph [ ] of *Schedule 8 to the Government of Wales Act 1998.*

It is further ordered that the proceedings be stayed until the [High Court] [Court of Appeal] [Judicial Committee of the Privy Council] determine the devolution issue[s] or until further order.

Dated

Judge/clerk to the magistrates' court
Chairman of the Tribunal [Address]

Skeleton Reference to be Attached to Form DI 4

In the [court]

[case name]

(a) [The question referred.]
(b) [The addresses of the parties]
(c) [A concise statement of the background to the matters including—
  (i) The facts of the case including any relevant findings of fact by the referring court or lower courts; and
  (ii) The main issues in the case and the contentions of the parties with regard to them;]
(d) [the relevant law including the relevant provisions of the *Government of Wales Act 1998*]
(e) [the reasons why an answer to the question is considered necessary for the purpose of disposing of the proceedings.]

[All judgments already given in the proceedings are annexed to this reference.]

Annex 2

Addresses

1. Notices to the National Assembly for Wales (*Cynulliad Cenedlaethol Cymru*) must be sent to the Counsel General to the National Assembly for Wales, Crown Buildings, Cathays Park, Cardiff CF99 INA.

2. Notices to the Attorney General must be sent to the Attorney General's Chambers, 9 Buckingham Gate, London, SW1E 6JP. Fax number [0207 271 2433].

3. References to the Crown Office under paragraph 9.3(1)c of the Practice Direction may be sent to the Crown Office, Royal Courts of Justice, Strand, London WC2A 2LL; or the Law Courts, Cathays Park, Cardiff, CF10 3PG (2 copies).

Explanatory Note

4. The addresses and fax numbers above are the best information available, however it is possible that these (particularly the fax numbers and address for Notices to the Assembly) may change, it would therefore be advisable to confirm the numbers before sending information.

APPENDIX E

Convention for the Protection of Human Rights and Fundamental Freedoms[1]

Rome, 4.XI.1950

The governments signatory hereto, being members of the Council of Europe,

Considering the Universal Declaration of Human Rights proclaimed by the General Assembly of the United Nations on 10th December 1948;

Considering that this Declaration aims at securing the universal and effective recognition and observance of the Rights therein declared;

Considering that the aim of the Council of Europe is the achievement of greater unity between its members and that one of the methods by which that aim is to be pursued is the maintenance and further realisation of human rights and fundamental freedoms;

Reaffirming their profound belief in those fundamental freedoms which are the foundation of justice and peace in the world and are best maintained on the one hand by an effective political democracy and on the other by a common understanding and observance of the human rights upon which they depend;

Being resolved, as the governments of European countries which are like-minded and have a common heritage of political traditions, ideals, freedom and the rule of law, to take the first steps for the collective enforcement of certain of the rights stated in the Universal Declaration,

Have agreed as follows:

Article 1

Obligation to respect human rights

The High Contracting Parties shall secure to everyone within their jurisdiction the rights and freedoms defined in Section I of this Convention.

Section I
Rights and Freedoms

Article 2

Right to life

1. Everyone's right to life shall be protected by law. No one shall be deprived of his life intentionally save in the execution of a sentence of a court following his conviction of a crime for which this penalty is provided by law.

---

[1] The text of the Convention had been amended according to the provisions of Protocol No 3 (ETS No 45), which entered into force on 21 September 1970, of Protocol No 5 (ETS No 55), which entered into force on 20 December 1971 and of Protocol No 8 (ETS No 118), which entered into force on 1 January 1990, and comprised also the text of Protocol No 2 (ETS No 44) which, in accordance with Article 5, paragraph 3 thereof, had been an integral part of the Convention since its entry into force on 21 September 1970. All provisions which had been amended or added by these Protocols are replaced by Protocol No 11 (ETS No 155), as from the date of its entry into force on 1 November 1998. As from that date, Protocol No 9 (ETS No 140), which entered into force on 1 October 1994, is repealed and Protocol No 10 (ETS No 146), which has not entered into force, has lost its purpose.

2. Deprivation of life shall not be regarded as inflicted in contravention of this article when it results from the use of force which is no more than absolutely necessary:
   (a) in defence of any person from unlawful violence;
   (b) in order to effect a lawful arrest or to prevent the escape of a person lawfully detained;
   (c) in action lawfully taken for the purpose of quelling a riot or insurrection.

Article 3

Prohibition of torture

No one shall be subjected to torture or to inhuman or degrading treatment or punishment.

Article 4

Prohibition of slavery and forced labour

1. No one shall be held in slavery or servitude.
2. No one shall be required to perform forced or compulsory labour.
3. For the purpose of this article the term 'forced or compulsory labour' shall not include:
   (a) any work required to be done in the ordinary course of detention imposed according to the provisions of Article 5 of this Convention or during conditional release from such detention;
   (b) any service of a military character or, in case of conscientious objectors in countries where they are recognised, service exacted instead of compulsory military service;
   (c) any service exacted in case of an emergency or calamity threatening the life or well-being of the community;
   (d) any work or service which forms part of normal civic obligations.

Article 5

Right to liberty and security

1. Everyone has the right to liberty and security of person. No one shall be deprived of his liberty save in the following cases and in accordance with a procedure prescribed by law:
   (a) the lawful detention of a person after conviction by a competent court;
   (b) the lawful arrest or detention of a person for non-compliance with the lawful order of a court or in order to secure the fulfilment of any obligation prescribed by law;
   (c) the lawful arrest or detention of a person effected for the purpose of bringing him before the competent legal authority on reasonable suspicion of having committed an offence or when it is reasonably considered necessary to prevent his committing an offence or fleeing after having done so;
   (d) the detention of a minor by lawful order for the purpose of educational supervision or his lawful detention for the purpose of bringing him before the competent legal authority;
   (e) the lawful detention of persons for the prevention of the spreading of infectious diseases, of persons of unsound mind, alcoholics or drug addicts or vagrants;
   (f) the lawful arrest or detention of a person to prevent his effecting an unauthorised entry into the country or of a person against whom action is being taken with a view to deportation or extradition.
2. Everyone who is arrested shall be informed promptly, in a language which he understands, of the reasons for his arrest and of any charge against him.
3. Everyone arrested or detained in accordance with the provisions of paragraph 1(c) of this article shall be brought promptly before a judge or other officer authorised by law to exercise judicial power and shall be

entitled to trial within a reasonable time or to release pending trial. Release may be conditioned by guarantees to appear for trial.

4. Everyone who is deprived of his liberty by arrest or detention shall be entitled to take proceedings by which the lawfulness of his detention shall be decided speedily by a court and his release ordered if the detention is not lawful.

5. Everyone who has been the victim of arrest or detention in contravention of the provisions of this article shall have an enforceable right to compensation.

Article 6

Right to a fair trial

1. In the determination of his civil rights and obligations or of any criminal charge against him, everyone is entitled to a fair and public hearing within a reasonable time by an independent and impartial tribunal established by law. Judgment shall be pronounced publicly but the press and public may be excluded from all or part of the trial in the interests of morals, public order or national security in a democratic society, where the interests of juveniles or the protection of the private life of the parties so require, or to the extent strictly necessary in the opinion of the court in special circumstances where publicity would prejudice the interests of justice.

2. Everyone charged with a criminal offence shall be presumed innocent until proved guilty according to law.

3. Everyone charged with a criminal offence has the following minimum rights:
   (a) to be informed promptly, in a language which he understands and in detail, of the nature and cause of the accusation against him;
   (b) to have adequate time and facilities for the preparation of his defence;
   (c) to defend himself in person or through legal assistance of his own choosing or, if he has not sufficient means to pay for legal assistance, to be given it free when the interests of justice so require;
   (d) to examine or have examined witnesses against him and to obtain the attendance and examination of witnesses on his behalf under the same conditions as witnesses against him;
   (e) to have the free assistance of an interpreter if he cannot understand or speak the language used in court.

Article 7

No punishment without law

1. No one shall be held guilty of any criminal offence on account of any act or omission which did not constitute a criminal offence under national or international law at the time when it was committed. Nor shall a heavier penalty be imposed than the one that was applicable at the time the criminal offence was committed.

2. This article shall not prejudice the trial and punishment of any person for any act or omission which, at the time when it was committed, was criminal according to the general principles of law recognised by civilised nations.

Article 8

Right to respect for private and family life

1. Everyone has the right to respect for his private and family life, his home and his correspondence.

2. There shall be no interference by a public authority with the exercise of this right except such as is in accordance with the law and is necessary in a democratic society in the interests of national security, public safety or the economic well-being of the country, for the prevention of disorder or crime, for the protection of health or morals, or for the protection of the rights and freedoms of others.

Article 9

Freedom of thought, conscience and religion

1. Everyone has the right to freedom of thought, conscience and religion; this right includes freedom to change his religion or belief and freedom, either alone or in community with others and in public or private, to manifest his religion or belief, in worship, teaching, practice and observance.

2. Freedom to manifest one's religion or beliefs shall be subject only to such limitations as are prescribed by law and are necessary in a democratic society in the interests of public safety, for the protection of public order, health or morals, or for the protection of the rights and freedoms of others.

Article 10

Freedom of expression

1. Everyone has the right to freedom of expression. This right shall include freedom to hold opinions and to receive and impart information and ideas without interference by public authority and regardless of frontiers. This article shall not prevent States from requiring the licensing of broadcasting, television or cinema enterprises.

2. The exercise of these freedoms, since it carries with it duties and responsibilities, may be subject to such formalities, conditions, restrictions or penalties as are prescribed by law and are necessary in a democratic society, in the interests of national security, territorial integrity or public safety, for the prevention of disorder or crime, for the protection of health or morals, for the protection of the reputation or rights of others, for preventing the disclosure of information received in confidence, or for maintaining the authority and impartiality of the judiciary.

Article 11

Freedom of assembly and association

1. Everyone has the right to freedom of peaceful assembly and to freedom of association with others, including the right to form and to join trade unions for the protection of his interests.

2. No restrictions shall be placed on the exercise of these rights other than such as are prescribed by law and are necessary in a democratic society in the interests of national security or public safety, for the prevention of disorder or crime, for the protection of health or morals or for the protection of the rights and freedoms of others. This article shall not prevent the imposition of lawful restrictions on the exercise of these rights by members of the armed forces, of the police or of the administration of the State.

Article 12

Right to marry

Men and women of marriageable age have the right to marry and to found a family, according to the national laws governing the exercise of this right.

Article 13

Right to an effective remedy

Everyone whose rights and freedoms as set forth in this Convention are violated shall have an effective remedy before a national authority notwithstanding that the violation has been committed by persons acting in an official capacity.

Article 14

Prohibition of discrimination

The enjoyment of the rights and freedoms set forth in this Convention shall be secured without discrimination on any ground such as sex, race, colour, language, religion, political or other opinion, national or social origin, association with a national minority, property, birth or other status.

Article 15

Derogation in time of emergency

1. In time of war or other public emergency threatening the life of the nation any High Contracting Party may take measures derogating from its obligations under this Convention to the extent strictly required by the exigencies of the situation, provided that such measures are not inconsistent with its other obligations under international law.

2. No derogation from Article 2, except in respect of deaths resulting from lawful acts of war, or from Articles 3, 4 (paragraph 1) and 7 shall be made under this provision.

3. Any High Contracting Party availing itself of this right of derogation shall keep the Secretary General of the Council of Europe fully informed of the measures which it has taken and the reasons therefor. It shall also inform the Secretary General of the Council of Europe when such measures have ceased to operate and the provisions of the Convention are again being fully executed.

Article 16

Restrictions on political activity of aliens

Nothing in Articles 10, 11 and 14 shall be regarded as preventing the High Contracting Parties from imposing restrictions on the political activity of aliens.

Article 17

Prohibition of abuse of rights

Nothing in this Convention may be interpreted as implying for any State, group or person any right to engage in any activity or perform any act aimed at the destruction of any of the rights and freedoms set forth herein or at their limitation to a greater extent than is provided for in the Convention.

Article 18

Limitation on use of restrictions on rights

The restrictions permitted under this Convention to the said rights and freedoms shall not be applied for any purpose other than those for which they have been prescribed.

Section II
European Court of Human Rights

Article 19

Establishment of the Court

To ensure the observance of the engagements undertaken by the High Contracting Parties in the Convention and the Protocols thereto, there shall be set up a European Court of Human Rights, hereinafter referred to as 'the Court'. It shall function on a permanent basis.

Article 20

Number of judges

The Court shall consist of a number of judges equal to that of the High Contracting Parties.

Article 21

Criteria for office

1. The judges shall be of high moral character and must either possess the qualifications required for appointment to high judicial office or be jurisconsults of recognised competence.

2. The judges shall sit on the Court in their individual capacity.

3. During their term of office the judges shall not engage in any activity which is incompatible with their independence, impartiality or with the demands of a full-time office; all questions arising from the application of this paragraph shall be decided by the Court.

Article 22

Election of judges

1. The judges shall be elected by the Parliamentary Assembly with respect to each High Contracting Party by a majority of votes cast from a list of three candidates nominated by the High Contracting Party.

2. The same procedure shall be followed to complete the Court in the event of the accession of new High Contracting Parties and in filling casual vacancies.

Article 23

Terms of office

1. The judges shall be elected for a period of six years. They may be re-elected. However, the terms of office of one-half of the judges elected at the first election shall expire at the end of three years.

2. The judges whose terms of office are to expire at the end of the initial period of three years shall be chosen by lot by the Secretary General of the Council of Europe immediately after their election.

3. In order to ensure that, as far as possible, the terms of office of one-half of the judges are renewed every three years, the Parliamentary Assembly may decide, before proceeding to any subsequent election, that the term or terms of office of one or more judges to be elected shall be for a period other than six years but not more than nine and not less than three years.

4. In cases where more than one term of office is involved and where the Parliamentary Assembly applies the preceding paragraph, the allocation of the terms of office shall be effected by a drawing of lots by the Secretary General of the Council of Europe immediately after the election.

5. A judge elected to replace a judge whose term of office has not expired shall hold office for the remainder of his predecessor's term.

6. The terms of office of judges shall expire when they reach the age of 70.

7. The judges shall hold office until replaced. They shall, however, continue to deal with such cases as they already have under consideration.

Article 24

Dismissal

No judge may be dismissed from his office unless the other judges decide by a majority of two-thirds that he has ceased to fulfil the required conditions.

Article 25

Registry and legal secretaries

The Court shall have a registry, the functions and organisation of which shall be laid down in the rules of the Court. The Court shall be assisted by legal secretaries.

Article 26

Plenary Court

The plenary Court shall

(a) elect its President and one or two Vice-Presidents for a period of three years; they may be re-elected;
(b) set up Chambers, constituted for a fixed period of time;
(c) elect the Presidents of the Chambers of the Court; they may be re-elected;
(d) adopt the rules of the Court, and
(e) elect the Registrar and one or more Deputy Registrars.

Article 27

Committees, Chambers and Grand Chamber

1. To consider cases brought before it, the Court shall sit in committees of three judges, in Chambers of seven judges and in a Grand Chamber of seventeen judges. The Court's Chambers shall set up committees for a fixed period of time.

2. There shall sit as an *ex officio* member of the Chamber and the Grand Chamber the judge elected in respect of the State Party concerned or, if there is none or if he is unable to sit, a person of its choice who shall sit in the capacity of judge.

3. The Grand Chamber shall also include the President of the Court, the Vice-Presidents, the Presidents of the Chambers and other judges chosen in accordance with the rules of the Court. When a case is referred to the Grand Chamber under Article 43, no judge from the Chamber which rendered the judgment shall sit in the Grand Chamber, with the exception of the President of the Chamber and the judge who sat in respect of the State Party concerned.

Article 28

Declarations of inadmissibility by committees

A committee may, by a unanimous vote, declare inadmissible or strike out of its list of cases an application submitted under Article 34 where such a decision can be taken without further examination. The decision shall be final.

Article 29

Decisions by Chambers on admissibility and merits

1. If no decision is taken under Article 28, a Chamber shall decide on the admissibility and merits of individual applications submitted under Article 34.

2. A Chamber shall decide on the admissibility and merits of inter-State applications submitted under Article 33.

3. The decision on admissibility shall be taken separately unless the Court, in exceptional cases, decides otherwise.

Article 30

Relinquishment of jurisdiction to the Grand Chamber

Where a case pending before a Chamber raises a serious question affecting the interpretation of the Convention or the protocols thereto, or where the resolution of a question before the Chamber might have a result inconsistent with a judgment previously delivered by the Court, the Chamber may, at any time before it has rendered its judgment, relinquish jurisdiction in favour of the Grand Chamber, unless one of the parties to the case objects.

Article 31

Powers of the Grand Chamber

The Grand Chamber shall

(a) determine applications submitted either under Article 33 or Article 34 when a Chamber has relinquished jurisdiction under Article 30 or when the case has been referred to it under Article 43; and
(b) consider requests for advisory opinions submitted under Article 47.

Article 32

Jurisdiction of the Court

1. The jurisdiction of the Court shall extend to all matters concerning the interpretation and application of the Convention and the protocols thereto which are referred to it as provided in Articles 33, 34 and 47.

2. In the event of dispute as to whether the Court has jurisdiction, the Court shall decide.

Article 33

Inter-State cases

Any High Contracting Party may refer to the Court any alleged breach of the provisions of the Convention and the protocols thereto by another High Contracting Party.

Article 34

Individual applications

The Court may receive applications from any person, non-governmental organisation or group of individuals claiming to be the victim of a violation by one of the High Contracting Parties of the rights set forth in the Convention or the protocols thereto. The High Contracting Parties undertake not to hinder in any way the effective exercise of this right.

Article 35

Admissibility criteria

1. The Court may only deal with the matter after all domestic remedies have been exhausted, according to the generally recognised rules of international law, and within a period of six months from the date on which the final decision was taken.

2. The Court shall not deal with any application submitted under Article 34 that
   (a) is anonymous; or
   (b) is substantially the same as a matter that has already been examined by the Court or has already been submitted to another procedure of international investigation or settlement and contains no relevant new information.

3. The Court shall declare inadmissible any individual application submitted under Article 34 which it considers incompatible with the provisions of the Convention or the protocols thereto, manifestly ill-founded, or an abuse of the right of application.

4. The Court shall reject any application which it considers inadmissible under this Article. It may do so at any stage of the proceedings.

Article 36

Third party intervention

1. In all cases before a Chamber or the Grand Chamber, a High Contracting Party one of whose nationals is an applicant shall have the right to submit written comments and to take part in hearings.

2. The President of the Court may, in the interest of the proper administration of justice, invite any High Contracting Party which is not a party to the proceedings or any person concerned who is not the applicant to submit written comments or take part in hearings.

Article 37

Striking out applications

1. The Court may at any stage of the proceedings decide to strike an application out of its list of cases where the circumstances lead to the conclusion that
   (a) the applicant does not intend to pursue his application; or
   (b) the matter has been resolved; or
   (c) for any other reason established by the Court, it is no longer justified to continue the examination of the application.

However, the Court shall continue the examination of the application if respect for human rights as defined in the Convention and the protocols thereto so requires.

2. The Court may decide to restore an application to its list of cases if it considers that the circumstances justify such a course.

Article 38

Examination of the case and friendly settlement proceedings

1. If the Court declares the application admissible, it shall
   (a) pursue the examination of the case, together with the representatives of the parties, and if need be, undertake an investigation, for the effective conduct of which the States concerned shall furnish all necessary facilities;
   (b) place itself at the disposal of the parties concerned with a view to securing a friendly settlement of the matter on the basis of respect for human rights as defined in the Convention and the protocols thereto.

2. Proceedings conducted under paragraph 1(b) shall be confidential.

Article 39

Finding of a friendly settlement

If a friendly settlement is effected, the Court shall strike the case out of its list by means of a decision which shall be confined to a brief statement of the facts and of the solution reached.

Article 40

Public hearings and access to documents

1. Hearings shall be in public unless the Court in exceptional circumstances decides otherwise.
2. Documents deposited with the Registrar shall be accessible to the public unless the President of the Court decides otherwise.

Article 41

Just satisfaction

If the Court finds that there has been a violation of the Convention or the protocols thereto, and if the internal law of the High Contracting Party concerned allows only partial reparation to be made, the Court shall, if necessary, afford just satisfaction to the injured party.

Article 42

Judgments of Chambers

Judgments of Chambers shall become final in accordance with the provisions of Article 44, paragraph 2.

Article 43

Referral to the Grand Chamber

1. Within a period of three months from the date of the judgment of the Chamber, any party to the case may, in exceptional cases, request that the case be referred to the Grand Chamber.
2. A panel of five judges of the Grand Chamber shall accept the request if the case raises a serious question affecting the interpretation or application of the Convention or the protocols thereto, or a serious issue of general importance.
3. If the panel accepts the request, the Grand Chamber shall decide the case by means of a judgment.

Article 44

Final judgments

1. The judgment of the Grand Chamber shall be final.
2. The judgment of a Chamber shall become final
   (a) when the parties declare that they will not request that the case be referred to the Grand Chamber; or
   (b) three months after the date of the judgment, if reference of the case to the Grand Chamber has not been requested; or
   (c) when the panel of the Grand Chamber rejects the request to refer under Article 43.
3. The final judgment shall be published.

Article 45

Reasons for judgments and decisions

1. Reasons shall be given for judgments as well as for decisions declaring applications admissible or inadmissible.

2. If a judgment does not represent, in whole or in part, the unanimous opinion of the judges, any judge shall be entitled to deliver a separate opinion.

Article 46

Binding force and execution of judgments

1. The High Contracting Parties undertake to abide by the final judgment of the Court in any case to which they are parties.

2. The final judgment of the Court shall be transmitted to the Committee of Ministers, which shall supervise its execution.

Article 47

Advisory opinions

1. The Court may, at the request of the Committee of Ministers, give advisory opinions on legal questions concerning the interpretation of the Convention and the protocols thereto.

2. Such opinions shall not deal with any question relating to the content or scope of the rights or freedoms defined in Section I of the Convention and the protocols thereto, or with any other question which the Court or the Committee of Ministers might have to consider in consequence of any such proceedings as could be instituted in accordance with the Convention.

3. Decisions of the Committee of Ministers to request an advisory opinion of the Court shall require a majority vote of the representatives entitled to sit on the Committee.

Article 48

Advisory jurisdiction of the Court

The Court shall decide whether a request for an advisory opinion submitted by the Committee of Ministers is within its competence as defined in Article 47.

Article 49

Reasons for advisory opinions

1. Reasons shall be given for advisory opinions of the Court.

2. If the advisory opinion does not represent, in whole or in part, the unanimous opinion of the judges, any judge shall be entitled to deliver a separate opinion.

3. Advisory opinions of the Court shall be communicated to the Committee of Ministers.

Article 50

Expenditure on the Court

The expenditure on the Court shall be borne by the Council of Europe.

Article 51

Privileges and immunities of judges

The judges shall be entitled, during the exercise of their functions, to the privileges and immunities provided for in Article 40 of the Statute of the Council of Europe and in the agreements made thereunder.

Section III
Miscellaneous Provisions

Article 52

Inquiries by the Secretary General

On receipt of a request from the Secretary General of the Council of Europe any High Contracting Party shall furnish an explanation of the manner in which its internal law ensures the effective implementation of any of the provisions of the Convention.

Article 53

Safeguard for existing human rights

Nothing in this Convention shall be construed as limiting or derogating from any of the human rights and fundamental freedoms which may be ensured under the laws of any High Contracting Party or under any other agreement to which it is a Party.

Article 54

Powers of the Committee of Ministers

Nothing in this Convention shall prejudice the powers conferred on the Committee of Ministers by the Statute of the Council of Europe.

Article 55

Exclusion of other means of dispute settlement

The High Contracting Parties agree that, except by special agreement, they will not avail themselves of treaties, conventions or declarations in force between them for the purpose of submitting, by way of petition, a dispute arising out of the interpretation or application of this Convention to a means of settlement other than those provided for in this Convention.

Article 56

Territorial application

1. Any State may at the time of its ratification or at any time thereafter declare by notification addressed to the Secretary General of the Council of Europe that the present Convention shall, subject to paragraph 4 of this Article, extend to all or any of the territories for whose international relations it is responsible.

2. The Convention shall extend to the territory or territories named in the notification as from the thirtieth day after the receipt of this notification by the Secretary General of the Council of Europe.

3. The provisions of this Convention shall be applied in such territories with due regard, however, to local requirements.

4. Any State which has made a declaration in accordance with paragraph 1 of this article may at any time thereafter declare on behalf of one or more of the territories to which the declaration relates that it accepts the competence of the Court to receive applications from individuals, non-governmental organisations or groups of individuals as provided by Article 34 of the Convention.

Article 57

Reservations

1. Any State may, when signing this Convention or when depositing its instrument of ratification, make a reservation in respect of any particular provision of the Convention to the extent that any law then in force in its territory is not in conformity with the provision. Reservations of a general character shall not be permitted under this article.

2. Any reservation made under this article shall contain a brief statement of the law concerned.

Article 58

Denunciation

1. A High Contracting Party may denounce the present Convention only after the expiry of five years from the date on which it became a party to it and after six months' notice contained in a notification addressed to the Secretary General of the Council of Europe, who shall inform the other High Contracting Parties.

2. Such a denunciation shall not have the effect of releasing the High Contracting Party concerned from its obligations under this Convention in respect of any act which, being capable of constituting a violation of such obligations, may have been performed by it before the date at which the denunciation became effective.

3. Any High Contracting Party which shall cease to be a member of the Council of Europe shall cease to be a Party to this Convention under the same conditions.

4. The Convention may be denounced in accordance with the provisions of the preceding paragraphs in respect of any territory to which it has been declared to extend under the terms of Article 56.

Article 59

Signature and ratification

1. This Convention shall be open to the signature of the members of the Council of Europe. It shall be ratified. Ratifications shall be deposited with the Secretary General of the Council of Europe.

2. The present Convention shall come into force after the deposit of ten instruments of ratification.

3. As regards any signatory ratifying subsequently, the Convention shall come into force at the date of the deposit of its instrument of ratification.

4. The Secretary General of the Council of Europe shall notify all the members of the Council of Europe of the entry into force of the Convention, the names of the High Contracting Parties who have ratified it, and the deposit of all instruments of ratification which may be effected subsequently.

Done at Rome this 4th day of November 1950, in English and French, both texts being equally authentic, in a single copy which shall remain deposited in the archives of the Council of Europe. The Secretary General shall transmit certified copies to each of the signatories.

Protocol to the Convention for the Protection of Human Rights and Fundamental Freedoms, as amended by Protocol No 11

Paris, 20.III.1952

The governments signatory hereto, being members of the Council of Europe,

Being resolved to take steps to ensure the collective enforcement of certain rights and freedoms other than those already included in Section I of the Convention for the Protection of Human Rights and Fundamental Freedoms signed at Rome on 4 November 1950 (hereinafter referred to as 'the Convention'),

Have agreed as follows:

Article 1

Protection of property

Every natural or legal person is entitled to the peaceful enjoyment of his possessions. No one shall be deprived of his possessions except in the public interest and subject to the conditions provided for by law and by the general principles of international law.

The preceding provisions shall not, however, in any way impair the right of a State to enforce such laws as it deems necessary to control the use of property in accordance with the general interest or to secure the payment of taxes or other contributions or penalties.

Article 2

Right to education

No person shall be denied the right to education. In the exercise of any functions which it assumes in relation to education and to teaching, the State shall respect the right of parents to ensure such education and teaching in conformity with their own religious and philosophical convictions.

Article 3

Right to free elections

The High Contracting Parties undertake to hold free elections at reasonable intervals by secret ballot, under conditions which will ensure the free expression of the opinion of the people in the choice of the legislature.

Article 4

Territorial application

Any High Contracting Party may at the time of signature or ratification or at any time thereafter communicate to the Secretary General of the Council of Europe a declaration stating the extent to which it undertakes that the provisions of the present Protocol shall apply to such of the territories for the international relations of which it is responsible as are named therein.

Any High Contracting Party which has communicated a declaration in virtue of the preceding paragraph may from time to time communicate a further declaration modifying the terms of any former declaration or terminating the application of the provisions of this Protocol in respect of any territory.

A declaration made in accordance with this article shall be deemed to have been made in accordance with paragraph 1 of Article 56 of the Convention.

Article 5

Relationship to the Convention

As between the High Contracting Parties the provisions of Articles 1, 2, 3 and 4 of this Protocol shall be regarded as additional articles to the Convention and all the provisions of the Convention shall apply accordingly.

Article 6

Signature and ratification

This Protocol shall be open for signature by the members of the Council of Europe, who are the signatories of the Convention; it shall be ratified at the same time as or after the ratification of the Convention. It shall enter into force after the deposit of ten instruments of ratification. As regards any signatory ratifying subsequently, the Protocol shall enter into force at the date of the deposit of its instrument of ratification.

The instruments of ratification shall be deposited with the Secretary General of the Council of Europe, who will notify all members of the names of those who have ratified.

Done at Paris on the 20th day of March 1952, in English and French, both texts being equally authentic, in a single copy which shall remain deposited in the archives of the Council of Europe. The Secretary General shall transmit certified copies to each of the signatory governments.

Protocol No 4 to the Convention for the Protection of Human Rights and Fundamental Freedoms, Securing Certain Rights and Freedoms other than those already included in the Convention and in the First Protocol thereto, as amended by Protocol No 11

Strasbourg, 16.IX.1963

The governments signatory hereto, being members of the Council of Europe,

Being resolved to take steps to ensure the collective enforcement of certain rights and freedoms other than those already included in Section 1 of the Convention for the Protection of Human Rights and Fundamental Freedoms signed at Rome on 4th November 1950 (hereinafter referred to as the 'Convention') and in Articles 1 to 3 of the First Protocol to the Convention, signed at Paris on 20th March 1952,

Have agreed as follows:

Article 1

Prohibition of imprisonment for debt

No one shall be deprived of his liberty merely on the ground of inability to fulfil a contractual obligation.

Article 2

Freedom of movement

1. Everyone lawfully within the territory of a State shall, within that territory, have the right to liberty of movement and freedom to choose his residence.

2. Everyone shall be free to leave any country, including his own.

3. No restrictions shall be placed on the exercise of these rights other than such as are in accordance with law and are necessary in a democratic society in the interests of national security or public safety, for the maintenance of *ordre public*, for the prevention of crime, for the protection of health or morals, or for the protection of the rights and freedoms of others.

4. The rights set forth in paragraph 1 may also be subject, in particular areas, to restrictions imposed in accordance with law and justified by the public interest in a democratic society.

Article 3

Prohibition of expulsion of nationals

1. No one shall be expelled, by means either of an individual or of a collective measure, from the territory of the State of which he is a national.

2. No one shall be deprived of the right to enter the territory of the state of which he is a national.

Article 4

Prohibition of collective expulsion of aliens

Collective expulsion of aliens is prohibited.

Article 5

Territorial application

1. Any High Contracting Party may, at the time of signature or ratification of this Protocol, or at any time thereafter, communicate to the Secretary General of the Council of Europe a declaration stating the extent to which it undertakes that the provisions of this Protocol shall apply to such of the territories for the international relations of which it is responsible as are named therein.

2. Any High Contracting Party which has communicated a declaration in virtue of the preceding paragraph may, from time to time, communicate a further declaration modifying the terms of any former declaration or terminating the application of the provisions of this Protocol in respect of any territory.

3. A declaration made in accordance with this article shall be deemed to have been made in accordance with paragraph 1 of Article 56 of the Convention.

4. The territory of any State to which this Protocol applies by virtue of ratification or acceptance by that State, and each territory to which this Protocol is applied by virtue of a declaration by that State under this article, shall be treated as separate territories for the purpose of the references in Articles 2 and 3 to the territory of a State.

5. Any State which has made a declaration in accordance with paragraph 1 or 2 of this Article may at any time thereafter declare on behalf of one or more of the territories to which the declaration relates that it accepts the competence of the Court to receive applications from individuals, non-governmental organisations or groups of individuals as provided in Article 34 of the Convention in respect of all or any of Articles 1 to 4 of this Protocol.

Article 6

Relationship to the Convention

As between the High Contracting Parties the provisions of Articles 1 to 5 of this Protocol shall be regarded as additional Articles to the Convention, and all the provisions of the Convention shall apply accordingly.

Article 7

Signature and ratification

1. This Protocol shall be open for signature by the members of the Council of Europe who are the signatories of the Convention; it shall be ratified at the same time as or after the ratification of the Convention. It shall enter into force after the deposit of five instruments of ratification. As regards any signatory ratifying subsequently, the Protocol shall enter into force at the date of the deposit of its instrument of ratification.

2. The instruments of ratification shall be deposited with the Secretary General of the Council of Europe, who will notify all members of the names of those who have ratified.

In witness whereof the undersigned, being duly authorised thereto, have signed this Protocol.

Done at Strasbourg, this 16th day of September 1963, in English and in French, both texts being equally authoritative, in a single copy which shall remain deposited in the archives of the Council of Europe. The Secretary General shall transmit certified copies to each of the signatory states.

Protocol No 6 to the Convention for the Protection of Human Rights and Fundamental Freedoms Concerning the Abolition of the Death Penalty, as amended by Protocol No 11

Strasbourg, 28.IV.1983

The member States of the Council of Europe, signatory to this Protocol to the Convention for the Protection of Human Rights and Fundamental Freedoms, signed at Rome on 4 November 1950 (hereinafter referred to as 'the Convention'),

Considering that the evolution that has occurred in several member States of the Council of Europe expresses a general tendency in favour of abolition of the death penalty;

Have agreed as follows:

Article 1

Abolition of the death penalty

The death penalty shall be abolished. No-one shall be condemned to such penalty or executed.

Article 2

Death penalty in time of war

A State may make provision in its law for the death penalty in respect of acts committed in time of war or of imminent threat of war; such penalty shall be applied only in the instances laid down in the law and in accordance with its provisions. The State shall communicate to the Secretary General of the Council of Europe the relevant provisions of that law.

Article 3

Prohibition of derogations

No derogation from the provisions of this Protocol shall be made under Article 15 of the Convention.

Article 4

Prohibition of reservations

No reservation may be made under Article 57 of the Convention in respect of the provisions of this Protocol.

Article 5

Territorial application

1. Any State may at the time of signature or when depositing its instrument of ratification, acceptance or approval, specify the territory or territories to which this Protocol shall apply.

2. Any State may at any later date, by a declaration addressed to the Secretary General of the Council of Europe, extend the application of this Protocol to any other territory specified in the declaration. In respect of such territory the Protocol shall enter into force on the first day of the month following the date of receipt of such declaration by the Secretary General.

3. Any declaration made under the two preceding paragraphs may, in respect of any territory specified in such declaration, be withdrawn by a notification addressed to the Secretary General. The withdrawal shall become effective on the first day of the month following the date of receipt of such notification by the Secretary General.

Article 6

Relationship to the Convention

As between the States Parties the provisions of Articles 1 to 5 of this Protocol shall be regarded as additional articles to the Convention and all the provisions of the Convention shall apply accordingly.

Article 7

Signature and ratification

The Protocol shall be open for signature by the member States of the Council of Europe, signatories to the Convention. It shall be subject to ratification, acceptance or approval. A member State of the Council of Europe may not ratify, accept or approve this Protocol unless it has, simultaneously or previously, ratified the Convention. Instruments of ratification, acceptance or approval shall be deposited with the Secretary General of the Council of Europe.

Article 8

Entry into force

1. This Protocol shall enter into force on the first day of the month following the date on which five member States of the Council of Europe have expressed their consent to be bound by the Protocol in accordance with the provisions of Article 7.

2. In respect of any member State which subsequently expresses its consent to be bound by it, the Protocol shall enter into force on the first day of the month following the date of the deposit of the instrument of ratification, acceptance or approval.

Article 9

Depositary functions

The Secretary General of the Council of Europe shall notify the member States of the Council of:

(a) any signature;
(b) the deposit of any instrument of ratification, acceptance or approval;
(c) any date of entry into force of this Protocol in accordance with Articles 5 and 8;
(d) any other act, notification or communication relating to this Protocol.

In witness whereof the undersigned, being duly authorised thereto, have signed this Protocol.

Done at Strasbourg, this 28th day of April 1983, in English and in French, both texts being equally authentic, in a single copy which shall be deposited in the archives of the Council of Europe. The Secretary General of the Council of Europe shall transmit certified copies to each member State of the Council of Europe.

Protocol No 7 to the Convention for the Protection of Human Rights and Fundamental Freedoms, as amended by Protocol No 11

Strasbourg, 22.XI.1984

The member States of the Council of Europe signatory hereto,

Being resolved to take further steps to ensure the collective enforcement of certain rights and freedoms by means of the Convention for the Protection of Human Rights and Fundamental Freedoms signed at Rome on 4 November 1950 (hereinafter referred to as 'the Convention'),

Have agreed as follows:

Article 1

Procedural safeguards relating to expulsion of aliens

1. An alien lawfully resident in the territory of a State shall not be expelled therefrom except in pursuance of a decision reached in accordance with law and shall be allowed:

(a) to submit reasons against his expulsion,

(b) to have his case reviewed, and

(c) to be represented for these purposes before the competent authority or a person or persons designated by that authority.

2. An alien may be expelled before the exercise of his rights under paragraph 1(a), (b) and (c) of this Article, when such expulsion is necessary in the interests of public order or is grounded on reasons of national security.

Article 2

Right of appeal in criminal matters

1. Everyone convicted of a criminal offence by a tribunal shall have the right to have his conviction or sentence reviewed by a higher tribunal. The exercise of this right, including the grounds on which it may be exercised, shall be governed by law.

2. This right may be subject to exceptions in regard to offences of a minor character, as prescribed by law, or in cases in which the person concerned was tried in the first instance by the highest tribunal or was convicted following an appeal against acquittal.

Article 3

Compensation for wrongful conviction

When a person has by a final decision been convicted of a criminal offence and when subsequently his conviction has been reversed, or he has been pardoned, on the ground that a new or newly discovered fact shows conclusively that there has been a miscarriage of justice, the person who has suffered punishment as a result of such conviction shall be compensated according to the law or the practice of the State concerned, unless it is proved that the non-disclosure of the unknown fact in time is wholly or partly attributable to him.

Article 4

Right not to be tried or punished twice

1. No one shall be liable to be tried or punished again in criminal proceedings under the jurisdiction of the same State for an offence for which he has already been finally acquitted or convicted in accordance with the law and penal procedure of that State.

2. The provisions of the preceding paragraph shall not prevent the reopening of the case in accordance with the law and penal procedure of the State concerned, if there is evidence of new or newly discovered facts, or if there has been a fundamental defect in the previous proceedings, which could affect the outcome of the case.

3. No derogation from this Article shall be made under Article 15 of the Convention.

Article 5

Equality between spouses

Spouses shall enjoy equality of rights and responsibilities of a private law character between them, and in their relations with their children, as to marriage, during marriage and in the event of its dissolution. This Article shall not prevent States from taking such measures as are necessary in the interests of the children.

Article 6

Territorial application

1. Any State may at the time of signature or when depositing its instrument of ratification, acceptance or approval, specify the territory or territories to which the Protocol shall apply and state the extent to which it undertakes that the provisions of this Protocol shall apply to such territory or territories.

2. Any State may at any later date, by a declaration addressed to the Secretary General of the Council of Europe, extend the application of this Protocol to any other territory specified in the declaration. In respect of such territory the Protocol shall enter into force on the first day of the month following the expiration of a period of two months after the date of receipt by the Secretary General of such declaration.

3. Any declaration made under the two preceding paragraphs may, in respect of any territory specified in such declaration, be withdrawn or modified by a notification addressed to the Secretary General. The withdrawal or modification shall become effective on the first day of the month following the expiration of a period of two months after the date of receipt of such notification by the Secretary General.

4. A declaration made in accordance with this Article shall be deemed to have been made in accordance with paragraph 1 of Article 56 of the Convention.

5. The territory of any State to which this Protocol applies by virtue of ratification, acceptance or approval by that State, and each territory to which this Protocol is applied by virtue of a declaration by that State under this Article, may be treated as separate territories for the purpose of the reference in Article 1 to the territory of a State.

6. Any State which has made a declaration in accordance with paragraph 1 or 2 of this Article may at any time thereafter declare on behalf of one or more of the territories to which the declaration relates that it accepts the competence of the Court to receive applications from individuals, non-governmental organisations or groups of individuals as provided in Article 34 of the Convention in respect of Articles 1 to 5 of this Protocol.

Article 7

Relationship to the Convention

As between the States Parties, the provisions of Article 1 to 6 of this Protocol shall be regarded as additional Articles to the Convention, and all the provisions of the Convention shall apply accordingly.

Article 8

Signature and ratification

This Protocol shall be open for signature by member States of the Council of Europe which have signed the Convention. It is subject to ratification, acceptance or approval. A member State of the Council of Europe may not ratify, accept or approve this Protocol without previously or simultaneously ratifying the Convention. Instruments of ratification, acceptance or approval shall be deposited with the Secretary General of the Council of Europe.

Article 9

Entry into force

1. This Protocol shall enter into force on the first day of the month following the expiration of a period of

two months after the date on which seven member States of the Council of Europe have expressed their consent to be bound by the Protocol in accordance with the provisions of Article 8.

2. In respect of any member State which subsequently expresses its consent to be bound by it, the Protocol shall enter into force on the first day of the month following the expiration of a period of two months after the date of the deposit of the instrument of ratification, acceptance or approval.

Article 10

Depositary functions

The Secretary General of the Council of Europe shall notify all the member States of the Council of Europe of:

(a) any signature;
(b) the deposit of any instrument of ratification, acceptance or approval;
(c) any date of entry into force of this Protocol in accordance with Articles 6 and 9;
(d) any other act, notification or declaration relating to this Protocol.

In witness whereof the undersigned, being duly authorised thereto, have signed this Protocol.

Done at Strasbourg, this 22nd day of November 1984, in English and French, both texts being equally authentic, in a single copy which shall be deposited in the archives of the Council of Europe. The Secretary General of the Council of Europe shall transmit certified copies to each member State of the Council of Europe.

APPENDIX F

European Court of Human Rights
Rules of Court

STRASBOURG 1999
(AS IN FORCE AT 1 NOVEMBER 1998)

Contents

Rule 1—Definitions

TITLE I—Organisation and Working of the Court

Chapter I—Judges

Rule 2—Calculation of term of office
Rule 3—Oath or solemn declaration
Rule 4—Incompatible activities
Rule 5—Precedence
Rule 6—Resignation
Rule 7—Dismissal from office

Chapter II—Presidency of the Court

Rule 8—Election of the President and Vice-Presidents of the Court and the Presidents and Vice-Presidents of the Sections
Rule 9—Functions of the President of the Court
Rule 10—Functions of the Vice-Presidents of the Court
Rule 11—Replacement of the President and the Vice-Presidents of the Court
Rule 12—Presidency of Sections and Chambers
Rule 13—Inability to preside
Rule 14—Balanced representation of the sexes

Chapter III—The Registry

Rule 15—Election of the Registrar
Rule 16—Election of the Deputy Registrars
Rule 17—Functions of the Registrar
Rule 18—Organisation of the Registry

Chapter IV—The Working of the Court

Rule 19—Seat of the Court
Rule 20—Sessions of the plenary Court
Rule 21—Other sessions of the Court
Rule 22—Deliberations
Rule 23—Votes

Chapter V—The Composition of the Court

Rule 24—Composition of the Grand Chamber
Rule 25—Setting up of Sections
Rule 26—Constitution of Chambers
Rule 27—Committees
Rule 28—Inability to sit, withdrawal or exemption
Rule 29—*Ad hoc* judges
Rule 30—Common interest

TITLE II—Procedure

Chapter I—General Rules

Rule 31—Possibility of particular derogations
Rule 32—Practice directions
Rule 33—Public character of proceedings
Rule 34—Use of languages
Rule 35—Representation of Contracting Parties
Rule 36—Representation of applicants
Rule 37—Communications, notifications and summonses
Rule 38—Written pleadings
Rule 39—Interim measures
Rule 40—Urgent notification of an application
Rule 41—Case priority
Rule 42—Measures for taking evidence
Rule 43—Joinder and simultaneous examination of applications
Rule 44—Striking out and restoration to the list

Chapter II—Institution of Proceedings

Rule 45—Signatures
Rule 46—Contents of an inter-State application
Rule 47—Contents of an individual application

Chapter III—Judge Rapporteurs

Rule 48—Inter-State applications
Rule 49—Individual applications
Rule 50—Grand Chamber proceedings

Chapter IV—Proceedings on Admissibility

Inter-State applications

Rule 51

Individual applications

Rule 52—Assignment of applications to the Sections
Rule 53—Procedure before a Committee
Rule 54—Procedure before a Chamber

Inter-State and individual applications

Rule 55—Pleas of inadmissibility
Rule 56—Decision of a Chamber
Rule 57—Language of the decision

Chapter V—Proceedings after the Admission of an Application

Rule 58—Inter-State applications
Rule 59—Individual applications

Rule 60—Claims for just satisfaction
Rule 61—Third-party intervention
Rule 62—Friendly settlement

Chapter VI—Hearings

Rule 63—Conduct of hearings
Rule 64—Failure to appear at a hearing
Rule 65—Convocation of witnesses, experts and other persons; costs of their appearance
Rule 66—Oath or solemn declaration by witnesses and experts
Rule 67—Objection to a witness or expert; hearing of a person for information purposes
Rule 68—Questions put during hearings
Rule 69—Failure to appear, refusal to give evidence or false evidence
Rule 70—Verbatim record of hearings

Chapter VII—Proceedings before the Grand Chamber

Rule 71—Applicability of procedural provisions
Rule 72—Relinquishment of jurisdiction by a Chamber in favour of the Grand Chamber
Rule 73—Request by a party for referral to the Grand Chamber

Chapter VIII—Judgments

Rule 74—Contents of the judgment
Rule 75—Ruling on just satisfaction
Rule 76—Language of the judgment
Rule 77—Signature, delivery and notification of the judgment
Rule 78—Publication of judgments and other documents
Rule 79—Request for interpretation of a judgment
Rule 80—Request for revision of a judgment
Rule 81—Rectification of errors in decisions and judgments

Chapter IX—Advisory Opinions

Rule 82
Rule 83
Rule 84
Rule 85
Rule 86
Rule 87
Rule 88
Rule 89
Rule 90

Chapter X—Legal Aid

Rule 91
Rule 92
Rule 93
Rule 94
Rule 95
Rule 96

TITLE III—Transitional Rules

Rule 97—Judges' terms of office
Rule 98—Presidency of the Sections
Rule 99—Relations between the Court and the Commission

Rule 100—Chamber and Grand Chamber proceedings
Rule 101—Grant of legal aid
Rule 102—Request for interpretation or revision of a judgment

TITLE IV—Final Clauses

Rule 103—Amendment or suspension of a Rule
Rule 104—Entry into force of the Rules

The European Court of Human Rights,

Having regard to the Convention for the Protection of Human Rights and Fundamental Freedoms and the Protocols thereto,

Makes the present Rules:

Rule 1

Definitions

For the purposes of these Rules unless the context otherwise requires:

(a) the term 'Convention' means the Convention for the Protection of Human Rights and Fundamental Freedoms and the Protocols thereto;

(b) the expression 'plenary Court' means the European Court of Human Rights sitting in plenary session;

(c) the expression 'Grand Chamber' means the Grand Chamber of seventeen judges constituted in pursuance of Article 27 §1 of the Convention;

(d) the term 'Section' means a Chamber set up by the plenary Court for a fixed period in pursuance of Article 26 (b) of the Convention and the expression 'President of the Section' means the judge elected by the plenary Court in pursuance of Article 26 (c) of the Convention as President of such a Section;

(e) the term 'Chamber' means any Chamber of seven judges constituted in pursuance of Article 27 §1 of the Convention and the expression 'President of the Chamber' means the judge presiding over such a 'Chamber';

(f) the term 'Committee' means a Committee of three judges set up in pursuance of Article 27 §1 of the Convention;

(g) the term 'Court' means either the plenary Court, the Grand Chamber, a Section, a Chamber, a Committee or the panel of five judges referred to in Article 43 §2 of the Convention;

(h) the expression '*ad hoc* judge' means any person, other than an elected judge, chosen by a Contracting Party in pursuance of Article 27 §2 of the Convention to sit as a member of the Grand Chamber or as a member of a Chamber;

(i) the terms 'judge' and 'judges' mean the judges elected by the Parliamentary Assembly of the Council of Europe or *ad hoc* judges;

(j) the expression 'Judge Rapporteur' means a judge appointed to carry out the tasks provided for in Rules 48 and 49;

(k) the term 'Registrar' denotes the Registrar of the Court or the Registrar of a Section according to the context;

(l) the terms 'party' and 'parties' mean
— the applicant or respondent Contracting Parties;
— the applicant (the person, non-governmental organisation or group of individuals) that lodged a complaint under Article 34 of the Convention;

(m) the expression 'third party' means any Contracting State or any person concerned who, as provided for in Article 36 §§1 and 2 of the Convention, has exercised its right or been invited to submit written comments or take part in a hearing;

(n) the expression 'Committee of Ministers' means the Committee of Ministers of the Council of Europe;

(o) the terms 'former Court' and 'Commission' mean respectively the European Court and European Commission of Human Rights set up under former Article 19 of the Convention.

Title I
Organisation and Working of the Court

Chapter I
Judges

Rule 2

Calculation of term of office

1. The duration of the term of office of an elected judge shall be calculated as from the date of election. However, when a judge is re-elected on the expiry of the term of office or is elected to replace a judge whose term of office has expired or is about to expire, the duration of the term of office shall, in either case, be calculated as from the date of such expiry.

2. In accordance with Article 23 §5 of the Convention, a judge elected to replace a judge whose term of office has not expired shall hold office for the remainder of the predecessor's term.

3. In accordance with Article 23 §7 of the Convention, an elected judge shall hold office until a successor has taken the oath or made the declaration provided for in Rule 3.

Rule 3

Oath or solemn declaration

1. Before taking up office, each elected judge shall, at the first sitting of the plenary Court at which the judge is present or, in case of need, before the President of the Court, take the following oath or make the following solemn declaration:

> 'I swear'—or 'I solemnly declare'—'that I will exercise my functions as a judge honourably, independently and impartially and that I will keep secret all deliberations.'

2. This act shall be recorded in minutes.

Rule 4

Incompatible activities

In accordance with Article 21 §3 of the Convention, the judges shall not during their term of office engage in any political or administrative activity or any professional activity which is incompatible with their independence or impartiality or with the demands of a full-time office. Each judge shall declare to the President of the Court any additional activity. In the event of a disagreement between the President and the judge concerned, any question arising shall be decided by the plenary Court.

Rule 5

Precedence

1. Elected judges shall take precedence after the President and Vice-Presidents of the Court and the Presidents of the Sections, according to the date of their election; in the event of re-election, even if it is not an immediate re-election, the length of time during which the judge concerned previously held office as a judge shall be taken into account.

2. Vice-Presidents of the Court elected to office on the same date shall take precedence according to the length of time they have served as judges. If the length of time they have served as judges is the same, they shall take precedence according to age. The same rule shall apply to Presidents of Sections.

3. Judges who have served the same length of time as judges shall take precedence according to age.

4. *Ad hoc* judges shall take precedence after the elected judges according to age.

Rule 6

Resignation

Resignation of a judge shall be notified to the President of the Court, who shall transmit it to the Secretary General of the Council of Europe. Subject to the provisions of Rules 24 §3 *in fine* and 26 §2, resignation shall constitute vacation of office.

Rule 7

Dismissal from office

No judge may be dismissed from his or her office unless the other judges, meeting in plenary session, decide by a majority of two-thirds of the elected judges in office that he or she has ceased to fulfil the required conditions. He or she must first be heard by the plenary Court. Any judge may set in motion the procedure for dismissal from office.

Chapter II
Presidency of the Court

Rule 8

Election of the President and Vice-Presidents of the Court and the Presidents and Vice-Presidents of the Sections

1. The plenary Court shall elect its President, two Vice-Presidents and the Presidents of the Sections for a period of three years, provided that such period shall not exceed the duration of their terms of office as judges. They may be re-elected.

2. Each Section shall likewise elect for a renewable period of three years a Vice-President, who shall replace the President of the Section if the latter is unable to carry out his or her duties.

3. The Presidents and Vice-Presidents shall continue to hold office until the election of their successors.

4. If a President or a Vice-President ceases to be a member of the Court or resigns from office before its normal expiry, the plenary Court or the relevant Section, as the case may be, shall elect a successor for the remainder of the term of that office.

5. The elections referred to in this Rule shall be by secret ballot; only the elected judges who are present shall take part. If no judge receives an absolute majority of the elected judges present, a ballot shall take place between the two judges who have received most votes. In the event of a tie, preference shall be given to the judge having precedence in accordance with Rule 5.

Rule 9

Functions of the President of the Court

1. The President of the Court shall direct the work and administration of the Court. The President shall represent the Court and, in particular, be responsible for its relations with the authorities of the Council of Europe.

2. The President shall preside at plenary meetings of the Court, meetings of the Grand Chamber and meetings of the panel of five judges.

3. The President shall not take part in the consideration of cases being heard by Chambers except where he or she is the judge elected in respect of a Contracting Party concerned.

Rule 10

Functions of the Vice-Presidents of the Court

The Vice-Presidents of the Court shall assist the President of the Court. They shall take the place of the President if the latter is unable to carry out his or her duties or the office of President is vacant, or at the request of the President. They shall also act as Presidents of Sections.

Rule 11

Replacement of the President and the Vice-Presidents of the Court

If the President and the Vice-Presidents of the Court are at the same time unable to carry out their duties or if their offices are at the same time vacant, the office of President of the Court shall be assumed by a President of a Section or, if none is available, by another elected judge, in accordance with the order of precedence provided for in Rule 5.

Rule 12

Presidency of Sections and Chambers

The Presidents of the Sections shall preside at the sittings of the Section and Chambers of which they are members. The Vice-Presidents of the Sections shall take their place if they are unable to carry out their duties or if the office of President of the Section concerned is vacant, or at the request of the President of the Section. Failing that, the judges of the Section and the Chambers shall take their place, in the order of precedence provided for in Rule 5.

Rule 13

Inability to preside

Judges of the Court may not preside in cases in which the Contracting Party of which they are nationals or in respect of which they were elected is a party.

Rule 14

Balanced representation of the sexes

In relation to the making of appointments governed by this and the following chapter of the present Rules, the Court shall pursue a policy aimed at securing a balanced representation of the sexes.

Chapter III
The Registry

Rule 15

Election of the Registrar

1. The plenary Court shall elect its Registrar. The candidates shall be of high moral character and must possess the legal, managerial and linguistic knowledge and experience necessary to carry out the functions attaching to the post.

2. The Registrar shall be elected for a term of five years and may be re-elected. The Registrar may not be dismissed from office, unless the judges, meeting in plenary session, decide by a majority of two-thirds of the elected judges in office that the person concerned has ceased to fulfil the required conditions. He or she must first be heard by the plenary Court. Any judge may set in motion the procedure for dismissal from office.

3. The elections referred to in this Rule shall be by secret ballot; only the elected judges who are present shall take part. If no candidate receives an absolute majority of the elected judges present, a ballot shall take place between the two candidates who have received most votes. In the event of a tie, preference shall be given, firstly, to the female candidate, if any, and, secondly, to the older candidate.

4. Before taking up office, the Registrar shall take the following oath or make the following solemn declaration before the plenary Court or, if need be, before the President of the Court:

> 'I swear'—or 'I solemnly declare'—'that I will exercise loyally, discreetly and conscientiously the functions conferred upon me as Registrar of the European Court of Human Rights.'

This act shall be recorded in minutes.

Rule 16

Election of the Deputy Registrars

1. The plenary Court shall also elect two Deputy Registrars on the conditions and in the manner and for the term prescribed in the preceding Rule. The procedure for dismissal from office provided for in respect of the Registrar shall likewise apply. The Court shall first consult the Registrar in both these matters.

2. Before taking up office, a Deputy Registrar shall take an oath or make a solemn declaration before the plenary Court or, if need be, before the President of the Court, in terms similar to those prescribed in respect of the Registrar. This act shall be recorded in minutes.

Rule 17

Functions of the Registrar

1. The Registrar shall assist the Court in the performance of its functions and shall be responsible for the organisation and activities of the Registry under the authority of the President of the Court.

2. The Registrar shall have the custody of the archives of the Court and shall be the channel for all communications and notifications made by, or addressed to, the Court in connection with the cases brought or to be brought before it.

3. The Registrar shall, subject to the duty of discretion attaching to this office, reply to requests for information concerning the work of the Court, in particular to enquiries from the press.

4. General instructions drawn up by the Registrar, and approved by the President of the Court, shall regulate the working of the Registry.

Rule 18

Organisation of the Registry

1. The Registry shall consist of Section Registries equal to the number of Sections set up by the Court and of the departments necessary to provide the legal and administrative services required by the Court.

2. The Section Registrar shall assist the Section in the performance of its functions and may be assisted by a Deputy Section Registrar.

3. The officials of the Registry, including the legal secretaries but not the Registrar and the Deputy Registrars, shall be appointed by the Secretary General of the Council of Europe with the agreement of the President of the Court or of the Registrar acting on the President's instructions.

Chapter IV
The Working of the Court

Rule 19

Seat of the Court

1. The seat of the Court shall be at the seat of the Council of Europe at Strasbourg. The Court may, however, if it considers it expedient, perform its functions elsewhere in the territories of the member States of the Council of Europe.

2. The Court may decide, at any stage of the examination of an application, that it is necessary that an investigation or any other function be carried out elsewhere by it or one or more of its members.

Rule 20

Sessions of the plenary Court

1. The plenary sessions of the Court shall be convened by the President of the Court whenever the performance of its functions under the Convention and under these Rules so requires. The President of the Court shall convene a plenary session if at least one-third of the members of the Court so request, and in any event once a year to consider administrative matters.

2. The quorum of the plenary Court shall be two-thirds of the elected judges in office.

3. If there is no quorum, the President shall adjourn the sitting.

Rule 21

Other sessions of the Court

1. The Grand Chamber, the Chambers and the Committees shall sit full time. On a proposal by the President, however, the Court shall fix session periods each year.

2. Outside those periods the Grand Chamber and the Chambers shall be convened by their Presidents in cases of urgency.

Rule 22

Deliberations

1. The Court shall deliberate in private. Its deliberations shall remain secret.

2. Only the judges shall take part in the deliberations. The Registrar or the designated substitute, as well as such other officials of the Registry and interpreters whose assistance is deemed necessary, shall be present. No other person may be admitted except by special decision of the Court.

3. Before a vote is taken on any matter in the Court, the President may request the judges to state their opinions on it.

Rule 23

Votes

1. The decisions of the Court shall be taken by a majority of the judges present. In the event of a tie, a fresh vote shall be taken and, if there is still a tie, the President shall have a casting vote. This paragraph shall apply unless otherwise provided for in these Rules.

2. The decisions and judgments of the Grand Chamber and the Chambers shall be adopted by a majority of the sitting judges. Abstentions shall not be allowed in final votes on the admissibility and merits of cases.

3. As a general rule, votes shall be taken by a show of hands. The President may take a roll-call vote, in reverse order of precedence.

4. Any matter that is to be voted upon shall be formulated in precise terms.

Chapter V
The Composition of the Court

Rule 24

Composition of the Grand Chamber

1. The Grand Chamber shall be composed of seventeen judges and three substitute judges.

2. The Grand Chamber shall be constituted for three years with effect from the election of the presidential office-holders referred to in Rule 8.

3. The Grand Chamber shall include the President and Vice-Presidents of the Court and the Presidents of the Sections. In order to complete the Grand Chamber, the plenary Court shall, on a proposal by its President, divide all the other judges into two groups which shall alternate every nine months and whose membership shall be geographically as balanced as possible and reflect the different legal systems among the Contracting Parties. The judges and substitute judges who are to hear each case referred to the Grand Chamber during each nine-month period shall be designated in rotation within each group; they shall remain members of the Grand Chamber until the proceedings have been completed, even after their terms of office as judges have expired.

4. If he or she does not sit as a member of the Grand Chamber by virtue of paragraph 3 of this Rule, the judge elected in respect of any Contracting Party concerned shall sit as an *ex officio* member of the Grand Chamber in accordance with Article 27 §§2 and 3 of the Convention.

5. (a) Where any President of a Section is unable to sit as a member of the Grand Chamber, he or she shall be replaced by the Vice-President of the Section.
(b) If other judges are prevented from sitting, they shall be replaced by the substitute judges in the order in which the latter were selected under paragraph 3 of this Rule.
(c) If there are not enough substitute judges in the group concerned to complete the Grand Chamber, the substitute judges lacking shall be designated by a drawing of lots amongst the members of the other group.

6. (a) The panel of five judges of the Grand Chamber called upon to consider requests submitted under Article 43 of the Convention shall be composed of
— the President of the Court;
— the Presidents or, if they are prevented from sitting, the Vice-Presidents of the Sections other than the Section from which was constituted the Chamber that dealt with the case whose referral to the Grand Chamber is being sought;
— one further judge designated in rotation from among the judges other than those who dealt with the case in the Chamber.
(b) No judge elected in respect of, or who is a national of, a Contracting Party concerned may be a member of the panel.
(c) Any member of the panel unable to sit shall be replaced by another judge who did not deal with the case in the Chamber, who shall be designated in rotation.

Rule 25

Setting up of Sections

1. The Chambers provided for in Article 26(b) of the Convention (referred to in these Rules as 'Sections') shall be set up by the plenary Court, on a proposal by its President, for a period of three years with effect from the election of the presidential office-holders of the Court under Rule 8. There shall be at least four Sections.

2. Each judge shall be a member of a Section. The composition of the Sections shall be geographically and gender balanced and shall reflect the different legal systems among the Contracting Parties.

3. Where a judge ceases to be a member of the Court before the expiry of the period for which the Section has been constituted, the judge's place in the Section shall be taken by his or her successor as a member of the Court.

4. The President of the Court may exceptionally make modifications to the composition of the Sections if circumstances so require.

5. On a proposal by the President, the plenary Court may constitute an additional Section.

Rule 26

Constitution of Chambers

1. The Chambers of seven judges provided for in Article 27 §1 of the Convention for the consideration of cases brought before the Court shall be constituted from the Sections as follows.

(a) The Chamber shall in each case include the President of the Section and the judge elected in respect of any Contracting Party concerned. If the latter judge is not a member of the Section to which the application has been assigned under Rule 51 or 52, he or she shall sit as an *ex officio* member of the Chamber in accordance with Article 27 §2 of the Convention. Rule 29 shall apply if that judge is unable to sit or withdraws.

(b) The other members of the Chamber shall be designated by the President of the Section in rotation from among the members of the relevant Section.

(c) The members of the Section who are not so designated shall sit in the case as substitute judges.

2. Even after the end of their terms of office judges shall continue to deal with cases in which they have participated in the consideration of the merits.

Rule 27

Committees

1. Committees composed of three judges belonging to the same Section shall be set up under Article 27 §1 of the Convention. After consulting the Presidents of the Sections, the President of the Court shall decide on the number of Committees to be set up.

2. The Committees shall be constituted for a period of twelve months by rotation among the members of each Section, excepting the President of the Section.

3. The judges of the Section who are not members of a Committee may be called upon to take the place of members who are unable to sit.

4. Each Committee shall be chaired by the member having precedence in the Section.

Rule 28

Inability to sit, withdrawal or exemption

1. Any judge who is prevented from taking part in sittings for which he has been convoked shall, as soon as possible, give notice to the President of the Chamber.

2. A judge may not take part in the consideration of any case in which he or she has a personal interest or has previously acted either as the Agent, advocate or adviser of a party or of a person having an interest in the case, or as a member of a tribunal or commission of inquiry, or in any other capacity.

3. If a judge withdraws for one of the said reasons, or for some special reason, he or she shall inform the President of the Chamber, who shall exempt the judge from sitting.

4. If the President of the Chamber considers that a reason exists for a judge to withdraw, he or she shall consult with the judge concerned; in the event of disagreement, the Chamber shall decide.

Rule 29

Ad hoc judges

1. If the judge elected in respect of a Contracting Party concerned is unable to sit in the Chamber or withdraws, the President of the Chamber shall invite that Party to indicate within thirty days whether it wishes to appoint to sit as judge either another elected judge or, as an *ad hoc* judge, any other person possessing the qualifications required by Article 21 §1 of the Convention and, if so, to state at the same time the name of the person appointed. The same rule shall apply if the person so appointed is unable to sit or withdraws.

2. The Contracting Party concerned shall be presumed to have waived its right of appointment if it does not reply within thirty days.

3. An *ad hoc* judge shall, at the opening of the first sitting fixed for the consideration of the case after the judge has been appointed, take the oath or make the solemn declaration provided for in Rule 3. This act shall be recorded in minutes.

Rule 30

Common interest

1. If several applicant or respondent Contracting Parties have a common interest, the President of the Court may invite them to agree to appoint a single elected judge or *ad hoc* judge in accordance with Article 27 §2 of the Convention. If the Parties are unable to agree, the President shall choose by lot, from among the persons proposed as judges by these Parties, the judge called upon to sit *ex officio*.

2. In the event of a dispute as to the existence of a common interest, the plenary Court shall decide.

Title II
Procedure

Chapter I
General Rules

Rule 31

Possibility of particular derogations

The provisions of this Title shall not prevent the Court from derogating from them for the consideration of a particular case after having consulted the parties where appropriate.

Rule 32

Practice directions

The President of the Court may issue practice directions, notably in relation to such matters as appearance at hearings and the filing of pleadings and other documents.

Rule 33

Public character of proceedings

1. Hearings shall be public unless, in accordance with paragraph 2 of this Rule, the Chamber in exceptional circumstances decides otherwise, either of its own motion or at the request of a party or any other person concerned.

2. The press and the public may be excluded from all or part of a hearing in the interest of morals, public order or national security in a democratic society, where the interests of juveniles or the protection of the private life of the parties so require, or to the extent strictly necessary in the opinion of the Chamber in special circumstances where publicity would prejudice the interests of justice.

3. Following registration of an application, all documents deposited with the Registry, with the exception of those deposited within the framework of friendly-settlement negotiations as provided for in Rule 62, shall be accessible to the public unless the President of the Chamber, for the reasons set out in paragraph 2 of this Rule, decides otherwise, either of his or her own motion or at the request of a party or any other person concerned.

4. Any request for confidentiality made under paragraphs 1 or 3 of this Rule must give reasons and specify whether the hearing or the documents, as the case may be, should be inaccessible to the public in whole or in part.

Rule 34

Use of languages

1. The official languages of the Court shall be English and French.

2. Before the decision on the admissibility of an application is taken, all communications with and

pleadings by applicants under Article 34 of the Convention or their representatives, if not in one of the Court's official languages, shall be in one of the official languages of the Contracting Parties.

3. (a) All communications with and pleadings by such applicants or their representatives in respect of a hearing, or after a case has been declared admissible, shall be in one of the Court's official languages, unless the President of the Chamber authorises the continued use of the official language of a Contracting Party.
   (b) If such leave is granted, the Registrar shall make the necessary arrangements for the oral or written translation of the applicant's observations or statements.

4. (a) All communications with and pleadings by Contracting Parties or third parties shall be in one of the Court's official languages. The President of the Chamber may authorise the use of a non-official language.
   (b) If such leave is granted, it shall be the responsibility of the requesting party to provide for and bear the costs of interpreting or translation into English or French of the oral arguments or written statements made.

5. The President of the Chamber may invite the respondent Contracting Party to provide a translation of its written submissions in the or an official language of that Party in order to facilitate the applicant's understanding of those submissions.

6. Any witness, expert or other person appearing before the Court may use his or her own language if he or she does not have sufficient knowledge of either of the two official languages. In that event the Registrar shall make the necessary arrangements for interpreting or translation.

Rule 35

Representation of Contracting Parties

The Contracting Parties shall be represented by Agents, who may have the assistance of advocates or advisers.

Rule 36

Representation of applicants

1. Persons, non-governmental organisations or groups of individuals may initially present applications under Article 34 of the Convention themselves or through a representative appointed under paragraph 4 of this Rule.

2. Following notification of the application to the respondent Contracting Party under Rule 54 §3(b), the President of the Chamber may direct that the applicant should be represented in accordance with paragraph 4 of this Rule.

3. The applicant must be so represented at any hearing decided on by the Chamber or for the purposes of the proceedings following a decision declaring the application admissible, unless the President of the Chamber decides otherwise.

4. (a) The representative of the applicant shall be an advocate authorised to practise in any of the Contracting Parties and resident in the territory of one of them, or any other person approved by the President of the Chamber.
   (b) The President of the Chamber may, where representation would otherwise be obligatory, grant leave to the applicant to present his or her own case, subject, if necessary, to being assisted by an advocate or other approved representative.
   (c) In exceptional circumstances and at any stage of the procedure, the President of the Chamber may, where he or she considers that the circumstances or the conduct of the advocate or other person appointed under the preceding sub-paragraphs so warrant, direct that the latter may no longer represent or assist the applicant and that the applicant should seek alternative representation.

5. The advocate or other approved representative, or the applicant in person if he or she seeks leave to present his or her own case, must have an adequate knowledge of one of the Court's official languages. However, leave to use a non-official language may be given by the President of the Chamber under Rule 34 §3.

Rule 37

Communications, notifications and summonses

1. Communications or notifications addressed to the Agents or advocates of the parties shall be deemed to have been addressed to the parties.

2. If, for any communication, notification or summons addressed to persons other than the Agents or advocates of the parties, the Court considers it necessary to have the assistance of the Government of the State on whose territory such communication, notification or summons is to have effect, the President of the Court shall apply directly to that Government in order to obtain the necessary facilities.

3. The same rule shall apply when the Court desires to make or arrange for the making of an investigation on the spot in order to establish the facts or to procure evidence or when it orders the appearance of a person who is resident in, or will have to cross, that territory.

Rule 38

Written pleadings

1. No written observations or other documents may be filed after the time-limit set by the President of the Chamber or the Judge Rapporteur, as the case may be, in accordance with these Rules. No written observations or other documents filed outside that time-limit or contrary to any practice direction issued under Rule 32 shall be included in the case file unless the President of the Chamber decides otherwise.

2. For the purposes of observing the time-limit referred to in paragraph 1 of this Rule, the material date is the certified date of dispatch of the document or, if there is none, the actual date of receipt at the Registry.

Rule 39

Interim measures

1. The Chamber or, where appropriate, its President may, at the request of a party or of any other person concerned, or of its own motion, indicate to the parties any interim measure which it considers should be adopted in the interests of the parties or of the proper conduct of the proceedings before it.

2. Notice of these measures shall be given to the Committee of Ministers.

3. The Chamber may request information from the parties on any matter connected with the implementation of any interim measure it has indicated.

Rule 40

Urgent notification of an application

In any case of urgency the Registrar, with the authorisation of the President of the Chamber, may, without prejudice to the taking of any other procedural steps and by any available means, inform a Contracting Party concerned in an application of the introduction of the application and of a summary of its objects.

Rule 41

Case priority

The Chamber shall deal with applications in the order in which they become ready for examination. It may, however, decide to give priority to a particular application.

Rule 42

Measures for taking evidence

1. The Chamber may, at the request of a party or a third party, or of its own motion, obtain any evidence which it considers capable of providing clarification of the facts of the case. The Chamber may, *inter alia*, request the parties to produce documentary evidence and decide to hear as a witness or expert or in any other capacity any person whose evidence or statements seem likely to assist it in the carrying out of its tasks.

2. The Chamber may, at any time during the proceedings, depute one or more of its members or of the other judges of the Court to conduct an inquiry, carry out an investigation on the spot or take evidence in some other manner. It may appoint independent external experts to assist such a delegation.

3. The Chamber may ask any person or institution of its choice to obtain information, express an opinion or make a report on any specific point.

4. The parties shall assist the Chamber, or its delegation, in implementing any measures for taking evidence.

5. Where a report has been drawn up or some other measure taken in accordance with the preceding paragraphs at the request of an applicant or respondent Contracting Party, the costs entailed shall be borne by that Party unless the Chamber decides otherwise. In other cases the Chamber shall decide whether such costs are to be borne by the Council of Europe or awarded against the applicant or third party at whose request the report was drawn up or the other measure was taken. In all cases the costs shall be taxed by the President of the Chamber.

Rule 43

Joinder and simultaneous examination of applications

1. The Chamber may, either at the request of the parties or of its own motion, order the joinder of two or more applications.

2. The President of the Chamber may, after consulting the parties, order that the proceedings in applications assigned to the same Chamber be conducted simultaneously, without prejudice to the decision of the Chamber on the joinder of the applications.

Rule 44

Striking out and restoration to the list

1. When an applicant Contracting Party notifies the Registrar of its intention not to proceed with the case, the Chamber may strike the application out of the Court's list under Article 37 of the Convention if the other Contracting Party or Parties concerned in the case agree to such discontinuance.

2. The decision to strike out an application which has been declared admissible shall be given in the form of a judgment. The President of the Chamber shall forward that judgment, once it has become final, to the Committee of Ministers in order to allow the latter to supervise, in accordance with Article 46 §2 of the Convention, the execution of any undertakings which may have been attached to the discontinuance, friendly settlement or solution of the matter.

3. When an application has been struck out, the costs shall be at the discretion of the Court. If an award of costs is made in a decision striking out an application which has not been declared admissible, the President of the Chamber shall forward the decision to the Committee of Ministers.

4. The Court may restore an application to its list if it considers that exceptional circumstances justify such a course.

Chapter II
Institution of Proceedings

Rule 45

Signatures

1. Any application made under Articles 33 or 34 of the Convention shall be submitted in writing and shall be signed by the applicant or by the applicant's representative.

2. Where an application is made by a non-governmental organisation or by a group of individuals, it shall be signed by those persons competent to represent that organisation or group. The Chamber or Committee concerned shall determine any question as to whether the persons who have signed an application are competent to do so.

3. Where applicants are represented in accordance with Rule 36, a power of attorney or written authority to act shall be supplied by their representative or representatives.

Rule 46

Contents of an inter-State application

Any Contracting Party or Parties intending to bring a case before the Court under Article 33 of the Convention shall file with the Registry an application setting out

(a) the name of the Contracting Party against which the application is made;
(b) a statement of the facts;
(c) a statement of the alleged violation(s) of the Convention and the relevant arguments;
(d) a statement on compliance with the admissibility criteria (exhaustion of domestic remedies and the six-month rule) laid down in Article 35 §1 of the Convention;
(e) the object of the application and a general indication of any claims for just satisfaction made under Article 41 of the Convention on behalf of the alleged injured party or parties; and
(f) the name and address of the person(s) appointed as Agent; and accompanied by
(g) copies of any relevant documents and in particular the decisions, whether judicial or not, relating to the object of the application.

Rule 47

Contents of an individual application

1. Any application under Article 34 of the Convention shall be made on the application form provided by the Registry, unless the President of the Section concerned decides otherwise. It shall set out

(a) the name, date of birth, nationality, sex, occupation and address of the applicant;
(b) the name, occupation and address of the representative, if any;
(c) the name of the Contracting Party or Parties against which the application is made;
(d) a succinct statement of the facts;
(e) a succinct statement of the alleged violation(s) of the Convention and the relevant arguments;
(f) a succinct statement on the applicant's compliance with the admissibility criteria (exhaustion of domestic remedies and the six-month rule) laid down in Article 35 §1 of the Convention; and
(g) the object of the application as well as a general indication of any claims for just satisfaction which the applicant may wish to make under Article 41 of the Convention;

and be accompanied by

(h) copies of any relevant documents and in particular the decisions, whether judicial or not, relating to the object of the application.

2. Applicants shall furthermore

(a) provide information, notably the documents and decisions referred to in paragraph 1(h) of this Rule, enabling it to be shown that the admissibility criteria (exhaustion of domestic remedies and the six-month rule) laid down in Article 35 §1 of the Convention have been satisfied; and
(b) indicate whether they have submitted their complaints to any other procedure of international investigation or settlement.

3. Applicants who do not wish their identity to be disclosed to the public shall so indicate and shall submit a statement of the reasons justifying such a departure from the normal rule of public access to information in proceedings before the Court. The President of the Chamber may authorise anonymity in exceptional and duly justified cases.

4. Failure to comply with the requirements set out in paragraphs 1 and 2 of this Rule may result in the application not being registered and examined by the Court.

5. The date of introduction of the application shall as a general rule be considered to be the date of the first communication from the applicant setting out, even summarily, the object of the application. The Court may for good cause nevertheless decide that a different date shall be considered to be the date of introduction.

6. Applicants shall keep the Court informed of any change of address and of all circumstances relevant to the application.

Chapter III
Judge Rapporteurs

Rule 48

Inter-State applications

1. Where an application is made under Article 33 of the Convention, the Chamber constituted to consider the case shall designate one or more of its judges as Judge Rapporteur(s), who shall submit a report on admissibility when the written observations of the Contracting Parties concerned have been received. Rule 49 §4 shall, in so far as appropriate, be applicable to this report.

2. After an application made under Article 33 of the Convention has been declared admissible, the Judge Rapporteur(s) shall submit such reports, drafts and other documents as may assist the Chamber in the carrying out of its functions.

Rule 49

Individual applications

1. Where an application is made under Article 34 of the Convention, the President of the Section to which the case has been assigned shall designate a judge as Judge Rapporteur, who shall examine the application.

2. In their examination of applications Judge Rapporteurs
   (a) may request the parties to submit, within a specified time, any factual information, documents or other material which they consider to be relevant;
   (b) shall, subject to the President of the Section directing that the case be considered by a Chamber, decide whether the application is to be considered by a Committee or by a Chamber.

3. Where a case is considered by a Committee in accordance with Article 28 of the Convention, the report of the Judge Rapporteur shall contain
   (a) a brief statement of the relevant facts;
   (b) a brief statement of the reasons underlying the proposal to declare the application inadmissible or to strike it out of the list.

4. Where a case is considered by a Chamber pursuant to Article 29 §1 of the Convention, the report of the Judge Rapporteur shall contain
   (a) a statement of the relevant facts, including any information obtained under paragraph 2 of this Rule;
   (b) an indication of the issues arising under the Convention in the application;
   (c) a proposal on admissibility and on any other action to be taken, together, if need be, with a provisional opinion on the merits.

5. After an application made under Article 34 of the Convention has been declared admissible, the Judge Rapporteur shall submit such reports, drafts and other documents as may assist the Chamber in the carrying out of its functions.

Rule 50

Grand Chamber proceedings

Where a case has been submitted to the Grand Chamber either under Article 30 or under Article 43 of the Convention, the President of the Grand Chamber shall designate as Judge Rapporteur(s) one or, in the case of an inter-State application, one or more of its members.

Chapter IV
Proceedings on Admissibility

Inter-State applications

Rule 51

1. When an application is made under Article 33 of the Convention, the President of the Court shall immediately give notice of the application to the respondent Contracting Party and shall assign the application to one of the Sections.

2. In accordance with Rule 26 §1(a), the judges elected in respect of the applicant and respondent Contracting Parties shall sit as *ex officio* members of the Chamber constituted to consider the case. Rule 30 shall apply if the application has been brought by several Contracting Parties or if applications with the same object brought by several Contracting Parties are being examined jointly under Rule 43 §2.

3. On assignment of the case to a Section, the President of the Section shall constitute the Chamber in accordance with Rule 26 §1 and shall invite the respondent Contracting Party to submit its observations in writing on the admissibility of the application. The observations so obtained shall be communicated by the Registrar to the applicant Contracting Party, which may submit written observations in reply.

4. Before ruling on the admissibility of the application, the Chamber may decide to invite the Parties to submit further observations in writing.

5. A hearing on the admissibility shall be held if one or more of the Contracting Parties concerned so requests or if the Chamber so decides of its own motion.

6. After consulting the Parties, the President of the Chamber shall fix the written and, where appropriate, oral procedure and for that purpose shall lay down the time-limit within which any written observations are to be filed.

7. In its deliberations the Chamber shall take into consideration the report submitted by the Judge Rapporteur(s) under Rule 48 §1.

Individual applications

Rule 52

Assignment of applications to the Sections

1. Any application made under Article 34 of the Convention shall be assigned to a Section by the President of the Court, who in so doing shall endeavour to ensure a fair distribution of cases between the Sections.

2. The Chamber of seven judges provided for in Article 27 §1 of the Convention shall be constituted by the President of the Section concerned in accordance with Rule 26 §1 once it has been decided that the application is to be considered by a Chamber.

3. Pending the constitution of a Chamber in accordance with paragraph 2 of this Rule, the President of the Section shall exercise any powers conferred on the President of the Chamber by these Rules.

Rule 53

Procedure before a Committee

1. In its deliberations the Committee shall take into consideration the report submitted by the Judge Rapporteur under Rule 49 §3.

2. The Judge Rapporteur, if he or she is not a member of the Committee, may be invited to attend the deliberations of the Committee.

3. In accordance with Article 28 of the Convention, the Committee may, by a unanimous vote, declare inadmissible or strike out of the Court's list of cases an application where such a decision can be taken without further examination. This decision shall be final.

4. If no decision pursuant to paragraph 3 of this Rule is taken, the application shall be forwarded to the Chamber constituted under Rule 52 §2 to examine the case.

Rule 54

Procedure before a Chamber

1. In its deliberations the Chamber shall take into consideration the report submitted by the Judge Rapporteur under Rule 49 §4.

2. The Chamber may at once declare the application inadmissible or strike it out of the Court's list of cases.

3. Alternatively, the Chamber may decide to
   (a) request the parties to submit any factual information, documents or other material which it considers to be relevant;
   (b) give notice of the application to the respondent Contracting Party and invite that Party to submit written observations on the application;
   (c) invite the parties to submit further observations in writing.

4. Before taking its decision on admissibility, the Chamber may decide, either at the request of the parties or of its own motion, to hold a hearing. In that event, unless the Chamber shall exceptionally decide otherwise, the parties shall be invited also to address the issues arising in relation to the merits of the application.

5. The President of the Chamber shall fix the procedure, including time-limits, in relation to any decisions taken by the Chamber under paragraphs 3 and 4 of this Rule.

Inter-State and individual applications

Rule 55

Pleas of inadmissibility

Any plea of inadmissibility must, in so far as its character and the circumstances permit, be raised by the respondent Contracting Party in its written or oral observations on the admissibility of the application submitted as provided in Rule 51 or 54, as the case may be.

Rule 56

Decision of a Chamber

1. The decision of the Chamber shall state whether it was taken unanimously or by a majority and shall be accompanied or followed by reasons.

2. The decision of the Chamber shall be communicated by the Registrar to the applicant and to the Contracting Party or Parties concerned.

Rule 57

Language of the decision

1. Unless the Court decides that a decision shall be given in both official languages, all decisions shall be given either in English or in French. Decisions given shall be accessible to the public.

2. Publication of such decisions in the official reports of the Court, as provided for in Rule 78, shall be in both official languages of the Court.

Chapter V
Proceedings after the Admission of an Application

Rule 58

Inter-State applications

1. Once the Chamber has decided to admit an application made under Article 33 of the Convention, the President of the Chamber shall, after consulting the Contracting Parties concerned, lay down the time-limits for the filing of written observations on the merits and for the production of any further evidence. The President may however, with the agreement of the Contracting Parties concerned, direct that a written procedure is to be dispensed with.

2. A hearing on the merits shall be held if one or more of the Contracting Parties concerned so requests or if the Chamber so decides of its own motion. The President of the Chamber shall fix the oral procedure.

3. In its deliberations the Chamber shall take into consideration any reports, drafts and other documents submitted by the Judge Rapporteur(s) under Rule 48 §2.

Rule 59

Individual applications

1. Once the Chamber has decided to admit an application made under Article 34 of the Convention, it may invite the parties to submit further evidence and written observations.

2. A hearing on the merits shall be held if the Chamber so decides of its own motion or, provided that no hearing also addressing the merits has been held at the admissibility stage under Rule 54 §4, if one of the parties so requests. However, the Chamber may exceptionally decide that the discharging of its functions under Article 38 §1(a) of the Convention does not require a hearing to be held.

3. The President of the Chamber shall, where appropriate, fix the written and oral procedure.

4. In its deliberations the Chamber shall take into consideration any reports, drafts and other documents submitted by the Judge Rapporteur under Rule 49 §5.

Rule 60

Claims for just satisfaction

1. Any claim which the applicant Contracting Party or the applicant may wish to make for just satisfaction under Article 41 of the Convention shall, unless the President of the Chamber directs otherwise, be set out in the written observations on the merits or, if no such written observations are filed, in a special document filed no later than two months after the decision declaring the application admissible.

2. Itemised particulars of all claims made, together with the relevant supporting documents or vouchers, shall be submitted, failing which the Chamber may reject the claim in whole or in part.

3. The Chamber may, at any time during the proceedings, invite any party to submit comments on the claim for just satisfaction.

Rule 61

Third-party intervention

1. The decision declaring an application admissible shall be notified by the Registrar to any Contracting Party one of whose nationals is an applicant in the case, as well as to the respondent Contracting Party or Parties under Rule 56 §2.

2. Where a Contracting Party seeks to exercise its right to submit written comments or to take part in a hearing, pursuant to Article 36 §1 of the Convention, the President of the Chamber shall fix the procedure to be followed.

3. In accordance with Article 36 §2 of the Convention, the President of the Chamber may, in the interests of the proper administration of justice, invite or grant leave to any Contracting State which is not a

party to the proceedings, or any person concerned who is not the applicant, to submit written comments or, in exceptional cases, to take part in a hearing. Requests for leave for this purpose must be duly reasoned and submitted in one of the official languages, within a reasonable time after the fixing of the written procedure.

4. Any invitation or grant of leave referred to in paragraph 3 of this Rule shall be subject to any conditions, including time-limits, set by the President of the Chamber. Where such conditions are not complied with, the President may decide not to include the comments in the case file.

5. Written comments submitted in accordance with this Rule shall be submitted in one of the official languages, save where leave to use another language has been granted under Rule 34 §4. They shall be transmitted by the Registrar to the parties to the case, who shall be entitled, subject to any conditions, including time-limits, set by the President of the Chamber, to file written observations in reply.

Rule 62

Friendly settlement

1. Once an application has been declared admissible, the Registrar, acting on the instructions of the Chamber or its President, shall enter into contact with the parties with a view to securing a friendly settlement of the matter in accordance with Article 38 §1(b) of the Convention. The Chamber shall take any steps that appear appropriate to facilitate such a settlement.

2. In accordance with Article 38 §2 of the Convention, the friendly-settlement negotiations shall be confidential and without prejudice to the parties' arguments in the contentious proceedings. No written or oral communication and no offer or concession made in the framework of the attempt to secure a friendly settlement may be referred to or relied on in the contentious proceedings.

3. If the Chamber is informed by the Registrar that the parties have agreed to a friendly settlement, it shall, after verifying that the settlement has been reached on the basis of respect for human rights as defined in the Convention and the Protocols thereto, strike the case out of the Court's list in accordance with Rule 44 §2.

Chapter VI
Hearings

Rule 63

Conduct of hearings

1. The President of the Chamber shall direct hearings and shall prescribe the order in which Agents and advocates or advisers of the parties shall be called upon to speak.

2. Where a fact-finding hearing is being carried out by a delegation of the Chamber under Rule 42, the head of the delegation shall conduct the hearing and the delegation shall exercise any relevant power conferred on the Chamber by the Convention or these Rules.

Rule 64

Failure to appear at a hearing

Where, without showing sufficient cause, a party fails to appear, the Chamber may, provided that it is satisfied that such a course is consistent with the proper administration of justice, nonetheless proceed with the hearing.

Rule 65

Convocation of witnesses, experts and other persons; costs of their appearance

1. Witnesses, experts and other persons whom the Chamber or the President of the Chamber decides to hear shall be summoned by the Registrar.

2. The summons shall indicate
   (a) the case in connection with which it has been issued;
   (b) the object of the inquiry, expert opinion or other measure ordered by the Chamber or the President of the Chamber;
   (c) any provisions for the payment of the sum due to the person summoned.

3. If the persons concerned appear at the request or on behalf of an applicant or respondent Contracting Party, the costs of their appearance shall be borne by that Party unless the Chamber decides otherwise. In other cases, the Chamber shall decide whether such costs are to be borne by the Council of Europe or awarded against the applicant or third party at whose request the person summoned appeared. In all cases the costs shall be taxed by the President of the Chamber.

Rule 66

Oath or solemn declaration by witnesses and experts

1. After the establishment of the identity of the witness and before testifying, every witness shall take the following oath or make the following solemn declaration:

> 'I swear'—or 'I solemnly declare upon my honour and conscience'—'that I shall speak the truth, the whole truth and nothing but the truth.'

This act shall be recorded in minutes.

2. After the establishment of the identity of the expert and before carrying out his or her task, every expert shall take the following oath or make the following solemn declaration:

> 'I swear'—or 'I solemnly declare'—'that I will discharge my duty as an expert honourably and conscientiously.'

This act shall be recorded in minutes.

3. This oath may be taken or this declaration made before the President of the Chamber, or before a judge or any public authority nominated by the President.

Rule 67

Objection to a witness or expert; hearing of a person for information purposes

The Chamber shall decide in the event of any dispute arising from an objection to a witness or expert. It may hear for information purposes a person who cannot be heard as a witness.

Rule 68

Questions put during hearings

1. Any judge may put questions to the Agents, advocates or advisers of the parties, to the applicant, witnesses and experts, and to any other persons appearing before the Chamber.

2. The witnesses, experts and other persons referred to in Rule 42 §1 may, subject to the control of the President of the Chamber, be examined by the Agents and advocates or advisers of the parties. In the event of an objection as to the relevance of a question put, the President of the Chamber shall decide.

Rule 69

Failure to appear, refusal to give evidence or false evidence

If, without good reason, a witness or any other person who has been duly summoned fails to appear or refuses to give evidence, the Registrar shall, on being so required by the President of the Chamber, inform the Contracting Party to whose jurisdiction the witness or other person is subject. The same provisions shall apply if a witness or expert has, in the opinion of the Chamber, violated the oath or solemn declaration provided for in Rule 66.

Rule 70

Verbatim record of hearings

1. The Registrar shall, if the Chamber so directs, be responsible for the making of a verbatim record of a hearing. The verbatim record shall include

(a) the composition of the Chamber at the hearing;

(b) a list of those appearing before the Court, that is to say Agents, advocates and advisers of the parties and any third party taking part;

(c) the surname, forenames, description and address of each witness, expert or other person heard;

(d) the text of statements made, questions put and replies given;

(e) the text of any decision delivered during the hearing by the Chamber or the President of the Chamber.

2. If all or part of the verbatim record is in a non-official language, the Registrar shall, if the Chamber so directs, arrange for its translation into one of the official languages.

3. The representatives of the parties shall receive a copy of the verbatim record in order that they may, subject to the control of the Registrar or the President of the Chamber, make corrections, but in no case may such corrections affect the sense and bearing of what was said. The Registrar shall lay down, in accordance with the instructions of the President of the Chamber, the time-limits granted for this purpose.

4. The verbatim record, once so corrected, shall be signed by the President and the Registrar and shall then constitute certified matters of record.

Chapter VII
Proceedings before the Grand Chamber

Rule 71

Applicability of procedural provisions

Any provisions governing proceedings before the Chambers shall apply, *mutatis mutandis*, to proceedings before the Grand Chamber.

Rule 72

Relinquishment of jurisdiction by a Chamber in favour of the Grand Chamber

1. In accordance with Article 30 of the Convention, where a case pending before a Chamber raises a serious question affecting the interpretation of the Convention or the Protocols thereto or where the resolution of a question before it might have a result inconsistent with a judgment previously delivered by the Court, the Chamber may, at any time before it has rendered its judgment, relinquish jurisdiction in favour of the Grand Chamber, unless one of the parties to the case has objected in accordance with paragraph 2 of this Rule. Reasons need not be given for the decision to relinquish.

2. The Registrar shall notify the parties of the Chamber's intention to relinquish jurisdiction. The parties shall have one month from the date of that notification within which to file at the Registry a duly reasoned objection. An objection which does not fulfil these conditions shall be considered invalid by the Chamber.

Rule 73

Request by a party for referral of a case to the Grand Chamber

1. In accordance with Article 43 of the Convention, any party to a case may exceptionally, within a period of three months from the date of delivery of the judgment of a Chamber, file in writing at the Registry a request that the case be referred to the Grand Chamber. The party shall specify in its request the serious question affecting the interpretation or application of the Convention or the Protocols thereto, or the serious issue of general importance, which in its view warrants consideration by the Grand Chamber.

2. A panel of five judges of the Grand Chamber constituted in accordance with Rule 24 §6 shall examine the request solely on the basis of the existing case file. It shall accept the request only if it considers that the case does raise such a question or issue. Reasons need not be given for a refusal of the request.

3. If the panel accepts the request, the Grand Chamber shall decide the case by means of a judgment.

Chapter VIII
Judgments

Rule 74

Contents of the judgment

1. A judgment as referred to in Articles 42 and 44 of the Convention shall contain
   (a) the names of the President and the other judges constituting the Chamber concerned, and the name of the Registrar or the Deputy Registrar;
   (b) the dates on which it was adopted and delivered;
   (c) a description of the parties;
   (d) the names of the Agents, advocates or advisers of the parties;
   (e) an account of the procedure followed;
   (f) the facts of the case;
   (g) a summary of the submissions of the parties;
   (h) the reasons in point of law;
   (i) the operative provisions;
   (j) the decision, if any, in respect of costs;
   (k) the number of judges constituting the majority;
   (l) where appropriate, a statement as to which text is authentic.

2. Any judge who has taken part in the consideration of the case shall be entitled to annex to the judgment either a separate opinion, concurring with or dissenting from that judgment, or a bare statement of dissent.

Rule 75

Ruling on just satisfaction

1. Where the Chamber finds that there has been a violation of the Convention or the Protocols thereto, it shall give in the same judgment a ruling on the application of Article 41 of the Convention if that question, after being raised in accordance with Rule 60, is ready for decision; if the question is not ready for decision, the Chamber shall reserve it in whole or in part and shall fix the further procedure.

2. For the purposes of ruling on the application of Article 41 of the Convention, the Chamber shall, as far as possible, be composed of those judges who sat to consider the merits of the case. Where it is not possible to constitute the original Chamber, the President of the Court shall complete or compose the Chamber by drawing lots.

3. The Chamber may, when affording just satisfaction under Article 41 of the Convention, direct that if settlement is not made within a specified time, interest is to be payable on any sums awarded.

4. If the Court is informed that an agreement has been reached between the injured party and the Contracting Party liable, it shall verify the equitable nature of the agreement and, where it finds the agreement to be equitable, strike the case out of the list in accordance with Rule 44 §2.

Rule 76

Language of the judgment

1. Unless the Court decides that a judgment shall be given in both official languages, all judgments shall be given either in English or in French. Judgments given shall be accessible to the public.

2. Publication of such judgments in the official reports of the Court, as provided for in Rule 78, shall be in both official languages of the Court.

Rule 77

Signature, delivery and notification of the judgment

1. Judgments shall be signed by the President of the Chamber and the Registrar.

2. The judgment may be read out at a public hearing by the President of the Chamber or by another judge delegated by him or her. The Agents and representatives of the parties shall be informed in due time of the date of the hearing. Otherwise the notification provided for in paragraph 3 of this Rule shall constitute delivery of the judgment.

3. The judgment shall be transmitted to the Committee of Ministers. The Registrar shall send certified copies to the parties, to the Secretary General of the Council of Europe, to any third party and to any other person directly concerned. The original copy, duly signed and sealed, shall be placed in the archives of the Court.

Rule 78

Publication of judgments and other documents

In accordance with Article 44 §3 of the Convention, final judgments of the Court shall be published, under the responsibility of the Registrar, in an appropriate form. The Registrar shall in addition be responsible for the publication of official reports of selected judgments and decisions and of any document which the President of the Court considers it useful to publish.

Rule 79

Request for interpretation of a judgment

1. A party may request the interpretation of a judgment within a period of one year following the delivery of that judgment.

2. The request shall be filed with the Registry. It shall state precisely the point or points in the operative provisions of the judgment on which interpretation is required.

3. The original Chamber may decide of its own motion to refuse the request on the ground that there is no reason to warrant considering it. Where it is not possible to constitute the original Chamber, the President of the Court shall complete or compose the Chamber by drawing lots.

4. If the Chamber does not refuse the request, the Registrar shall communicate it to the other party or parties and shall invite them to submit any written comments within a time-limit laid down by the President of the Chamber. The President of the Chamber shall also fix the date of the hearing should the Chamber decide to hold one. The Chamber shall decide by means of a judgment.

Rule 80

Request for revision of a judgment

1. A party may, in the event of the discovery of a fact which might by its nature have a decisive influence and which, when a judgment was delivered, was unknown to the Court and could not reasonably have been known to that party, request the Court, within a period of six months after that party acquired knowledge of the fact, to revise that judgment.

2. The request shall mention the judgment of which revision is requested and shall contain the information necessary to show that the conditions laid down in paragraph 1 of this Rule have been complied with. It shall be accompanied by a copy of all supporting documents. The request and supporting documents shall be filed with the Registry.

3. The original Chamber may decide of its own motion to refuse the request on the ground that there is no

reason to warrant considering it. Where it is not possible to constitute the original Chamber, the President of the Court shall complete or compose the Chamber by drawing lots.

4. If the Chamber does not refuse the request, the Registrar shall communicate it to the other party or parties and shall invite them to submit any written comments within a time-limit laid down by the President of the Chamber. The President of the Chamber shall also fix the date of the hearing should the Chamber decide to hold one. The Chamber shall decide by means of a judgment.

Rule 81

Rectification of errors in decisions and judgments

Without prejudice to the provisions on revision of judgments and on restoration to the list of applications, the Court may, of its own motion or at the request of a party made within one month of the delivery of a decision or a judgment, rectify clerical errors, errors in calculation or obvious mistakes.

Chapter IX
Advisory Opinions

Rule 82

In proceedings relating to advisory opinions the Court shall apply, in addition to the provisions of Articles 47, 48 and 49 of the Convention, the provisions which follow. It shall also apply the other provisions of these Rules to the extent to which it considers this to be appropriate.

Rule 83

The request for an advisory opinion shall be filed with the Registry. It shall state fully and precisely the question on which the opinion of the Court is sought, and also

(a) the date on which the Committee of Ministers adopted the decision referred to in Article 47 §3 of the Convention;

(b) the names and addresses of the person or persons appointed by the Committee of Ministers to give the Court any explanations which it may require.

The request shall be accompanied by all documents likely to elucidate the question.

Rule 84

1. On receipt of a request, the Registrar shall transmit a copy of it to all members of the Court.

2. The Registrar shall inform the Contracting Parties that the Court is prepared to receive their written comments.

Rule 85

1. The President of the Court shall lay down the time-limits for filing written comments or other documents.

2. Written comments or other documents shall be filed with the Registry. The Registrar shall transmit copies of them to all the members of the Court, to the Committee of Ministers and to each of the Contracting Parties.

Rule 86

After the close of the written procedure, the President of the Court shall decide whether the Contracting Parties which have submitted written comments are to be given an opportunity to develop them at a hearing held for the purpose.

Rule 87

If the Court considers that the request for an advisory opinion is not within its consultative competence as defined in Article 47 of the Convention, it shall so declare in a reasoned decision.

Rule 88

1. Advisory opinions shall be given by a majority vote of the Grand Chamber. They shall mention the number of judges constituting the majority.

2. Any judge may, if he or she so desires, attach to the opinion of the Court either a separate opinion, concurring with or dissenting from the advisory opinion, or a bare statement of dissent.

Rule 89

The advisory opinion shall be read out in one of the two official languages by the President of the Court, or by another judge delegated by the President, at a public hearing, prior notice having been given to the Committee of Ministers and to each of the Contracting Parties.

Rule 90

The opinion, or any decision given under Rule 87, shall be signed by the President of the Court and by the Registrar. The original copy, duly signed and sealed, shall be placed in the archives of the Court. The Registrar shall send certified copies to the Committee of Ministers, to the Contracting Parties and to the Secretary General of the Council of Europe.

Chapter X
Legal Aid

Rule 91

1. The President of the Chamber may, either at the request of an applicant having lodged an application under Article 34 of the Convention or of his or her own motion, grant free legal aid to the applicant in connection with the presentation of the case from the moment when observations in writing on the admissibility of that application are received from the respondent Contracting Party in accordance with Rule 54 §3(b), or where the time-limit for their submission has expired.

2. Subject to Rule 96, where the applicant has been granted legal aid in connection with the presentation of his or her case before the Chamber, that grant shall continue in force for the purposes of his or her representation before the Grand Chamber.

Rule 92

Legal aid shall be granted only where the President of the Chamber is satisfied

(a) that it is necessary for the proper conduct of the case before the Chamber;

(b) that the applicant has insufficient means to meet all or part of the costs entailed.

Rule 93

1. In order to determine whether or not applicants have sufficient means to meet all or part of the costs entailed, they shall be required to complete a form of declaration stating their income, capital assets and any financial commitments in respect of dependants, or any other financial obligations. The declaration shall be certified by the appropriate domestic authority or authorities.

2. The Contracting Party concerned shall be requested to submit its comments in writing.

3. After receiving the information mentioned in paragraphs 1 and 2 of this Rule, the President of the Chamber shall decide whether or not to grant legal aid. The Registrar shall inform the parties accordingly.

Rule 94

1. Fees shall be payable to the advocates or other persons appointed in accordance with Rule 36 §4. Fees may, where appropriate, be paid to more than one such representative.

2. Legal aid may be granted to cover not only representatives' fees but also travelling and subsistence expenses and other necessary expenses incurred by the applicant or appointed representative.

Rule 95

On a decision to grant legal aid, the Registrar shall fix

(a) the rate of fees to be paid in accordance with the legal-aid scales in force;

(b) the level of expenses to be paid.

Rule 96

The President of the Chamber may, if satisfied that the conditions stated in Rule 92 are no longer fulfilled, revoke or vary a grant of legal aid at any time.

Title III
Transitional Rules

Rule 97

Judges' terms of office

The duration of the terms of office of the judges who were members of the Court at the date of the entry into force of Protocol No 11 to the Convention shall be calculated as from that date.

Rule 98

Presidency of the Sections

For a period of three years from the entry into force of Protocol No 11 to the Convention,

(a) the two Presidents of Sections who are not simultaneously Vice-Presidents of the Court and the Vice-Presidents of the Sections shall be elected for a term of office of eighteen months;

(b) the Vice-Presidents of the Sections may not be immediately re-elected.

Rule 99

Relations between the Court and the Commission

1. In cases brought before the Court under Article 5 §§4 and 5 of Protocol No 11 to the Convention the Court may invite the Commission to delegate one or more of its members to take part in the consideration of the case before the Court.

2. In cases referred to in paragraph 1 of this Rule the Court shall take into consideration the report of the Commission adopted pursuant to former Article 31 of the Convention.

3. Unless the President of the Chamber decides otherwise, the said report shall be made available to the public through the Registrar as soon as possible after the case has been brought before the Court.

4. The remainder of the case file of the Commission, including all pleadings, in cases brought before the Court under Article 5 §§2 to 5 of Protocol No 11 shall remain confidential unless the President of the Chamber decides otherwise.

5. In cases where the Commission has taken evidence but has been unable to adopt a report in accordance with former Article 31 of the Convention, the Court shall take into consideration the verbatim records, documentation and opinion of the Commission's delegations arising from such investigations.

Rule 100

Chamber and Grand Chamber proceedings

1. In cases referred to the Court under Article 5 §4 of Protocol No 11 to the Convention, a panel of the Grand Chamber constituted in accordance with Rule 24 §6 shall determine, solely on the basis of the existing case file, whether a Chamber or the Grand Chamber is to decide the case.

2. If the case is decided by a Chamber, the judgment of the Chamber shall, in accordance with Article 5 §4 of Protocol No 11, be final and Rule 73 shall be inapplicable.

3. Cases transmitted to the Court under Article 5 §5 of Protocol No 11 shall be forwarded by the President of the Court to the Grand Chamber.

4. For each case transmitted to the Grand Chamber under Article 5 §5 of Protocol No 11, the Grand Chamber shall be completed by judges designated by rotation within one of the groups mentioned in Rule 24 §3, the cases being allocated to the groups on an alternate basis.

Rule 101

Grant of legal aid

Subject to Rule 96, in cases brought before the Court under Article 5 §§2 to 5 of Protocol No 11 to the Convention, a grant of legal aid made to an applicant in the proceedings before the Commission or the former Court shall continue in force for the purposes of his or her representation before the Court.

Rule 102

Request for interpretation or revision of a judgment

1. Where a party requests interpretation or revision of a judgment delivered by the former Court, the President of the Court shall assign the request to one of the Sections in accordance with the conditions laid down in Rule 51 or 52, as the case may be.

2. The President of the relevant Section shall, notwithstanding Rules 79 §3 and 80 §3, constitute a new Chamber to consider the request.

3. The Chamber to be constituted shall include as *ex officio* members

(a) the President of the Section;

and, whether or not they are members of the relevant Section,

(b) the judge elected in respect of any Contracting Party concerned or, if he or she is unable to sit, any judge appointed under Rule 29;

(c) any judge of the Court who was a member of the original Chamber that delivered the judgment in the former Court.

4. (a) The other members of the Chamber shall be designated by the President of the Section by means of a drawing of lots from among the members of the relevant Section.

(b) The members of the Section who are not so designated shall sit in the case as substitute judges.

Title IV
Final Clauses

Rule 103

Amendment or suspension of a Rule

1. Any Rule may be amended upon a motion made after notice where such a motion is carried at the next session of the plenary Court by a majority of all the members of the Court. Notice of such a motion shall be delivered in writing to the Registrar at least one month before the session at which it is to be discussed. On receipt of such a notice of motion, the Registrar shall inform all members of the Court at the earliest possible moment.

2. A Rule relating to the internal working of the Court may be suspended upon a motion made without notice, provided that this decision is taken unanimously by the Chamber concerned. The suspension of a Rule shall in this case be limited in its operation to the particular purpose for which it was sought.

Rule 104

Entry into force of the Rules

The present Rules shall enter into force on 1 November 1998.

APPENDIX G

European Social Charter 1961

(*Revised Version: see note on p 125*)

The Governments signatory hereto, being members of the Council of Europe,

Considering that the aim of the Council of Europe is the achievement of greater unity between its members for the purpose of safeguarding and realising the ideals and principles which are their common heritage and of facilitating their economic and social progress, in particular by the maintenance and further realisation of human rights and fundamental freedoms;

Considering that in the European Convention for the Protection of Human Rights and Fundamental Freedoms signed at Rome on 4 November 1950, and the Protocols thereto, the member States of the Council of Europe agreed to secure to their populations the civil and political rights and freedoms therein specified;

Considering that in the European Social Charter opened for signature in Turin on 18 October 1961 and the Protocols thereto, the member States of the Council of Europe agreed to secure to their populations the social rights specified therein in order to improve their standard of living and their social well-being;

Recalling that the Ministerial Conference on Human Rights held in Rome on 5 November 1990 stressed the need, on the one hand, to preserve the indivisible nature of all human rights, be they civil, political, economic, social or cultural and, on the other hand, to give the European Social Charter fresh impetus;

Resolved, as was decided during the Ministerial Conference held in Turin on 21 and 22 October 1991, to update and adapt the substantive contents of the Charter in order to take account in particular of the fundamental social changes which have occurred since the text was adopted;

Recognising the advantage of embodying in a Revised Charter, designed progressively to take the place of the European Social Charter, the rights guaranteed by the Charter as amended, the rights guaranteed by the Additional Protocol of 1988 and to add new rights,

Have agreed as follows:

Part I

The Parties accept as the aim of their policy, to be pursued by all appropriate means both national and international in character, the attainment of conditions in which the following rights and principles may be effectively realised:

(1) Everyone shall have the opportunity to earn his living in an occupation freely entered upon.

(2) All workers have the right to just conditions of work.

(3) All workers have the right to safe and healthy working conditions.

(4) All workers have the right to a fair remuneration sufficient for a decent standard of living for themselves and their families.

(5) All workers and employers have the right to freedom of association in national or international organisations for the protection of their economic and social interests.

(6) All workers and employers have the right to bargain collectively.

(7) Children and young persons have the right to a special protection against the physical and moral hazards to which they are exposed.

(8) Employed women, in case of maternity, have the right to a special protection.

(9) Everyone has the right to appropriate facilities for vocational guidance with a view to helping him choose an occupation suited to his personal aptitude and interests.
(10) Everyone has the right to appropriate facilities for vocational training.
(11) Everyone has the right to benefit from any measures enabling him to enjoy the highest possible standard of health attainable.
(12) All workers and their dependents have the right to social security.
(13) Anyone without adequate resources has the right to social and medical assistance.
(14) Everyone has the right to benefit from social welfare services.
(15) Disabled persons have the right to independence, social integration and participation in the life of the community.
(16) The family as a fundamental unit of society has the right to appropriate social, legal and economic protection to ensure its full development.
(17) Children and young persons have the right to appropriate social, legal and economic protection.
(18) The nationals of any one of the Parties have the right to engage in any gainful occupation in the territory of any one of the others on a footing of equality with the nationals of the latter, subject to restrictions based on cogent economic or social reasons.
(19) Migrant workers who are nationals of a Party and their families have the right to protection and assistance in the territory of any other Party.
(20) All workers have the right to equal opportunities and equal treatment in matters of employment and occupation without discrimination on the grounds of sex.
(21) Workers have the right to be informed and to be consulted within the undertaking.
(22) Workers have the right to take part in the determination and improvement of the working conditions and working environment in the undertaking.
(23) Every elderly person has the right to social protection.
(24) All workers have the right to protection in cases of termination of employment.
(25) All workers have the right to protection of their claims in the event of the insolvency of their employer.
(26) All workers have the right to dignity at work.
(27) All persons with family responsibilities and who are engaged or wish to engage in employment have a right to do so without being subject to discrimination and as far as possible without conflict between their employment and family responsibilities.
(28) Workers' representatives in undertakings have the right to protection against acts prejudicial to them and should be afforded appropriate facilities to carry out their functions.
(29) All workers have the right to be informed and consulted in collective redundancy procedures.
(30) Everyone has the right to protection against poverty and social exclusion.
(31) Everyone has the right to housing.

Part II

The Parties undertake, as provided for in Part III, to consider themselves bound by the obligations laid down in the following articles and paragraphs.

Article 1

The right to work

With a view to ensuring the effective exercise of the right to work, the Parties undertake:

(1) to accept as one of their primary aims and responsibilities the achievement and maintenance of as high and stable a level of employment as possible, with a view to the attainment of full employment;
(2) to protect effectively the right of the worker to earn his living in an occupation freely entered upon;
(3) to establish or maintain free employment services for all workers;
(4) to provide or promote appropriate vocational guidance, training and rehabilitation.

Article 2

The right to just conditions of work

With a view to ensuring the effective exercise of the right to just conditions of work, the Parties undertake:

(1) to provide for reasonable daily and weekly working hours, the working week to be progressively reduced to the extent that the increase of productivity and other relevant factors permit;

(2) to provide for public holidays with pay;

(3) to provide for a minimum of four weeks' annual holiday with pay;

(4) to eliminate risks in inherently dangerous or unhealthy occupations, and where it has not yet been possible to eliminate or reduce sufficiently these risks, to provide for either a reduction of working hours or additional paid holidays for workers engaged in such occupations;

(5) to ensure a weekly rest period which shall, as far as possible, coincide with the day recognised by tradition or custom in the country or region concerned as a day of rest;

(6) to ensure that workers are informed in written form, as soon as possible, and in any event not later than two months after the date of commencing their employment, of the essential aspects of the contract or employment relationship;

(7) to ensure that workers performing night work benefit from measures which take account of the special nature of the work.

Article 3

The right to safe and healthy working conditions

With a view to ensuring the effective exercise of the right to safe and healthy working conditions, the Parties undertake, in consultation with employers' and workers' organisations:

(1) to formulate, implement and periodically review a coherent national policy on occupational safety, occupational health and the working environment. The primary aim of this policy shall be to improve occupational safety and health and to prevent accidents and injury to health arising out of, linked with or occurring in the course of work, particularly by minimising the causes of hazards inherent in the working environment;

(2) to issue safety and health regulations;

(3) to provide for the enforcement of such regulations by measures of supervision;

(4) to promote the progressive development of occupational health services for all workers with essentially preventive and advisory functions.

Article 4

The right to a fair remuneration

With a view to ensuring the effective exercise of the right to a fair remuneration, the Parties undertake:

(1) to recognise the right of workers to a remuneration such as will give them and their families a decent standard of living;

(2) to recognise the right of workers to an increased rate of remuneration for overtime work, subject to exceptions in particular cases;

(3) to recognise the right of men and women workers to equal pay for work of equal value;

(4) to recognise the right of all workers to a reasonable period of notice for termination of employment;

(5) to permit deductions from wages only under conditions and to the extent prescribed by national laws or regulations or fixed by collective agreements or arbitration awards.

The exercise of these rights shall be achieved by freely concluded collective agreements, by statutory wage-fixing machinery, or by other means appropriate to national conditions.

Article 5

The right to organise

With a view to ensuring or promoting the freedom of workers and employers to form local, national or international organisations for the protection of their economic and social interests and to join those organisations, the Parties undertake that national law shall not be such as to impair, nor shall it be so applied as to impair, this freedom. The extent to which the guarantees provided for in this article shall apply to the police shall be determined by national laws or regulations. The principle governing the application to the members of the armed forces of these guarantees and the extent to which they shall apply to persons in this category shall equally be determined by national laws or regulations.

Article 6

The right to bargain collectively

With a view to ensuring the effective exercise of the right to bargain collectively, the Parties undertake:

(1) to promote joint consultation between workers and employers;

(2) to promote, where necessary and appropriate, machinery for voluntary negotiations between employers or employers' organisations and workers' organisations, with a view to the regulation of terms and conditions of employment by means of collective agreements;

(3) to promote the establishment and use of appropriate machinery for conciliation and voluntary arbitration for the settlement of labour disputes;

and recognise:

(4) the right of workers and employers to collective action in cases of conflicts of interest, including the right to strike, subject to obligations that might arise out of collective agreements previously entered into.

Article 7

The right of children and young persons to protection

With a view to ensuring the effective exercise of the right of children and young persons to protection, the Parties undertake:

(1) to provide that the minimum age of admission to employment shall be 15 years, subject to exceptions for children employed in prescribed light work without harm to their health, morals or education;

(2) to provide that the minimum age of admission to employment shall be 18 years with respect to prescribed occupations regarded as dangerous or unhealthy;

(3) to provide that persons who are still subject to compulsory education shall not be employed in such work as would deprive them of the full benefit of their education;

(4) to provide that the working hours of persons under 18 years of age shall be limited in accordance with the needs of their development, and particularly with their need for vocational training;

(5) to recognise the right of young workers and apprentices to a fair wage or other appropriate allowances;

(6) to provide that the time spent by young persons in vocational training during the normal working hours with the consent of the employer shall be treated as forming part of the working day;

(7) to provide that employed persons of under 18 years of age shall be entitled to a minimum of four weeks' annual holiday with pay;

(8) to provide that persons under 18 years of age shall not be employed in night work with the exception of certain occupations provided for by national laws or regulations;

(9) to provide that persons under 18 years of age employed in occupations prescribed by national laws or regulations shall be subject to regular medical control;

(10) to ensure special protection against physical and moral dangers to which children and young persons are exposed, and particularly against those resulting directly or indirectly from their work.

Article 8

The right of employed women to protection of maternity

With a view to ensuring the effective exercise of the right of employed women to the protection of maternity, the Parties undertake:

(1) to provide either by paid leave, by adequate social security benefits or by benefits from public funds for employed women to take leave before and after childbirth up to a total of at least fourteen weeks;
(2) to consider it as unlawful for an employer to give a woman notice of dismissal during the period from the time she notifies her employer that she is pregnant until the end of her maternity leave, or to give her notice of dismissal at such a time that the notice would expire during such a period;
(3) to provide that mothers who are nursing their infants shall be entitled to sufficient time off for this purpose;
(4) to regulate the employment in night work of pregnant women, women who have recently given birth and women nursing their infants;
(5) to prohibit the employment of pregnant women, women who have recently given birth or who are nursing their infants in underground mining and all other work which is unsuitable by reason of its dangerous, unhealthy or arduous nature and to take appropriate measures to protect the employment rights of these women.

Article 9

The right to vocational guidance

With a view to ensuring the effective exercise of the right to vocational guidance, the Parties undertake to provide or promote, as necessary, a service which will assist all persons, including the handicapped, to solve problems related to occupational choice and progress, with due regard to the individual's characteristics and their relation to occupational opportunity: this assistance should be available free of charge, both to young persons, including schoolchildren, and to adults.

Article 10

The right to vocational training

With a view to ensuring the effective exercise of the right to vocational training, the Parties undertake:

(1) to provide or promote, as necessary, the technical and vocational training of all persons, including the handicapped, in consultation with employers' and workers' organisations, and to grant facilities for access to higher technical and university education, based solely on individual aptitude;
(2) to provide or promote a system of apprenticeship and other systematic arrangements for training young boys and girls in their various employments;
(3) to provide or promote, as necessary:
   (a) adequate and readily available training facilities for adult workers;
   (b) special facilities for the retraining of adult workers needed as a result of technological development or new trends in employment;
(4) to provide or promote, as necessary, special measures for the retraining and reintegration of the long-term unemployed;
(5) to encourage the full utilisation of the facilities provided by appropriate measures such as:
   (a) reducing or abolishing any fees or charges;
   (b) granting financial assistance in appropriate cases;

(c) including in the normal working hours time spent on supplementary training taken by the worker, at the request of his employer, during employment;
(d) ensuring, through adequate supervision, in consultation with the employers' and workers' organisations, the efficiency of apprenticeship and other training arrangements for young workers, and the adequate protection of young workers generally.

Article 11

The right to protection of health

With a view to ensuring the effective exercise of the right to protection of health, the Parties undertake, either directly or in co-operation with public or private organisations, to take appropriate measures designed *inter alia*:

(1) to remove as far as possible the causes of ill-health;
(2) to provide advisory and educational facilities for the promotion of health and the encouragement of individual responsibility in matters of health;
(3) to prevent as far as possible epidemic, endemic and other diseases, as well as accidents.

Article 12

The right to social security

With a view to ensuring the effective exercise of the right to social security, the Parties undertake:

(1) to establish or maintain a system of social security;
(2) to maintain the social security system at a satisfactory level at least equal to that necessary for the ratification of the European Code of Social Security;
(3) to endeavour to raise progressively the system of social security to a higher level;
(4) to take steps, by the conclusion of appropriate bilateral and multilateral agreements or by other means, and subject to the conditions laid down in such agreements, in order to ensure:
   (a) equal treatment with their own nationals of the nationals of other Parties in respect of social security rights, including the retention of benefits arising out of social security legislation, whatever movements the persons protected may undertake between the territories of the Parties;
   (b) the granting, maintenance and resumption of social security rights by such means as the accumulation of insurance or employment periods completed under the legislation of each of the Parties.

Article 13

The right to social and medical assistance

With a view to ensuring the effective exercise of the right to social and medical assistance, the Parties undertake:

(1) to ensure that any person who is without adequate resources and who is unable to secure such resources either by his own efforts or from other sources, in particular by benefits under a social security scheme, be granted adequate assistance, and, in case of sickness, the care necessitated by his condition;
(2) to ensure that persons receiving such assistance shall not, for that reason, suffer from a diminution of their political or social rights;
(3) to provide that everyone may receive by appropriate public or private services such advice and personal help as may be required to prevent, to remove, or to alleviate personal or family want;
(4) to apply the provisions referred to in paragraphs 1, 2 and 3 of this article on an equal footing with their nationals to nationals of other Parties lawfully within their territories, in accordance with their

obligations under the European Convention on Social and Medical Assistance, signed at Paris on 11 December 1953.

Article 14

The right to benefit from social welfare services

With a view to ensuring the effective exercise of the right to benefit from social welfare services, the Parties undertake:

(1) to promote or provide services which, by using methods of social work, would contribute to the welfare and development of both individuals and groups in the community, and to their adjustment to the social environment;

(2) to encourage the participation of individuals and voluntary or other organisations in the establishment and maintenance of such services.

Article 15

The right of persons with disabilities to independence, social integration and participation in the life of the community

With a view to ensuring to persons with disabilities, irrespective of age and the nature and origin of their disabilities, the effective exercise of the right to independence, social integration and participation in the life of the community, the Parties undertake, in particular:

(1) to take the necessary measures to provide persons with disabilities with guidance, education and vocational training in the framework of general schemes wherever possible or, where this is not possible, through specialised bodies, public or private;

(2) to promote their access to employment through all measures tending to encourage employers to hire and keep in employment persons with disabilities in the ordinary working environment and to adjust the working conditions to the needs of the disabled or, where this is not possible by reason of the disability, by arranging for or creating sheltered employment according to the level of disability. In certain cases, such measures may require recourse to specialised placement and support services;

(3) to promote their full social integration and participation in the life of the community in particular through measures, including technical aids, aiming to overcome barriers to communication and mobility and enabling access to transport, housing, cultural activities and leisure.

Article 16

The right of the family to social, legal and economic protection

With a view to ensuring the necessary conditions for the full development of the family, which is a fundamental unit of society, the Parties undertake to promote the economic, legal and social protection of family life by such means as social and family benefits, fiscal arrangements, provision of family housing, benefits for the newly married and other appropriate means.

Article 17

The right of children and young persons to social, legal and economic protection

With a view to ensuring the effective exercise of the right of children and young persons to grow up in an environment which encourages the full development of their personality and of their physical and mental capacities, the Parties undertake, either directly or in co-operation with public and private organisations, to take all appropriate and necessary measures designed:

(1)(a) to ensure that children and young persons, taking account of the rights and duties of their parents, have the care, the assistance, the education and the training they need, in particular by providing for the establishment or maintenance of institutions and services sufficient and adequate for this purpose;

(b) to protect children and young persons against negligence, violence or exploitation;

(c) to provide protection and special aid from the state for children and young persons temporarily or definitively deprived of their family's support;

(2) to provide to children and young persons a free primary and secondary education as well as to encourage regular attendance at schools.

Article 18

The right to engage in a gainful occupation in the territory of other Parties

With a view to ensuring the effective exercise of the right to engage in a gainful occupation in the territory of any other Party, the Parties undertake:

(1) to apply existing regulations in a spirit of liberality;

(2) to simplify existing formalities and to reduce or abolish chancery dues and other charges payable by foreign workers or their employers;

(3) to liberalise, individually or collectively, regulations governing the employment of foreign workers;

and recognise:

(4) the right of their nationals to leave the country to engage in a gainful occupation in the territories of the other Parties.

Article 19

The right of migrant workers and their families to protection and assistance

With a view to ensuring the effective exercise of the right of migrant workers and their families to protection and assistance in the territory of any other Party, the Parties undertake:

(1) to maintain or to satisfy themselves that there are maintained adequate and free services to assist such workers, particularly in obtaining accurate information, and to take all appropriate steps, so far as national laws and regulations permit, against misleading propaganda relating to emigration and immigration;

(2) to adopt appropriate measures within their own jurisdiction to facilitate the departure, journey and reception of such workers and their families, and to provide, within their own jurisdiction, appropriate services for health, medical attention and good hygienic conditions during the journey;

(3) to promote co-operation, as appropriate, between social services, public and private, in emigration and immigration countries;

(4) to secure for such workers lawfully within their territories, insofar as such matters are regulated by law or regulations or are subject to the control of administrative authorities, treatment not less favourable than that of their own nationals in respect of the following matters:

(a) remuneration and other employment and working conditions;

(b) membership of trade unions and enjoyment of the benefits of collective bargaining;

(c) accommodation;

(5) to secure for such workers lawfully within their territories treatment not less favourable than that of their own nationals with regard to employment taxes, dues or contributions payable in respect of employed persons;

(6) to facilitate as far as possible the reunion of the family of a foreign worker permitted to establish himself in the territory;

(7) to secure for such workers lawfully within their territories treatment not less favourable than that of their own nationals in respect of legal proceedings relating to matters referred to in this article;

(8) to secure that such workers lawfully residing within their territories are not expelled unless they endanger national security or offend against public interest or morality;
(9) to permit, within legal limits, the transfer of such parts of the earnings and savings of such workers as they may desire;
(10) to extend the protection and assistance provided for in this article to self-employed migrants insofar as such measures apply;
(11) to promote and facilitate the teaching of the national language of the receiving state or, if there are several, one of these languages, to migrant workers and members of their families;
(12) to promote and facilitate, as far as practicable, the teaching of the migrant worker's mother tongue to the children of the migrant worker.

Article 20

The right to equal opportunities and equal treatment in matters of employment and occupation without discrimination on the grounds of sex

With a view to ensuring the effective exercise of the right to equal opportunities and equal treatment in matters of employment and occupation without discrimination on the grounds of sex, the Parties undertake to recognise that right and to take appropriate measures to ensure or promote its application in the following fields:

(a) access to employment, protection against dismissal and occupational reintegration;
(b) vocational guidance, training, retraining and rehabilitation;
(c) terms of employment and working conditions, including remuneration;
(d) career development, including promotion.

Article 21

The right to information and consultation

With a view to ensuring the effective exercise of the right of workers to be informed and consulted within the undertaking, the Parties undertake to adopt or encourage measures enabling workers or their representatives, in accordance with national legislation and practice:

(a) to be informed regularly or at the appropriate time and in a comprehensible way about the economic and financial situation of the undertaking employing them, on the understanding that the disclosure of certain information which could be prejudicial to the undertaking may be refused or subject to confidentiality; and
(b) to be consulted in good time on proposed decisions which could substantially affect the interests of workers, particularly on those decisions which could have an important impact on the employment situation in the undertaking.

Article 22

The right to take part in the determination and improvement of the working conditions and working environment

With a view to ensuring the effective exercise of the right of workers to take part in the determination and improvement of the working conditions and working environment in the undertaking, the Parties undertake to adopt or encourage measures enabling workers or their representatives, in accordance with national legislation and practice, to contribute:

(a) to the determination and the improvement of the working conditions, work organisation and working environment;
(b) to the protection of health and safety within the undertaking;

(c) to the organisation of social and socio-cultural services and facilities within the undertaking;
(d) to the supervision of the observance of regulations on these matters.

Article 23

The right of elderly persons to social protection

With a view to ensuring the effective exercise of the right of elderly persons to social protection, the Parties undertake to adopt or encourage, either directly or in co-operation with public or private organisations, appropriate measures designed in particular:

(1) to enable elderly persons to remain full members of society for as long as possible, by means of:
  (a) adequate resources enabling them to lead a decent life and play an active part in public, social and cultural life;
  (b) provision of information about services and facilities available for elderly persons and their opportunities to make use of them;

(2) to enable elderly persons to choose their life-style freely and to lead independent lives in their familiar surroundings for as long as they wish and are able, by means of:
  (a) provision of housing suited to their needs and their state of health or of adequate support for adapting their housing;
  (b) the health care and the services necessitated by their state;

(3) to guarantee elderly persons living in institutions appropriate support, while respecting their privacy, and participation in decisions concerning living conditions in the institution.

Article 24

The right to protection in cases of termination of employment

With a view to ensuring the effective exercise of the right of workers to protection in cases of termination of employment, the Parties undertake to recognise:

(a) the right of all workers not to have their employment terminated without valid reasons for such termination connected with their capacity or conduct or based on the operational requirements of the undertaking, establishment or service;
(b) the right of workers whose employment is terminated without a valid reason to adequate compensation or other appropriate relief.

To this end the Parties undertake to ensure that a worker who considers that his employment has been terminated without a valid reason shall have the right to appeal to an impartial body.

Article 25

The right of workers to the protection of their claims in the event of the insolvency of their employer

With a view to ensuring the effective exercise of the right of workers to the protection of their claims in the event of the insolvency of their employer, the Parties undertake to provide that workers' claims arising from contracts of employment or employment relationships be guaranteed by a guarantee institution or by any other effective form of protection.

Article 26

The right to dignity at work

With a view to ensuring the effective exercise of the right of all workers to protection of their dignity at work, the Parties undertake, in consultation with employers' and workers' organisations:

(1) to promote awareness, information and prevention of sexual harassment in the workplace or in relation to work and to take all appropriate measures to protect workers from such conduct;

(2) to promote awareness, information and prevention of recurrent reprehensible or distinctly negative and offensive actions directed against individual workers in the workplace or in relation to work and to take all appropriate measures to protect workers from such conduct.

Article 27

The right of workers with family responsibilities to equal opportunities and equal treatment

With a view to ensuring the exercise of the right to equality of opportunity and treatment for men and women workers with family responsibilities and between such workers and other workers, the Parties undertake:

(1) to take appropriate measures:
  (a) to enable workers with family responsibilities to enter and remain in employment, as well as to re-enter employment after an absence due to those responsibilities, including measures in the field of vocational guidance and training;
  (b) to take account of their needs in terms of conditions of employment and social security;
  (c) to develop or promote services, public or private, in particular child daycare services and other childcare arrangements;

(2) to provide a possibility for either parent to obtain, during a period after maternity leave, parental leave to take care of a child, the duration and conditions of which should be determined by national legislation, collective agreements or practice;

(3) to ensure that family responsibilities shall not, as such, constitute a valid reason for termination of employment.

Article 28

The right of workers' representatives to protection in the undertaking and facilities to be accorded to them

With a view to ensuring the effective exercise of the right of workers' representatives to carry out their functions, the Parties undertake to ensure that in the undertaking:

(a) they enjoy effective protection against acts prejudicial to them, including dismissal, based on their status or activities as workers' representatives within the undertaking;

(b) they are afforded such facilities as may be appropriate in order to enable them to carry out their functions promptly and efficiently, account being taken of the industrial relations system of the country and the needs, size and capabilities of the undertaking concerned.

Article 29

The right to information and consultation in collective redundancy procedures

With a view to ensuring the effective exercise of the right of workers to be informed and consulted in situations of collective redundancies, the Parties undertake to ensure that employers shall inform and consult workers' representatives, in good time prior to such collective redundancies, on ways and means of avoiding collective redundancies or limiting their occurrence and mitigating their consequences, for example by recourse to accompanying social measures aimed, in particular, at aid for the redeployment or retraining of the workers concerned.

Article 30

The right to protection against poverty and social exclusion

With a view to ensuring the effective exercise of the right to protection against poverty and social exclusion, the Parties undertake:

(a) to take measures within the framework of an overall and co-ordinated approach to promote the effective access of persons who live or risk living in a situation of social exclusion or poverty, as well as their families, to, in particular, employment, housing, training, education, culture and social and medical assistance;

(b) to review these measures with a view to their adaptation if necessary.

Article 31

The right to housing

With a view to ensuring the effective exercise of the right to housing, the Parties undertake to take measures designed:

(1) to promote access to housing of an adequate standard;

(2) to prevent and reduce homelessness with a view to its gradual elimination;

(3) to make the price of housing accessible to those without adequate resources.

Part III

Article A

Undertakings

1. Subject to the provisions of Article B below, each of the Parties undertakes:

(a) to consider Part I of this Charter as a declaration of the aims which it will pursue by all appropriate means, as stated in the introductory paragraph of that part;

(b) to consider itself bound by at least six of the following nine articles of Part II of this Charter: Articles 1, 5, 6, 7, 12, 13, 16, 19 and 20;

(c) to consider itself bound by an additional number of articles or numbered paragraphs of Part II of the Charter which it may select, provided that the total number of articles or numbered paragraphs by which it is bound is not less than sixteen articles or sixty-three numbered paragraphs.

2. The articles or paragraphs selected in accordance with sub-paragraphs b and c of paragraph 1 of this article shall be notified to the Secretary General of the Council of Europe at the time when the instrument of ratification, acceptance or approval is deposited.

3. Any Party may, at a later date, declare by notification addressed to the Secretary General that it considers itself bound by any articles or any numbered paragraphs of Part II of the Charter which it has not already accepted under the terms of paragraph 1 of this article. Such undertakings subsequently given shall be deemed to be an integral part of the ratification, acceptance or approval and shall have the same effect as from the first day of the month following the expiration of a period of one month after the date of the notification.

4. Each Party shall maintain a system of labour inspection appropriate to national conditions.

Article B

Links with the European Social Charter and the 1988 Additional Protocol

No Contracting Party to the European Social Charter or Party to the Additional Protocol of 5 May 1988 may ratify, accept or approve this Charter without considering itself bound by at least the provisions corresponding to the provisions of the European Social Charter and, where appropriate, of the Additional Protocol, to which it was bound.

Acceptance of the obligations of any provision of this Charter shall, from the date of entry into force of those obligations for the Party concerned, result in the corresponding provision of the European Social Charter and, where appropriate, of its Additional Protocol of 1988 ceasing to apply to the Party concerned in the event of that Party being bound by the first of those instruments or by both instruments.

Part IV

Article C

Supervision of the implementation of the undertakings contained in this Charter

The implementation of the legal obligations contained in this Charter shall be submitted to the same supervision as the European Social Charter.

Article D

Collective complaints

1. The provisions of the Additional Protocol to the European Social Charter providing for a system of collective complaints shall apply to the undertakings given in this Charter for the States which have ratified the said Protocol.

2. Any State which is not bound by the Additional Protocol to the European Social Charter providing for a system of collective complaints may when depositing its instrument of ratification, acceptance or approval of this Charter or at any time thereafter, declare by notification addressed to the Secretary General of the Council of Europe, that it accepts the supervision of its obligations under this Charter following the procedure provided for in the said Protocol.

Part V

Article E

Non-discrimination

The enjoyment of the rights set forth in this Charter shall be secured without discrimination on any ground such as race, colour, sex, language, religion, political or other opinion, national extraction or social origin, health, association with a national minority, birth or other status.

Article F

Derogations in time of war or public emergency

1. In time of war or other public emergency threatening the life of the nation any Party may take measures derogating from its obligations under this Charter to the extent strictly required by the exigencies of the situation, provided that such measures are not inconsistent with its other obligations under international law.

2. Any Party which has availed itself of this right of derogation shall, within a reasonable lapse of time, keep the Secretary General of the Council of Europe fully informed of the measures taken and of the reasons therefor. It shall likewise inform the Secretary General when such measures have ceased to operate and the provisions of the Charter which it has accepted are again being fully executed.

Article G

Restrictions

1. The rights and principles set forth in Part I when effectively realised, and their effective exercise as provided for in Part II, shall not be subject to any restrictions or limitations not specified in those parts, except such as are prescribed by law and are necessary in a democratic society for the protection of the rights and freedoms of others or for the protection of public interest, national security, public health, or morals.

2. The restrictions permitted under this Charter to the rights and obligations set forth herein shall not be applied for any purpose other than that for which they have been prescribed.

Article H

Relations between the Charter and domestic law or international agreements

The provisions of this Charter shall not prejudice the provisions of domestic law or of any bilateral or multilateral treaties, conventions or agreements which are already in force, or may come into force, under which more favourable treatment would be accorded to the persons protected.

Article I

Implementation of the undertakings given

1. Without prejudice to the methods of implementation foreseen in these articles the relevant provisions of Articles 1 to 31 of Part II of this Charter shall be implemented by:

(a) laws or regulations;
(b) agreements between employers or employers' organisations and workers' organisations;
(c) a combination of those two methods;
(d) other appropriate means.

2. Compliance with the undertakings deriving from the provisions of paragraphs 1, 2, 3, 4, 5 and 7 of Article 2, paragraphs 4, 6 and 7 of Article 7, paragraphs 1, 2, 3 and 5 of Article 10 and Articles 21 and 22 of Part II of this Charter shall be regarded as effective if the provisions are applied, in accordance with paragraph 1 of this article, to the great majority of the workers concerned.

Article J

Amendments

1. Any amendment to Parts I and II of this Charter with the purpose of extending the rights guaranteed in this Charter as well as any amendment to Parts III to VI, proposed by a Party or by the Governmental Committee, shall be communicated to the Secretary General of the Council of Europe and forwarded by the Secretary General to the Parties to this Charter.

2. Any amendment proposed in accordance with the provisions of the preceding paragraph shall be examined by the Governmental Committee which shall submit the text adopted to the Committee of Ministers for approval after consultation with the Parliamentary Assembly. After its approval by the Committee of Ministers this text shall be forwarded to the Parties for acceptance.

3. Any amendment to Part I and to Part II of this Charter shall enter into force, in respect of those Parties which have accepted it, on the first day of the month following the expiration of a period of one month after the date on which three Parties have informed the Secretary General that they have accepted it.

In respect of any Party which subsequently accepts it, the amendment shall enter into force on the first day of the month following the expiration of a period of one month after the date on which that Party has informed the Secretary General of its acceptance.

4. Any amendment to Parts III to VI of this Charter shall enter into force on the first day of the month following the expiration of a period of one month after the date on which all Parties have informed the Secretary General that they have accepted it.

Part VI

Article K

Signature, ratification and entry into force

1. This Charter shall be open for signature by the member States of the Council of Europe. It shall be subject to ratification, acceptance or approval. Instruments of ratification, acceptance or approval shall be deposited with the Secretary General of the Council of Europe.

2. This Charter shall enter into force on the first day of the month following the expiration of a period of one month after the date on which three member States of the Council of Europe have expressed their consent to be bound by this Charter in accordance with the preceding paragraph.
3. In respect of any member State which subsequently expresses its consent to be bound by this Charter, it shall enter into force on the first day of the month following the expiration of a period of one month after the date of the deposit of the instrument of ratification, acceptance or approval.

Article L

Territorial application

1. This Charter shall apply to the metropolitan territory of each Party. Each signatory may, at the time of signature or of the deposit of its instrument of ratification, acceptance or approval, specify, by declaration addressed to the Secretary General of the Council of Europe, the territory which shall be considered to be its metropolitan territory for this purpose.
2. Any signatory may, at the time of signature or of the deposit of its instrument of ratification, acceptance or approval, or at any time thereafter, declare by notification addressed to the Secretary General of the Council of Europe, that the Charter shall extend in whole or in part to a non-metropolitan territory or territories specified in the said declaration for whose international relations it is responsible or for which it assumes international responsibility. It shall specify in the declaration the articles or paragraphs of Part II of the Charter which it accepts as binding in respect of the territories named in the declaration.
3. The Charter shall extend its application to the territory or territories named in the aforesaid declaration as from the first day of the month following the expiration of a period of one month after the date of receipt of the notification of such declaration by the Secretary General.
4. Any Party may declare at a later date by notification addressed to the Secretary General of the Council of Europe that, in respect of one or more of the territories to which the Charter has been applied in accordance with paragraph 2 of this article, it accepts as binding any articles or any numbered paragraphs which it has not already accepted in respect of that territory or territories. Such undertakings subsequently given shall be deemed to be an integral part of the original declaration in respect of the territory concerned, and shall have the same effect as from the first day of the month following the expiration of a period of one month after the date of receipt of such notification by the Secretary General.

Article M

Denunciation

1. Any Party may denounce this Charter only at the end of a period of five years from the date on which the Charter entered into force for it, or at the end of any subsequent period of two years, and in either case after giving six months' notice to the Secretary General of the Council of Europe who shall inform the other Parties accordingly.
2. Any Party may, in accordance with the provisions set out in the preceding paragraph, denounce any article or paragraph of Part II of the Charter accepted by it provided that the number of articles or paragraphs by which this Party is bound shall never be less than sixteen in the former case and sixty-three in the latter and that this number of articles or paragraphs shall continue to include the articles selected by the Party among those to which special reference is made in Article A, paragraph 1, sub-paragraph b.
3. Any Party may denounce the present Charter or any of the articles or paragraphs of Part II of the Charter under the conditions specified in paragraph 1 of this article in respect of any territory to which the said Charter is applicable, by virtue of a declaration made in accordance with paragraph 2 of Article L.

Article N

Appendix

The appendix to this Charter shall form an integral part of it.

Article O

Notifications

The Secretary General of the Council of Europe shall notify the member States of the Council and the Director General of the International Labour Office of:

(a) any signature;
(b) the deposit of any instrument of ratification, acceptance or approval;
(c) any date of entry into force of this Charter in accordance with Article K;
(d) any declaration made in application of Articles A, paragraphs 2 and 3, D, paragraphs 1 and 2, F, paragraph 2, L, paragraphs 1, 2, 3 and 4;
(e) any amendment in accordance with Article J;
(f) any denunciation in accordance with Article M;
(g) any other act, notification or communication relating to this Charter.

In witness whereof, the undersigned, being duly authorised thereto, have signed this revised Charter.

Done at Strasbourg, this 3rd day of May 1996, in English and French, both texts being equally authentic, in a single copy which shall be deposited in the archives of the Council of Europe. The Secretary General of the Council of Europe shall transmit certified copies to each member State of the Council of Europe and to the Director General of the International Labour Office.

Appendix to the Revised European Social Charter

Scope of the Revised European Social Charter in Terms of Persons Protected

1. Without prejudice to Article 12, paragraph 4, and Article 13, paragraph 4, the persons covered by Articles 1 to 17 and 20 to 31 include foreigners only in so far as they are nationals of other Parties lawfully resident or working regularly within the territory of the Party concerned, subject to the understanding that these articles are to be interpreted in the light of the provisions of Articles 18 and 19. This interpretation would not prejudice the extension of similar facilities to other persons by any of the Parties.

2. Each Party will grant to refugees as defined in the Convention relating to the Status of Refugees, signed in Geneva on 28 July 1951 and in the Protocol of 31 January 1967, and lawfully staying in its territory, treatment as favourable as possible, and in any case not less favourable than under the obligations accepted by the Party under the said convention and under any other existing international instruments applicable to those refugees.

3. Each Party will grant to stateless persons as defined in the Convention on the Status of Stateless Persons done in New York on 28 September 1954 and lawfully staying in its territory, treatment as favourable as possible and in any case not less favourable than under the obligations accepted by the Party under the said instrument and under any other existing international instruments applicable to those stateless persons.

Part I paragraph 18 and Part II Article 18, paragraph 1

It is understood that these provisions are not concerned with the question of entry into the territories of the Parties and do not prejudice the provisions of the European Convention on Establishment, signed in Paris on 13 December 1955.

Part II

Article 1, paragraph 2

This provision shall not be interpreted as prohibiting or authorising any union security clause or practice.

Article 2, paragraph 6

Parties may provide that this provision shall not apply:

(a) to workers having a contract or employment relationship with a total duration not exceeding one month and/or with a working week not exceeding eight hours;
(b) where the contract or employment relationship is of a casual and/or specific nature, provided, in these cases, that its non-application is justified by objective considerations.

Article 3, paragraph 4

It is understood that for the purposes of this provision the functions, organisation and conditions of operation of these services shall be determined by national laws or regulations, collective agreements or other means appropriate to national conditions.

Article 4, paragraph 4

This provision shall be so understood as not to prohibit immediate dismissal for any serious offence.

Article 4, paragraph 5

It is understood that a Party may give the undertaking required in this paragraph if the great majority of workers are not permitted to suffer deductions from wages either by law or through collective agreements or arbitration awards, the exceptions being those persons not so covered.

Article 6, paragraph 4

It is understood that each Party may, insofar as it is concerned, regulate the exercise of the right to strike by law, provided that any further restriction that this might place on the right can be justified under the terms of Article G.

Article 7, paragraph 2

This provision does not prevent Parties from providing in their legislation that young persons not having reached the minimum age laid down may perform work in so far as it is absolutely necessary for their vocational training where such work is carried out in accordance with conditions prescribed by the competent authority and measures are taken to protect the health and safety of these young persons.

Article 7, paragraph 8

It is understood that a Party may give the undertaking required in this paragraph if it fulfils the spirit of the undertaking by providing by law that the great majority of persons under eighteen years of age shall not be employed in night work.

Article 8, paragraph 2

This provision shall not be interpreted as laying down an absolute prohibition. Exceptions could be made, for instance, in the following cases:

(a) if an employed woman has been guilty of misconduct which justifies breaking off the employment relationship;
(b) if the undertaking concerned ceases to operate;
(c) if the period prescribed in the employment contract has expired.

Article 12, paragraph 4

The words 'and subject to the conditions laid down in such agreements' in the introduction to this paragraph are taken to imply *inter alia* that with regard to benefits which are available independently of any insurance contribution, a Party may require the completion of a prescribed period of residence before granting such benefits to nationals of other Parties.

Article 13, paragraph 4

Governments not Parties to the European Convention on Social and Medical Assistance may ratify the Charter in respect of this paragraph provided that they grant to nationals of other Parties a treatment which is in conformity with the provisions of the said convention.

Article 16

It is understood that the protection afforded in this provision covers single-parent families.

Article 17

It is understood that this provision covers all persons below the age of 18 years, unless under the law applicable to the child majority is attained earlier, without prejudice to the other specific provisions provided by the Charter, particularly Article 7.

This does not imply an obligation to provide compulsory education up to the above-mentioned age.

Article 19, paragraph 6

For the purpose of applying this provision, the term 'family of a foreign worker' is understood to mean at least the worker's spouse and unmarried children, as long as the latter are considered to be minors by the receiving State and are dependent on the migrant worker.

Article 20

1. It is understood that social security matters, as well as other provisions relating to unemployment benefit, old age benefit and survivor's benefit, may be excluded from the scope of this article.

2. Provisions concerning the protection of women, particularly as regards pregnancy, confinement and the post-natal period, shall not be deemed to be discrimination as referred to in this article.

3. This article shall not prevent the adoption of specific measures aimed at removing *de facto* inequalities.

4. Occupational activities which, by reason of their nature or the context in which they are carried out, can be entrusted only to persons of a particular sex may be excluded from the scope of this article or some of its provisions. This provision is not to be interpreted as requiring the Parties to embody in laws or regulations a list of occupations which, by reason of their nature or the context in which they are carried out, may be reserved to persons of a particular sex.

Articles 21 and 22

1. For the purpose of the application of these articles, the term 'workers' representatives' means persons who are recognised as such under national legislation or practice.

2. The terms 'national legislation and practice' embrace as the case may be, in addition to laws and regulations, collective agreements, other agreements between employers and workers' representatives, customs as well as relevant case law.

3. For the purpose of the application of these articles, the term 'undertaking' is understood as referring to a set of tangible and intangible components, with or without legal personality, formed to produce goods or provide services for financial gain and with power to determine its own market policy.

4. It is understood that religious communities and their institutions may be excluded from the application of these articles, even if these institutions are 'undertakings' within the meaning of paragraph 3. Establishments pursuing activities which are inspired by certain ideals or guided by certain moral concepts, ideals and concepts which are protected by national legislation, may be excluded from the application of these articles to such an extent as is necessary to protect the orientation of the undertaking.

5. It is understood that where in a state the rights set out in these articles are exercised in the various establishments of the undertaking, the Party concerned is to be considered as fulfilling the obligations deriving from these provisions.

6. The Parties may exclude from the field of application of these articles, those undertakings employing less than a certain number of workers, to be determined by national legislation or practice.

Article 22

1. Part I, paragraph 18, and Part II, Article 18, paragraph 1

It is understood that these provisions are not concerned with the question of entry into the territories of the Parties and do not prejudice the provisions of the European Convention on Establishment, signed in Paris on 13 December 1955.

NOTE

The version of the European Social Charter reproduced here is the revised version adopted at Strasbourg in 1996, which substantially augmented the original version adopted at Turin in 1961. The United Kingdom has yet to rafity the revised version, although it is expected to do so in the near future. In the meantime, those seeking the original 1961 version can find it reproduced in Brownlie's *Basic Documents on Human Rights* (Clarendon Press, 1992) or on the Council of Europe website at 'www.coe.fr/eng/legaltxt/35e.htm'.

APPENDIX H

Universal Declaration of Human Rights 1948

PREAMBLE

Whereas recognition of the inherent dignity and of the equal and inalienable rights of all members of the human family is the foundation of freedom, justice and peace in the world,

Whereas disregard and contempt for human rights have resulted in barbarous acts which have outraged the conscience of mankind, and the advent of a world in which human beings shall enjoy freedom of speech and belief and freedom from fear and want has been proclaimed as the highest aspiration of the common people,

Whereas it is essential, if man is not to be compelled to have recourse, as a last resort, to rebellion against tyranny and oppression, that human rights should be protected by the rule of law,

Whereas it is essential to promote the development of friendly relations between nations,

Whereas the peoples of the United Nations have in the Charter reaffirmed their faith in fundamental human rights, in the dignity and worth of the human person and in the equal rights of men and women and have determined to promote social progress and better standards of life in larger freedom,

Whereas Member States have pledged themselves to achieve, in co-operation with the United Nations, the promotion of universal respect for and observance of human rights and fundamental freedoms,

Whereas a common understanding of these rights and freedoms is of the greatest importance for the full realization of this pledge,

Now, Therefore

THE GENERAL ASSEMBLY

proclaims

This universal declaration of human rights as a common standard of achievement for all peoples and all nations, to the end that every individual and every organ of society, keeping this Declaration constantly in mind, shall strive by teaching and education to promote respect for these rights and freedoms and by progressive measures, national and international, to secure their universal and effective recognition and observance, both among the peoples of Member States themselves and among the peoples of territories under their jurisdiction.

Article 1

All human beings are born free and equal in dignity and rights.They are endowed with reason and conscience and should act towards one another in a spirit of brotherhood.

Article 2

Everyone is entitled to all the rights and freedoms set forth in this Declaration, without distinction of any kind, such as race, colour, sex, language, religion, political or other opinion, national or social origin, property, birth or other status.

Furthermore, no distinction shall be made on the basis of the political, jurisdictional or international status of the country or territory to which a person belongs, whether it be independent, trust, non-self-governing or under any other limitation of sovereignty.

Article 3

Everyone has the right to life, liberty and security of person.

Article 4

No one shall be held in slavery or servitude; slavery and the slave trade shall be prohibited in all their forms.

Article 5

No one shall be subjected to torture or to cruel, inhuman or degrading treatment or punishment.

Article 6

Everyone has the right to recognition everywhere as a person before the law.

Article 7

All are equal before the law and are entitled without any discrimination to equal protection of the law. All are entitled to equal protection against any discrimination in violation of this Declaration and against any incitement to such discrimination.

Article 8

Everyone has the right to an effective remedy by the competent national tribunals for acts violating the fundamental rights granted him by the constitution or by law.

Article 9

No one shall be subjected to arbitrary arrest, detention or exile.

Article 10

Everyone is entitled in full equality to a fair and public hearing by an independent and impartial tribunal, in the determination of his rights and obligations and of any criminal charge against him.

Article 11

1. Everyone charged with a penal offence has the right to be presumed innocent until proved guilty according to law in a public trial at which he has had all the guarantees necessary for his defence.

2. No one shall be held guilty of any penal offence on account of any act or omission which did not constitute a penal offence, under national or international law, at the time when it was committed. Nor shall a heavier penalty be imposed than the one that was applicable at the time the penal offence was committed.

Article 12

No one shall be subjected to arbitrary interference with his privacy, family, home or correspondence, nor to attacks upon his honour and reputation. Everyone has the right to the protection of the law against such interference or attacks.

Article 13

1. Everyone has the right to freedom of movement and residence within the borders of each state.

2. Everyone has the right to leave any country, including his own, and to return to his country.

Article 14

1. Everyone has the right to seek and to enjoy in other countries asylum from persecution.

2. This right may not be invoked in the case of prosecutions genuinely arising from non-political crimes or from acts contrary to the purposes and principles of the United Nations.

Article 15

1. Everyone has the right to a nationality.

2. No one shall be arbitrarily deprived of his nationality nor denied the right to change his nationality.

Article 16

1. Men and women of full age, without any limitation due to race, nationality or religion, have the right to marry and to found a family. They are entitled to equal rights as to marriage, during marriage and at its dissolution.

2. Marriage shall be entered into only with the free and full consent of the intending spouses.

3. The family is the natural and fundamental group unit of society and is entitled to protection by society and the State.

Article 17

1. Everyone has the right to own property alone as well as in association with others.

2. No one shall be arbitrarily deprived of his property.

Article 18

Everyone has the right to freedom of thought, conscience and religion; this right includes freedom to change his religion or belief, and freedom, either alone or in community with others and in public or private, to manifest his religion or belief in teaching, practice, worship and observance.

Article 19

Everyone has the right to freedom of opinion and expression; this right includes freedom to hold opinions without interference and to seek, receive and impart information and ideas through any media and regardless of frontiers.

Article 20

1. Everyone has the right to freedom of peaceful assembly and association.

2. No one may be compelled to belong to an association.

Article 21

1. Everyone has the right to take part in the government of his country, directly or through freely chosen representatives.

2. Everyone has the right of equal access to public service in his country.

3. The will of the people shall be the basis of the authority of government; this will shall be expressed in periodic and genuine elections which shall be by universal and equal suffrage and shall be held by secret vote or by equivalent free voting procedures.

Article 22

Everyone, as a member of society, has the right to social security and is entitled to realisation, through national effort and international co-operation and in accordance with the organisation and resources of each State, of the economic, social and cultural rights indispensable for his dignity and the free development of his personality.

Article 23

1. Everyone has the right to work, to free choice of employment, to just and favourable conditions of work and to protection against unemployment.

2. Everyone, without any discrimination, has the right to equal pay for equal work.

3. Everyone who works has the right to just and favourable remuneration ensuring for himself and his family an existence worthy of human dignity, and supplemented, if necessary, by other means of social protection.

4. Everyone has the right to form and to join trade unions for the protection of his interests.

Article 24

Everyone has the right to rest and leisure, including reasonable limitation of working hours and periodic holidays with pay.

Article 25

1. Everyone has the right to a standard of living adequate for the health and well-being of himself and of his family, including food, clothing, housing and medical care and necessary social services, and the right to security in the event of unemployment, sickness, disability, widowhood, old age or other lack of livelihood in circumstances beyond his control.

2. Motherhood and childhood are entitled to special care and assistance. All children, whether born in or out of wedlock, shall enjoy the same social protection.

Article 26

1. Everyone has the right to education. Education shall be free, at least in the elementary and fundamental stages. Elementary education shall be compulsory. Technical and professional education shall be made generally available and higher education shall be equally accessible to all on the basis of merit.

2. Education shall be directed to the full development of the human personality and to the strengthening of respect for human rights and fundamental freedoms. It shall promote understanding, tolerance and friendship among all nations, racial or religious groups, and shall further the activities of the United Nations for the maintenance of peace.

3. Parents have a prior right to choose the kind of education that shall be given to their children.

Article 27

1. Everyone has the right freely to participate in the cultural life of the community, to enjoy the arts and to share in scientific advancement and its benefits.

2. Everyone has the right to the protection of the moral and material interests resulting from any scientific, literary or artistic production of which he is the author.

Article 28

Everyone is entitled to a social and international order in which the rights and freedoms set forth in this Declaration can be fully realised.

Article 29

1. Everyone has duties to the community in which alone the free and full development of his personality is possible.

2. In the exercise of his rights and freedoms, everyone shall be subject only to such limitations as are determined by law solely for the purpose of securing due recognition and respect for the rights and freedoms of others and of meeting the just requirements of morality, public order and the general welfare in a democratic society.

3. These rights and freedoms may in no case be exercised contrary to the purposes and principles of the United Nations.

Article 30

Nothing in this Declaration may be interpreted as implying for any State, group or person any right to engage in any activity or to perform any act aimed at the destruction of any of the rights and freedoms set forth herein.

APPENDIX I

Convention Relating to the Status of Refugees 1951

Preamble

The High Contracting Parties,

Considering that the Charter of the United Nations and the Universal Declaration of Human Rights approved on 10 December 1948 by the General Assembly have affirmed the principle that human beings shall enjoy fundamental rights and freedoms without discrimination,

Considering that the United Nations has, on various occasions, manifested its profound concern for refugees and endeavoured to assure refugees the widest possible exercise of these fundamental rights and freedoms,

Considering that it is desirable to revise and consolidate previous international agreements relating to the status of refugees and to extend the scope of and the protection accorded by such instruments by means of a new agreement,

Considering that the grant of asylum may place unduly heavy burdens on certain countries, and that a satisfactory solution of a problem of which the United Nations has recognised the international scope and nature cannot therefore be achieved without international co-operation,

Expressing the wish that all States, recognising the social and humanitarian nature of the problem of refugees, will do everything within their power to prevent this problem from becoming a cause of tension between States,

Noting that the United Nations High Commissioner for Refugees is charged with the task of supervising international conventions providing for the protection of refugees, and recognising that the effective co-ordination of measures taken to deal with this problem will depend upon the co-operation of States with the High Commissioner,

Have agreed as follows:

Chapter I
General Provisions

Article 1

Definition of the term 'refugee'

A. For the purposes of the present Convention, the term 'refugee' shall apply to any person who:

(1) Has been considered a refugee under the Arrangements of 12 May 1926 and 30 June 1928 or under the Conventions of 28 October 1933 and 10 February 1938, the Protocol of 14 September 1939 or the Constitution of the International Refugee Organisation;

Decisions of non-eligibility taken by the International Refugee Organisation during the period of its activities shall not prevent the status of refugee being accorded to persons who fulfil the conditions of paragraph 2 of this section;

(2) [As a result of events occurring before I January 1951 and] owing to well-founded fear of being persecuted for reasons of race, religion, nationality, membership of a particular social group or political opinion, is outside the country of his nationality and is unable, or owing to such fear, is unwilling to avail

himself of the protection of that country; or who, not having a nationality and being outside the country of his former habitual residence [as a result of such events], is unable or, owing to such fear, is unwilling to return to it.

In the case of a person who has more than one nationality, the term 'the country of his nationality' shall mean each of the countries of which he is a national, and a person shall not be deemed to be lacking the protection of the country of his nationality if, without any valid reason based on well-founded fear, he has not availed himself of the protection of one of the countries of which he is a national.

B.(1) For the purposes of this Convention, the words 'events occurring before I January 1951' in Article 1, Section A, shall be understood to mean either

(a) 'events occurring in Europe before I January 1951'; or

(b) 'events occurring in Europe or elsewhere before I January 1951';

and each Contracting State shall make a declaration at the time of signature, ratification or accession, specifying which of these meanings it applies for the purpose of its obligations under this Convention.

(2) Any Contracting State which has adopted alternative (a) may at any time extend its obligations by adopting alternative (b) by means of a notification addressed to the Secretary-General of the United Nations.

C. This Convention shall cease to apply to any person falling under the terms of section A if:

(1) He has voluntarily re-availed himself of the protection of the country of his nationality; or

(2) Having lost his nationality, he has voluntarily reacquired it; or

(3) He has acquired a new nationality, and enjoys the protection of the country of his new nationality; or

(4) He has voluntarily re-established himself in the country which he left or outside which he remained owing to fear of persecution; or

(5) He can no longer, because the circumstances in connection with which he has been recognised as a refugee have ceased to exist, continue to refuse to avail himself of the protection of the country of his nationality;

Provided that this paragraph shall not apply to a refugee falling under section A (I) of this article who is able to invoke compelling reasons arising out of previous persecution for refusing to avail himself of the protection of the country of nationality;

(6) Being a person who has no nationality he is, because the circumstances in connection with which he has been recognised as a refugee have ceased to exist, able to return to the country of his former habitual residence;

Provided that this paragraph shall not apply to a refugee falling under section A (I) of this article who is able to invoke compelling reasons arising out of previous persecution for refusing to return to the country of his former habitual residence.

D. This Convention shall not apply to persons who are at present receiving from organs or agencies of the United Nations other than the United Nations High Commissioner for Refugees protection or assistance.

When such protection or assistance has ceased for any reason, without the position of such persons being definitively settled in accordance with the relevant resolutions adopted by the General Assembly of the United Nations, these persons shall *ipso facto* be entitled to the benefits of this Convention.

E. This Convention shall not apply to a person who is recognised by the competent authorities of the country in which he has taken residence as having the rights and obligations which are attached to the possession of the nationality of that country.

F. The provisions of this Convention shall not apply to any person with respect to whom there are serious reasons for considering that.

(a) He has committed a crime against peace, a war crime, or a crime against humanity, as defined in the international instruments drawn up to make provision in respect of such crimes;

(b) He has committed a serious non-political crime outside the country of refuge prior to his admission to that country as a refugee;

(c) He has been guilty of acts contrary to the purposes and principles of the United Nations.

Article 2

General obligations

Every refugee has duties to the country in which he finds himself, which require in particular that he conform to its laws and regulations as well as to measures taken for the maintenance of public order.

Article 3

Non-discrimination

The Contracting States shall apply the provisions of this Convention to refugees without discrimination as to race, religion or country of origin.

Article 4

Religion

The Contracting States shall accord to refugees within their territories treatment at least as favourable as that accorded to their nationals with respect to freedom to practise their religion and freedom as regards the religious education of their children.

Article 5

Rights granted apart from this Convention

Nothing in this Convention shall be deemed to impair any rights and benefits granted by a Contracting State to refugees apart from this Convention.

Article 6

The term 'in the same circumstances'

For the purposes of this Convention, the term 'in the same circumstances,, implies that any requirements (including requirements as to length and conditions of sojourn or residence) which the particular individual would have to fulfil for the enjoyment of the right in question, if he were not a refugee, must be fulfilled by him, with the exception of requirements which by their nature a refugee is incapable of fulfilling.

Article 7

Exemption from reciprocity

1. Except where this Convention contains more favourable provisions, a Contracting State shall accord to refugees the same treatment as is accorded to aliens generally.

2. After a period of three years' residence, all refugees shall enjoy exemption from legislative reciprocity in the territory of the Contracting States.

3. Each Contracting State shall continue to accord to refugees the rights and benefits to which they were already entitled, in the absence of reciprocity, at the date of entry into force of this Convention for that State.

4. The Contracting States shall consider favourably the possibility of according to refugees, in the absence of reciprocity, rights and benefits beyond those to which they are entitled according to paragraphs 2 and 3, and to extending exemption from reciprocity to refugees who do not fulfil the conditions provided for in paragraphs 2 and 3.

5. The provisions of paragraphs 2 and 3 apply both to the rights and benefits referred to in Articles 13, 18, 19, 21 and 22 of this Convention and to rights and benefits for which this Convention does not provide.

Article 8

Exemption from exceptional measures

With regard to exceptional measures which may be taken against the person, property or interests of nationals of a foreign State, the Contracting States shall not apply such measures to a refugee who is formally a national of the said State solely on account of such nationality. Contracting States which, under their legislation, are prevented from applying the general principle expressed in this article, shall, in appropriate cases, grant exemptions in favour of such refugees.

Article 9

Provisional measures

Nothing in this Convention shall prevent a Contracting State, in time of war or other grave and exceptional circumstances, from taking provisionally measures which it considers to be essential to the national security in the case of a particular person, pending a determination by the Contracting State that that person is in fact a refugee and that the continuance of such measures is necessary in his case in the interests of national security.

Article 10

Continuity of residence

1. Where a refugee has been forcibly displaced during the Second World War and removed to the territory of a Contracting State, and is resident there, the period of such enforced sojourn shall be considered to have been lawful residence within that territory.

2. Where a refugee has been forcibly displaced during the Second World War from the territory of a Contracting State and has, prior to the date of entry into force of this Convention, returned there for the purpose of taking up residence, the period of residence before and after such enforced displacement shall be regarded as one uninterrupted period for any purposes for which uninterrupted residence is required.

Article 11

Refugee seamen

In the case of refugees regularly serving as crew members on board a ship flying the flag of a Contracting State, that State shall give sympathetic consideration to their establishment on its territory and the issue of travel documents to them or their temporary admission to its territory particularly with a view to facilitating their establishment in another country.

Chapter II
Juridical Status

Article 12

Personal status

1. The personal status of a refugee shall be governed by the law of the country of his domicile or, if he has no domicile, by the law of the country of his residence.

2. Rights previously acquired by a refugee and dependent on personal status, more particularly rights attaching to marriage, shall be respected by a Contracting State, subject to compliance, if this be necessary, with the formalities required by the law of that State, provided that the right in question is one which would have been recognised by the law of that State had he not become a refugee.

Article 13

Movable and immovable property

The Contracting States shall accord to a refugee treatment as favourable as possible and, in any event, not less favourable than that accorded to aliens generally in the same circumstances, as regards the acquisition of movable and immovable property and other rights pertaining thereto, and to leases and other contracts relating to movable and immovable property.

Article 14

Artistic rights and industrial property

In respect of the protection of industrial property, such as inventions, designs or models, trade marks, trade names, and of rights in literary, artistic and scientific works, a refugee shall be accorded in the country in which he has his habitual residence the same protection as is accorded to nationals of that country. In the territory of any other Contracting States, he shall be accorded the same protection as is accorded in that territory to nationals of the country in which he has his habitual residence.

Article 15

Right of association

As regards non-political and non-profit-making associations and trade unions the Contracting States shall accord to refugees lawfully staying in their territory the most favourable treatment accorded to nationals of a foreign country, in the same circumstances.

Article 16

Access to courts

1. A refugee shall have free access to the courts of law on the territory of all Contracting States.

2. A refugee shall enjoy in the Contracting State in which he has his habitual residence the same treatment as a national in matters pertaining to access to the courts, including legal assistance and exemption from *cautio judicatum solvi.*

3. A refugee shall be accorded in the matters referred to in paragraph 2 in countries other than that in which he has his habitual residence the treatment granted to a national of the country of his habitual residence.

Chapter III
Gainful Employment

Article 17

Wage-earning employment

1. The Contracting States shall accord to refugees lawfully staying in their territory the most favourable treatment accorded to nationals of a foreign country in the same circumstances, as regards the right to engage in wage-earning employment.

2. In any case, restrictive measures imposed on aliens or the employment of aliens for the protection of the national labour market shall not be applied to a refugee who was already exempt from them at the date of entry into force of this Convention for the Contracting State concerned, or who fulfils one of the following conditions:

(a) He has completed three years' residence in the country;

(b) He has a spouse possessing the nationality of the country of residence. A refugee may not invoke the benefit of this provision if he has abandoned his spouse;

(c) He has one or more children possessing the nationality of the country of residence.

3. The Contracting States shall give sympathetic consideration to assimilating the rights of all refugees with regard to wage-earning employment to those of nationals, and in particular of those refugees who have entered their territory pursuant to programmes of labour recruitment or under immigration schemes.

Article 18

Self-employment

The Contracting States shall accord to a refugee lawfully in their territory treatment as favourable as possible and, in any event, not less favourable than that accorded to aliens generally in the same circumstances, as regards the right to engage on his own account in agriculture, industry, handicrafts and commerce and to establish commercial and industrial companies.

Article 19

Liberal professions

1. Each Contracting State shall accord to refugees lawfully staying in their territory who hold diplomas recognised by the competent authorities of that State, and who are desirous of practising a liberal profession, treatment as favourable as possible and, in any event, not less favourable than that accorded to aliens generally in the same circumstances.

2. The Contracting States shall use their best endeavours consistently with their laws and constitutions to secure the settlement of such refugees in the territories, other than the metropolitan territory, for whose international relations they are responsible.

Chapter IV
Welfare

Article 20

Rationing

Where a rationing system exists, which applies to the population at large and regulates the general distribution of products in short supply, refugees shall be accorded the same treatment as nationals.

Article 21

Housing

As regards housing, the Contracting States, in so far as the matter is regulated by laws or regulations or is subject to the control of public authorities, shall accord to refugees lawfully staying in their territory treatment as favourable as possible and, in any event, not less favourable than that accorded to aliens generally in the same circumstances.

Article 22

Public education

1. The Contracting States shall accord to refugees the same treatment as is accorded to nationals with respect to elementary education.

2. The Contracting States shall accord to refugees treatment as favourable as possible, and, in any event, not less favourable than that accorded to aliens generally in the same circumstances, with respect to education other than elementary education and, in particular, as regards access to studies, the recognition of foreign school certificates, diplomas and degrees, the remission of fees and charges and the award of scholarships.

Article 23

Public relief

The Contracting States shall accord to refugees lawfully staying in their territory the same treatment with respect to public relief and assistance as is accorded to their nationals.

Article 24

Labour legislation and social security

1. The Contracting States shall accord to refugees lawfully staying in their territory the same treatment as is accorded to nationals in respect of the following matters:

(a) In so far as such matters are governed by laws or regulations or are subject to the control of administrative authorities: remuneration, including family allowances where these form part of remuneration, hours of work, overtime arrangements, holidays with pay, restrictions on home work, minimum age of employment, apprenticeship and training, women's work and the work of young persons, and the enjoyment of the benefits of collective bargaining;

(b) Social security (legal provisions in respect of employment injury, occupational diseases, maternity, sickness, disability, old age, death, unemployment, family responsibilities and any other contingency which, according to national laws or regulations, is covered by a social security scheme), subject to the following limitations:

(i) There may be appropriate arrangements for the maintenance of acquired rights and rights in course of acquisition;

(ii) National laws or regulations of the country of residence may prescribe special arrangements concerning benefits or portions of benefits which are payable wholly out of public funds, and concerning allowances paid to persons who do not fulfil the contribution conditions prescribed for the award of a normal pension.

2. The right to compensation for the death of a refugee resulting from employment injury or from occupational disease shall not be affected by the fact that the residence of the beneficiary is outside the territory of the Contracting State.

3. The Contracting States shall extend to refugees the benefits of agreements concluded between them, or which may be concluded between them in the future, concerning the maintenance of acquired rights in the process of acquisition in regard to social security, subject only to the conditions which apply to nationals of the States signatory to the agreements in question.

4. The Contracting States will give sympathetic consideration to extending to refugees so far as possible the benefits of similar agreements which may at any time be in force between such Contracting States and non-contracting States.

Chapter V
Administrative Measures

Article 25

Administrative assistance

1. When the exercise of a right by a refugee would normally require the assistance of authorities of a foreign country to whom he cannot have recourse, the Contracting States in whose territory he is residing shall arrange that such assistance be afforded to him by their own authorities or by an international authority.

2. The authority or authorities mentioned in paragraph 1 shall deliver or cause to be delivered under their supervision to refugees such documents or certifications as would normally be delivered to aliens by or through their national authorities.

3. Documents or certifications so delivered shall stand in the stead of the official instruments delivered to aliens by or through their national authorities, and shall be given credence in the absence of proof to the contrary.

4. Subject to such exceptional treatment as may be granted to indigent persons, fees may be charged for the services mentioned herein, but such fees shall be moderate and commensurate with those charged to nationals for similar services.

5. The provisions of this article shall be without prejudice to Articles 27 and 28.

Article 26

Freedom of movement

Each Contracting State shall accord to refugees lawfully in its territory the right to choose their place of residence and to move freely within its territory, subject to any regulations applicable to aliens generally in the same circumstances.

Article 27

Identity papers

The Contracting States shall issue identity papers to any refugee in their territory who does not possess a valid travel document.

Article 28

Travel documents

1. The Contracting States shall issue to refugees lawfully staying in their territory travel documents for the purpose of travel outside their territory, unless compelling reasons of national security or public order otherwise require, and the provisions of the Schedule to this Convention shall apply with respect to such documents. The Contracting States may issue such a travel document to any other refugee in their territory; they shall in particular give sympathetic consideration to the issue of such a travel document to refugees in their territory who are unable to obtain a travel document from the country of their lawful residence.

2. Travel documents issued to refugees under previous international agreements by parties thereto shall be recognised and treated by the Contracting States in the same way as if they had been issued pursuant to this Article.

Article 29

Fiscal charges

1. The Contracting States shall not impose upon refugees duties, charges or taxes, of any description whatsoever, other or higher than those which are or may be levied on their nationals in similar situations.

2. Nothing in the above paragraph shall prevent the application to refugees of the laws and regulations concerning charges in respect of the issue to aliens of administrative documents including identity papers.

Article 30

Transfer of assets

1. A Contracting State shall, in conformity with its laws and regulations, permit refugees to transfer assets which they have brought into its territory, to another country where they have been admitted for the purposes of resettlement.

2. A Contracting State shall give sympathetic consideration to the application of refugees for permission to transfer assets wherever they may be and which are necessary for their resettlement in another country to which they have been admitted.

Article 31

Refugees unlawfully in the country of refuge

1. The Contracting States shall not impose penalties, on account of their illegal entry or presence, on refugees who, coming directly from a territory where their life or freedom was threatened in the sense of Article 1, enter or are present in their territory without authorisation, provided they present themselves without delay to the authorities and show good cause for their illegal entry or presence.

2. The Contracting States shall not apply to the movements of such refugees restrictions other than those which are necessary and such restrictions shall only be applied until their status in the country is regularised

or they obtain admission into another country. The Contracting States shall allow such refugees a reasonable period and all the necessary facilities to obtain admission into another country.

Article 32

Expulsion

1. The Contracting States shall not expel a refugee lawfully in their territory save on grounds of national security or public order.

2. The expulsion of such a refugee shall be only in pursuance of a decision reached in accordance with due process of law. Except where compelling reasons of national security otherwise require, the refugee shall be allowed to submit evidence to clear himself, and to appeal to and be represented for the purpose before competent authority or a person or persons specially designated by the competent authority.

3. The Contracting States shall allow such a refugee a reasonable period within which to seek legal admission into another country. The Contracting States reserve the right to apply during that period such internal measures as they may deem necessary.

Article 33

Prohibition of expulsion or return ('refoulement')

1. No Contracting State shall expel or return ('refouler') a refugee in any manner whatsoever to the frontiers of territories where his life or freedom would be threatened on account of his race, religion, nationality, membership of a particular social group or political opinion.

2. The benefit of the present provision may not, however, be claimed by a refugee whom there are reasonable grounds for regarding as a danger to the security of the country in which he is, or who, having been convicted by a final judgment of a particularly serious crime, constitutes a danger to the community of that country.

Article 34

Naturalisation

The Contracting States shall as far as possible facilitate the assimilation and naturalisation of refugees. They shall in particular make every effort to expedite naturalisation proceedings and to reduce as far as possible the charges and costs of such proceedings.

Chapter VI
Executory and Transitory Provisions

Article 35

Co-operation of the national authorities with the United Nations

1. The Contracting States undertake to co-operate with the Office of the United Nations High Commissioner for Refugees, or any other agency of the United Nations which may succeed it, in the exercise of its functions, and shall in particular facilitate its duty of supervising the application of the provisions of this Convention.

2. In order to enable the Office of the High Commissioner or any other agency of the United Nations which may succeed it, to make reports to the competent organs of the United Nations, the Contracting States undertake to provide them in the appropriate form with information and statistical data requested concerning:

(a) The condition of refugees,
(b) The implementation of this Convention, and
(c) Laws, regulations and decrees which are, or may hereafter be, in force relating to refugees.

Article 36

Information on national legislation

The Contracting States shall communicate to the Secretary-General of the United Nations the laws and regulations which they may adopt to ensure the application of this Convention.

Article 37

Relation to previous conventions

Without prejudice to Article 28, paragraph 2, of this Convention, this Convention replaces, as between Parties to it, the Arrangements of 5 July 1922, 31 May 1924, 12 May 1926, 30 June 1928 and 30 July 1935, the Conventions of 28 October 1933 and 10 February 1938, the Protocol of 14 September 1939 and the Agreement of 15 October 1946.

Chapter VII
Final Clauses

Article 38

Settlement of disputes

Any dispute between Parties to this Convention relating to its interpretation or application, which cannot be settled by other means, shall be referred to the International Court of Justice at the request of any one of the parties to the dispute.

Article 39

Signature, ratification and accession

1. This Convention shall be opened for signature at Geneva on 28 July 1951 and shall thereafter be deposited with the Secretary-General of the United Nations. It shall be open for signature at the European Office of the United Nations from 28 July to 31 August 1951 and shall be re-opened for signature at the Headquarters of the United Nations from 17 September 1951 to 31 December 1952.

2. This Convention shall be open for signature on behalf of all States Members of the United Nations, and also on behalf of any other State invited to attend the Conference of Plenipotentiaries on the Status of Refugees and Stateless Persons or to which an invitation to sign will have been addressed by the General Assembly. It shall be ratified and the instruments of ratification shall be deposited with the Secretary-General of the United Nations.

3. This Convention shall be open from 28 July 1951 for accession by the States referred to in paragraph 2 of this Article. Accession shall be effected by the deposit of an instrument of accession with the Secretary-General of the United Nations.

Article 40

Territorial application clause

1. Any State may, at the time of signature, ratification or accession, declare that this Convention shall extend to all or any of the territories for the international relations of which it is responsible. Such a declaration shall take effect when the Convention enters into force for the State concerned.

2. At any time thereafter any such extension shall be made by notification addressed to the Secretary-General of the United Nations and shall take effect as from the ninetieth day after the day of receipt by the Secretary-General of the United Nations of this notification, or as from the date of entry into force of the Convention for the State concerned, whichever is the later.

3. With respect to those territories to which this Convention is not extended at the time of signature, ratification or accession, each State concerned shall consider the possibility of taking the necessary steps in

order to extend the application of this Convention to such territories, subject, where necessary for constitutional reasons, to the consent of the Governments of such territories.

Article 41

Federal clause

In the case of a Federal or non-unitary State, the following provisions shall apply:

(a) With respect to those articles of this Convention that come within the legislative jurisdiction of the federal legislative authority, the obligations of the Federal Government shall to this extent be the same as those of parties which are not Federal States;

(b) With respect to those articles of this Convention that come within the legislative jurisdiction of constituent States, provinces or cantons which are not, under the constitutional system of the federation, bound to take legislative action, the Federal Government shall bring such Articles with a favourable recommendation to the notice of the appropriate authorities of States, provinces or cantons at the earliest possible moment;

(c) A Federal State Party to this Convention shall, at the request of any other Contracting State transmitted through the Secretary-General of the United Nations, supply a statement of the law and practice of the Federation and its constituent units in regard to any particular provision of the Convention showing the extent to which effect has been given to that provision by legislative or other action.

Article 42

Reservations

1. At the time of signature, ratification or accession, any State may make reservations to Articles of the Convention other than to Articles 1, 3, 4, 16(1), 33, 36–46 inclusive.

2. Any State making a reservation in accordance with paragraph 1 of this article may at any time withdraw the reservation by a communication to that effect addressed to the Secretary-General of the United Nations.

Article 43

Entry into force

1. This Convention shall come into force on the ninetieth day following the day of deposit of the sixth instrument of ratification or accession.

2. For each State ratifying or acceding to the Convention after the deposit of the sixth instrument of ratification or accession, the Convention shall enter into force on the ninetieth day following the date of deposit by such State of its instrument of ratification or accession.

Article 44

Denunciation

1. Any Contracting State may denounce this Convention at any time by a notification addressed to the Secretary-General of the United Nations.

2. Such denunciation shall take effect for the Contracting State concerned one year from the date upon which it is received by the Secretary-General of the United Nations.

3. Any State which has made a declaration or notification under Article 40 may, at any time thereafter, by a notification to the Secretary-General of the United Nations, declare that the Convention shall cease to extend to such territory one year after the date of receipt of the notification by the Secretary-General.

Article 45

Revision

1. Any Contracting State may request revision of this Convention at any time by a notification addressed to the Secretary-General of the United Nations.

2. The General Assembly of the United Nations shall recommend the steps, if any, to be taken in respect of such request.

Article 46

Notifications by the Secretary-General of the United Nations

The Secretary-General of the United Nations shall inform all Members of the United Nations and non-member States referred to in article 39:

(a) Of declarations and notifications in accordance with section B of Article 1;
(b) Of signatures, ratifications and accessions in accordance with Article 39;
(c) Of declarations and notifications in accordance with Article 40;
(d) Of reservations and withdrawals in accordance with Article 42;
(e) Of the date on which this Convention will come into force in accordance with Article 43;
(f) Of denunciations and notifications in accordance with Article 44;
(g) Of requests for revision in accordance with Article 45.

In faith whereof the undersigned, duly authorised, have signed this Convention on behalf of their respective Governments.

Done at Geneva, this twenty-eighth day of July, one thousand nine hundred and fifty-one, in a single copy, of which the English and French texts are equally authentic and which shall remain deposited in the archives of the United Nations, and certified true copies of which shall be delivered to all Members of the United Nations and to the non-member States referred to in Article 39.

APPENDIX J

International Covenant on Civil and Political Rights 1966

Preamble

The States Parties to the present Covenant,

Considering that, in accordance with the principles proclaimed in the Charter of the United Nations, recognition of the inherent dignity and of the equal and inalienable rights of all members of the human family is the foundation of freedom, justice and peace in the world,

Recognizing that these rights derive from the inherent dignity of the human person,

Recognizing that, in accordance with the Universal Declaration of Human Rights, the ideal of free human beings enjoying civil and political freedom and freedom from fear and want can only be achieved if conditions are created whereby everyone may enjoy his civil and political rights, as well as his economic, social and cultural rights,

Considering the obligation of States under the Charter of the United Nations to promote universal respect for, and observance of, human rights and freedoms,

Realizing that the individual, having duties to other individuals and to the community to which he belongs, is under a responsibility to strive for the promotion and observance of the rights recognized in the present Covenant,

Agree upon the following articles:

Part I

Article 1

1. All peoples have the right of self-determination. By virtue of that right they freely determine their political status and freely pursue their economic, social and cultural development.

2. All peoples may, for their own ends, freely dispose of their natural wealth and resources without prejudice to any obligations arising out of international economic co-operation, based upon the principle of mutual benefit, and international law. In no case may a people be deprived of its own means of subsistence.

3. The States Parties to the present Covenant, including those having responsibility for the administration of Non-Self-Governing and Trust Territories, shall promote the realization of the right of self-determination, and shall respect that right, in conformity with the provisions of the Charter of the United Nations.

Part II

Article 2

1. Each State Party to the present Covenant undertakes to respect and to ensure to all individuals within its territory and subject to its jurisdiction the rights recognized in the present Covenant, without distinction of any kind, such as race, colour, sex, language, religion, political or other opinion, national or social origin, property, birth or other status.

2. Where not already provided for by existing legislative or other measures, each State Party to the present Covenant undertakes to take the necessary steps, in accordance with its constitutional processes and with the provisions of the present Covenant, to adopt such legislative or other measures as may be necessary to give effect to the rights recognized in the present Covenant.

3. Each State Party to the present Covenant undertakes:

(a) To ensure that any person whose rights or freedoms as herein recognized are violated shall have an effective remedy, notwithstanding that the violation has been committed by persons acting in an official capacity;

(b) To ensure that any person claiming such a remedy shall have his right thereto determined by competent judicial, administrative or legislative authorities, or by any other competent authority provided for by the legal system of the State, and to develop the possibilities of judicial remedy;

(c) To ensure that the competent authorities shall enforce such remedies when granted.

Article 3

The States Parties to the present Covenant undertake to ensure the equal right of men and women to the enjoyment of all civil and political rights set forth in the present Covenant.

Article 4

1. In time of public emergency which threatens the life of the nation and the existence of which is officially proclaimed, the States Parties to the present Covenant may take measures derogating from their obligations under the present Covenant to the extent strictly required by the exigencies of the situation, provided that such measures are not inconsistent with their other obligations under international law and do not involve discrimination solely on the ground of race, colour, sex, language, religion or social origin.

2. No derogation from Articles 6, 7, 8 (paragraphs 1 and 2), 11, 15, 16 and 18 may be made under this provision.

3. Any State Party to the present Covenant availing itself of the right of derogation shall immediately inform the other States Parties to the present Covenant, through the intermediary of the Secretary-General of the United Nations, of the provisions from which it has derogated and of the reasons by which it was actuated. A further communication shall be made, through the same intermediary, on the date on which it terminates such derogation.

Article 5

1. Nothing in the present Covenant may be interpreted as implying for any State, group or person any right to engage in any activity or perform any act aimed at the destruction of any of the rights and freedoms recognized herein or at their limitation to a greater extent than is provided for in the present Covenant.

2. There shall be no restriction upon or derogation from any of the fundamental human rights recognized or existing in any State Party to the present Covenant pursuant to law, conventions, regulations or custom on the pretext that the present Covenant does not recognize such rights or that it recognizes them to a lesser extent.

Part III

Article 6

1. Every human being has the inherent right to life. This right shall be protected by law. No one shall be arbitrarily deprived of his life.

2. In countries which have not abolished the death penalty, sentence of death may be imposed only for the most serious crimes in accordance with the law in force at the time of the commission of the crime and not contrary to the provisions of the present Covenant and to the Convention on the Prevention and Punishment of the Crime of Genocide. This penalty can only be carried out pursuant to a final judgement rendered by a competent court.

3. When deprivation of life constitutes the crime of genocide, it is understood that nothing in this Article shall authorize any State Party to the present Covenant to derogate in any way from any obligation assumed under the provisions of the Convention on the Prevention and Punishment of the Crime of Genocide.

4. Anyone sentenced to death shall have the right to seek pardon or commutation of the sentence. Amnesty, pardon or commutation of the sentence of death may be granted in all cases.

5. Sentence of death shall not be imposed for crimes committed by persons below eighteen years of age and shall not be carried out on pregnant women.

6. Nothing in this Article shall be invoked to delay or to prevent the abolition of capital punishment by any State Party to the present Covenant.

Article 7

No one shall be subjected to torture or to cruel, inhuman or degrading treatment or punishment. In particular, no one shall be subjected without his free consent to medical or scientific experimentation.

Article 8

1. No one shall be held in slavery; slavery and the slave-trade in all their forms shall be prohibited.

2. No one shall be held in servitude.

3. (a) No one shall be required to perform forced or compulsory labour;
   (b) Paragraph 3 (a) shall not be held to preclude, in countries where imprisonment with hard labour may be imposed as a punishment for a crime, the performance of hard labour in pursuance of a sentence to such punishment by a competent court;
   (c) For the purpose of this paragraph the term 'forced or compulsory labour' shall not include:
      (i) Any work or service, not referred to in sub-paragraph (b), normally required of a person who is under detention in consequence of a lawful order of a court, or of a person during conditional release from such detention;
      (ii) Any service of a military character and, in countries where conscientious objection is recognized, any national service required by law of conscientious objectors;
      (iii) Any service exacted in cases of emergency or calamity threatening the life or well-being of the community;
      (iv) Any work or service which forms part of normal civil obligations.

Article 9

1. Everyone has the right to liberty and security of person. No one shall be subjected to arbitrary arrest or detention. No one shall be deprived of his liberty except on such grounds and in accordance with such procedure as are established by law.

2. Anyone who is arrested shall be informed, at the time of arrest, of the reasons for his arrest and shall be promptly informed of any charges against him.

3. Anyone arrested or detained on a criminal charge shall be brought promptly before a judge or other officer authorized by law to exercise judicial power and shall be entitled to trial within a reasonable time or to release. It shall not be the general rule that persons awaiting trial shall be detained in custody, but release may be subject to guarantees to appear for trial, at any other stage of the judicial proceedings, and, should occasion arise, for execution of the judgment.

4. Anyone who is deprived of his liberty by arrest or detention shall be entitled to take proceedings before a court, in order that that court may decide without delay on the lawfulness of his detention and order his release if the detention is not lawful.

5. Anyone who has been the victim of unlawful arrest or detention shall have an enforceable right to compensation.

Article 10

1. All persons deprived of their liberty shall be treated with humanity and with respect for the inherent dignity of the human person.

2. (a) Accused persons shall, save in exceptional circumstances, be segregated from convicted persons and shall be subject to separate treatment appropriate to their status as unconvicted persons;
   (b) Accused juvenile persons shall be separated from adults and brought as speedily as possible for adjudication.

3. The penitentiary system shall comprise treatment of prisoners the essential aim of which shall be their reformation and social rehabilitation. Juvenile offenders shall be segregated from adults and be accorded treatment appropriate to their age and legal status.

Article 11

No one shall be imprisoned merely on the ground of inability to fulfil a contractual obligation.

Article 12

1. Everyone lawfully within the territory of a State shall, within that territory, have the right to liberty of movement and freedom to choose his residence.

2. Everyone shall be free to leave any country, including his own.

3. The above-mentioned rights shall not be subject to any restrictions except those which are provided by law, are necessary to protect national security, public order (*ordre public*), public health or morals or the rights and freedoms of others, and are consistent with the other rights recognized in the present Covenant.

4. No one shall be arbitrarily deprived of the right to enter his own country.

Article 13

An alien lawfully in the territory of a State Party to the present Covenant may be expelled therefrom only in pursuance of a decision reached in accordance with law and shall, except where compelling reasons of national security otherwise require, be allowed to submit the reasons against his expulsion and to have his case reviewed by, and be represented for the purpose before, the competent authority or a person or persons especially designated by the competent authority.

Article 14

1. All persons shall be equal before the courts and tribunals. In the determination of any criminal charge against him, or of his rights and obligations in a suit at law, everyone shall be entitled to a fair and public hearing by a competent, independent and impartial tribunal established by law. The Press and the public may be excluded from all or part of a trial for reasons of morals, public order (*ordre public*) or national security in a democratic society, or when the interest of the private lives of the parties so requires, or to the extent strictly necessary in the opinion of the court in special circumstances where publicity would prejudice the interests of justice; but any judgement rendered in a criminal case or in a suit at law shall be made public except where the interest of juvenile persons otherwise requires or the proceedings concern matrimonial disputes or the guardianship of children.

2. Everyone charged with a criminal offence shall have the right to be presumed innocent until proved guilty according to law.

3. In the determination of any criminal charge against him, everyone shall be entitled to the following minimum guarantees, in full equality:
   (a) To be informed promptly and in detail in a language which he understands of the nature and cause of the charge against him;
   (b) To have adequate time and facilities for the preparation of his defence and to communicate with counsel of his own choosing;
   (c) To be tried without undue delay;

(d) To be tried in his presence, and to defend himself in person or through legal assistance of his own choosing; to be informed, if he does not have legal assistance, of this right; and to have legal assistance assigned to him, in any case where the interests of justice so require, and without payment by him in any such case if he does not have sufficient means to pay for it;

(e) To examine, or have examined, the witnesses against him and to obtain the attendance and examination of witnesses on his behalf under the same conditions as witnesses against him;

(f) To have the free assistance of an interpreter if he cannot understand or speak the language used in court;

(g) Not to be compelled to testify against himself or to confess guilt.

4. In the case of juvenile persons, the procedure shall be such as will take account of their age and the desirability of promoting their rehabilitation.

5. Everyone convicted of a crime shall have the right to his conviction and sentence being reviewed by a higher tribunal according to law.

6. When a person has by a final decision been convicted of a criminal offence and when subsequently his conviction has been reversed or he has been pardoned on the ground that a new or newly discovered fact shows conclusively that there has been a miscarriage of justice, the person who has suffered punishment as a result of such conviction shall be compensated according to law, unless it is proved that the non-disclosure of the unknown fact in time is wholly or partly attributable to him.

7. No one shall be liable to be tried or punished again for an offence for which he has already been finally convicted or acquitted in accordance with the law and penal procedure of each country.

Article 15

1. No one shall be held guilty of any criminal offence on account of any act or omission which did not constitute a criminal offence, under national or international law, at the time when it was committed. Nor shall a heavier penalty be imposed than the one that was applicable at the time when the criminal offence was committed. If, subsequent to the commission of the offence, provision is made by law for the imposition of the lighter penalty, the offender shall benefit thereby.

2. Nothing in this Article shall prejudice the trial and punishment of any person for any act or omission which, at the time when it was committed, was criminal according to the general principles of law recognized by the community of nations.

Article 16

Everyone shall have the right to recognition everywhere as a person before the law.

Article 17

1. No one shall be subjected to arbitrary or unlawful interference with his privacy, family, home or correspondence, nor to unlawful attacks on his honour and reputation.

2. Everyone has the right to the protection of the law against such interference or attacks.

Article 18

1. Everyone shall have the right to freedom of thought, conscience and religion. This right shall include freedom to have or to adopt a religion or belief of his choice, and freedom, either individually or in community with others and in public or private, to manifest his religion or belief in worship, observance, practice and teaching.

2. No one shall be subject to coercion which would impair his freedom to have or to adopt a religion or belief of his choice.

3. Freedom to manifest one's religion or beliefs may be subject only to such limitations as are prescribed by law and are necessary to protect public safety, order, health, or morals or the fundamental rights and freedoms of others.

4. The States Parties to the present Covenant undertake to have respect for the liberty of parents and, when applicable, legal guardians to ensure the religious and moral education of their children in conformity with their own convictions.

Article 19

1. Everyone shall have the right to hold opinions without interference.

2. Everyone shall have the right to freedom of expression; this right shall include freedom to seek, receive and impart information and ideas of all kinds, regardless of frontiers, either orally, in writing or in print, in the form of art, or through any other media of his choice.

3. The exercise of the rights provided for in paragraph 2 of this article carries with it special duties and responsibilities. It may therefore be subject to certain restrictions, but these shall only be such as are provided by law and are necessary:

(a) For respect of the rights or reputations of others;

(b) For the protection of national security or of public order (*ordre public*), or of public health or morals.

Article 20

1. Any propaganda for war shall be prohibited by law.

2. Any advocacy of national, racial or religious hatred that constitutes incitement to discrimination, hostility or violence shall be prohibited by law.

Article 21

The right of peaceful assembly shall be recognized. No restrictions may be placed on the exercise of this right other than those imposed in conformity with the law and which are necessary in a democratic society in the interests of national security or public safety, public order (*ordre public*), the protection of public health or morals or the protection of the rights and freedoms of others.

Article 22

1. Everyone shall have the right to freedom of association with others, including the right to form and join trade unions for the protection of his interests.

2. No restrictions may be placed on the exercise of this right other than those which are prescribed by law and which are necessary in a democratic society in the interests of national security or public safety, public order (*ordre public*), the protection of public health or morals or the protection of the rights and freedoms of others. This Article shall not prevent the imposition of lawful restrictions on members of the armed forces and of the police in their exercise of this right.

3. Nothing in this Article shall authorize States Parties to the International Labour Organisation Convention of 1948 concerning Freedom of Association and Protection of the Right to Organize to take legislative measures which would prejudice, or to apply the law in such a manner as to prejudice, the guarantees provided for in that Convention.

Article 23

1. The family is the natural and fundamental group unit of society and is entitled to protection by society and the State.

2. The right of men and women of marriageable age to marry and to found a family shall be recognized.

3. No marriage shall be entered into without the free and full consent of the intending spouses.

4. States Parties to the present Covenant shall take appropriate steps to ensure equality of rights and responsibilities of spouses as to marriage, during marriage and at its dissolution. In the case of dissolution, provision shall be made for the necessary protection of any children.

Article 24

1. Every child shall have, without any discrimination as to race, colour, sex, language, religion, national or social origin, property or birth, the right to such measures of protection as are required by his status as a minor, on the part of his family, society and the State.

2. Every child shall be registered immediately after birth and shall have a name.

3. Every child has the right to acquire a nationality.

Article 25

Every citizen shall have the right and the opportunity, without any of the distinctions mentioned in Article 2 and without unreasonable restrictions:

(a) To take part in the conduct of public affairs, directly or through freely chosen representatives;

(b) To vote and to be elected at genuine periodic elections which shall be by universal and equal suffrage and shall be held by secret ballot, guaranteeing the free expression of the will of the electors;

(c) To have access, on general terms of equality, to public service in his country.

Article 26

All persons are equal before the law and are entitled without any discrimination to the equal protection of the law. In this respect, the law shall prohibit any discrimination and guarantee to all persons equal and effective protection against discrimination on any ground such as race, colour, sex, language, religion, political or other opinion, national or social origin, property, birth or other status.

Article 27

In those States in which ethnic, religious or linguistic minorities exist, persons belonging to such minorities shall not be denied the right, in community with the other members of their group, to enjoy their own culture, to profess and practise their own religion, or to use their own language.

Part IV

Article 28

1. There shall be established a Human Rights Committee (hereafter referred to in the present Covenant as the Committee). It shall consist of eighteen members and shall carry out the functions hereinafter provided.

2. The Committee shall be composed of nationals of the States Parties to the present Covenant who shall be persons of high moral character and recognized competence in the field of human rights, consideration being given to the usefulness of the participation of some persons having legal experience.

3. The members of the Committee shall be elected and shall serve in their personal capacity.

Article 29

1. The members of the Committee shall be elected by secret ballot from a list of persons possessing the qualifications prescribed in Article 28 and nominated for the purpose by the States Parties to the present Covenant.

2. Each State Party to the present Covenant may nominate not more than two persons. These persons shall be nationals of the nominating State.

3. A person shall be eligible for renomination.

Article 30

1. The initial election shall be held no later than six months after the date of the entry into force of the present Covenant.

2. At least four months before the date of each election to the Committee, other than an election to fill a vacancy declared in accordance with Article 34, the Secretary-General of the United Nations shall address a written invitation to the States Parties to the present Covenant to submit their nominations for membership of the Committee within three months.

3. The Secretary-General of the United Nations shall prepare a list in alphabetical order of all the persons thus nominated, with an indication of the States Parties which have nominated them, and shall submit it to the States Parties to the present Covenant no later than one month before the date of each election.

4. Elections of the members of the Committee shall be held at a meeting of the States Parties to the present Covenant convened by the Secretary-General of the United Nations at the Headquarters of the United Nations. At that meeting, for which two thirds of the States Parties to the present Covenant shall constitute a quorum, the persons elected to the Committee shall be those nominees who obtain the largest number of votes and an absolute majority of the votes of the representatives of States Parties present and voting.

Article 31

1. The Committee may not include more than one national of the same State.

2. In the election of the Committee, consideration shall be given to equitable geographical distribution of membership and to the representation of the different forms of civilization and of the principal legal systems.

Article 32

1. The members of the Committee shall be elected for a term of four years. They shall be eligible for re-election if renominated. However, the terms of nine of the members elected at the first election shall expire at the end of two years; immediately after the first election, the names of these nine members shall be chosen by lot by the Chairman of the meeting referred to in Article 30, paragraph 4.

2. Elections at the expiry of office shall be held in accordance with the preceding Articles of this part of the present Covenant.

Article 33

1. If, in the unanimous opinion of the other members, a member of the Committee has ceased to carry out his functions for any cause other than absence of a temporary character, the Chairman of the Committee shall notify the Secretary-General of the United Nations, who shall then declare the seat of that member to be vacant.

2. In the event of the death or the resignation of a member of the Committee, the Chairman shall immediately notify the Secretary-General of the United Nations, who shall declare the seat vacant from the date of death or the date on which the resignation takes effect.

Article 34

1. When a vacancy is declared in accordance with Article 33 and if the term of office of the member to be replaced does not expire within six months of the declaration of the vacancy, the Secretary-General of the United Nations shall notify each of the States Parties to the present Covenant, which may within two months submit nominations in accordance with Article 29 for the purpose of fulfilling the vacancy.

2. The Secretary-General of the United Nations shall prepare a list in alphabetical order of the persons thus nominated and shall submit it to the States Parties to the present Covenant. The election to fill the vacancy shall then take place in accordance with the relevant provisions of this part of the present Covenant.

3. A member of the Committee elected to fill a vacancy declared in accordance with Article 33 shall hold office for the remainder of the term of the member who vacated the seat on the Committee under the provisions of that Article.

Article 35

The members of the Committee shall, with the approval of the General Assembly of the United Nations, receive emoluments from United Nations resources on such terms and conditions as the General Assembly may decide, having regard to the importance of the Committee's responsibilities.

Article 36

The Secretary-General of the United Nations shall provide the necessary staff and facilities for the effective performance of the functions of the Committee under the present Covenant.

Article 37

1. The Secretary-General of the United Nations shall convene the initial meeting of the Committee at the Headquarters of the United Nations.

2. After its initial meeting, the Committee shall meet at such times as shall be provided in its rules of procedure.

3. The Committee shall normally meet at the Headquarters of the United Nations or at the United Nations Office at Geneva.

Article 38

Every member of the Committee shall, before taking up his duties, make a solemn declaration in open committee that he will perform his functions impartially and conscientiously.

Article 39

1. The Committee shall elect its officers for a term of two years. They may be re-elected.

2. The Committee shall establish its own rules of procedure, but these rules shall provide, *inter alia*, that:
   (a) Twelve members shall constitute a quorum;
   (b) Decisions of the Committee shall be made by a majority vote of the members present.

Article 40

1. The States Parties to the present Covenant undertake to submit reports on the measures they have adopted which give effect to the rights recognized herein and on the progress made in the enjoyment of those rights:
   (a) Within one year of the entry into force of the present Covenant for the States Parties concerned;
   (b) Thereafter whenever the Committee so requests.

2. All reports shall be submitted to the Secretary-General of the United Nations, who shall transmit them to the Committee for consideration. Reports shall indicate the factors and difficulties, if any, affecting the implementation of the present Covenant.

3. The Secretary-General of the United Nations may, after consultation with the Committee, transmit to the specialized agencies concerned copies of such parts of the reports as may fall within their field of competence.

4. The Committee shall study the reports submitted by the States Parties to the present Covenant. It shall transmit its reports, and such general comments as it may consider appropriate, to the States Parties. The Committee may also transmit to the Economic and Social Council these comments along with the copies of the reports it has received from States Parties to the present Covenant.

5. The States Parties to the present Covenant may submit to the Committee observations on any comments that may be made in accordance with paragraph 4 of this Article.

Article 41

1. A State Party to the present Covenant may at any time declare under this Article that it recognizes the competence of the Committee to receive and consider communications to the effect that a State Party claims that another State Party is not fulfilling its obligations under the present Covenant. Communications under this Article may be received and considered only if submitted by a State Party which has made a declaration recognizing in regard to itself the competence of the Committee. No communication shall be received by the Committee if it concerns a State Party which has not made such a declaration. Communications received under this Article shall be dealt with in accordance with the following procedure:

(a) If a State Party to the present Covenant considers that another State Party is not giving effect to the provisions of the present Covenant, it may, by written communication, bring the matter to the attention of that State Party. Within three months after the receipt of the communication the receiving State shall afford the State which sent the communication an explanation, or any other statement in writing clarifying the matter which should include, to the extent possible and pertinent, reference to domestic procedures and remedies taken, pending, or available in the matter.

(b) If the matter is not adjusted to the satisfaction of both States Parties concerned within six months after the receipt by the receiving State of the initial communication, either State shall have the right to refer the matter to the Committee, by notice given to the Committee and to the other State.

(c) The Committee shall deal with a matter referred to it only after it has ascertained that all available domestic remedies have been invoked and exhausted in the matter, in conformity with the generally recognized principles of international law. This shall not be the rule where the application of the remedies is unreasonably prolonged.

(d) The Committee shall hold closed meetings when examining communications under this Article.

(e) Subject to the provisions of sub-paragraph (c), the Committee shall make available its good offices to the States Parties concerned with a view to a friendly solution of the matter on the basis of respect for human rights and fundamental freedoms as recognized in the present Covenant.

(f) In any matter referred to it, the Committee may call upon the States Parties concerned, referred to in sub-paragraph (b), to supply any relevant information.

(g) The States Parties concerned, referred to in sub-paragraph (b), shall have the right to be represented when the matter is being considered in the Committee and to make submissions orally and/or in writing.

(h) The Committee shall, within twelve months after the date of receipt of notice under sub-paragraph (b), submit a report:

(i) If a solution within the terms of sub-paragraph (e) is reached, the Committee shall confine its report to a brief statement of the facts and of the solution reached;

(ii) If a solution within the terms of sub-paragraph (e) is not reached, the Committee shall confine its report to a brief statement of the facts; the written submissions and record of the oral submissions made by the States Parties concerned shall be attached to the report.

In every matter, the report shall be communicated to the States Parties concerned.

2. The provisions of this Article shall come into force when ten States Parties to the present Covenant have made declarations under paragraph 1 of this Article. Such declarations shall be deposited by the States Parties with the Secretary-General of the United Nations, who shall transmit copies thereof to the other States Parties. A declaration may be withdrawn at any time by notification to the Secretary-General. Such a withdrawal shall not prejudice the consideration of any matter which is the subject of a communication already transmitted under this Article; no further communication by any State Party shall be received after the notification of withdrawal of the declaration has been received by the Secretary-General, unless the State Party concerned has made a new declaration.

Article 42

1. (a) If a matter referred to the Committee in accordance with Article 41 is not resolved to the satisfaction of the States Parties concerned, the Committee may, with the prior consent of the States Parties concerned, appoint an *ad hoc* Conciliation Commission (hereinafter referred to as the Commission). The good offices of the Commission shall be made available to the States Parties concerned with a view to an amicable solution of the matter on the basis of respect for the present Covenant;

(b) The Commission shall consist of five persons acceptable to the States Parties concerned. If the States Parties concerned fail to reach agreement within three months on all or part of the composition of the Commission, the members of the Commission concerning whom no agreement has been reached shall be elected by secret ballot by a two-thirds majority vote of the Committee from among its members.

2. The members of the Commission shall serve in their personal capacity. They shall not be nationals of the States Parties concerned, or of a State not party to the present Covenant, or of a State Party which has not made a declaration under Article 41.

3. The Commission shall elect its own Chairman and adopt its own rules of procedure.

4. The meetings of the Commission shall normally be held at the Headquarters of the United Nations or at the United Nations Office at Geneva. However, they may be held at such other convenient places as the Commission may determine in consultation with the Secretary-General of the United Nations and the States Parties concerned.

5. The secretariat provided in accordance with Article 36 shall also service the commissions appointed under this Article.

6. The information received and collated by the Committee shall be made available to the Commission and the Commission may call upon the States Parties concerned to supply any other relevant information.

7. When the Commission has fully considered the matter, but in any event not later than twelve months after having been seized of the matter, it shall submit to the Chairman of the Committee a report for communication to the States Parties concerned.

(a) If the Commission is unable to complete its consideration of the matter within twelve months, it shall confine its report to a brief statement of the status of its consideration of the matter.

(b) If an amicable solution to the matter on the basis of respect for human rights as recognized in the present Covenant is reached, the Commission shall confine its report to a brief statement of the facts and of the solution reached.

(c) If a solution within the terms of sub-paragraph (b) is not reached, the Commission's report shall embody its findings on all questions of fact relevant to the issues between the States Parties concerned, and its views on the possibilities of an amicable solution of the matter. This report shall also contain the written submissions and a record of the oral submissions made by the States Parties concerned.

(d) If the Commission's report is submitted under sub-paragraph (c), the States Parties concerned shall, within three months of the receipt of the report, notify the Chairman of the Committee whether or not they accept the contents of the report of the Commission.

8. The provisions of this Article are without prejudice to the responsibilities of the Committee under Article 41.

9. The States Parties concerned shall share equally all the expenses of the members of the Commission in accordance with estimates to be provided by the Secretary-General of the United Nations.

10. The Secretary-General of the United Nations shall be empowered to pay the expenses of the members of the Commission, if necessary, before reimbursement by the States Parties concerned, in accordance with paragraph 9 of this Article.

Article 43

The members of the Committee, and of the *ad hoc* conciliation commissions which may be appointed under Article 42, shall be entitled to the facilities, privileges and immunities of experts on mission for the United Nations as laid down in the relevant sections of the Convention on the Privileges and Immunities of the United Nations.

Article 44

The provisions for the implementation of the present Covenant shall apply without prejudice to the procedures prescribed in the field of human rights by or under the constituent instruments and the conventions of the United Nations and of the specialized agencies and shall not prevent the States Parties to the present Covenant from having recourse to other procedures for settling a dispute in accordance with general or special international agreements in force between them.

Article 45

The Committee shall submit to the General Assembly of the United Nations, through the Economic and Social Council, an annual report on its activities.

Part V

Article 46

Nothing in the present Covenant shall be interpreted as impairing the provisions of the Charter of the United Nations and of the constitutions of the specialized agencies which define the respective responsibilities of the various organs of the United Nations and of the specialized agencies in regard to the matters dealt with in the present Covenant.

Article 47

Nothing in the present Covenant shall be interpreted as impairing the inherent right of all peoples to enjoy and utilize fully and freely their natural wealth and resources.

Part VI

Article 48

1. The present Covenant is open for signature by any State Member of the United Nations or member of any of its specialized agencies, by any State Party to the Statute of the International Court of Justice, and by any other State which has been invited by the General Assembly of the United Nations to become a party to the present Covenant.

2. The present Covenant is subject to ratification. Instruments of ratification shall be deposited with the Secretary-General of the United Nations.

3. The present Covenant shall be open to accession by any State referred to in paragraph 1 of this article.

4. Accession shall be effected by the deposit of an instrument of accession with the Secretary-General of the United Nations.

5. The Secretary-General of the United Nations shall inform all States which have signed this Covenant or acceded to it of the deposit of each instrument of ratification or accession.

Article 49

1. The present Covenant shall enter into force three months after the date of the deposit with the Secretary-General of the United Nations of the thirty-fifth instrument of ratification or instrument of accession.

2. For each State ratifying the present Covenant or acceding to it after the deposit of the thirty-fifth instrument of ratification or instrument of accession, the present Covenant shall enter into force three months after the date of the deposit of its own instrument of ratification or instrument of accession.

Article 50

The provisions of the present Covenant shall extend to all parts of federal States without any limitations or exceptions.

Article 51

1. Any State Party to the present Covenant may propose an amendment and file it with the Secretary-General of the United Nations. The Secretary-General of the United Nations shall thereupon communicate any proposed amendments to the States Parties to the present Covenant with a request that they notify him

whether they favour a conference of States Parties for the purpose of considering and voting upon the proposals. In the event that at least one third of the States Parties favours such a conference, the Secretary-General shall convene the conference under the auspices of the United Nations. Any amendment adopted by a majority of the States Parties present and voting at the conference shall be submitted to the General Assembly of the United Nations for approval.

2. Amendments shall come into force when they have been approved by the General Assembly of the United Nations and accepted by a two-thirds majority of the States Parties to the present Covenant in accordance with their respective constitutional processes.

3. When amendments come into force, they shall be binding on those States Parties which have accepted them, other States Parties still being bound by the provisions of the present Covenant and any earlier amendment which they have accepted.

Article 52

Irrespective of the notifications made under Article 48, paragraph 5, the Secretary-General of the United Nations shall inform all States referred to in paragraph 1 of the same Article of the following particulars:

(a) Signatures, ratifications and accessions under Article 48;

(b) The date of the entry into force of the present Covenant under Article 49 and the date of the entry into force of any amendments under Article 51.

Article 53

1. The present Covenant, of which the Chinese, English, French, Russian and Spanish texts are equally authentic, shall be deposited in the archives of the United Nations.

2. The Secretary-General of the United Nations shall transmit certified copies of the present Covenant to all States referred to in Article 48.

Optional Protocol to the International Covenant on Civil and Political Rights, 1966

The States Parties to the present Protocol,

Considering that in order further to achieve the purposes of the International Covenant on Civil and Political Rights (hereinafter referred to as the Covenant) and the implemenation of its provisions it would be appropriate to enable the Human Rights Committee set up in Part IV of the Covenant (hereinafter referred to as the Committee) to receive and consider, as provided in the present Protocol, communications from individuals claiming to be victims of violations of any of the rights set forth in the Covenant.

Have agreed as follows:

Article I

A State Party to the Covenant that becomes a party to the present Protocol recognizes the competence of the Committee to receive and consider communications from individuals subject to its jurisdiction who claim to be victims of a violation by that State Party of any of the rights set forth in the Covenant. No communication shall be received by the Committee if it concerns a State Party to the Covenant which is not a Party to the present Protocol.

Article 2

Subject to the provisions of Article 1, individuals who claim that any of their rights enumerated in the Covenant have been violated and who have exhausted all available domestic remedies may submit a written communication to the Committee for consideration.

Article 3

The Committee shall consider inadmissible any communciation under the present Protocol which is anonymous, or which it considers to be an abuse of the right of submission of such communications or to be incompatible with the provisions of the Covenant.

Article 4

1. Subject to the provisions of Article 3, the Committee shall bring any communications submitted to it under the present Protocol to the attention of the State Party to the present Protocol alleged to be violating any provision of the Covenant.

2. Within six months, the receiving State shall submit to the Committee written explanations or statements clarifying the matter and the remedy, if any, that may have been taken by that State.

Article 5

1. The Committee shall consider communications received under the present Protocol in the light of all written information made available to it by the individual and by the State Party concerned.

2. The Committee shall not consider any communication from an individual unless it has ascertained that:
   (a) The same matter is not being examined under another procedure of international investigation or settlement;
   (b) The individual has exhausted all available domestic remedies. This shall not be the rule where the application of the remedies is unreasonably prolonged.

3. The Committee shall hold closed meetings when examining communications under the present Protocol.

4. The Committee shall forward its views to the State Party concerned and to the individual.

Article 6

The Committee shall include in its annual report under Article 45 of the Covenant a summary of its activities under the present Protocol.

Article 7

Pending the achievement of the objectives of resolution 1514 (XV) adopted by the General Assembly of the United Nations on 14 December 1960 concerning the Declaration on the Granting of Independence to Colonial Countries and Peoples, the provisions of the present Protocol shall in no way limit the right of petition granted to these peoples by the Charter of the United Nations and other international conventions and instruments under the United Nations and its specialized agencies.

Article 8

1. The present Protocol is open for signature by any State which has signed the Covenant.

2. The present Protocol is subject to ratification by any State which has ratified or acceded to the Covenant. Instruments of ratification shall be deposited with the Secretary-General of the United Nations.

3. The present Protocol shall be open to accession by any State which has ratified or acceded to the Covenant.

4. Accession shall be effected by the deposit of an instrument of accession with the Secretary-General of the United Nations.

5. The Secretary-General of the United Nations shall inform all States which have signed the present Protocol or acceded to it of the deposit of each instrument of ratification or accession.

Article 9

1. Subject to the entry into force of the Covenant, the present Protocol shall enter into force three months after the date of the deposit with the Secretary-General of the United Nations of the tenth instrument of ratification or instrument of accession.

2. For each State ratifying the present Protocol or acceding to it after the deposit of the tenth instrument of ratification or instrument of accession, the present Protocol shall enter into force three months after the date of the deposit of its own instrument of ratification or instrument of accession.

Article 10

The provisions of the present Protocol shall extend to all parts of federal States without any limitations or exceptions.

Article 11

1. Any State Party to the present Protocol may propose an amendment and file it with the Secretary-General of the United Nations. The Secretary-General shall thereupon communicate any proposed amendments to the States Parties to the present Protocol with a request that they notify him whether they favour a conference of States Parties for the purpose of considering and voting upon the proposal. In the event that at least one third of the States Parties favours such a conference, the Secretary-General shall convene the conference under the auspices of the United Nations. Any amendment adopted by a majority of the States Parties present and voting at the conference shall be submitted to the General Assembly of the United Nations for approval.

2. Amendments shall come into force when they have been approved by the General Assembly of the United Nations and accepted by a two-thirds majority of the States Parties to the present Protocol in accordance with their respective constitutional processes.

3. When amendments come into force, they shall be binding on those States Parties which have accepted them, other States Parties still being bound by the provisions of the present Protocol and any earlier amendment which they have accepted.

Article 12

1. Any State Party may denounce the present Protocol at any time by written notification addressed to the Secretary-General of the United Nations. Denunciation shall take effect three months after the date of receipt of the notification by the Secretary-General.

2. Denunciation shall be without prejudice to the continued application of the provisions of the present Protocol to any communication submitted under Article 2 before the effective date of denunciation.

Article 13

Irrespective of the notifications made under Article 8, paragraph 5, of the present Protocol, the Secretary-General of the United Nations shall inform all States referred to in Article 48, paragraph 1, of the Covenant of the following particulars:

- (a) Signatures, ratifications and accessions under Article 8;
- (b) The date of the entry into force of the present Protocol under Article 9 and the date of the entry into force of any amendments under Article 11;
- (c) Denunciations under article 12.

Article 14

1. The present Protocol, of which the Chinese, English, French, Russian and Spanish texts are equally authentic, shall be deposited in the archives of the United Nations.

2. The Secretary-General of the United Nations shall transmit certified copies of the present Protocol to all States referred to in Article 48 of the Covenant.

APPENDIX K

International Covenant on Economic, Social and Cultural Rights, 1966

Preamble

The States Parties to the present Covenant,

Considering that, in accordance with the principles proclaimed in the Charter of the United Nations, recognition of the inherent dignity and of the equal and inalienable rights of all members of the human family is the foundation of freedom, justice and peace in the world,

Recognizing that these rights derive from the inherent dignity of the human person,

Recognizing that, in accordance with the Universal Declaration of Human Rights, the ideal of free human beings enjoying freedom from fear and want can only be achieved if conditions are created whereby everyone may enjoy his economic, social and cultural rights, as well as his civil and political rights,

Considering the obligation of States under the Charter of the United Nations to promote universal respect for, and observance of, human rights and freedoms,

Realizing that the individual, having duties to other individuals and to the community to which he belongs, is under a responsibility to strive for the promotion and observance of the rights recognized in the present Covenant,

Agree upon the following articles:

Part I

Article 1

1. All peoples have the right of self-determination. By virtue of that right they freely determine their political status and freely pursue their economic, social and cultural development.

2. All peoples may, for their own ends, freely dispose of their natural wealth and resources without prejudice to any obligations arising out of international economic co-operation, based upon the principle of mutual benefit, and international law. In no case may a people be deprived of its own means of subsistence.

3. The States Parties to the present Covenant, including those having responsibility for the administration of Non-Self-Governing and Trust Territories, shall promote the realization of the right of self-determination, and shall respect that right, in conformity with the provisions of the Charter of the United Nations.

Part II

Article 2

1. Each State Party to the present Covenant undertakes to take steps, individually and through international assistance and co-operation, especially economic and technical, to the maximum of its available resources, with a view to achieving progressively the full realization of the rights recognized in the present Covenant by all appropriate means, including particularly the adoption of legislative measures.

2. The States Parties to the present Covenant undertake to guarantee that the rights enunciated in the present Covenant will be exercised without discrimination of any kind as to race, colour, sex, language, religion, political or other opinion, national or social origin, property, birth or other status.

3. Developing countries, with due regard to human rights and their national economy, may determine to what extent they would guarantee the economic rights recognized in the present Covenant to non-nationals.

Article 3

The States Parties to the present Covenant undertake to ensure the equal right of men and women to the enjoyment of all economic, social and cultural rights set forth in the present Covenant.

Article 4

The States Parties to the present Covenant recognize that, in the enjoyment of those rights provided by the State in conformity with the present Covenant, the State may subject such rights only to such limitations as are determined by law only in so far as this may be compatible with the nature of these rights and solely for the purpose of promoting the general welfare in a democratic society.

Article 5

1. Nothing in the present Covenant may be interpreted as implying for any State, group or person any right to engage in any activity or to perform any act aimed at the destruction of any of the rights or freedoms recognized herein, or at their limitation to a greater extent than is provided for in the present Covenant.

2. No restriction upon or derogation from any of the fundamental human rights recognized or existing in any country in virtue of law, conventions, regulations or custom shall be admitted on the pretext that the present Covenant does not recognize such rights or that it recognizes them to a lesser extent.

Part III

Article 6

1. The States Parties to the present Covenant recognize the right to work, which includes the right of everyone to the opportunity to gain his living by work which he freely chooses or accepts, and will take appropriate steps to safeguard this right.

2. The steps to be taken by a State Party to the present Covenant to achieve the full realization of this right shall include technical and vocational guidance and training programmes, policies and techniques to achieve steady economic, social and cultural development and full and productive employment under conditions safeguarding fundamental political and economic freedoms to the individual.

Article 7

The States Parties to the present Covenant recognize the right of everyone to the enjoyment of just and favourable conditions of work which ensure, in particular:

(a) Remuneration which provides all workers, as a minimum, with:
   (i) Fair wages and equal remuneration for work of equal value without distinction of any kind, in particular women being guaranteed conditions of work not inferior to those enjoyed by men, with equal pay for equal work;
   (ii) A decent living for themselves and their families in accordance with the provisions of the present Covenant;

(b) Safe and healthy working conditions;

(c) Equal opportunity for everyone to be promoted in his employment to an appropriate higher level, subject to no considerations other than those of seniority and competence;

(d) Rest, leisure and reasonable limitation of working hours and periodic holidays with pay, as well as remuneration for public holidays.

Article 8

1. The States Parties to the present Covenant undertake to ensure:

(a) The right of everyone to form trade unions and join the trade union of his choice, subject only to the rules of the organization concerned, for the promotion and protection of his economic and social interests. No restrictions may be placed on the exercise of this right other than those prescribed by law and which are necessary in a democratic society in the interests of national security or public order or for the protection of the rights and freedoms of others;

(b) The right of trade unions to establish national federations or confederations and the right of the latter to form or join international trade-union organizations;

(c) The right of trade unions to function freely subject to no limitations other than those prescribed by law and which are necessary in a democratic society in the interests of national security or public order or for the protection of the rights and freedoms of others;

(d) The right to strike, provided that it is exercised in conformity with the laws of the particular country.

2. This article shall not prevent the imposition of lawful restrictions on the exercise of these rights by members of the armed forces or of the police or of the administration of the State.

3. Nothing in this article shall authorize States Parties to the International Labour Organization Convention of 1948 concerning Freedom of Association and Protection of the Right to Organize to take legislative measures which would prejudice, or apply the law in such a manner as would prejudice, the guarantees provided for in that Convention.

Article 9

The States Parties to the present Covenant recognize the right of everyone to social security, including social insurance.

Article 10

The States Parties to the present Covenant recognize that:

1. The widest possible protection and assistance should be accorded to the family, which is the natural and fundamental group unit of society, particularly for its establishment and while it is responsible for the care and education of dependent children. Marriage must be entered into with the free consent of the intending spouses.

2. Special protection should be accorded to mothers during a reasonable period before and after childbirth. During such period working mothers should be accorded paid leave or leave with adequate social security benefits.

3. Special measures of protection and assistance should be taken on behalf of all children and young persons without any discrimination for reasons of parentage or other conditions. Children and young persons should be protected from economic and social exploitation. Their employment in work harmful to their morals or health or dangerous to life or likely to hamper their normal development should be punishable by law. States should also set age limits below which the paid employment of child labour should be prohibited and punishable by law.

Article 11

1. The States Parties to the present Covenant recognize the right of everyone to an adequate standard of living for himself and his family, including adequate food, clothing and housing, and to the continuous improvement of living conditions. The States Parties will take appropriate steps to ensure the realization of this right, recognizing to this effect the essential importance of international co-operation based on free consent.

2. The States Parties to the present Covenant, recognizing the fundamental right of everyone to be free from hunger, shall take, individually and through international co-operation, the measures, including specific programmes, which are needed:

(a) To improve methods of production, conservation and distribution of food by making full use of technical and scientific knowledge, by disseminating knowledge of the principles of nutrition and by developing or reforming agrarian systems in such a way as to achieve the most efficient development and utilization of natural resources;

(b) Taking into account the problems of both food-importing and food-exporting countries, to ensure an equitable distribution of world food supplies in relation to need.

Article 12

1. The States Parties to the present Covenant recognize the right of everyone to the enjoyment of the highest attainable standard of physical and mental health.

2. The steps to be taken by the States Parties to the present Covenant to achieve the full realization of this right shall include those necessary for:

(a) The provision for the reduction of the stillbirth-rate and of infant mortality and for the healthy development of the child;

(b) The improvement of all aspects of environmental and industrial hygiene;

(c) The prevention, treatment and control of epidemic, endemic, occupational and other diseases;

(d) The creation of conditions which would assure to all medical service and medical attention in the event of sickness.

Article 13

1. The States Parties to the present Covenant recognize the right of everyone to education. They agree that education shall be directed to the full development of the human personality and the sense of its dignity, and shall strengthen the respect for human rights and fundamental freedoms. They further agree that education shall enable all persons to participate effectively in a free society, promote understanding, tolerance and friendship among all nations and all racial, ethnic or religious groups, and further the activities of the United Nations for the maintenance of peace.

2. The States Parties to the present Covenant recognize that, with a view to achieving the full realization of this right:

(a) Primary education shall be compulsory and available free to all;

(b) Secondary education in its different forms, including technical and vocational secondary education, shall be made generally available and accessible to all by every appropriate means, and in particular by the progressive introduction of free education;

(c) Higher education shall be made equally accessible to all, on the basis of capacity, by every appropriate means, and in particular by the progressive introduction of free education;

(d) Fundamental education shall be encouraged or intensified as far as possible for those persons who have not received or completed the whole period of their primary education;

(e) The development of a system of schools at all levels shall be actively pursued, an adequate fellowship system shall be established, and the material conditions of teaching staff shall be continuously improved.

3. The States Parties to the present Covenant undertake to have respect for the liberty of parents and, when applicable, legal guardians to choose for their children schools, other than those established by the public authorities, which conform to such minimum educational standards as may be laid down or approved by the State and to ensure the religious and moral education of their children in conformity with their own convictions.

4. No part of this article shall be construed so as to interfere with the liberty of individuals and bodies to establish and direct educational institutions, subject always to the observance of the principles set forth in paragraph 1 of this article and to the requirement that the education given in such institutions shall conform to such minimum standards as may be laid down by the State.

Article 14

Each State Party to the present Covenant which, at the time of becoming a Party, has not been able to secure in its metropolitan territory or other territories under its jurisdiction compulsory primary education, free of charge, undertakes, within two years, to work out and adopt a detailed plan of action for the progressive implementation, within a reasonable number of years, to be fixed in the plan, of the principle of compulsory education free of charge for all.

Article 15

1. The States Parties to the present Covenant recognize the right of everyone:
   (a) To take part in cultural life;
   (b) To enjoy the benefits of scientific progress and its applications;
   (c) To benefit from the protection of the moral and material interests resulting from any scientific, literary or artistic production of which he is the author.

2. The steps to be taken by the States Parties to the present Covenant to achieve the full realization of this right shall include those necessary for the conservation, the development and the diffusion of science and culture.

3. The States Parties to the present Covenant undertake to respect the freedom indispensable for scientific research and creative activity.

4. The States Parties to the present Covenant recognize the benefits to be derived from the encouragement and development of international contacts and co-operation in the scientific and cultural fields.

Part IV

Article 16

1. The States Parties to the present Covenant undertake to submit in conformity with this part of the Covenant reports on the measures which they have adopted and the progress made in achieving the observance of the rights recognized herein.

2. (a) All reports shall be submitted to the Secretary-General of the United Nations, who shall transmit copies to the Economic and Social Council for consideration in accordance with the provisions of the present Covenant.
   (b) The Secretary-General of the United Nations shall also transmit to the specialized agencies copies of the reports, or any relevant parts therefrom, from States Parties to the present Covenant which are also members of these specialized agencies in so far as these reports, or parts therefrom, relate to any matters which fall within the responsibilities of the said agencies in accordance with their constitutional instruments.

Article 17

1. The States Parties to the present Covenant shall furnish their reports in stages, in accordance with a programme to be established by the Economic and Social Council within one year of the entry into force of the present Covenant after consultation with the States Parties and the specialized agencies concerned.

2. Reports may indicate factors and difficulties affecting the degree of fulfilment of obligations under the present Covenant.

3. Where relevant information has previously been furnished to the United Nations or to any specialized agency by any State Party to the present Covenant, it will not be necessary to reproduce that information, but a precise reference to the information so furnished will suffice.

Article 18

Pursuant to its responsibilities under the Charter of the United Nations in the field of human rights and fundamental freedoms, the Economic and Social Council may make arrangements with the specialized agencies in respect of their reporting to it on the progress made in achieving the observance of the provisions of the present Covenant falling within the scope of their activities. These reports may include particulars of decisions and recommendations on such implementation adopted by their competent organs.

Article 19

The Economic and Social Council may transmit to the Commission on Human Rights for study and general recommendation or, as appropriate, for information the reports concerning human rights submitted by States in accordance with Articles 16 and 17, and those concerning human rights submitted by the specialized agencies in accordance with Article 18.

Article 20

The States Parties to the present Covenant and the specialized agencies concerned may submit comments to the Economic and Social Council on any general recommendation under Article 19 or reference to such general recommendation in any report of the Commission on Human Rights or any documentation referred to therein.

Article 21

The Economic and Social Council may submit from time to time to the General Assembly reports with recommendations of a general nature and a summary of the information received from the States Parties to the present Covenant and the specialized agencies on the measures taken and the progress made in achieving general observance of the rights recognized in the present Covenant.

Article 22

The Economic and Social Council may bring to the attention of other organs of the United Nations, their subsidiary organs and specialized agencies concerned with furnishing technical assistance any matters arising out of the reports referred to in this part of the present Covenant which may assist such bodies in deciding, each within its field of competence, on the advisability of international measures likely to contribute to the effective progressive implementation of the present Covenant.

Article 23

The States Parties to the present Covenant agree that international action for the achievement of the rights recognized in the present Covenant includes such methods as the conclusion of conventions, the adoption of recommendations, the furnishing of technical assistance and the holding of regional meetings and technical meetings for the purpose of consultation and study organized in conjunction with the Governments concerned.

Article 24

Nothing in the present Covenant shall be interpreted as impairing the provisions of the Charter of the United Nations and of the constitutions of the specialized agencies which define the respective responsibilities of the various organs of the United Nations and of the specialized agencies in regard to the matters dealt with in the present Covenant.

Article 25

Nothing in the present Covenant shall be interpreted as impairing the inherent right of all peoples to enjoy and utilize fully and freely their natural wealth and resources.

Part V

Article 26

1. The present Covenant is open for signature by any State Member of the United Nations or member of any of its specialized agencies, by any State Party to the Statute of the International Court of Justice, and by any other State which has been invited by the General Assembly of the United Nations to become a party to the present Covenant.

2. The present Covenant is subject to ratification. Instruments of ratification shall be deposited with the Secretary-General of the United Nations.

3. The present Covenant shall be open to accession by any State referred to in paragraph 1 of this Article.

4. Accession shall be effected by the deposit of an instrument of accession with the Secretary-General of the United Nations.

5. The Secretary-General of the United Nations shall inform all States which have signed the present Covenant or acceded to it of the deposit of each instrument of ratification or accession.

Article 27

1. The present Covenant shall enter into force three months after the date of the deposit with the Secretary-General of the United Nations of the thirty-fifth instrument of ratification or instrument of accession.

2. For each State ratifying the present Covenant or acceding to it after the deposit of the thirty-fifth instrument of ratification or instrument of accession, the present Covenant shall enter into force three months after the date of the deposit of its own instrument of ratification or instrument of accession.

Article 28

The provisions of the present Covenant shall extend to all parts of federal States without any limitations or exceptions.

Article 29

1. Any State Party to the present Covenant may propose an amendment and file it with the Secretary-General of the United Nations. The Secretary-General shall thereupon communicate any proposed amendments to the States Parties to the present Covenant with a request that they notify him whether they favour a conference of States Parties for the purpose of considering and voting upon the proposals. In the event that at least one third of the States Parties favours such a conference, the Secretary-General shall convene the conference under the auspices of the United Nations. Any amendment adopted by a majority of the States Parties present and voting at the conference shall be submitted to the General Assembly of the United Nations for approval.

2. Amendments shall come into force when they have been approved by the General Assembly of the United Nations and accepted by a two-thirds majority of the States Parties to the present Covenant in accordance with their respective constitutional processes.

3. When amendments come into force they shall be binding on those States Parties which have accepted them, other States Parties still being bound by the provisions of the present Covenant and any earlier amendment which they have accepted.

Article 30

Irrespective of the notifications made under Article 26, paragraph 5, the Secretary-General of the United Nations shall inform all States referred to in paragraph 1 of the same Article of the following particulars:

(a) Signatures, ratifications and accessions under Article 26;

(b) The date of the entry into force of the present Covenant under Article 27 and the date of the entry into force of any amendments under Article 29.

Article 31

1. The present Covenant, of which the Chinese, English, French, Russian and Spanish texts are equally authentic, shall be deposited in the archives of the United Nations.

2. The Secretary-General of the United Nations shall transmit certified copies of the present Covenant to all States referred to in Article 26.

APPENDIX L

International Convention on the Elimination of All Forms of Racial Discrimination, 1966

The States Parties to this Convention,

Considering that the Charter of the United Nations is based on the principles of the dignity and equality inherent in all human beings, and that all Member States have pledged themselves to take joint and separate action, in co-operation with the Organization, for the achievement of one of the purposes of the United Nations which is to promote and encourage universal respect for and observance of human rights and fundamental freedoms for all, without distinction as to race, sex, language or religion,

Considering that the Universal Declaration of Human Rights proclaims that all human beings are born free and equal in dignity and rights and that everyone is entitled to all the rights and freedoms set out therein, without distinction of any kind, in particular as to race, colour or national origin,

Considering that all human beings are equal before the law and are entitled to equal protection of the law against any discrimination and against any incitement to discrimination,

Considering that the United Nations has condemned colonialism and all practices of segregation and discrimination associated therewith, in whatever form and wherever they exist, and that the Declaration on the Granting of Independence to Colonial Countries and Peoples of 14 December 1960 (General Assembly resolution 1514 (XV)) has affirmed and solemnly proclaimed the necessity of bringing them to a speedy and unconditional end,

Considering that the United Nations Declaration on the Elimination of All Forms of Racial Discrimination of 20 November 1963 (General Assembly resolution 1904 (XVIII)) solemnly affirms the necessity of speedily eliminating racial discrimination throughout the world in all its forms and manifestations and of securing understanding of and respect for the dignity of the human person,

Convinced that any doctrine of superiority based on racial differentiation is scientifically false, morally condemnable, socially unjust and dangerous, and that there is no justification for racial discrimination, in theory or in practice, anywhere,

Reaffirming that discrimination between human beings on the grounds of race, colour or ethnic origin is an obstacle to friendly and peaceful relations among nations and is capable of disturbing peace and security among peoples and the harmony of persons living side by side even within one and the same State,

Convinced that the existence of racial barriers is repugnant to the ideals of any human society,

Alarmed by manifestations of racial discrimination still in evidence in some areas of the world and by governmental policies based on racial superiority or hatred, such as policies of *apartheid*, segregation or separation,

Resolved to adopt all necessary measures for speedily eliminating racial discrimination in all its forms and manifestations, and to prevent and combat racist doctrines and practices in order to promote understanding between races and to build an international community free from all forms of racial segregation and racial discrimination,

Bearing in mind the Convention concerning Discrimination in respect of Employment and Occupation adopted by the International Labour Organisation in 1958, and the Convention against Discrimination in Education adopted by the United Nations Educational, Scientific and Cultural Organization in 1960,

Desiring to implement the principles embodied in the United Nations Declaration on the Elimination of All Forms of Racial Discrimination and to secure the earliest adoption of practical measures to that end,

Have agreed as follows:

Part I

Article I

1. In this Convention, the term 'racial discrimination' shall mean any distinction, exclusion, restriction or preference based on race, colour, descent, or national or ethnic origin which has the purpose or effect of nullifying or impairing the recognition, enjoyment or exercise, on an equal footing, of human rights and fundamental freedoms in the political, economic, social, cultural or any other field of public life.

2. This Convention shall not apply to distinctions, exclusions, restrictions or preferences made by a State Party to this Convention between citizens and non-citizens.

3. Nothing in this Convention may be interpreted as affecting in any way the legal provisions of States Parties concerning nationality, citizenship or naturalization, provided that such provisions do not discriminate against any particular nationality.

4. Special measures taken for the sole purpose of securing adequate advancement of certain racial or ethnic groups or individuals requiring such protection as may be necessary in order to ensure such groups or individuals equal enjoyment or exercise of human rights and fundamental freedoms shall not be deemed racial discrimination, provided, however, that such measures do not, as a consequence, lead to the maintenance of separate rights for different racial groups and that they shall not be continued after the objectives for which they were taken have been achieved.

Article 2

1. States Parties condemn racial discrimination and undertake to pursue by all appropriate means and without delay a policy of eliminating racial discrimination in all its forms and promoting understanding among all races, and, to this end:

(a) Each State Party undertakes to engage in no act or practice of racial discrimination against persons, groups of persons or institutions and to ensure that all public authorities and public institutions, national and local, shall act in conformity with this obligation;

(b) Each State Party undertakes not to sponsor, defend or support racial discrimination by any persons or organizations;

(c) Each State Party shall take effective measures to review governmental, national and local policies, and to amend, rescind or nullify any laws and regulations which have the effect of creating or perpetuating racial discrimination wherever it exists;

(d) Each State Party shall prohibit and bring to an end, by all appropriate means, including legislation as required by circumstances, racial discrimination by any persons, group or organization;

(e) Each State Party undertakes to encourage, where appropriate, integrationist multi-racial organizations and movements and other means of eliminating barriers between races, and to discourage anything which tends to strengthen racial division.

2. States Parties shall, when the circumstances so warrant, take, in the social, economic, cultural and other fields, special and concrete measures to ensure the adequate development and protection of certain racial groups or individuals belonging to them, for the purpose of guaranteeing them the full and equal enjoyment of human rights and fundamental freedoms. These measures shall in no case entail as a consequence the maintenance of unequal or separate rights for different racial groups after the objectives for which they were taken have been achieved.

Article 3

States Parties particularly condemn racial segregation and *apartheid* and undertake to prevent, prohibit and eradicate all practices of this nature in territories under their jurisdiction.

Article 4

States Parties condemn all propaganda and all organizations which are based on ideas or theories of superiority of one race or group of persons of one colour or ethnic origin, or which attempt to justify or promote racial hatred and discrimination in any form, and undertake to adopt immediate and positive measures designed to eradicate all incitement to, or acts of, such discrimination and, to this end, with due regard to the principles embodied in the Universal Declaration of Human Rights and the rights expressly set forth in Article 5 of this Convention, *inter alia*:

(a) Shall declare an offence punishable by law all dissemination of ideas based on racial superiority or hatred, incitement to racial discrimination, as well as all acts of violence or incitement to such acts against any race or group of persons of another colour or ethnic origin, and also the provision of any assistance to racist activities, including the financing thereof;

(b) Shall declare illegal and prohibit organizations, and also organized and all other propaganda activities, which promote and incite racial discrimination, and shall recognize participation in such organizations or activities as an offence punishable by law;

(c) Shall not permit public authorities or public institutions, national or local, to promote or incite racial discrimination.

Article 5

In compliance with the fundamental obligations laid down in Article 2 of this Convention, States Parties undertake to prohibit and to eliminate racial discrimination in all its forms and to guarantee the right of everyone, without distinction as to race, colour, or national or ethnic origin, to equality before the law, notably in the enjoyment of the following rights:

(a) The right to equal treatment before the tribunals and all other organs administering justice;

(b) The right to security of person and protection by the State against violence or bodily harm, whether inflicted by government officials or by any individual group or institution;

(c) Political rights, in particular the right to participate in elections—to vote and to stand for election—on the basis of universal and equal suffrage, to take part in the Government as well as in the conduct of public affairs at any level and to have equal access to public service;

(d) Other civil rights, in particular:

(i) The right to freedom of movement and residence within the border of the State;

(ii) The right to leave any country, including one's own, and to return to one's country;

(iii) The right to nationality;

(iv) The right to marriage and choice of spouse;

(v) The right to own property alone as well as in association with others;

(vi) The right to inherit;

(vii) The right to freedom of thought, conscience and religion;

(viii) The right to freedom of opinion and expression;

(ix) The right to freedom of peaceful assembly and association;

(e) Economic, social and cultural rights, in particular:

(i) The rights to work, to free choice of employment, to just and favourable conditions of work, to protection against unemployment, to equal pay for equal work, to just and favourable remuneration;

(ii) The right to form and join trade unions;

(iii) The right to housing;

(iv) The right to public health, medical care, social security and social services;

(v) The right to education and training;

(vi) The right to equal participation in cultural activities;

(f) The right of access to any place or service intended for use by the general public, such as transport, hotels, restaurants, cafés, theatres and parks.

Article 6

States Parties shall assure to everyone within their jurisdiction effective protection and remedies, through the competent national tribunals and other State institutions, against any acts of racial discrimination which violate his human rights and fundamental freedoms contrary to this Convention, as well as the right to seek from such tribunals just and adequate reparation or satisfaction for any damage suffered as a result of such discrimination.

Article 7

States Parties undertake to adopt immediate and effective measures, particularly in the fields of teaching, education, culture and information, with a view to combating prejudices which lead to racial discrimination and to promoting understanding, tolerance and friendship among nations and racial or ethnical groups, as well as to propagating the purposes and principles of the Charter of the United Nations, the Universal Declaration of Human Rights, the United Nations Declaration on the Elimination of All Forms of Racial Discrimination, and this Convention.

Part II

Article 8

1. There shall be established a Committee on the Elimination of Racial Discrimination (hereinafter referred to as the Committee) consisting of eighteen experts of high moral standing and acknowledged impartiality elected by States Parties from among their nationals, who shall serve in their personal capacity, consideration being given to equitable geographical distribution and to the representation of the different forms of civilization as well as of the principal legal systems.

2. The members of the Committee shall be elected by secret ballot from a list of persons nominated by the States Parties. Each State Party may nominate one person from among its own nationals.

3. The initial election shall be held six months after the date of the entry into force of this Convention. At least three months before the date of each election the Secretary-General of the United Nations shall address a letter to the States Parties inviting them to submit their nominations within two months. The Secretary-General shall prepare a list in alphabetical order of all persons thus nominated, indicating the States Parties which have nominated them, and shall submit it to the States Parties.

4. Elections of the members of the Committee shall be held at a meeting of States Parties convened by the Secretary-General at United Nations Headquarters. At that meeting, for which two thirds of the States Parties shall constitute a quorum, the persons elected to the Committee shall be nominees who obtain the largest number of votes and an absolute majority of the votes of the representatives of States Parties present and voting.

5. (a) The members of the Committee shall be elected for a term of four years. However, the terms of nine of the members elected at the first election shall expire at the end of two years; immediately after the first election the names of these nine members shall be chosen by lot by the Chairman of the Committee.
   (b) For the filling of casual vacancies, the State Party whose expert has ceased to function as a member of the Committee shall appoint another expert from among its nationals, subject to the approval of the Committee.

6. States Parties shall be responsible for the expenses of the members of the Committee while they are in performance of Committee duties.

Article 9

1. States Parties undertake to submit to the Secretary-General of the United Nations, for consideration by the Committee, a report on the legislative, judicial, administrative or other measures which they have adopted and which give effect to the provisions of this Convention:
   (a) within one year after the entry into force of the Convention for the State concerned; and
   (b) thereafter every two years and whenever the Committee so requests. The Committee may request further information from the States Parties.

2. The Committee shall report annually, through the Secretary General, to the General Assembly of the United Nations on its activities and may make suggestions and general recommendations based on the

examination of the reports and information received from the States Parties. Such suggestions and general recommendations shall be reported to the General Assembly together with comments, if any, from States Parties.

Article 10

1. The Committee shall adopt its own rules of procedure.

2. The Committee shall elect its officers for a term of two years.

3. The secretariat of the Committee shall be provided by the Secretary-General of the United Nations.

4. The meetings of the Committee shall normally be held at United Nations Headquarters.

Article 11

1. If a State Party considers that another State Party is not giving effect to the provisions of this Convention, it may bring the matter to the attention of the Committee. The Committee shall then transmit the communication to the State Party concerned. Within three months, the receiving State shall submit to the Committee written explanations or statements clarifying the matter and the remedy, if any, that may have been taken by that State.

2. If the matter is not adjusted to the satisfaction of both parties, either by bilateral negotiations or by any other procedure open to them, within six months after the receipt by the receiving State of the initial communication, either State shall have the right to refer the matter again to the Committee by notifying the Committee and also the other State.

3. The Committee shall deal with a matter referred to it in accordance with paragraph 2 of this article after it has ascertained that all available domestic remedies have been invoked and exhausted in the case, in conformity with the generally recognized principles of international law. This shall not be the rule where the application of the remedies is unreasonably prolonged.

4. In any matter referred to it, the Committee may call upon the States Parties concerned to supply any other relevant information.

5. When any matter arising out of this Article is being considered by the Committee, the States Parties concerned shall be entitled to send a representative to take part in the proceedings of the Committee, without voting rights, while the matter is under consideration.

Article 12

1. (a) After the Committee has obtained and collated all the information it deems necessary, the Chairman shall appoint an *ad hoc* Conciliation Commission (hereinafter referred to as the Commission) comprising five persons who may or may not be members of the Committee. The members of the Commission shall be appointed with the unanimous consent of the parties to the dispute, and its good offices shall be made available to the States concerned with a view to an amicable solution of the matter on the basis of respect for this Convention.

   (b) If the States parties to the dispute fail to reach agreement within three months on all or part of the composition of the Commission, the members of the Commission not agreed upon by the States parties to the dispute shall be elected by secret ballot by a two-thirds majority vote of the Committee from among its own members.

2. The members of the Commission shall serve in their personal capacity. They shall not be nationals of the States Parties to the dispute or of a State not Party to this Convention.

3. The Commission shall elect its own Chairman and adopt its own rules of procedure.

4. The meetings of the Commission shall normally be held at United Nations Headquarters or at any other convenient place as determined by the Commission.

5. The secretariat provided in accordance with Article 10, paragraph 3, of this Convention shall also service the Commission whenever a dispute among States Parties brings the Commission into being.

6. The States Parties to the dispute shall share equally all the expenses of the members of the Commission in accordance with estimates to be provided by the Secretary-General of the United Nations.

7. The Secretary-General shall be empowered to pay the expenses of the members of the Commission, if necessary, before reimbursement by the States Parties to the dispute in accordance with paragraph 6 of this Article.

8. The information obtained and collated by the Committee shall be made available to the Commission, and the Commission may call upon the States concerned to supply any other relevant information.

Article 13

1. When the Commission has fully considered the matter, it shall prepare and submit to the Chairman of the Committee a report embodying its findings on all questions of fact relevant to the issue between the parties and containing such recommendations as it may think proper for the amicable solution of the dispute.

2. The Chairman of the Committee shall communicate the report of the Commission to each of the States Parties to the dispute. These States shall, within three months, inform the Chairman of the Committee whether or not they accept the recommendations contained in the report of the Commission.

3. After the period provided for in paragraph 2 of this Article, the Chairman of the Committee shall communicate the report of the Commission and the declarations of the States Parties concerned to the other States Parties to this Convention.

Article 14

1. A State Party may at any time declare that it recognizes the competence of the Committee to receive and consider communications from individuals or groups of individuals within its jurisdiction claiming to be victims of a violation by that State Party of any of the rights set forth in this Convention. No communication shall be received by the Committee if it concerns a State Party which has not made such a declaration.

2. Any State Party which makes a declaration as provided for in paragraph 1 of this Article may establish or indicate a body within its national legal order which shall be competent to receive and consider petitions from individuals and groups of individuals within its jurisdiction who claim to be victims of a violation of any of the rights set forth in this Convention and who have exhausted other available local remedies.

3. A declaration made in accordance with paragraph 1 of this Article and the name of any body established or indicated in accordance with paragraph 2 of this Article shall be deposited by the State Party concerned with the Secretary-General of the United Nations, who shall transmit copies thereof to the other States Parties. A declaration may be withdrawn at any time by notification to the Secretary-General, but such a withdrawal shall not affect communications pending before the Committee.

4. A register of petitions shall be kept by the body established or indicated in accordance with paragraph 2 of this Article, and certified copies of the register shall be filed annually through appropriate channels with the Secretary-General on the understanding that the contents shall not be publicly disclosed.

5. In the event of failure to obtain satisfaction from the body established or indicated in accordance with paragraph 2 of this Article, the petitioner shall have the right to communicate the matter to the Committee within six months.

6. (a) The Committee shall confidentially bring any communication referred to it to the attention of the State Party alleged to be violating any provision of this Convention, but the identity of the individual or groups of individuals concerned shall not be revealed without his or their express consent. The Committee shall not receive anonymous communications.

   (b) Within three months, the receiving State shall submit to the Committee written explanations or statements clarifying the matter and the remedy, if any, that may have been taken by that State.

7. (a) The Committee shall consider communications in the light of all information made available to it by the State Party concerned and by the petitioner. The Committee shall not consider any communication from a petitioner unless it has ascertained that the petitioner has exhausted all

available domestic remedies. However, this shall not be the rule where the application of the remedies is unreasonably prolonged.

(b) The Committee shall forward its suggestions and recommendations, if any, to the State Party concerned and to the petitioner.

8. The Committee shall include in its annual report a summary of such communications and, where appropriate, a summary of the explanations and statements of the States Parties concerned and of its own suggestions and recommendations.

9. The Committee shall be competent to exercise the functions provided for in this Article only when at least ten States Parties to this Convention are bound by declarations in accordance with paragraph 1of this Article.

Article 15

1. Pending the achievement of the objectives of the Declaration on the Granting of Independence to Colonial Countries and Peoples, contained in General Assembly resolution 1514 (XV) of 14 December 1960, the provisions of this Convention shall in no way limit the right of petition granted to these peoples by other international instruments or by the United Nations and its specialized agencies.

2. (a) The Committee established under Article 8, paragraph 1, of this Convention shall receive copies of the petitions from, and submit expressions of opinion and recommendations on these petitions to, the bodies of the United Nations which deal with matters directly related to the principles and objectives of this Convention in their consideration of petitions from the inhabitants of Trust and Non-Self-Governing Territories and all other territories to which General Assembly resolution 1514 (XV) applies, relating to matters covered by this Convention which are before these bodies.

(b) The Committee shall receive from the competent bodies of the United Nations copies of the reports concerning the legislative, judicial, administrative or other measures directly related to the principles and objectives of this Convention applied by the administering Powers within the Territories mentioned in sub-paragraph (a) of this paragraph, and shall express opinions and make recommendations to these bodies.

3. The Committee shall include in its report to the General Assembly a summary of the petitions and reports it has received from United Nations bodies, and the expressions of opinion and recommendations of the Committee relating to the said petitions and reports.

4. The Committee shall request from the Secretary-General of the United Nations all information relevant to the objectives of this Convention and available to him regarding the Territories mentioned in paragraph 2 (a) of this Article.

Article 16

The provisions of this Convention concerning the settlement of disputes or complaints shall be applied without prejudice to other procedures for settling disputes or complaints in the field of discrimination laid down in the constituent instruments of, or in conventions adopted by, the United Nations and its specialized agencies, and shall not prevent the States Parties from having recourse to other procedures for settling a dispute in accordance with general or special international agreements in force between them.

Part III

Article 17

1. This Convention is open for signature by any State Member of the United Nations or member of any of its specialized agencies, by any State Party to the Statute of the International Court of Justice, and by any other State which has been invited by the General Assembly of the United Nations to become a Party to this Convention.

2. This Convention is subject to ratification. Instruments of ratification shall be deposited with the Secretary-General of the United Nations.

Article 18

1. This Convention shall be open to accession by any State referred to in Article 17, paragraph 1, of the Convention.

2. Accession shall be effected by the deposit of an instrument of accession with the Secretary-General of the United Nations.

Article 19

1. This Convention shall enter into force on the thirtieth day after the date of the deposit with the Secretary-General of the United Nations of the twenty-seventh instrument of ratification or instrument of accession.

2. For each State ratifying this Convention or acceding to it after the deposit of the twenty-seventh instrument of ratification or instrument of accession, the Convention shall enter into force on the thirtieth day after the date of the deposit of its own instrument of ratification or instrument of accession.

Article 20

1. The Secretary-General of the United Nations shall receive and circulate to all States which are or may become Parties to this Convention reservations made by States at the time of ratification or accession. Any State which objects to the reservation shall, within a period of ninety days from the date of the said communication, notify the Secretary-General that it does not accept it.

2. A reservation incompatible with the object and purpose of this Convention shall not be permitted, nor shall a reservation the effect of which would inhibit the operation of any of the bodies established by this Convention be allowed. A reservation shall be considered incompatible or inhibitive if at least two thirds of the States Parties to this Convention object to it.

3. Reservations may be withdrawn at any time by notification to this effect addressed to the Secretary-General. Such notification shall take effect on the date on which it is received.

Article 21

A State Party may denounce this Convention by written notification to the Secretary-General of the United Nations. Denunciation shall take effect one year after the date of receipt of the notification by the Secretary- General.

Article 22

Any dispute between two or more States Parties with respect to the interpretation or application of this Convention, which is not settled by negotiation or by the procedures expressly provided for in this Convention, shall, at the request of any of the parties to the dispute, be referred to the International Court of Justice for decision, unless the disputants agree to another mode of settlement.

Article 23

1. A request for the revision of this Convention may be made at any time by any State Party by means of a notification in writing addressed to the Secretary-General of the United Nations.

2. The General Assembly of the United Nations shall decide upon the steps, if any, to be taken in respect of such a request.

Article 24

The Secretary-General of the United Nations shall inform all States referred to in Article 17, paragraph 1, of this Convention of the following particulars:

(a) Signatures, ratifications and accessions under Articles 17 and 18;
(b) The date of entry into force of this Convention under Article 19;
(c) Communications and declarations received under Articles 14, 20 and 23;
(d) Denunciations under Article 21.

Article 25

1. This Convention, of which the Chinese, English, French, Russian and Spanish texts are equally authentic, shall be deposited in the archives of the United Nations.

2. The Secretary-General of the United Nations shall transmit certified copies of this Convention to all States belonging to any of the categories mentioned in Article 17, paragraph 1, of the Convention.

In faith whereof the undersigned, being duly authorized thereto by their respective Governments, have signed the present Convention, opened for signature at New York, on the seventh day of March, one thousand nine hundred and sixty-six.

Annex

The General Assembly,

Recalling the Declaration on the Granting of Independence to Colonial Countries and Peoples contained in its resolution 1514 (XV) of 14 December 1960,

Bearing in mind its resolution 1654 (XVI) of 27 November 1962, which established the Special Committee on the Situation with regard to the Implementation of the Declaration on the Granting of Independence to Colonial Countries and Peoples to examine the application of the Declaration and to carry out its provisions by all means at its disposal,

Bearing in mind also the provisions of Article 15 of the International Convention on the Elimination of All Forms of Racial Discrimination contained in the annex to resolution 2106 A (XX) above,

Recalling that the General Assembly has established other bodies to receive and examine petitions from the peoples of colonial countries,

Convinced that close co-operation between the Committee on the Elimination of Racial Discrimination, established by the International Convention on the Elimination of All Forms of Racial Discrimination, and the bodies of the United Nations charged with receiving and examining petitions from the peoples of colonial countries will facilitate the achievement of the objectives of both the Convention and the Declaration on the Granting of Independence to Colonial Countries and Peoples,

Recognizing that the elimination of racial discrimination in all its forms is vital to the achievement of fundamental human rights and to the assurance of the dignity and worth of the human person, and thus constitutes a pre-emptory obligation under the Charter of the United Nations,

1. *Calls upon* the Secretary-General to make available to the Committee on the Elimination of Racial Discrimination, periodically or at its request, all information in his possession relevant to Article 15 of the International Convention on the Elimination of All Forms of Racial Discrimination;

2. *Requests* the Special Committee on the Situation with regard to the Implementation of the Granting of Independence to Colonial Countries and Peoples, and all other bodies of the United Nations authorized to receive and examine petitions from the peoples of the colonial countries, to transmit to the Committee on the Elimination of Racial Discrimination, periodically or at its request, copies of petitions from those peoples relevant to the Convention, for the comments and recommendations of the said Committee;

3. *Requests* the bodies referred to in paragraph 2 above to include in their annual reports to the General Assembly a summary of the action taken by them under the terms of the present resolution.

1406th plenary meeting
21 December 1965

APPENDIX M

Convention on the Elimination of All Forms of Discrimination against Women 1979

The States Parties to the present Convention,

Noting that the Charter of the United Nations reaffirms faith in fundamental human rights, in the dignity and worth of the human person and in the equal rights of men and women,

Noting that the Universal Declaration of Human Rights affirms the principle of the inadmissibility of discrimination and proclaims that all human beings are born free and equal in dignity and rights and that everyone is entitled to all the rights and freedoms set forth therein, without distinction of any kind, including distinction based on sex,

Noting that the States Parties to the International Covenants on Human Rights have the obligation to ensure the equal rights of men and women to enjoy all economic, social, cultural, civil and political rights,

Considering the international conventions concluded under the auspices of the United Nations and the specialized agencies promoting equality of rights of men and women,

Noting also the resolutions, declarations and recommendations adopted by the United Nations and the specialized agencies promoting equality of rights of men and women,

Concerned, however, that despite these various instruments extensive discrimination against women continues to exist,

Recalling that discrimination against women violates the principles of equality of rights and respect for human dignity, is an obstacle to the participation of women, on equal terms with men, in the political, social, economic and cultural life of their countries, hampers the growth of the prosperity of society and the family and makes more difficult the full development of the potentialities of women in the service of their countries and of humanity,

Concerned that in situations of poverty women have the least access to food, health, education, training and opportunities for employment and other needs,

Convinced that the establishment of the new international economic order based on equity and justice will contribute significantly towards the promotion of equality between men and women,

Emphasizing that the eradication of *apartheid*, all forms of racism, racial discrimination, colonialism, neo-colonialism, aggression, foreign occupation and domination and interference in the internal affairs of States is essential to the full enjoyment of the rights of men and women,

Affirming that the strengthening of international peace and security, the relaxation of international tension, mutual co-operation among all States irrespective of their social and economic systems, general and complete disarmament, in particular nuclear disarmament under strict and effective international control, the affirmation of the principles of justice, equality and mutual benefit in relations among countries and the realization of the right of peoples under alien and colonial domination and foreign occupation to self-determination and independence, as well as respect for national sovereignty and territorial integrity, will promote social progress and development and as a consequence will contribute to the attainment of full equality between men and women,

Convinced that the full and complete development of a country, the welfare of the world and the cause of peace require the maximum participation of women on equal terms with men in all fields,

Bearing in mind the great contribution of women to the welfare of the family and to the development of society, so far not fully recognized, the social significance of maternity and the role of both parents in the family and in the upbringing of children, and aware that the role of women in procreation should not be a basis for discrimination but that the upbringing of children requires a sharing of responsibility between men and women and society as a whole,

Aware that a change in the traditional role of men as well as the role of women in society and in the family is needed to achieve full equality between men and women,

Determined to implement the principles set forth in the Declaration on the Elimination of Discrimination against Women and, for that purpose, to adopt the measures required for the elimination of such discrimination in all its forms and manifestations,

Have agreed on the following:

Part I

Article I

For the purposes of the present Convention, the term 'discrimination against women' shall mean any distinction, exclusion or restriction made on the basis of sex which has the effect or purpose of impairing or nullifying the recognition, enjoyment or exercise by women, irrespective of their marital status, on a basis of equality of men and women, of human rights and fundamental freedoms in the political, economic, social, cultural, civil or any other field.

Article 2

States Parties condemn discrimination against women in all its forms, agree to pursue by all appropriate means and without delay a policy of eliminating discrimination against women and, to this end, undertake:

(a) To embody the principle of the equality of men and women in their national constitutions or other appropriate legislation if not yet incorporated therein and to ensure, through law and other appropriate means, the practical realization of this principle;

(b) To adopt appropriate legislative and other measures, including sanctions where appropriate, prohibiting all discrimination against women;

(c) To establish legal protection of the rights of women on an equal basis with men and to ensure through competent national tribunals and other public institutions the effective protection of women against any act of discrimination;

(d) To refrain from engaging in any act or practice of discrimination against women and to ensure that public authorities and institutions shall act in conformity with this obligation;

(e) To take all appropriate measures to eliminate discrimination against women by any person, organization or enterprise;

(f) To take all appropriate measures, including legislation, to modify or abolish existing laws, regulations, customs and practices which constitute discrimination against women;

(g) To repeal all national penal provisions which constitute discrimination against women.

Article 3

States Parties shall take in all fields, in particular in the political, social, economic and cultural fields, all appropriate measures, including legislation, to ensure the full development and advancement of women , for the purpose of guaranteeing them the exercise and enjoyment of human rights and fundamental freedoms on a basis of equality with men.

Article 4

1. Adoption by States Parties of temporary special measures aimed at accelerating *de facto* equality between men and women shall not be considered discrimination as defined in the present Convention, but shall in no way entail as a consequence the maintenance of unequal or separate standards; these measures shall be discontinued when the objectives of equality of opportunity and treatment have been achieved.

2. Adoption by States Parties of special measures, including those measures contained in the present Convention, aimed at protecting maternity shall not be considered discriminatory.

Article 5

States Parties shall take all appropriate measures:

(a) To modify the social and cultural patterns of conduct of men and women, with a view to achieving the elimination of prejudices and customary and all other practices which are based on the idea of the inferiority or the superiority of either of the sexes or on stereotyped roles for men and women;

(b) To ensure that family education includes a proper understanding of maternity as a social function and the recognition of the common responsibility of men and women in the upbringing and development of their children, it being understood that the interest of the children is the primordial consideration in all cases.

Article 6

States Parties shall take all appropriate measures, including legislation, to suppress all forms of traffic in women and exploitation of prostitution of women.

Part II

Article 7

States Parties shall take all appropriate measures to eliminate discrimination against women in the political and public life of the country and, in particular, shall ensure to women, on equal terms with men, the right:

(a) To vote in all elections and public referenda and to be eligible for election to all publicly elected bodies;

(b) To participate in the formulation of government policy and the implementation thereof and to hold public office and perform all public functions at all levels of government;

(c) To participate in non-governmental organizations and associations concerned with the public and political life of the country.

Article 8

States Parties shall take all appropriate measures to ensure to women, on equal terms with men and without any discrimination, the opportunity to represent their Governments at the international level and to participate in the work of international organizations.

Article 9

1. States Parties shall grant women equal rights with men to acquire, change or retain their nationality. They shall ensure in particular that neither marriage to an alien nor change of nationality by the husband during marriage shall automatically change the nationality of the wife, render her stateless or force upon her the nationality of the husband.
2. States Parties shall grant women equal rights with men with respect to the nationality of their children.

Part II

Article 10

States Parties shall take all appropriate measures to eliminate discrimination against women in order to ensure to them equal rights with men in the field of education and in particular to ensure, on a basis of equality of men and women:

(a) The same conditions for career and vocational guidance, for access to studies and for the achievement of diplomas in educational establishments of all categories in rural as well as in urban areas; this equality shall be ensured in pre-school, general, technical, professional and higher technical education, as well as in all types of vocational training;

(b) Access to the same curricula, the same examinations, teaching staff with qualifications of the same standard and school premises and equipment of the same quality;

(c) The elimination of any stereotyped concept of the roles of men and women at all levels and in all forms of education by encouraging co-education and other types of education which will help to achieve this aim and, in particular, by the revision of textbooks and school programmes and the adaptation of teaching methods;
(d) The same opportunities to benefit from scholarships and other study grants;
(e) The same opportunities for access to programmes of continuing education, including adult and functional literacy programmes, particulary those aimed at reducing, at the earliest possible time, any gap in education existing between men and women;
(f) The reduction of female student drop-out rates and the organization of programmes for girls and women who have left school prematurely;
(g) The same opportunities to participate actively in sports and physical education;
(h) Access to specific educational information to help to ensure the health and well-being of families, including information and advice on family planning.

Article 11

1. States Parties shall take all appropriate measures to eliminate discrimination against women in the field of employment in order to ensure, on a basis of equality of men and women, the same rights, in particular:
(a) The right to work as an inalienable right of all human beings;
(b) The right to the same employment opportunities, including the application of the same criteria for selection in matters of employment;
(c) The right to free choice of profession and employment, the right to promotion, job security and all benefits and conditions of service and the right to receive vocational training and retraining, including apprenticeships, advanced vocational training and recurrent training;
(d) The right to equal remuneration, including benefits, and to equal treatment in respect of work of equal value, as well as equality of treatment in the evaluation of the quality of work;
(e) The right to social security, particularly in cases of retirement, unemployment, sickness, invalidity and old age and other incapacity to work, as well as the right to paid leave;
(f) The right to protection of health and to safety in working conditions, including the safeguarding of the function of reproduction.

2. In order to prevent discrimination against women on the grounds of marriage or maternity and to ensure their effective right to work, States Parties shall take appropriate measures:
(a) To prohibit, subject to the imposition of sanctions, dismissal on the grounds of pregnancy or of maternity leave and discrimination in dismissals on the basis of marital status;
(b) To introduce maternity leave with pay or with comparable social benefits without loss of former employment, seniority or social allowances;
(c) To encourage the provision of the necessary supporting social services to enable parents to combine family obligations with work responsibilities and participation in public life, in particular through promoting the establishment and development of a network of child-care facilities;
(d) To provide special protection to women during pregnancy in types of work proved to be harmful to them.

3. Protective legislation relating to matters covered in this Article shall be reviewed periodically in the light of scientific and technological knowledge and shall be revised, repealed or extended as necessary.

Article 12

1. States Parties shall take all appropriate measures to eliminate discrimination against women in the field of health care in order to ensure, on a basis of equality of men and women, access to health care services, including those related to family planning.

2. Notwithstanding the provisions of paragraph I of this Article, States Parties shall ensure to women appropriate services in connection with pregnancy, confinement and the post-natal period, granting free services where necessary, as well as adequate nutrition during pregnancy and lactation.

Article 13

States Parties shall take all appropriate measures to eliminate discrimination against women in other areas of economic and social life in order to ensure, on a basis of equality of men and women, the same rights, in particular:

(a) The right to family benefits;
(b) The right to bank loans, mortgages and other forms of financial credit;
(c) The right to participate in recreational activities, sports and all aspects of cultural life.

Article 14

1. States Parties shall take into account the particular problems faced by rural women and the significant roles which rural women play in the economic survival of their families, including their work in the non-monetized sectors of the economy, and shall take all appropriate measures to ensure the application of the provisions of the present Convention to women in rural areas.

2. States Parties shall take all appropriate measures to eliminate discrimination against women in rural areas in order to ensure, on a basis of equality of men and women, that they participate in and benefit from rural development and, in particular, shall ensure to such women the right:

(a) To participate in the elaboration and implementation of development planning at all levels;
(b) To have access to adequate health care facilities, including information, counselling and services in family planning;
(c) To benefit directly from social security programmes;
(d) To obtain all types of training and education, formal and non-formal, including that relating to functional literacy, as well as, *inter alia*, the benefit of all community and extension services, in order to increase their technical proficiency;
(e) To organize self-help groups and co-operatives in order to obtain equal access to economic opportunities through employment or self employment;
(f) To participate in all community activities;
(g) To have access to agricultural credit and loans, marketing facilities, appropriate technology and equal treatment in land and agrarian reform as well as in land resettlement schemes;
(h) To enjoy adequate living conditions, particularly in relation to housing, sanitation, electricity and water supply, transport and communications.

Part IV

Article 15

1. States Parties shall accord to women equality with men before the law.

2. States Parties shall accord to women, in civil matters, a legal capacity identical to that of men and the same opportunities to exercise that capacity. In particular, they shall give women equal rights to conclude contracts and to administer property and shall treat them equally in all stages of procedure in courts and tribunals.

3. States Parties agree that all contracts and all other private instruments of any kind with a legal effect which is directed at restricting the legal capacity of women shall be deemed null and void.

4. States Parties shall accord to men and women the same rights with regard to the law relating to the movement of persons and the freedom to choose their residence and domicile.

Article 16

1. States Parties shall take all appropriate measures to eliminate discrimination against women in all matters relating to marriage and family relations and in particular shall ensure, on a basis of equality of men and women:

(a) The same right to enter into marriage;
(b) The same right freely to choose a spouse and to enter into marriage only with their free and full consent;

(c) The same rights and responsibilities during marriage and at its dissolution;
(d) The same rights and responsibilities as parents, irrespective of their marital status, in matters relating to their children; in all cases the interests of the children shall be paramount;
(e) The same rights to decide freely and responsibly on the number and spacing of their children and to have access to the information, education and means to enable them to exercise these rights;
(f) The same rights and responsibilities with regard to guardianship, wardship, trusteeship and adoption of children, or similar institutions where these concepts exist in national legislation; in all cases the interests of the children shall be paramount;
(g) The same personal rights as husband and wife, including the right to choose a family name, a profession and an occupation;
(h) The same rights for both spouses in respect of the ownership, acquisition, management, administration, enjoyment and disposition of property, whether free of charge or for a valuable consideration.

2. The betrothal and the marriage of a child shall have no legal effect, and all necessary action, including legislation, shall be taken to specify a minimum age for marriage and to make the registration of marriages in an official registry compulsory.

Part V

Article 17

1. For the purpose of considering the progress made in the implementation of the present Convention, there shall be established a Committee on the Elimination of Discrimination against Women (hereinafter referred to as the Committee) consisting, at the time of entry into force of the Convention, of eighteen and, after ratification of or accession to the Convention by the thirty-fifth State Party, of twenty-three experts of high moral standing and competence in the field covered by the Convention. The experts shall be elected by States Parties from among their nationals and shall serve in their personal capacity, consideration being given to equitable geographical distribution and to the representation of the different forms of civilization as well as the principal legal system.

2. The members of the Committee shall be elected by secret ballot from a list of persons nominated by States Parties. Each State Party may nominate one person from among its own nationals.

3. The initial election shall be held six months after the date of the entry into force of the present Convention. At least three months before the date of each election the Secretary-General of the United Nations shall address a letter to the States Parties inviting them to submit their nominations within two months. The Secretary-General shall prepare a list in alphabetical order of all persons thus nominated, indicating the States Parties which have nominated them, and shall submit it to the States Parties.

4. Elections of the members of the Committee shall be held at a meeting of States Parties convened by the Secretary-General at United Nations Headquarters. At that meeting, for which two thirds of the States Parties shall constitute a quorum, the persons elected to the Committee shall be those nominees who obtain the largest number of votes and an absolute majority of the votes of the representatives of States Parties present and voting.

5. The members of the Committee shall be elected for a term of four years. However, the terms of nine of the members elected at the first election shall expire at the end of two years; immediately after the first election the names of these nine members shall be chosen by lot by the Chairman of the Committee.

6. The election of the five additional members of the Committee shall be held in accordance with the provisions of paragraphs 2, 3 and 4 of this Article, following the thirty-fifth ratification or accession. The terms of two of the additional members elected on this occasion shall expire at the end of two years, the names of these two members having been chosen by lot by the Chairman of the Committee.

7. For the filling of casual vacancies, the State Party whose expert has ceased to function as a member of the Committee shall appoint another expert from among its nationals, subject to the approval of the Committee.

8. The members of the Committee shall, with the approval of the General Assembly, receive emoluments from United Nations resources on such terms and conditions as the Assembly may decide, having regard to the importance of the Committee's responsibilities.

9. The Secretary-General of the United Nations shall provide the necessary staff and facilities for the effective performance of the functions of the Committee under the present Convention.

Article 18

1. States Parties undertake to submit to the Secretary-General of the United Nations, for consideration by the Committee, a report on the legislative, judicial, administrative or other measures which they have adopted to give effect to the provisions of the present Convention and on the progress made in this respect:

   (a) Within one year after the entry into force for the State concerned; and

   (b) Thereafter at least every four years and further whenever the Committee so requests.

2. Reports may indicate factors and difficulties affecting the degree of fulfilment of obligations under the present Convention.

Article 19

1. The Committee shall adopt its own rules of procedure.

2. The Committee shall elect its officers for a term of two years.

Article 20

1. The Committee shall normally meet for a period of not more than two weeks annually in order to consider the reports submitted in accordance with Article 18 of the present Convention.

2. The meetings of the Committee shall normally be held at United Nations Headquarters or at any other convenient place as determined by the Committee.

Article 21

1. The Committee shall, through the Economic and Social Council, report annually to the General Assembly of the United Nations on its activities and may make suggestions and general recommendations based on the examination of reports and information received from the States Parties. Such suggestions and general recommendations shall be included in the report of the Committee together with comments, if any, from States Parties.

2. The Secretary-General of the United Nations shall transmit the reports of the Committee to the Commission on the Status of Women for its information.

Article 22

The specialized agencies shall be entitled to be represented at the consideration of the implementation of such provisions of the present Convention as fall within the scope of their activities. The Committee may invite the specialized agencies to submit reports on the implementation of the Convention in areas falling within the scope of their activities.

Part VI

Article 23

Nothing in the present Convention shall affect any provisions that are more conducive to the achievement of equality between men and women which may be contained:

   (a) In the legislation of a State Party; or

   (b) In any other international convention, treaty or agreement in force for that State.

Article 24

States Parties undertake to adopt all necessary measures at the national level aimed at achieving the full realization of the rights recognized in the present Convention.

Article 25

1. The present Convention shall be open for signature by all States.

2. The Secretary-General of the United Nations is designated as the depositary of the present Convention.

3. The present Convention is subject to ratification. Instruments of ratification shall be deposited with the Secretary-General of the United Nations.

4. The present Convention shall be open to accession by all States. Accession shall be effected by the deposit of an instrument of accession with the Secretary-General of the United Nations.

Article 26

1. A request for the revision of the present Convention may be made at any time by any State Party by means of a notification in writing addressed to the Secretary-General of the United Nations.

2. The General Assembly of the United Nations shall decide upon the steps, if any, to be taken in respect of such a request.

Article 27

1. The present Convention shall enter into force on the thirtieth day after the date of deposit with the Secretary-General of the United Nations of the twentieth instrument of ratification or accession.

2. For each State ratifying the present Convention or acceding to it after the deposit of the twentieth instrument of ratification or accession, the Convention shall enter into force on the thirtieth day after the date of the deposit of its own instrument of ratification or accession.

Article 28

1. The Secretary-General of the United Nations shall receive and circulate to all States the text of reservations made by States at the time of ratification or accession.

2. A reservation incompatible with the object and purpose of the present Convention shall not be permitted.

3. Reservations may be withdrawn at any time by notification to this effect addressed to the Secretary-General of the United Nations, who shall then inform all States thereof. Such notification shall take effect on the date on which it is received.

Article 29

1. Any dispute between two or more States Parties concerning the interpretation or application of the present Convention which is not settled by negotiation shall, at the request of one of them, be submitted to arbitration. If within six months from the date of the request for arbitration the parties are unable to agree on the organization of the arbitration, any one of those parties may refer the dispute to the International Court of Justice by request in conformity with the Statute of the Court.

2. Each State Party may at the time of signature or ratification of the present Convention or accession thereto declare that it does not consider itself bound by paragraph 1 of this Article. The other States Parties shall not be bound by that paragraph with respect to any State Party which has made such a reservation.

3. Any State Party which has made a reservation in accordance with paragraph 2 of this Article may at any time withdraw that reservation by notification to the Secretary-General of the United Nations.

Article 30

The present Convention, the Arabic, Chinese, English, French, Russian and Spanish texts of which are equally authentic, shall be deposited with the Secretary-General of the United Nations.

IN WITNESS WHEREOF the undersigned, duly authorized, have signed the present Convention.

APPENDIX N

Convention on the Rights of the Child, 1989

CONVENTION ON THE RIGHTS OF THE CHILD
PREAMBLE

The States Parties to the present Convention,

Considering that, in accordance with the principles proclaimed in the Charter of the United Nations, recognition of the inherent dignity and of the equal and inalienable rights of all members of the human family is the foundation of freedom, justice and peace in the world,

Bearing in mind that the peoples of the United Nations have, in the Charter, reaffirmed their faith in fundamental human rights and in the dignity and worth of the human person, and have determined to promote social progress and better standards of life in larger freedom,

Recognizing that the United Nations has, in the Universal Declaration of Human Rights and in the International Covenants on Human Rights, proclaimed and agreed that everyone is entitled to all the rights and freedoms set forth therein, without distinction of any kind, such as race, colour, sex, language, religion, political or other opinion, national or social origin, property, birth or other status,

Recalling that, in the Universal Declaration of Human Rights, the United Nations has proclaimed that childhood is entitled to special care and assistance,

Convinced that the family, as the fundamental group of society and the natural environment for the growth and well-being of all its members and particularly children, should be afforded the necessary protection and assistance so that it can fully assume its responsibilities within the community,

Recognizing that the child, for the full and harmonious development of his or her personality, should grow up in a family environment, in an atmosphere of happiness, love and understanding,

Considering that the child should be fully prepared to live an individual life in society, and brought up in the spirit of the ideals proclaimed in the Charter of the United Nations, and in particular in the spirit of peace, dignity, tolerance, freedom, equality and solidarity,

Bearing in mind that the need to extend particular care to the child has been stated in the Geneva Declaration of the Rights of the Child of 1924 and in the Declaration of the Rights of the Child adopted by the General Assembly on 20 November 1959 and recognized in the Universal Declaration of Human Rights, in the International Covenant on Civil and Political Rights (in particular in Articles 23 and 24), in the International Covenant on Economic, Social and Cultural Rights (in particular in Article 10) and in the statutes and relevant instruments of specialized agencies and international organizations concerned with the welfare of children,

Bearing in mind that, as indicated in the Declaration of the Rights of the Child, 'the child, by reason of his physical and mental immaturity, needs special safeguards and care, including appropriate legal protection, before as well as after birth',

Recalling the provisions of the Declaration on Social and Legal Principles relating to the Protection and Welfare of Children, with Special Reference to Foster Placement and Adoption Nationally and Internationally; the United Nations Standard Minimum Rules for the Administration of Juvenile Justice (The Beijing Rules); and the Declaration on the Protection of Women and Children in Emergency and Armed Conflict,

Recognizing that, in all countries in the world, there are children living in exceptionally difficult conditions, and that such children need special consideration,

Taking due account of the importance of the traditions and cultural values of each people for the protection and harmonious development of the child,

Recognizing the importance of international co-operation for improving the living conditions of children in every country, in particular in the developing countries,

Have agreed as follows:

Part I

Article 1

For the purposes of the present Convention, a child means every human being below the age of eighteen years unless under the law applicable to the child, majority is attained earlier.

Article 2

1. States Parties shall respect and ensure the rights set forth in the present Convention to each child within their jurisdiction without discrimination of any kind, irrespective of the child's or his or her parent's or legal guardian's race, colour, sex, language, religion, political or other opinion, national, ethnic or social origin, property, disability, birth or other status.

2. States Parties shall take all appropriate measures to ensure that the child is protected against all forms of discrimination or punishment on the basis of the status, activities, expressed opinions, or beliefs of the child's parents, legal guardians, or family members.

Article 3

1. In all actions concerning children, whether undertaken by public or private social welfare institutions, courts of law, administrative authorities or legislative bodies, the best interests of the child shall be a primary consideration.

2. States Parties undertake to ensure the child such protection and care as is necessary for his or her well-being, taking into account the rights and duties of his or her parents, legal guardians, or other individuals legally responsible for him or her, and, to this end, shall take all appropriate legislative and administrative measures.

3. States Parties shall ensure that the institutions, services and facilities responsible for the care or protection of children shall conform with the standards established by competent authorities, particularly in the areas of safety, health, in the number and suitability of their staff, as well as competent supervision.

Article 4

States Parties shall undertake all appropriate legislative, administrative, and other measures for the implementation of the rights recognized in the present Convention. With regard to economic, social and cultural rights, States Parties shall undertake such measures to the maximum extent of their available resources and, where needed, within the framework of international co-operation.

Article 5

States Parties shall respect the responsibilities, rights and duties of parents or, where applicable, the members of the extended family or community as provided for by local custom, legal guardians or other persons legally responsible for the child, to provide, in a manner consistent with the evolving capacities of the child, appropriate direction and guidance in the exercise by the child of the rights recognized in the present Convention.

Article 6

1. States Parties recognize that every child has the inherent right to life.

2. States Parties shall ensure to the maximum extent possible the survival and development of the child.

Article 7

1. The child shall be registered immediately after birth and shall have the right from birth to a name, the right to acquire a nationality and. as far as possible, the right to know and be cared for by his or her parents.

2. States Parties shall ensure the implementation of these rights in accordance with their national law and their obligations under the relevant international instruments in this field, in particular where the child would otherwise be stateless.

Article 8

1. States Parties undertake to respect the right of the child to preserve his or her identity, including nationality, name and family relations as recognized by law without unlawful interference.

2. Where a child is illegally deprived of some or all of the elements of his or her identity, States Parties shall provide appropriate assistance and protection, with a view to re-establishing speedily his or her identity.

Article 9

1. States Parties shall ensure that a child shall not be separated from his or her parents against their will, except when competent authorities subject to judicial review determine, in accordance with applicable law and procedures, that such separation is necessary for the best interests of the child. Such determination may be necessary in a particular case such as one involving abuse or neglect of the child by the parents, or one where the parents are living separately and a decision must be made as to the child's place of residence.

2. In any proceedings pursuant to paragraph 1 of the present Article, all interested parties shall be given an opportunity to participate in the proceedings and make their views known.

3. States Parties shall respect the right of the child who is separated from one or both parents to maintain personal relations and direct contact with both parents on a regular basis, except if it is contrary to the child's best interests.

4. Where such separation results from any action initiated by a State Party, such as the detention, imprisonment, exile, deportation or death (including death arising from any cause while the person is in the custody of the State) of one or both parents or of the child, that State Party shall, upon request, provide the parents, the child or, if appropriate, another member of the family with the essential information concerning the whereabouts of the absent member(s) of the family unless the provision of the information would be detrimental to the well-being of the child. States Parties shall further ensure that the submission of such a request shall of itself entail no adverse consequences for the person(s) concerned.

Article 10

1. In accordance with the obligation of States Parties under Article 9, paragraph 1, applications by a child or his or her parents to enter or leave a State Party for the purpose of family reunification shall be dealt with by States Parties in a positive, humane and expeditious manner. States Parties shall further ensure that the submission of such a request shall entail no adverse consequences for the applicants and for the members of their family.

2. A child whose parents reside in different States shall have the right to maintain on a regular basis, save in exceptional circumstances personal relations and direct contacts with both parents. Towards that end and in accordance with the obligation of States Parties under Article 9, paragraph 1, States Parties shall respect the right of the child and his or her parents to leave any country, including their own, and to enter their own country. The right to leave any country shall be subject only to such restrictions as are prescribed by law and which are necessary to protect the national security, public order (*ordre public*), public health or morals or the rights and freedoms of others and are consistent with the other rights recognized in the present Convention.

Article 11

1. States Parties shall take measures to combat the illicit transfer and non-return of children abroad.

2. To this end, States Parties shall promote the conclusion of bilateral or multilateral agreements or accession to existing agreements.

Article 12

1. States Parties shall assure to the child who is capable of forming his or her own views the right to express those views freely in all matters affecting the child, the views of the child being given due weight in accordance with the age and maturity of the child.

2. For this purpose, the child shall in particular be provided the opportunity to be heard in any judicial and administrative proceedings affecting the child, either directly, or through a representative or an appropriate body, in a manner consistent with the procedural rules of national law.

Article 13

1. The child shall have the right to freedom of expression; this right shall include freedom to seek, receive and impart information and ideas of all kinds, regardless of frontiers, either orally, in writing or in print, in the form of art, or through any other media of the child's choice.

2. The exercise of this right may be subject to certain restrictions, but these shall only be such as are provided by law and are necessary:

(a) For respect of the rights or reputations of others; or

(b) For the protection of national security or of public order (*ordre public*), or of public health or morals.

Article 14

1. States Parties shall respect the right of the child to freedom of thought, conscience and religion.

2. States Parties shall respect the rights and duties of the parents and, when applicable, legal guardians, to provide direction to the child in the exercise of his or her right in a manner consistent with the evolving capacities of the child.

3. Freedom to manifest one's religion or beliefs may be subject only to such limitations as are prescribed by law and are necessary to protect public safety, order, health or morals, or the fundamental rights and freedoms of others.

Article 15

1. States Parties recognize the rights of the child to freedom of association and to freedom of peaceful assembly.

2. No restrictions may be placed on the exercise of these rights other than those imposed in conformity with the law and which are necessary in a democratic society in the interests of national security or public safety, public order (*ordre public*), the protection of public health or morals or the protection of the rights and freedoms of others.

Article 16

1. No child shall be subjected to arbitrary or unlawful interference with his or her privacy, family, home or correspondence, nor to unlawful attacks on his or her honour and reputation.

2. The child has the right to the protection of the law against such interference or attacks.

Article 17

States Parties recognize the important function performed by the mass media and shall ensure that the child has access to information and material from a diversity of national and international sources, especially those aimed at the promotion of his or her social, spiritual and moral well-being and physical and mental health. To this end, States Parties shall:

(a) Encourage the mass media to disseminate information and material of social and cultural benefit to the child and in accordance with the spirit of Article 29;

(b) Encourage international co-operation in the production, exchange and dissemination of such information and material from a diversity of cultural, national and international sources;

(c) Encourage the production and dissemination of children's books;

(d) Encourage the mass media to have particular regard to the linguistic needs of the child who belongs to a minority group or who is indigenous;

(e) Encourage the development of appropriate guidelines for the protection of the child from information and material injurious to his or her well-being, bearing in mind the provisions of Articles 13 and 18.

Article 18

1. States Parties shall use their best efforts to ensure recognition of the principle that both parents have common responsibilities for the upbringing and development of the child. Parents or, as the case may be, legal guardians, have the primary responsibility for the upbringing and development of the child. The best interests of the child will be their basic concern.

2. For the purpose of guaranteeing and promoting the rights set forth in the present Convention, States Parties shall render appropriate assistance to parents and legal guardians in the performance of their child-rearing responsibilities and shall ensure the development of institutions, facilities and services for the care of children.

3. States Parties shall take all appropriate measures to ensure that children of working parents have the right to benefit from child-care services and facilities for which they are eligible.

Article 19

1. States Parties shall take all appropriate legislative, administrative, social and educational measures to protect the child from all forms of physical or mental violence, injury or abuse, neglect or negligent treatment, maltreatment or exploitation, including sexual abuse, while in the care of parent(s), legal guardian(s) or any other person who has the care of the child.

2. Such protective measures should, as appropriate, include effective procedures for the establishment of social programmes to provide necessary support for the child and for those who have the care of the child, as well as for other forms of prevention and for identification, reporting, referral, investigation, treatment and follow-up of instances of child maltreatment described heretofore, and, as appropriate, for judicial involvement.

Article 20

1. A child temporarily or permanently deprived of his or her family environment, or in whose own best interests cannot be allowed to remain in that environment, shall be entitled to special protection and assistance provided by the State.

2. States Parties shall in accordance with their national laws ensure alternative care for such a child.

3. Such care could include, *inter alia*, foster placement, *kafalah* of Islamic law, adoption or if necessary placement in suitable institutions for the care of children. When considering solutions, due regard shall be paid to the desirability of continuity in a child's upbringing and to the child's ethnic, religious, cultural and linguistic background.

Article 21

States Parties that recognize and/or permit the system of adoption shall ensure that the best interests of the child shall be the paramount consideration and they shall:

(a) Ensure that the adoption of a child is authorized only by competent authorities who determine, in accordance with applicable law and procedures and on the basis of all pertinent and reliable information, that the adoption is permissible in view of the child's status concerning parents, relatives and legal guardians and that, if required, the persons concerned have given their informed consent to the adoption on the basis of such counselling as may be necessary;

(b) Recognize that inter-country adoption may be considered as an alternative means of child's care, if the child cannot be placed in a foster or an adoptive family or cannot in any suitable manner be cared for in the child's country of origin;

(c) Ensure that the child concerned by inter-country adoption enjoys safeguards and standards equivalent to those existing in the case of national adoption;

(d) Take all appropriate measures to ensure that, in inter-country adoption, the placement does not result in improper financial gain for those involved in it;

(e) Promote, where appropriate, the objectives of the present article by concluding bilateral or multilateral arrangements or agreements, and endeavour, within this framework, to ensure that the placement of the child in another country is carried out by competent authorities or organs.

Article 22

1. States Parties shall take appropriate measures to ensure that a child who is seeking refugee status or who is considered a refugee in accordance with applicable international or domestic law and procedures shall, whether unaccompanied or accompanied by his or her parents or by any other person, receive appropriate protection and humanitarian assistance in the enjoyment of applicable rights set forth in the present Convention and in other international human rights or humanitarian instruments to which the said States are Parties.

2. For this purpose, States Parties shall provide, as they consider appropriate, co-operation in any efforts by the United Nations and other competent inter-governmental organizations or non-governmental organizations co-operating with the United Nations to protect and assist such a child and to trace the parents or other members of the family of any refugee child in order to obtain information necessary for reunification with his or her family. In cases where no parents or other members of the family can be found, the child shall be accorded the same protection as any other child permanently or temporarily deprived of his or her family environment for any reason , as set forth in the present Convention.

Article 23

1. States Parties recognize that a mentally or physically disabled child should enjoy a full and decent life, in conditions which ensure dignity, promote self-reliance and facilitate the child's active participation in the community.

2. States Parties recognize the right of the disabled child to special care and shall encourage and ensure the extension, subject to available resources, to the eligible child and those responsible for his or her care, of assistance for which application is made and which is appropriate to the child's condition and to the circumstances of the parents or others caring for the child.

3. Recognizing the special needs of a disabled child, assistance extended in accordance with paragraph 2 of the present article shall be provided free of charge, whenever possible, taking into account the financial resources of the parents or others caring for the child, and shall be designed to ensure that the disabled child has effective access to and receives education, training, health care services, rehabilitation services, preparation for employment and recreation opportunities in a manner conducive to the child's achieving the fullest possible social integration and individual development, including his or her cultural and spiritual development

4. States Parties shall promote, in the spirit of international co-operation, the exchange of appropriate information in the field of preventive health care and of medical, psychological and functional treatment of disabled children, including dissemination of and access to information concerning methods of rehabilitation, education and vocational services, with the aim of enabling States Parties to improve their capabilities and skills and to widen their experience in these areas. In this regard, particular account shall be taken of the needs of developing countries.

Article 24

1. States Parties recognize the right of the child to the enjoyment of the highest attainable standard of health and to facilities for the treatment of illness and rehabilitation of health. States Parties shall strive to ensure that no child is deprived of his or her right of access to such health care services.

2. States Parties shall pursue full implementation of this right and, in particular, shall take appropriate measures:

(a) To diminish infant and child mortality;
(b) To ensure the provision of necessary medical assistance and health care to all children with emphasis on the development of primary health care;
(c) To combat disease and malnutrition, including within the framework of primary health care, through, *inter alia*, the application of readily available technology and through the provision of adequate nutritious foods and clean drinking-water, taking into consideration the dangers and risks of environmental pollution;
(d) To ensure appropriate pre-natal and post-natal health care for mothers;
(e) To ensure that all segments of society, in particular parents and children, are informed, have access to education and are supported in the use of basic knowledge of child health and nutrition, the advantages of breast-feeding, hygiene and environmental sanitation and the prevention of accidents;
(f) To develop preventive health care, guidance for parents and family planning education and services.

3. States Parties shall take all effective and appropriate measures with a view to abolishing traditional practices prejudicial to the health of children.

4. States Parties undertake to promote and encourage international co-operation with a view to achieving progressively the full realization of the right recognized in the present article. In this regard, particular account shall be taken of the needs of developing countries.

Article 25

States Parties recognize the right of a child who has been placed by the competent authorities for the purposes of care, protection or treatment of his or her physical or mental health, to a periodic review of the treatment provided to the child and all other circumstances relevant to his or her placement.

Article 26

1. States Parties shall recognize for every child the right to benefit from social security, including social insurance, and shall take the necessary measures to achieve the full realization of this right in accordance with their national law.

2. The benefits should, where appropriate, be granted, taking into account the resources and the circumstances of the child and persons having responsibility for the maintenance of the child, as well as any other consideration relevant to an application for benefits made by or on behalf of the child.

Article 27

1. States Parties recognize the right of every child to a standard of living adequate for the child's physical, mental, spiritual, moral and social development.

2. The parent(s) or others responsible for the child have the primary responsibility to secure, within their abilities and financial capacities, the conditions of living necessary for the child's development.

3. States Parties, in accordance with national conditions and within their means, shall take appropriate measures to assist parents and others responsible for the child to implement this right and shall in case of need provide material assistance and support programmes, particularly with regard to nutrition, clothing and housing.

4. States Parties shall take all appropriate measures to secure the recovery of maintenance for the child from the parents or other persons having financial responsibility for the child, both within the State Party and from abroad. In particular, where the person having financial responsibility for the child lives in a State different from that of the child, States Parties shall promote the accession to international agreements or the conclusion of such agreements, as well as the making of other appropriate arrangements.

Article 28

1. States Parties recognize the right of the child to education, and with a view to achieving this right progressively and on the basis of equal opportunity, they shall, in particular:

(a) Make primary education compulsory and available free to all;
(b) Encourage the development of different forms of secondary education, including general and vocational education, make them available and accessible to every child, and take appropriate measures such as the introduction of free education and offering financial assistance in case of need;
(c) Make higher education accessible to all on the basis of capacity by every appropriate means;
(d) Make educational and vocational information and guidance available and accessible to all children;
(e) Take measures to encourage regular attendance at schools and the reduction of drop-out rates.

2. States Parties shall take all appropriate measures to ensure that school discipline is administered in a manner consistent with the child's human dignity and in conformity with the present Convention.

3. States Parties shall promote and encourage international co-operation in matters relating to education, in particular with a view to contributing to the elimination of ignorance and illiteracy throughout the world and facilitating access to scientific and technical knowledge and modern teaching methods. In this regard, particular account shall be taken of the needs of developing countries.

Article 29

1. States Parties agree that the education of the child shall be directed to:
(a) The development of the child's personality, talents and mental and physical abilities to their fullest potential;
(b) The development of respect for human rights and fundamental freedoms, and for the principles enshrined in the Charter of the United Nations;
(c) The development of respect for the child's parents, his or her own cultural identity, language and values, for the national values of the country in which the child is living, the country from which he or she may originate, and for civilizations different from his or her own;
(d) The preparation of the child for responsible life in a free society, in the spirit of understanding, peace, tolerance, equality of sexes, and friendship among all peoples, ethnic, national and religious groups and persons of indigenous origin;
(e) The development of respect for the natural environment.

2. No part of the present Article or Article 28 shall be construed so as to interfere with the liberty of individuals and bodies to establish and direct educational institutions, subject always to the observance of the principle set forth in paragraph 1 of the present Article and to the requirements that the education given in such institutions shall conform to such minimum standards as may be laid down by the State.

Article 30

In those States in which ethnic, religious or linguistic minorities or persons of indigenous origin exist, a child belonging to such a minority or who is indigenous shall not be denied the right, in community with other members of his or her group, to enjoy his or her own culture, to profess and practise his or her own religion, or to use his or her own language.

Article 31

1. States Parties recognize the right of the child to rest and leisure, to engage in play and recreational activities appropriate to the age of the child and to participate freely in cultural life and the arts.

2. States Parties shall respect and promote the right of the child to participate fully in cultural and artistic life and shall encourage the provision of appropriate and equal opportunities for cultural, artistic, recreational and leisure activity.

Article 32

1. States Parties recognize the right of the child to be protected from economic exploitation and from performing any work that is likely to be hazardous or to interfere with the child's education, or to be harmful to the child's health or physical, mental, spiritual, moral or social development.

2. States Parties shall take legislative, administrative, social and educational measures to ensure the implementation of the present article. To this end, and having regard to the relevant provisions of other international instruments, States Parties shall in particular:

(a) Provide for a minimum age or minimum ages for admission to employment;
(b) Provide for appropriate regulation of the hours and conditions of employment;
(c) Provide for appropriate penalties or other sanctions to ensure the effective enforcement of the present article.

Article 33

States Parties shall take all appropriate measures, including legislative, administrative, social and educational measures, to protect children from the illicit use of narcotic drugs and psychotropic substances as defined in the relevant international treaties, and to prevent the use of children in the illicit production and trafficking of such substances.

Article 34

States Parties undertake to protect the child from all forms of sexual exploitation and sexual abuse. For these purposes, States Parties shall in particular take all appropriate national, bilateral and multilateral measures to prevent:

(a) The inducement or coercion of a child to engage in any unlawful sexual activity;
(b) The exploitative use of children in prostitution or other unlawful sexual practices;
(c) The exploitative use of children in pornographic performances and materials.

Article 35

States Parties shall take all appropriate national, bilateral and multilateral measures to prevent the abduction of, the sale of or traffic in children for any purpose or in any form.

Article 36

States Parties shall protect the child against all other forms of exploitation prejudicial to any aspects of the child's welfare.

Article 37

States Parties shall ensure that:

(a) No child shall be subjected to torture or other cruel, inhuman or degrading treatment or punishment. Neither capital punishment nor life imprisonment without possibility of release shall be imposed for offences committed by persons below eighteen years of age;
(b) No child shall be deprived of his or her liberty unlawfully or arbitrarily. The arrest, detention or imprisonment of a child shall be in conformity with the law and shall be used only as a measure of last resort and for the shortest appropriate period of time;
(c) Every child deprived of liberty shall be treated with humanity and respect for the inherent dignity of the human person, and in a manner which takes into account the needs of persons of his or her age. In particular, every child deprived of liberty shall be separated from adults unless it is considered in the child's best interest not to do so and shall have the right to maintain contact with his or her family through correspondence and visits, save in exceptional circumstances;
(d) Every child deprived of his or her liberty shall have the right to prompt access to legal and other appropriate assistance, as well as the right to challenge the legality of the deprivation of his or her liberty before a court or other competent, independent and impartial authority, and to a prompt decision on any such action.

Article 38

1. States Parties undertake to respect and to ensure respect for rules of international humanitarian law applicable to them in armed conflicts which are relevant to the child.

2. States Parties shall take all feasible measures to ensure that persons who have not attained the age of fifteen years do not take a direct part in hostilities.

3. States Parties shall refrain from recruiting any person who has not attained the age of fifteen years into their armed forces. In recruiting among those persons who have attained the age of fifteen years but who have not attained the age of eighteen years, States Parties shall endeavour to give priority to those who are oldest.

4. In accordance with their obligations under international humanitarian law to protect the civilian population in armed conflicts, States Parties shall take all feasible measures to ensure protection and care of children who are affected by an armed conflict.

Article 39

States Parties shall take all appropriate measures to promote physical and psychological recovery and social reintegration of a child victim of: any form of neglect, exploitation, or abuse; torture or any other form of cruel, inhuman or degrading treatment or punishment; or armed conflicts. Such recovery and reintegration shall take place in an environment which fosters the health, self-respect and dignity of the child.

Article 40

1. States Parties recognize the right of every child alleged as, accused of, or recognized as having infringed the penal law to be treated in a manner consistent with the promotion of the child's sense of dignity and worth, which reinforces the child's respect for the human rights and fundamental freedoms of others and which takes into account the child's age and the desirability of promoting the child's reintegration and the child's assuming a constructive role in society.

2. To this end, and having regard to the relevant provisions of international instruments, States Parties shall, in particular, ensure that:

- (a) No child shall be alleged as, be accused of, or recognized as having infringed the penal law by reason of acts or omissions that were not prohibited by national or international law at the time they were committed;
- (b) Every child alleged as or accused of having infringed the penal law has at least the following guarantees:
  - (i) To be presumed innocent until proven guilty according to law;
  - (ii) To be informed promptly and directly of the charges against him or her, and, if appropriate, through his or her parents or legal guardians, and to have legal or other appropriate assistance in the preparation and presentation of his or her defence;
  - (iii) To have the matter determined without delay by a competent, independent and impartial authority or judicial body in a fair hearing according to law, in the presence of legal or other appropriate assistance and, unless it is considered not to be in the best interest of the child, in particular, taking into account his or her age or situation, his or her parents or legal guardians;
  - (iv) Not to be compelled to give testimony or to confess guilt; to examine or have examined adverse witnesses and to obtain the participation and examination of witnesses on his or her behalf under conditions of equality;
  - (v) If considered to have infringed the penal law, to have this decision and any measures imposed in consequence thereof reviewed by a higher competent, independent and impartial authority or judicial body according to law;
  - (vi) To have the free assistance of an interpreter if the child cannot understand or speak the language used;
  - (vii) To have his or her privacy fully respected at all stages of the proceedings.

3. States Parties shall seek to promote the establishment of laws, procedures, authorities and institutions specifically applicable to children alleged as, accused of, or recognized as having infringed the penal law, and, in particular:

(a) The establishment of a minimum age below which children shall be presumed not to have the capacity to infringe the penal law;
(b) Whenever appropriate and desirable, measures for dealing with such children without resorting to judicial proceedings, providing that human rights and legal safeguards are fully respected.

4. A variety of dispositions, such as care, guidance and supervision orders; counselling; probation; foster care; education and vocational training programmes and other alternatives to institutional care shall be available to ensure that children are dealt with in a manner appropriate to their well-being and proportionate both to their circumstances and the offence.

Article 41

Nothing in the present Convention shall affect any provisions which are more conducive to the realization of the rights of the child and which may be contained in:
(a) The law of a State party; or
(b) International law in force for that State.

Part II

Article 42

States Parties undertake to make the principles and provisions of the Convention widely known, by appropriate and active means, to adults and children alike.

Article 43

1. For the purpose of examining the progress made by States Parties in achieving the realization of the obligations undertaken in the present Convention, there shall be established a Committee on the Rights of the Child, which shall carry out the functions hereinafter provided.

2. The Committee shall consist of ten experts of high moral standing and recognized competence in the field covered by this Convention. The members of the Committee shall be elected by States Parties from among their nationals and shall serve in their personal capacity, consideration being given to equitable geographical distribution, as well as to the principal legal systems.

3. The members of the Committee shall be elected by secret ballot from a list of persons nominated by States Parties. Each State Party may nominate one person from among its own nationals.

4. The initial election to the Committee shall be held no later than six months after the date of the entry into force of the present Convention and thereafter every second year. At least four months before the date of each election, the Secretary-General of the United Nations shall address a letter to States Parties inviting them to submit their nominations within two months. The Secretary-General shall subsequently prepare a list in alphabetical order of all persons thus nominated, indicating States Parties which have nominated them, and shall submit it to the States Parties to the present Convention.

5. The elections shall be held at meetings of States Parties convened by the Secretary-General at United Nations Headquarters. At those meetings, for which two thirds of States Parties shall constitute a quorum, the persons elected to the Committee shall be those who obtain the largest number of votes and an absolute majority of the votes of the representatives of States Parties present and voting.

6. The members of the Committee shall be elected for a term of four years. They shall be eligible for re-election if renominated. The term of five of the members elected at the first election shall expire at the end of two years; immediately after the first election, the names of these five members shall be chosen by lot by the Chairman of the meeting.

7. If a member of the Committee dies or resigns or declares that for any other cause he or she can no longer perform the duties of the Committee, the State Party which nominated the member shall appoint another expert from among its nationals to serve for the remainder of the term, subject to the approval of the Committee.

8. The Committee shall establish its own rules of procedure.

9. The Committee shall elect its officers for a period of two years.

10. The meetings of the Committee shall normally be held at United Nations Headquarters or at any other convenient place as determined by the Committee. The Committee shall normally meet annually. The duration of the meetings of the Committee shall be determined, and reviewed, if necessary, by a meeting of the States Parties to the present Convention, subject to the approval of the General Assembly.

11. The Secretary-General of the United Nations shall provide the necessary staff and facilities for the effective performance of the functions of the Committee under the present Convention.

12. With the approval of the General Assembly, the members of the Committee established under the present Convention shall receive emoluments from United Nations resources on such terms and conditions as the Assembly may decide.

Article 44

1. States Parties undertake to submit to the Committee, through the Secretary-General of the United Nations, reports on the measures they have adopted which give effect to the rights recognized herein and on the progress made on the enjoyment of those rights:

(a) Within two years of the entry into force of the Convention for the State Party concerned;

(b) Thereafter every five years.

2. Reports made under the present Article shall indicate factors and difficulties, if any, affecting the degree of fulfilment of the obligations under the present Convention. Reports shall also contain sufficient information to provide the Committee with a comprehensive understanding of the implementation of the Convention in the country concerned.

3. A State Party which has submitted a comprehensive initial report to the Committee need not, in its subsequent reports submitted in accordance with paragraph 1(b) of the present article, repeat basic information previously provided.

4. The Committee may request from States Parties further information relevant to the implementation of the Convention.

5. The Committee shall submit to the General Assembly, through the Economic and Social Council, every two years, reports on its activities.

6. States Parties shall make their reports widely available to the public in their own countries.

Article 45

In order to foster the effective implementation of the Convention and to encourage international co-operation in the field covered by the Convention:

(a) The specialized agencies, the United Nations Children's Fund, and other United Nations organs shall be entitled to be represented at the consideration of the implementation of such provisions of the present Convention as fall within the scope of their mandate. The Committee may invite the specialized agencies, the United Nations Children's Fund and other competent bodies as it may consider appropriate to provide expert advice on the implementation of the Convention in areas falling within the scope of their respective mandates. The Committee may invite the specialized agencies, the United Nations Children's Fund, and other United Nations organs to submit reports on the implementation of the Convention in areas falling within the scope of their activities;

(b) The Committee shall transmit, as it may consider appropriate, to the specialized agencies, the United Nations Children's Fund and other competent bodies, any reports from States Parties that contain a request, or indicate a need, for technical advice or assistance, along with the Committee's observations and suggestions, if any, on these requests or indications;

(c) The Committee may recommend to the General Assembly to request the Secretary-General to undertake on its behalf studies on specific issues relating to the rights of the child;

(d) The Committee may make suggestions and general recommendations based on information received pursuant to Articles 44 and 45 of the present Convention. Such suggestions and general recommendations shall be transmitted to any State Party concerned and reported to the General Assembly, together with comments, if any, from States Parties.

Part III

Article 46

The present Convention shall be open for signature by all States.

Article 47

The present Convention is subject to ratification. Instruments of ratification shall be deposited with the Secretary-General of the United Nations.

Article 48

The present Convention shall remain open for accession by any State. The instruments of accession shall be deposited with the Secretary-General of the United Nations.

Article 49

1. The present Convention shall enter into force on the thirtieth day following the date of deposit with the Secretary-General of the United Nations of the twentieth instrument of ratification or accession.

2. For each State ratifying or acceding to the Convention after the deposit of the twentieth instrument of ratification or accession, the Convention shall enter into force on the thirtieth day after the deposit by such State of its instrument of ratification or accession.

Article 50

1. Any State Party may propose an amendment and file it with the Secretary-General of the United Nations. The Secretary-General shall thereupon communicate the proposed amendment to States Parties, with a request that they indicate whether they favour a conference of States Parties for the purpose of considering and voting upon the proposals. In the event that, within four months from the date of such communication, at least one third of the States Parties favour such a conference, the Secretary-General shall convene the conference under the auspices of the United Nations. Any amendment adopted by a majority of States Parties present and voting at the conference shall be submitted to the General Assembly for approval.

2. An amendment adopted in accordance with paragraph 1 of the present article shall enter into force when it has been approved by the General Assembly of the United Nations and accepted by a two-thirds majority of States Parties.

3. When an amendment enters into force, it shall be binding on those States Parties which have accepted it, other States Parties still being bound by the provisions of the present Convention and any earlier amendments which they have accepted.

Article 51

1. The Secretary-General of the United Nations shall receive and circulate to all States the text of reservations made by States at the time of ratification or accession.

2. A reservation incompatible with the object and purpose of the present Convention shall not be permitted.

3. Reservations may be withdrawn at any time by notification to that effect addressed to the Secretary-General of the United Nations, who shall then inform all States. Such notification shall take effect on the date on which it is received by the Secretary-General.

Article 52

A State Party may denounce the present Convention by written notification to the Secretary-General of the United Nations. Denunciation becomes effective one year after the date of receipt of the notification by the Secretary-General.

Article 53

The Secretary-General of the United Nations is designated as the depositary of the present Convention.

Article 54

The original of the present Convention, of which the Arabic, Chinese, English, French, Russian and Spanish texts are equally authentic, shall be deposited with the Secretary-General of the United Nations.

In witness thereof the undersigned plenipotentiaries, being duly authorized thereto by their respective governments, have signed the present Convention.

APPENDIX O

Canadian Charter of Rights and Freedoms

Schedule B
Constitution Act, 1982 (79)

Enacted as Schedule B to the *Canada Act 1982* (UK) 1982, c 11, which came into force on April 17,1982

Part I

Whereas Canada is founded upon principles that recognize the supremacy of God and the rule of law:

Guarantee of rights and freedoms

Rights and freedoms in Canada

1. The *Canadian Charter of Rights and Freedoms* guarantees the rights and freedoms set out in it subject only to such reasonable limits prescribed by law as can be demonstrably justified in a free and democratic society.

Fundamental freedoms

Fundamental freedoms

2. Everyone has the following fundamental freedoms:
   (a) freedom of conscience and religion;
   (b) freedom of thought, belief, opinion and expression, including freedom of the press and other media of communication;
   (c) freedom of peaceful assembly; and
   (d) freedom of association.

Democratic rights

Democratic rights of citizens

3. Every citizen of Canada has the right to vote in an election of members of the House of Commons or of a legislative assembly and to be qualified for membership therein.

Maximum duration of legislative bodies

4.(1) No House of Commons and no legislative assembly shall continue for longer than five years from the date fixed for the return of the writs of a general election of its members.

Continuation in special circumstances

(2) In time of real or apprehended war, invasion or insurrection, a House of Commons may be continued by Parliament and a legislative assembly may be continued by the legislature beyond five years if such continuation is not opposed by the votes of more than one-third of the members of the House of Commons or the legislative assembly, as the case may be.

Annual sitting of legislative bodies

5. There shall be a sitting of Parliament and of each legislature at least once every twelve months.

Mobility rights

Mobility of citizens

6.(1) Every citizen of Canada has the right to enter, remain in and leave Canada.

Rights to move and gain livelihood

(2) Every citizen of Canada and every person who has the status of a permanent resident of Canada has the right

(a) to move to and take up residence in any province; and
(b) to pursue the gaining of a livelihood in any province.

Limitation

(3) The rights specified in subsection (2) are subject to

(a) any laws or practices of general application in force in a province other than those that discriminate among persons primarily on the basis of province of present or previous residence; and
(b) any laws providing for reasonable residency requirements as a qualification for the receipt of publicly provided social services.

Affirmative action programs

(4) Subsections (2) and (3) do not preclude any law, program or activity that has as its object the amelioration in a province of conditions of individuals in that province who are socially or economically disadvantaged if the rate of employment in that province is below the rate of employment in Canada.

Legal rights

Life, liberty and security of person

7. Everyone has the right to life, liberty and security of the person and the right not to be deprived thereof except in accordance with the principles of fundamental justice.

Search or seizure

8. Everyone has the right to be secure against unreasonable search or seizure.

Detention or imprisonment

9. Everyone has the right not to be arbitrarily detained or imprisoned.

Arrest or detention

10. Everyone has the right on arrest or detention

(a) to be informed promptly of the reasons therefor;
(b) to retain and instruct counsel without delay and to be informed of that right; and
(c) to have the validity of the detention determined by way of *habeas corpus* and to be released if the detention is not lawful.

Proceedings in criminal and penal matters

11. Any person charged with an offence has the right

(a) to be informed without unreasonable delay of the specific offence;
(b) to be tried within a reasonable time;
(c) not to be compelled to be a witness in proceedings against that person in respect of the offence;
(d) to be presumed innocent until proven guilty according to law in a fair and public hearing by an independent and impartial tribunal;
(e) not to be denied reasonable bail without just cause;
(f) except in the case of an offence under military law tried before a military tribunal, to the benefit of trial by jury where the maximum punishment for the offence is imprisonment for five years or a more severe punishment;

(g) not to be found guilty on account of any act or omission unless, at the time of the act or omission, it constituted an offence under Canadian or international law or was criminal according to the general principles of law recognized by the community of nations;
(h) if finally acquitted of the offence, not to be tried for it again and, if finally found guilty and punished for the offence, not to be tried or punished for it again; and
(i) if found guilty of the offence and if the punishment for the offence has been varied between the time of commission and the time of sentencing, to the benefit of the lesser punishment.

Treatment or punishment

12. Everyone has the right not to be subjected to any cruel and unusual treatment or punishment.

Self-crimination

13. A witness who testifies in any proceedings has the right not to have any incriminating evidence so given used to incriminate that witness in any other proceedings, except in a prosecution for perjury or for the giving of contradictory evidence.

Interpreter

14. A party or witness in any proceedings who does not understand or speak the language in which the proceedings are conducted or who is deaf has the right to the assistance of an interpreter.

Equality rights

Equality before and under law and equal protection and benefit of law

15.(1) Every individual is equal before and under the law and has the right to the equal protection and equal benefit of the law without discrimination and, in particular, without discrimination based on race, national or ethnic origin, colour, religion, sex, age or mental or physical disability.

Affirmative action programmes

(2) Subsection (1) does not preclude any law, programme or activity that has as its object the amelioration of conditions of disadvantaged individuals or groups including those that are disadvantaged because of race, national or ethnic origin, colour, religion, sex, age or mental or physical disability.

Official languages of Canada

Official languages of Canada

16.(1) English and French are the official languages of Canada and have equality of status and equal rights and privileges as to their use in all institutions of the Parliament and government of Canada.

Official languages of New Brunswick

(2) English and French are the official languages of New Brunswick and have equality of status and equal rights and privileges as to their use in all institutions of the legislature and government of New Brunswick.

Advancement of status and use

(3) Nothing in this Charter limits the authority of Parliament or a legislature to advance the equality of status or use of English and French.

English and French linguistic communities in New Brunswick

16.1(1) The English linguistic community and the French linguistic community in New Brunswick have equality of status and equal rights and privileges, including the right to distinct educational institutions and such distinct cultural institutions as are necessary for the preservation and promotion of those communities.

Role of the legislature and government of New Brunswick

(2) The role of the legislature and government of New Brunswick to preserve and promote the status, rights and privileges referred to in subsection (1) is affirmed.

Proceedings of Parliament

17.(1) Everyone has the right to use English or French in any debates and other proceedings of Parliament.

Proceedings of New Brunswick legislature

(2) Everyone has the right to use English or French in any debates and other proceedings of the legislature of New Brunswick.

Parliamentary statutes and records

18.(1) The statutes, records and journals of Parliament shall be printed and published in English and French and both language versions are equally authoritative.

New Brunswick statutes and records

(2) The statutes, records and journals of the legislature of New Brunswick shall be printed and published in English and French and both language versions are equally authoritative.

Proceedings in courts established by Parliament

19.(1) Either English or French may be used by any person in, or in any pleading in or process issuing from, any court established by Parliament.

Proceedings in New Brunswick courts

(2) Either English or French may be used by any person in, or in any pleading in or process issuing from, any court of New Brunswick.

Communications by public with federal institutions

20.(1) Any member of the public in Canada has the right to communicate with, and to receive available services from, any head or central office of an institution of the Parliament or government of Canada in English or French, and has the same right with respect to any other office of any such institution where

(a) there is a significant demand for communications with and services from that office in such language; or

(b) due to the nature of the office, it is reasonable that communications with and services from that office be available in both English and French.

Communications by public with New Brunswick institutions

(2) Any member of the public in New Brunswick has the right to communicate with, and to receive available services from, any office of an institution of the legislature or government of New Brunswick in English or French.

Continuation of existing constitutional provisions

21. Nothing in sections 16 to 20 abrogates or derogates from any right, privilege or obligation with respect to the English and French languages, or either of them, that exists or is continued by virtue of any other provision of the Constitution of Canada.

Rights and privileges preserved

22. Nothing in sections 16 to 20 abrogates or derogates from any legal or customary right or privilege acquired or enjoyed either before or after the coming into force of this Charter with respect to any language that is not English or French.

Minority language educational rights

Language of instruction

23.(1) Citizens of Canada

(a) whose first language learned and still understood is that of the English or French linguistic minority population of the province in which they reside, or

(b) who have received their primary school instruction in Canada in English or French and reside in a province where the language in which they received that instruction is the language of the English or French linguistic minority population of the province,

have the right to have their children receive primary and secondary school instruction in that language in that province.

Continuity of language instruction

(2) Citizens of Canada of whom any child has received or is receiving primary or secondary school instruction in English or French in Canada, have the right to have all their children receive primary and secondary school instruction in the same language.

Application where numbers warrant

(3) The right of citizens of Canada under subsections (1) and (2) to have their children receive primary and secondary school instruction in the language of the English or French linguistic minority population of a province

(a) applies wherever in the province the number of children of citizens who have such a right is sufficient to warrant the provision to them out of public funds of minority language instruction; and
(b) includes, where the number of those children so warrants, the right to have them receive that instruction in minority language educational facilities provided out of public funds.

Enforcement

Enforcement of guaranteed rights and freedoms

24.(1) Anyone whose rights or freedoms, as guaranteed by this Charter, have been infringed or denied may apply to a court of competent jurisdiction to obtain such remedy as the court considers appropriate and just in the circumstances.

Exclusion of evidence bringing administration of justice into disrepute

(2) Where, in proceedings under subsection (1), a court concludes that evidence was obtained in a manner that infringed or denied any rights or freedoms guaranteed by this Charter, the evidence shall be excluded if it is established that, having regard to all the circumstances, the admission of it in the proceedings would bring the administration of justice into disrepute.

General

Aboriginal rights and freedoms not affected by Charter

25. The guarantee in this Charter of certain rights and freedoms shall not be construed so as to abrogate or derogate from any aboriginal, treaty or other rights or freedoms that pertain to the aboriginal peoples of Canada including

(a) any rights or freedoms that have been recognized by the Royal Proclamation of October 7, 1763; and
(b) any rights or freedoms that now exist by way of land claims agreements or may be so acquired.

Other rights and freedoms not affected by Charter

26. The guarantee in this Charter of certain rights and freedoms shall not be construed as denying the existence of any other rights or freedoms that exist in Canada.

Multicultural heritage

27. This Charter shall be interpreted in a manner consistent with the preservation and enhancement of the multicultural heritage of Canadians.

Rights guaranteed equally to both sexes

28. Notwithstanding anything in this Charter, the rights and freedoms referred to in it are guaranteed equally to male and female persons.

Rights respecting certain schools preserved

29. Nothing in this Charter abrogates or derogates from any rights or privileges guaranteed by or under the Constitution of Canada in respect of denominational, separate or dissentient schools.

Application to territories and territorial authorities

30. A reference in this Charter to a Province or to the legislative assembly or legislature of a province shall be deemed to include a reference to the Yukon Territory and the Northwest Territories, or to the appropriate legislative authority thereof, as the case may be.

Legislative powers not extended

31. Nothing in this Charter extends the legislative powers of any body or authority.

Application of Charter

Application of Charter

32.(1) This Charter applies

(a) to the Parliament and government of Canada in respect of all matters within the authority of Parliament including all matters relating to the Yukon Territory and Northwest Territories; and

(b) to the legislature and government of each province in respect of all matters within the authority of the legislature of each province.

Exception

(2) Notwithstanding subsection (1), section 15 shall not have effect until three years after this section comes into force.

Exception where express declaration

33.(1) Parliament or the legislature of a province may expressly declare in an Act of Parliament or of the legislature, as the case may be, that the Act or a provision thereof shall operate notwithstanding a provision included in section 2 or sections 7 to 15 of this Charter.

Operation of exception

(2) An Act or a provision of an Act in respect of which a declaration made under this section is in effect shall have such operation as it would have but for the provision of this Charter referred to in the declaration.

Five year limitation

(3) A declaration made under subsection (1) shall cease to have effect five years after it comes into force or on such earlier date as may be specified in the declaration.

Re-enactment

(4) Parliament or the legislature of a province may re-enact a declaration made under subsection (1).

Five year limitation

(5) Subsection (3) applies in respect of a re-enactment made under subsection (4).

Citation

Citation

34. This Part may be cited as the *Canadian Charter of Rights and Freedoms*.

APPENDIX P

Constitution of India

Part III
Fundamental Rights

Article 12

Definition

In this Part, unless the context otherwise required, 'the State' includes the Governmental and Parliament of India and the Government and the Legislature of each of the States and all local or other authorities within the territory of India or under the control of the Government of India.

Article 13

Laws inconsistent with or in derogation of the fundamental rights

(1) All laws in force in the territory of India immediately before the commencement of this Constitution, in so far as they are inconsistent with the provisions of this Part, shall, to the extent of such inconsistency, be void.

(2) The State shall not make any law which takes away or abridges the rights conferred by this Part and any law made in contravention of this clause shall, to the extent of the contravention, be void.

(3) In this article, unless the context otherwise required,

(a) 'law' includes any Ordinance, order, bye-law, rule, regulation, notification, custom or usage having in the territory of India the force of law;

(b) 'laws in force' includes laws passed or made by a Legislature or other competent authority in the territory of India before the commencement of this Constitution and not previously repealed, notwithstanding that any such law or any part thereof may not be then in operation either at all or in particular areas.

(4) Nothing in this article shall apply to any amendment of this Constitution made under article 368.

Article 14

Equality before law

The State shall not deny to any person equality before the law or the equal protection of the laws within the territory of India.

Article 15

Prohibition of discrimination on grounds of religion, race, caste, sex or place of birth

(1) The State shall not discriminate against any citizen on grounds only of religion, race, caste, sex, place of birth or any of them.

(2) No citizen shall, on ground only of religion, race, caste, sex, place of birth or any of them, be subject to any disability, liability, restriction or condition with regard to—

(a) access to shops, public restaurants, hotels and places of public entertainment; or

(b) the use of wells, tanks, bathing ghats, roads and places of public resort maintained whole or partly out of State funds or dedicated to the use of general public.

(3) Nothing in this article shall prevent the State from making any special provision for women and children.

(4) Nothing in this article or in clause (2) or article 29 shall prevent the State from making any special provision for the advancement of any socially and educationally backward classes of citizens or for the Scheduled Castes and the Scheduled Tribes.

Article 16

Equality of opportunity in matters of public employment

(1) There shall be equality of opportunity for all citizens in matters relating to employment or appointment to any office under the State.

(2) No citizen shall, on grounds only of religion, race, caste, sex, descent, place of birth, residence or any of them, be ineligible for, or discriminated against in respect of, any employment or office under the State.

(3) Nothing in this article shall prevent Parliament from making any law prescribing, in regard to a class or classes of employment or appointment to an office under the Government of, or any local or other authority within, a State or Union territory, any requirement as to residence within that State or Union territory prior to such employment or appointment.

(4) Nothing in this article shall prevent the State from making any provision for the reservation of appointments or posts in favour of any backward class of citizens which, in the opinion of the State, is not adequately represented in the services under the State.

(4A) Nothing in this article shall prevent the State from making any provision for reservation in matters of promotion to any class or classes of posts in the services under the State in favour of the Scheduled Castes and the Scheduled Tribes which, in the opinion of the State, are not adequately represented in the services under the State.

(5) Nothing in this article shall affect the operation of any law which provides that the incumbent of an office in connection with the affairs of any religious or denominational institution or any member of the governing body thereof shall be a person professing a particular religion or belonging to a particular denomination.

Article 17

Abolition of Untouchability

'Untouchability' is abolished and its practice in any form is forbidden. The enforcement of any disability arising out of 'Untouchability' shall be an offence punishable in accordance with law.

Article 18

Abolition of titles

(1) No title, not being a military or academic distinction, shall be conferred by the State.

(2) No citizen of India shall accept any title from any foreign State.

(3) No person who is not a citizen of India shall, while he holds any office of profit or trust under the State, accept without the consent of the President any title from any foreign State.

(4) No person holding any office of profit or trust under the State shall, without the consent of the President, accept any present, emolument, or office of any kind from or under any foreign State.

Article 19

Protection of certain rights regarding freedom of speech, etc.

(1) All citizens shall have the right—

(a) to freedom of speech and expression;

(b) to assemble peaceably and without arms;

(c) to form associations or unions;

(d) to move freely throughout the territory of India;

(e) to reside and settle in any part of the territory of India; and

(f) to practice any profession, or to carry on any occupation, trade or business.

(2) Nothing in sub-clause (a) of clause (1) shall affect the operation of any existing law, or prevent the State from making any law, in so far as such law imposes reasonable restrictions on the exercise of the right conferred by the said sub-clause in the interests of the sovereignty and integrity of India, the security of the State, friendly relations with foreign States, public order, decency or morality, or in relation to contempt of court, defamation or incitement to an offence.

(3) Nothing in sub-clause (b) of the said clause shall affect the operation of any existing law in so far as it imposes, or prevent the State from making any law imposing, in the interest of the sovereignty and integrity of India or public order, reasonable restrictions on the right conferred by the said sub-clause.

(4) Nothing in sub-clause (c) of the said clause shall affect the operation of any existing law in so far as it imposes, or prevent the State from making any law imposing, in the interests of the the sovereignty and integrity of India or public order or morality, reasonable restrictions on the exercise of the right conferred by the said sub-clause.

(5) Nothing in sub-clause (d) and (e) of the said clause shall affect the operation of any existing law in so far as it imposes, or prevent the State from making any law imposing, reasonable restrictions on the exercise of any of the rights conferred by the said sub-clauses either in the interests of the general public or for the protection of the interests of any Schedule Tribe.

(6) Nothing in sub-clause (f) of the said clause shall affect the operation of any existing law in so far as it imposes, or prevent the State from making any law imposing, in the interests of the general public, reasonable restrictions on the exercise of the right conferred by the said sub-clause, and, in particular, nothing in the said sub-clause shall affect the operation of any existing law in so far as it relates to, or prevent the State from making any law relating to—

(i) the professional or technical qualifications necessary for practicing any profession or carrying on any occupation, trade or business, or

(ii) the carrying on by the State, or by a corporation owned or controlled by the State, of any trade, business, industry or service, whether to the exclusion, complete or partial, of citizens or otherwise.

Article 20

Protection in respect of conviction for offences

(1) No person shall be convicted of any offence except for violation of a law in force at the time of the commission of the act charged as an offence, not be subjected to a penalty greater than that which might have been inflicted under the law in force at the time of the commission of the offence.

(2) No person shall be prosecuted and punished for the same offence more than once.

(3) No person accused of any offence shall be compelled to be a witness against himself.

Article 21

Protection of life and personal liberty

No person shall be deprived of his life or personal liberty except according to procedure established by law.

Article 22

Protection against arrest and detention in certain cases

(1) No person who is arrested shall be detained in custody without being informed, as soon as may be, of the grounds for such arrest nor shall he be denied the right to consult, and to be defended by, a legal practitioner of his choice.

(2) Every person who is arrested and detained in custody shall be produced before the nearest magistrate within a period of twenty-four hours of such arrest excluding the time necessary for the journey from the place of arrest to court of the magistrate and no such person shall be detained in custody beyond the said period without the authority of a magistrate.

(3) Nothing in clauses (1) and (2) shall apply—

(a) to any person who for the time being is an enemy alien; or

(b) to any person who is arrested or detained under any law providing for preventive detention.

(4) No law providing for preventive detention shall authorize the detention of a person for a longer period than three months unless—

(5) (a) an Advisory Board consisting of persons who are, or have been, or are qualified to be appointed as, Judges of a High Court has reported before the expiration of the said period of three months that there is in its opinion sufficient cause for such detention: Provided that nothing in this sub-clause shall authorise the detention of any person beyond the maximum period prescribed by any law made by Parliament under sub-clause (b) of clause (7); or

(b) such person is detained in accordance with the provisions of any law made by Parliament under sub-clauses (a) and (b) of clause (7).

(6) When any person is detained in pursuance of an order made under any law providing for preventive detention, the authority making the order shall, as soon as may be, communicate to such person the grounds on which the order has been made and shall afford him the earliest opportunity of making a representation against the order.

(7) Nothing in clause (5) shall require the authority making any such order as is referred to in that clause to disclose facts which such authority considers to be against the public interest to disclose.

(8) Parliament may by law prescribe—

(a) the circumstances under which, and the class or classes of cases in which, a person may be detained for a period longer than three months under any law providing for preventive detention without obtaining the opinion of an Advisory Board in accordance with the provisions of sub-clause (a) of clause (4);

(b) the maximum period for which any person may in any class or classes of cases be detained under any law providing for preventive detention; and

(c) the procedure to be followed by an Advisory Board in an inquiry under sub-clause (a) of clause (4).

Article 23

Prohibition of traffic in human beings and forced labour

(1) Traffic in human beings and begar and other similar forms of forced labour are prohibited and any contravention of this provision shall be an offence punishable in accordance with law.

(2) Nothing in this article shall prevent the State from imposing compulsory service for public purposes, and in imposing such service the State shall not make any discrimination on ground only of religion, race, caste or class or any of them.

Article 24

Prohibition of employment of children in factories, etc.

No child below the age of fourteen years shall be employed to work in any factory or mine or engaged in any other hazardous employment.

Article 25

Freedom of conscience and free profession, practice and propagation of religion

(1) Subject to public order, morality and health and to the other provisions of this Part, all persons are equally entitled to freedom of conscience and the right freely to profess, practice and propagate religion.

(2) Nothing in this article shall affect the operation of any existing law or prevent the State from making any law—

(a) regulating or restricting any economic, financial, political or other secular activity which may be associated with religious practice;

(b) providing for social welfare and reform or the throwing open of Hindu religious institutions of a public character to all classes and sections of Hindus.

Explanation I: The wearing and carrying of kirpans shall be deemed to be included in the profession of the Sikh religion.

Explanation II: In sub-Clause (b) of clause (2), the reference to Hindus shall be construed as including a reference to persons professing the Sikh, Jaina or Buddhist religion, and the reference to Hindu religious institutions shall be construed accordingly.

Article 26

Freedom to manage religious affairs

Subject to public order, morality and health, every religious denomination or any section thereof shall have the right—

(a) to establish and maintain institutions for religious and charitable purposes;

(b) to manage its own affairs in matters of religion;

(c) to own and acquire movable and immovable property; and

(d) to administer such property in accordance with law.

Article 27

Freedom as to payment of taxes for promotion of any particular religion

No person shall be compelled to pay any taxes, the proceeds of which are specifically appropriated in payment of expenses for the promotion or maintenance of any particular religion or religious denomination.

Article 28

Freedom as to attendance at religious instruction or religious worship in certain educational institutions

(1) No religious instruction shall be provided in any educational institution wholly maintained out of State funds.

(2) Nothing in clause (1) shall apply to an educational institution which is administered by the State but has been established under any endowment or trust which requires that religious instruction shall be imparted in such institution.

(3) No person attending any educational institution recognized by the State or receiving aid out of State funds shall be required to take part in any religious instruction that may be imparted in such institution or to attend any religious worship that may be conducted in such institution or in any premises attached thereto unless such person or, if such person is minor, his guardian has given his consent thereto.

Article 29

Protection of interests of minorities

(1) Any section of the citizens residing in the territory of India or any part thereof having a distinct language, script or culture of its own shall have the right to conserve the same.

(2) No citizen shall be denied admission into any educational institution maintained by the State or receiving aid out of State funds on grounds only of religion, race, caste, language or any of them.

Article 30

Right of minorities to establish and administer educational institutions

(1) All minorities, whether based on religion or language, shall have the right to establish and administer educational institutions of their choice.

(1A) In making any law providing for the compulsory acquisition of any property of an educational institution established and administered by a minority, referred to in clause (1), the State shall ensure that the amount fixed by or determined under such law for the acquisition of such property is such as would not restrict or abrogate the right guaranteed under that clause.

(2) The State shall not, in granting aid to educational institutions, discriminate against any educational institution on the ground that it is under the management of a minority, whether based on religion or language.

Article 31

Compulsory acquisition of property

. . .

Article 31A

Saving of laws providing for acquisition of estates, etc.

(1) Notwithstanding anything contained in article 13, no law providing for—

(a) the acquisition by the State of any estate or of any rights therein or the extinguishment or modification of any such rights, or

(b) the taking over of the management of any property by the State for a limited period either in the public interest or in order to secure the proper management of the property, or

(c) the amalgamation of two or more corporations either in the public interest or in order to secure the proper management of any of the corporations, or

(d) the extinguishment or modification of any rights of managing agents, secretaries and treasurers, managing directors, directors or managers of corporations, or of any voting rights of shareholders thereof, or

(e) the extinguishment or modification of any rights accruing by virtue of any agreement, lease or licence for the purpose of searching for, or winning, any mineral or mineral oil, or the premature termination or cancellation of and such agreement, lease or licence, shall be deemed to be void on the ground that it is inconsistent with, or takes away or abridges any of the rights conferred by article 14 or article 19: Provided that where such law is a law made by the Legislature of a State, the provisions of this article shall not apply thereto unless such law, having been reserved for the consideration of the President, has received his assent:

Provided further that where any law makes any provision for the acquisition by the State of any estate and where any land comprised therein is held by a person under his personal cultivation, it shall not be lawful for the State to acquire any portion of such land as is within the ceiling limit applicable to him under any law for the time being in force or any building or structure standing thereon or appurtenant thereto, unless the law relating to the acquisition of such land, building or structure, provides for payment of compensation at a rate which shall not be less than the market value thereof.

(2) In this article—

(a) the expression 'estate' shall, in relation to any local area, have the same meaning as that expression or its local equivalent has in the existing law relating to land tenure in force in that area and shall also include—

(i) any jagir, inam or muafi or other similar grant and in the States of Tamil Nadu and Kerala, any janmam right;

(ii) any land held under ryotwari settlement;

(iii) any land held or let for purposes of agriculture of for purposes ancillary thereto, including waste land, forest land, land for pasture or sites of buildings and other structures occupied by cultivators of land, agricultural labourers and village artisans;

(b) the expression 'rights', in relation to an estate, shall include any rights vesting in a proprietor, sub-proprietor, under-proprietor, tenure-holder, raiyat, under-raiyat or other intermediary and any rights or privileges in respect of land revenue.

Article 31B

Validation of certain Acts and Regulations

Without prejudice to the generality of the provisions contained in article 31A, none of the Acts and Regulations specified in the Ninth Schedule nor any of the provision thereof shall be deemed to be void, or even to have become void, on the ground that such Act, Regulation or provision is inconsistent with, or takes away or abridges any of the rights conferred by, any provisions of this part, and notwithstanding any judgment, decree or order of any court or tribunal to the contrary, each of the said Acts and Regulations shall, subject to the power of any competent Legislature to repeal or amend it, continue in force.

Article 31C

Saving of laws giving effect to certain directive principles

Notwithstanding anything contained in article 13, no law giving effect to the policy of the State towards securing all or any of the principles laid down in Part IV shall be deemed to be void on the ground that it is inconsistent with, or takes away or abridges any of the rights conferred by article 14 or article 19; and no law containing a declaration that it is for giving effect to such policy shall be called in question in any court on the ground that it does not give effect to such policy:

Provided that where such law is made by the Legislature of a State, the provisions of this article shall not apply thereto unless such law, having been reserved for the consideration of the President, has received his assent.

Article 31D

Saving of laws in respect of anti-national activities

. . .

Article 32

Remedies for enforcement of rights conferred by this Part

(1) The right to move the Supreme Court by appropriate proceedings for the enforcement of the rights conferred by this Part is guaranteed.

(2) The Supreme Court shall have power to issue directions or orders or writs, including writs in the nature of habeas corpus, mandamus, prohibition, quo warranto and certiorari, whichever may be appropriate, for the enforcement of any of the rights conferred by this Part.

(3) Without prejudice to the powers conferred on the Supreme Court by clauses (1) and (2), Parliament may by law empower any other court to exercise within the local limits of its jurisdiction all or any of the powers exercisable by the Supreme Court under clause (2).

(4) The right guaranteed by this article shall not be suspended except as otherwise provided for by this Constitution.

Article 32A

Constitutional validity of State laws not to be considered in proceedings under article 32

. . .

Article 33

Power of Parliament to modify the rights conferred by this Part in their application to Forces, etc.

Parliament may, by law, determine to what extent any of the rights conferred by this Part shall, in their application to—

(a) the members of the Armed Forces; or
(b) the members of the Forces charged with the maintenance of public order; or
(c) persons employed in any bureau or other organisation established by the State for purposes of intelligence or counter intelligence; or
(d) persons employed in, or in connection with, the telecommunication systems set up for the purposes of any Force, bureau or organisation referred to in clauses (a) to (c),

be restricted or abrogated so as to ensure the proper discharge of their duties and the maintenance of discipline among them.

Article 34

Restriction on rights conferred by this Part while marital law is in force in any area

Notwithstanding anything in the foregoing provisions of this Part, Parliament may by law indemnify any person in the service of the Union or of a State or any person in respect of any act done by him in connection with the maintenance or restoration or order in any area within the territory of India where martial law was in force or validate any sentence passed, punishment inflicted, forfeiture ordered or other act done under martial law in such area.

Article 35

Legislation to give effect to the provisions of this Part

Notwithstanding anything in this Constitution—

(a) Parliament shall have, and the Legislature of a State shall not have, power to make laws—

(i) With respect to any of the matters which under clause (3) of article 16, clause (3) of article 32, article 33 and article 34 may be provided for by law made by Parliament; and

(ii) for prescribing punishment for those acts which are declared to be offences under this part,

and Parliament shall, as soon as may be after the commencement of this Constitution, make laws for prescribing punishment for the acts referred to in sub-clause (ii);

(b) any law in force immediately before the commencement of this Constitution in the territory of India with respect to any of the matters referred to in sub-clause (i) of clause (a) or providing for punishment for any act referred to in sub-clause (ii) of that clause shall, subject to the terms thereof and to any adaptations and modifications that may be made therein under article 372, continue in force until altered or repealed or amended by Parliament.

Explanation: In this article, the expression 'law in force' has the same meaning as in article 372.

APPENDIX Q

Chapter XII of the Irish Constitution—Fundamental Rights

Article 40

Personal Rights

(1) All citizens shall, as human persons, be held equal before the law. This shall not be held to mean that the State shall not in its enactments have due regard to differences of capacity, physical and moral, and of social function.

(2.1) Titles of nobility shall not be conferred by the State.

(2.2) No title of nobility or of honor may be accepted by any citizen except with the prior approval of the Government.

(3.1) The State guarantees in its laws to respect, and, as far as practicable, by its laws to defend and vindicate the personal rights of the citizen.

(3.2) The State shall, in particular, by its laws protect as best it may from unjust attack and, in the case of injustice done, vindicate the life, person, good name, and property rights of every citizen.

(3.3) The State acknowledges the right to life of the unborn and, with due regard to the equal right to life of the mother, guarantees in its laws to respect, and, as far as practicable, by its laws to defend and vindicate that right. This subsection shall not limit freedom to travel between the State and another state. This subsection shall not limit freedom to obtain or make available, in the State, subject to such conditions as may be laid down by law, information relating to services lawfully available in another state.

(4.1) No citizen shall be deprived of his personal liberty save in accordance with law.

(4.2) Upon complaint being made by or on behalf of any person to the High Court or any judge thereof alleging that such person is being unlawfully detained, the High Court and any and every judge thereof to whom such complaint is made shall forthwith enquire into the said complaint and may order the person in whose custody such person is detained to produce the body of such person before the High Court on a named day and to certify in writing the grounds of his detention, and the High Court shall, upon the body of such person being produced before that Court and after giving the person in whose custody he is detained an opportunity of justifying the detention, order the release of such person from such detention unless satisfied that he is being detained in accordance with the law.

(4.3) Where the body of a person alleged to be unlawfully detained is produced before the High Court in pursuance of an order in that behalf made under this section and that Court is satisfied that such person is being detained in accordance with a law but that such law is invalid having regard to the provisions of this Constitution, the High Court shall refer the question of the validity of such law to the Supreme Court by way of case stated and may, at the time of such reference or at any time thereafter, allow the said person to be at liberty on such bail and subject to such conditions as the High Court shall fix until the Supreme Court has determined the question so referred to it.

(4.4) The High Court before which the body of a person alleged to be unlawfully detained is to be produced in pursuance of an order in that behalf made under this section shall, if the President of the High Court or, if he is not available, the senior judge of that Court who is available so directs in respect of any particular case, consist of three judges and shall, in every other case, consist of one judge only.

(4.5) Where an order is made under this section by the High Court or a judge thereof for the production of the body of a person who is under sentence of death, the High Court or such judge thereof shall further order that the execution of the said sentence of death shall be deferred until after the body of such person has been produced before the High Court and the lawfulness of his detention has been determined and if, after such deferment, the detention of such person is determined to be lawful, the High Court shall appoint a day for the execution of the said sentence of death and that sentence shall have effect with the substitution of the day so appointed for the day originally fixed for the execution thereof.

(4.6) Nothing in this section, however, shall be invoked to prohibit, control, or interfere with any act of the Defence Forces during the existence of a state of war or armed rebellion.

(5) The dwelling of every citizen is inviolable and shall not be forcibly entered save in accordance with law.

(6.1) The State guarantees liberty for the exercise of the following rights, subject to public order and morality:—

(i) The right of the citizens to express freely their convictions and opinions

The education of public opinion being, however, a matter of such grave import to the common good, the State shall endeavour to ensure that organs of public opinion, such as the radio, the press, the cinema, while preserving their rightful liberty of expression, including criticism of Government policy, shall not be used to undermine public order or morality or the authority of the State.

The publication or utterance of blasphemous, seditious, or indecent matter is an offence which shall be punishable in accordance with law.

(ii) The right of the citizens to assemble peaceably and without arms

Provision may be made by law to prevent or control meetings which are determined in accordance with law to be calculated to cause a breach of the peace or to be a danger or nuisance to the general public and to prevent or control meetings in the vicinity of either House of Parliament.

(iii) The right of the citizens to form associations and unions

Laws, however, may be enacted for the regulation and control in the public interest of the exercise of the foregoing right.

(6.2) Laws regulating the manner in which the right of forming associations and unions and the right of free assembly may be exercised shall contain no political, religious or class discrimination.

Article 41

Family

(1.1) The State recognises the Family as the natural primary and fundamental unit group of Society, and as a moral institution possessing inalienable and imprescriptible rights, antecedent and superior to all positive law.

(1.2) The State, therefore, guarantees to protect the Family in its constitution and authority, as the necessary basis of social order and as indispensable to the welfare of the Nation and the State.

(2.1) In particular, the State recognises that by her life within the home, woman gives to the State a support without which the common good cannot be achieved.

(2.2) The State shall, therefore, endeavor to ensure that mothers shall not be obliged by economic necessity to engage in labour to the neglect of their duties in the home.

(3.1) The State pledges itself to guard with special care the institution of Marriage, on which the Family is founded, and to protect it against attack.

(3.2) A Court designated by law may grant a dissolution of marriage where, but only where, it is satisfied that—

(i) at the date of the institution of the proceedings, the spouses have lived apart from one another for a period of, or periods amounting to, at least four years during the previous five years,
(ii) there is no reasonable prospect of a reconciliation between the spouses,
(iii) such provision as the Court considers proper having regard to the circumstances exists or will be made for the spouses, any children of either or both of them and any other person prescribed by law, and
(iv) any further conditions prescribed by law are complied with.

(3.3) No person whose marriage has been dissolved under the civil law of any other State but is a subsisting valid marriage under the law for the time being in force within the jurisdiction of the Government and Parliament established by this Constitution shall be capable of contracting a valid marriage within that jurisdiction during the lifetime of the other party to the marriage so dissolved.

Article 42

Education

(1) The State acknowledges that the primary and natural educator of the child is the Family and guarantees to respect the inalienable right and duty of parents to provide, according to their means, for the religious and moral, intellectual, physical and social education of their children.

(2) Parents shall be free to provide this education in their homes or in private schools or in schools recognised or established by the State.

(3.1) The State shall not oblige parents in violation of their conscience and lawful preference to send their children to schools established by the State, or to any particular type of school designated by the State.

(3.2) The State shall, however, as guardian of the common good, require in view of actual conditions that the children receive a certain minimum education. moral. intellectual and social.

(4) The State shall provide for free primary education and shall endeavour to supplement and give reasonable aid to private and corporate educational initiative, and, when the public good requires it, provide other educational facilities or institutions with due regard, however, for the rights of parents, especially in the matter of religious and moral formation.

(5) In exceptional cases, where the parents for physical or moral reasons fail in their duty towards their children, the State as guardian of the common good, by appropriate means shall endeavour to supply the place of the parents, but always with due regard for the natural and imprescriptible rights of the child.

Article 43

Private Property

(1.1) The State acknowledges that man, in virtue of his rational being, has the natural right, antecedent to positive law, to the private ownership of external goods.

(1.2) The State accordingly guarantees to pass no law attempting to abolish the right of private ownership or the general right to transfer, bequeath, and inherit property.

(2.1) The State recognises, however, that the exercise of the rights mentioned in the foregoing provisions of this article ought, in civil society, to be regulated by the principles of social justice.

(2.2) The State, accordingly, may as occasion requires delimit by law the exercise of the said rights with a view to reconciling their exercise with the exigencies of the common good.

Article 44

Religion

(1) The State acknowledges that the homage of public worship is due to Almighty God. It shall hold His Name in reverence, and shall respect and honour religion.

(2.1) Freedom of conscience and the free profession and practice of religion are, subject to public order and morality, guaranteed to every citizen.

(2.2) The State guarantees not to endow any religion.

(2.3) The State shall not impose any disabilities or make any discrimination on the ground of religious profession, belief or status.

(2.4) Legislation providing State aid for schools shall not discriminate between schools under the management of different religious denominations, nor be such as to affect prejudicially the right of any child to attend a school receiving public money without attending religious instruction at that school.

(2.5) Every religious denomination shall have the right to manage its own affairs, own, acquire and administer property, movable and immovable, and maintain institutions for religious or charitable purposes.

(2.6) The property of any religious denomination or any educational institution shall not be diverted save for necessary works of public utility and on payment of compensation.

APPENDIX R

New Zealand Bill of Rights Act 1990

Preamble

An Act

(a) To affirm, protect, and promote human rights and fundamental freedoms in New Zealand; and

(b) To affirm New Zealand's commitment to the International Covenant on Civil and Political Rights.

Part 0
Short Title

Section 1

Short title

(1) This Act may be cited as the New Zealand Bill of Rights Act 1990.

(2) This Act shall come into force on the 28th day after the date on which it recieves the Royal assent.

Part I
General Provisions

Section 2

Rights affirmed

The rights and freedoms contained in this Bill of Rights are affirmed.

Section 3

Application

This Bill of Rights applies only to acts done

(a) By the legislative, executive, or judicial branches of the government of New Zealand; or

(b) By any person or body in the performance of any public function, power, or duty conferred or imposed on that person or body by or pursuant to law.

Section 4

Other enactments

No court shall, in relation to any enactment (whether passed or made before or after the commencement of this Bill of Rights),

(a) Hold any provision of the enactment to be impliedly repealed or revoked, or to be in any way invalid or ineffective; or

(b) Decline to apply any provision of this enactment by reason only that the provision is inconsistent with any provision of this Bill of Rights.

Section 5

Justified limitations

Subject to Section 4 of this Bill of Rights, the rights and freedoms contained in this Bill of Rights may be subject only to such reasonable limits prescribed by law as can be demonstrably justified justified in a free and democratic society.

Section 6

Interpretation

Wherever an enactment can be given a meaning that is consistent with the rights and freedoms contained in this Bill of Rights, that meaning shall be preferred to any other meaning.

Section 7

Attorney-General's report

Where any Bill is introduced into the House of Representatives, the Attorney-General shall,

(a) In the case of a Government Bill, on the introduction of that Bill; or

(b) In any other case, as soon as practicable after the introduction of the Bill, bring to the attention of the House of Representatives any provision in the Bill that appears to be inconsistent with any of the rights and freedoms in this Bill of Rights.

Part II
Civil and Political Rights

Title 1
Life and the Security of the Person

Section 8

Life

No one shall be deprived of life except on such grounds as are established by law and are consistent with the principles of fundamental justice.

Section 9

Torture, cruel treatment

Everyone has the right not to be subjected to torture or to cruel, degrading, or disproportionately severe treatment or punishment.

Section 10

Experimentation

Every person has the right not to be subjected to medical or scientific experimentation without that person's consent.

Section 11

Medical Treatment

Everyone has the right to refuse to undergo any medical treatment.

Title 2
Democratic and Civil Rights

Section 12

Electoral rights

Every New Zealand citizen who is of or over the age of 18 years

(a) Has the right to vote in genuine periodic elections of members of the House of Representatives, which elections shall be by equal suffrage and by secret ballot; and

(b) Is qualified for membership of the House of Representatives.

Section 13

Freedom of thought, conscience, and religion

Everyone has the right to freedom of thought, conscience, religion, and belief, including the right to adopt and hold opinions without interference.

Section 14

Freedom of expression

Everyone has the right to freedom of expression, including the freedom to seek, receive, and impart information and opinions of any kind in any form.

Section 15

Religion and belief

Every person has the right to manifest that person's religion or belief in worship, observance, practice, or teaching, either individually or in community with others, and either in public or in private.

Section 16

Assembly

Everyone has the right of peaceful assembly.

Section 17

Association

Everyone has the right to freedom of association.

Section 18

Movement

(1) Everyone lawfully in New Zealand has the right to freedom of movement and residence in New Zealand.

(2) Every New Zealand citizen has the right to enter New Zealand.

(3) Everyone has the right to leave New Zealand.

(4) No one who is not a New Zealand citizen and who is lawfully in New Zealand shall be required to leave New Zealand except under a decision taken on grounds prescribed by law.

Title 3
Non-Discrimination and Minority Rights

Section 19

Freedom from discrimination

(1) Everyone has the right to freedom from discrimination on the grounds of discrimination in the Human Rights Act 1993.

(2) Measures taken in good faith for the purpose of assisting or advancing persons or groups of persons disadvantaged because of discrimination that is unlawful by virtue of Part II of the Human Rights Act 1993 do not constitute discrimination.

Section 20

Rights of minorities

A person who belongs to an ethnic, religious, or linguistic minority in New Zealand shall not be denied the right, in community with other members of that minority, to enjoy the culture, to profess and practise the religion, or to use the language, of that minority.

Title 4
Search, Arrest, and Detention

Section 21

Unreasonable search and seizure

Everyone has the right to be secure against unreasonable search or seizure, whether of the person, property, or correspondence, or otherwise.

Section 22

Personal liberty

Everyone has the right not to be arbitrarily arrested or detained.

Section 23

Arrest

(1) Everyone who is arrested or who is detained under any enactment
- (a) Shall be informed at the time of the arrest or detention of the reason for it; and
- (b) Shall have the right to consult and instruct a lawyer without delay and to be informed of that right; and
- (c) Shall have the right to have the validity of the arrest or detention determined without delay by way of habeas corpus and to be released if the arrest or detention is not lawful.

(2) Everyone who is arrested for an offence has the right to be charged promptly or to be released.

(3) Everyone who is arrested for an offence and is not released shall be brought as soon as possible before a court or competant tribunal.

(4) Everyone who is
- (a) Arrested; or
- (b) Detained under any enactment for any offence or suspected offence shall have the right to refrain from making any statement and to be informed of that right.

(5) Everyone deprived of liberty shall be treated with humanity and with respect for the inherent dignity of the person.

Section 24

Criminal justice

Everyone who is charged with an offence
- (a) Shall be informed promptly and in detail of the nature and cause of the charge; and
- (b) Shall be released on reasonable terms and conditions unless there is just cause for continued detention; and
- (c) Shall have the right to consult and instruct a lawyer; and
- (d) Shall have the right to adequate time and facilities to prepare a defence; and
- (e) Shall have the right, except in the case of an offence under military law tried before a military

tribunal, to the benefit of a trial by jury when the penalty for the offence is or includes imprisonment for more than 3 months; and

(f) Shall have the right to receive legal assistance without cost if the interests of justice so require and the person does not have sufficient means to provide for that assistance; and

(g) Shall have the right to have the free assistance of an interpreter if the person cannot understand or speak the language used in court.

Section 25

Fair trial

Everyone who is charged with an offence has, in relation to the determination of the charge, the following minimum rights:

(a) The right to a fair and public hearing by an independent and impartial court:

(b) The right to be tried without undue delay:

(c) The right to be presumed innocent until proved guilty according to law:

(d) The right not to be compelled to be a witness or to confess guilt:

(e) The right to be present at the trial and to present a defence:

(f) The right to examine the witnesses for the prosecution and to obtain the attendance and examination of witnesses for the defence under the same conditions as the prosecution:

(g) The right, if convicted of an offence in respect of which the penalty has been varied between the commission of the offence and sentencing, to the benefit of the lesser penalty:

(h) The right, if convicted of the offence, to appeal according to the law to a higher court against the conviction or against the sentence or against both:

(i) The right, in the case of a child, to be dealt with in a manner that takes account of the child's age.

Section 26

Nulla poena sine lege, double jepordy

(1) No one shall be liable to conviction of any offence on account of any act or omission which did not constitute an offence by such person under the law of New Zealand at the time it occurred.

(2) No one who has been finally acquitted or convicted of, or pardoned for, an offence shall be tried or punished for it again.

Section 27

Remedies

(1) Every person has the right to the observance of the principles of natural justice by any tribunal or other public authority which has the power to make a determination in respect of that person's right, obligations, or interests protected or recognised by law.

(2) Every person whose rights, obligations, or interests protected or recognised by law have been affected by a determination of any tribunal or other public authority has the right to apply, in accordance with law, or judicial review of that determination.

(3) Every person has the right to bring civil proceedings against, and to defend civil proceedings brought by, the Crown, and to have those proceedings heard, according to law, in the same way as civil proceedings between individuals.

Part III
Miscellaneous Provisions

Section 28

Other rights and Rreedoms

An existing right or freedom shall not be held to be abrogated or restricted by reason only that the right or freedom is not included in this Bill of Rights or is included only in part.

Section 29

Legal persons

Except where the provisions of this Bill of Rights otherwise provide, the provisions of this Bill of Rights apply, so far as practicable, for the benefit of all legal persons as well as for the benefit of all natural persons.

APPENDIX S

Constitution of the Republic of South Africa 1996

Chapter 2

Bill of Rights

Rights

7.(1) This Bill of Rights is a cornerstone of democracy in South Africa. It enshrines the rights of all people in our country and affirms the democratic values of human dignity, equality and freedom.

(2) The state must respect, protect, promote and fulfil the rights in the Bill of Rights.

(3) The rights in the Bill of Rights are subject to the limitations contained or referred to in section 36, or elsewhere in the Bill.

Application

8.(1) The Bill of Rights applies to all law, and binds the legislature, the executive, the judiciary and all organs of state.

(2) A provision of the Bill of Rights binds a natural or a juristic person if, and to the extent that, it is applicable, taking into account the nature of the right and the nature of any duty imposed by the right.

(3) When applying a provision of the Bill of Rights to a natural or juristic person in terms of subsection (2), a court—

- (a) in order to give effect to a right in the Bill, must apply, or if necessary develop, the common law to the extent that legislation does not give effect to that right; and
- (b) may develop rules of the common law to limit the right, provided that the limitation is in accordance with section 36(1).

(4) A juristic person is entitled to the rights in the Bill of Rights to the extent required by the nature of the rights and the nature of that juristic person.

Equality

9.(1) Everyone is equal before the law and has the right to equal protection and benefit of the law.

(2) Equality includes the full and equal enjoyment of all rights and freedoms. To promote the achievement of equality, legislative and other measures designed to protect or advance persons, or categories of persons, disadvantaged by unfair discrimination may be taken.

(3) The state may not unfairly discriminate directly or indirectly against anyone on one or more grounds, including race, gender, sex, pregnancy, marital status, ethnic or social origin, colour, sexual orientation, age, disability, religion, conscience, belief, culture, language and birth.

(4) No person may unfairly discriminate directly or indirectly against anyone on one or more grounds in terms of subsection (3). National legislation must be enacted to prevent or prohibit unfair discrimination.

(5) Discrimination on one or more of the grounds listed in subsection (3) is unfair unless it is established that the discrimination is fair.

Human dignity

10. Everyone has inherent dignity and the right to have their dignity respected and protected.

Life

11. Everyone has the right to life.

Freedom and security of the person

12.(1) Everyone has the right to freedom and security of the person, which includes the right—
(a) not to be deprived of freedom arbitrarily or without just cause;
(b) not to be detained without trial;
(c) to be free from all forms of violence from either public or private sources;
(d) not to be tortured in any way; and
(e) not to be treated or punished in a cruel, inhuman or degrading way.

(2) Everyone has the right to bodily and psychological integrity, which includes the right—
(a) to make decisions concerning reproduction;
(b) to security in and control over their body; and
(c) not to be subjected to medical or scientific experiments without their informed consent.

Slavery, servitude and forced labour

13. No one may be subjected to slavery, servitude or forced labour.

Privacy

14. Everyone has the right to privacy, which includes the right not to have—
(a) their person or home searched;
(b) their property searched;
(c) their possessions seized; or
(d) the privacy of their communications infringed.

Freedom of religion, belief and opinion

15.(1) Everyone has the right to freedom of conscience, religion, thought, belief and opinion.

(2) Religious observances may be conducted at state or state-aided institutions, provided that—
(a) those observances follow rules made by the appropriate public authorities;
(b) they are conducted on an equitable basis; and
(c) attendance at them is free and voluntary.

(3) (a) This section does not prevent legislation recognising—
(i) marriages concluded under any tradition, or a system of religious, personal or family law; or
(ii) systems of personal and family law under any tradition, or adhered to by persons professing a particular religion.

(b) Recognition in terms of paragraph (a) must be consistent with this section and the other provisions of the Constitution.

Freedom of expression

16.(1) Everyone has the right to freedom of expression, which includes—
(a) freedom of the press and other media;
(b) freedom to receive or impart information or ideas;
(c) freedom of artistic creativity; and
(d) academic freedom and freedom of scientific research.

(2) The right in subsection (1) does not extend to—
(a) propaganda for war;
(b) incitement of imminent violence; or

(c) advocacy of hatred that is based on race, ethnicity, gender or religion, and that constitutes incitement to cause harm.

Assembly, demonstration, picket and petition

17. Everyone has the right, peacefully and unarmed, to assemble, to demonstrate, to picket and to present petitions.

Freedom of association

18. Everyone has the right to freedom of association.

Political rights

19.(1) Every citizen is free to make political choices, which includes the right—

(a) to form a political party;
(b) to participate in the activities of, or recruit members for, a political party; and
(c) to campaign for a political party or cause.

(2) Every citizen has the right to free, fair and regular elections for any legislative body established in terms of the Constitution.

(3) Every adult citizen has the right—

(a) to vote in elections for any legislative body established in terms of the Constitution, and to do so in secret; and
(b) to stand for public office and, if elected, to hold office.

Citizenship

20. No citizen may be deprived of citizenship.

Freedom of movement and residence

21.(1) Everyone has the right to freedom of movement.

(2) Everyone has the right to leave the Republic.

(3) Every citizen has the right to enter, to remain in and to reside anywhere in, the Republic.

(4) Every citizen has the right to a passport.

Freedom of trade, occupation and profession

22. Every citizen has the right to choose their trade, occupation or profession freely. The practice of a trade, occupation or profession may be regulated by law.

Labour relations

23.(1) Everyone has the right to fair labour practices.

(2) Every worker has the right—

(a) to form and join a trade union;
(b) to participate in the activities and programmes of a trade union; and
(c) to strike.

(3) Every employer has the right—

(a) to form and join an employers' organisation; and
(b) to participate in the activities and programmes of an employers' organisation.

(4) Every trade union and every employers' organisation has the right—

(a) to determine its own administration, programmes and activities;
(b) to organise; and
(c) to form and join a federation.

(5) Every trade union, employers' organisation and employer has the right to engage in collective bargaining. National legislation may be enacted to regulate collective bargaining. To the extent that the legislation may limit a right in this Chapter, the limitation must comply with section 36(1).

(6) National legislation may recognise union security arrangements contained in collective agreements. To the extent that the legislation may limit a right in this Chapter, the limitation must comply with section 36(1).

Environment

24. Everyone has the right—

(a) to an environment that is not harmful to their health or well-being; and

(b) to have the environment protected, for the benefit of present and future generations, through reasonable legislative and other measures that—

(i) prevent pollution and ecological degradation;

(ii) promote conservation; and

(iii) secure ecologically sustainable development and use of natural resources while promoting justifiable economic and social development.

Property

25.(1) No one may be deprived of property except in terms of law of general application, and no law may permit arbitrary deprivation of property.

(2) Property may be expropriated only in terms of law of general application—

(a) for a public purpose or in the public interest; and

(b) subject to compensation, the amount of which and the time and manner of payment of which have either been agreed to by those affected or decided or approved by a court.

(3) The amount of the compensation and the time and manner of payment must be just and equitable, reflecting an equitable balance between the public interest and the interests of those affected, having regard to all relevant circumstances, including—

(a) the current use of the property;

(b) the history of the acquisition and use of the property;

(c) the market value of the property;

(d) the extent of direct state investment and subsidy in the acquisition and beneficial capital improvement of the property; and

(e) the purpose of the expropriation.

(4) For the purposes of this section—

(a) the public interest includes the nation's commitment to land reform, and to reforms to bring about equitable access to all South Africa's natural resources; and

(b) property is not limited to land.

(5) The state must take reasonable legislative and other measures, within its available resources, to foster conditions which enable citizens to gain access to land on an equitable basis.

(6) A person or community whose tenure of land is legally insecure as a result of past racially discriminatory laws or practices is entitled, to the extent provided by an Act of Parliament, either to tenure which is legally secure or to comparable redress.

(7) A person or community dispossessed of property after 19 June 1913 as a result of past racially discriminatory laws or practices is entitled, to the extent provided by an Act of Parliament, either to restitution of that property or to equitable redress.

(8) No provision of this section may impede the state from taking legislative and other measures to achieve land, water and related reform, in order to redress the results of past racial discrimination, provided that any departure from the provisions of this section is in accordance with the provisions of section 36(1).

(9) Parliament must enact the legislation referred to in subsection (6).

Housing

26.(1) Everyone has the right to have access to adequate housing.

(2) The state must take reasonable legislative and other measures, within its available resources, to achieve the progressive realisation of this right.

(3) No one may be evicted from their home, or have their home demolished, without an order of court made after considering all the relevant circumstances. No legislation may permit arbitrary evictions.

Health care, food, water and social security

27.(1) Everyone has the right to have access to—

(a) health care services, including reproductive health care;

(b) sufficient food and water; and

(c) social security, including, if they are unable to support themselves and their dependants, appropriate social assistance.

(2) The state must take reasonable legislative and other measures, within its available resources, to achieve the progressive realisation of each of these rights.

(3) No one may be refused emergency medical treatment.

Children

28.(1) Every child has the right—

(a) to a name and a nationality from birth;

(b) to family care or parental care, or to appropriate alternative care when removed from the family environment;

(c) to basic nutrition, shelter, basic health care services and social services;

(d) to be protected from maltreatment, neglect, abuse or degradation;

(e) to be protected from exploitative labour practices;

(f) not to be required or permitted to perform work or provide services that—

(i) are inappropriate for a person of that child's age; or

(ii) place at risk the child's well-being, education, physical or mental health or spiritual, moral or social development;

(g) not to be detained except as a measure of last resort, in which case, in addition to the rights a child enjoys under sections 12 and 35, the child may be detained only for the shortest appropriate period of time, and has the right to be—

(i) kept separately from detained persons over the age of 18 years; and

(ii) treated in a manner, and kept in conditions, that take account of the child's age;

(h) to have a legal practitioner assigned to the child by the state, and at state expense, in civil proceedings affecting the child, if substantial injustice would otherwise result; and

(i) not to be used directly in armed conflict, and to be protected in times of armed conflict.

(2) A child's best interests are of paramount importance in every matter concerning the child.

(3) In this section 'child' means a person under the age of 18 years.

Education

29.(1) Everyone has the right—

(a) to a basic education, including adult basic education; and

(b) to further education, which the state, through reasonable measures, must make progressively available and accessible.

(2) Everyone has the right to receive education in the official language or languages of their choice in public educational institutions where that education is reasonably practicable. In order to ensure the effective access to, and implementation of, this right, the state must consider all reasonable educational alternatives, including single medium institutions, taking into account—

(a) equity;
(b) practicability; and
(c) the need to redress the results of past racially discriminatory laws and practices.

(3) Everyone has the right to establish and maintain, at their own expense, independent educational institutions that—
(a) do not discriminate on the basis of race;
(b) are registered with the state; and
(c) maintain standards that are not inferior to standards at comparable public educational institutions.

(4) Subsection (3) does not preclude state subsidies for independent educational institutions.

Language and culture

30. Everyone has the right to use the language and to participate in the cultural life of their choice, but no one exercising these rights may do so in a manner inconsistent with any provision of the Bill of Rights.

Cultural, religious and linguistic communities

31.(1) Persons belonging to a cultural, religious or linguistic community may not be denied the right, with other members of that community—
(a) to enjoy their culture, practise their religion and use their language; and
(b) to form, join and maintain cultural, religious and linguistic associations and other organs of civil society.

(2) The rights in subsection (1) may not be exercised in a manner inconsistent with any provision of the Bill of Rights.

Access to information

32.(1) Everyone has the right of access to—
(a) any information held by the state; and
(b) any information that is held by another person and that is required for the exercise or protection of any rights.

(2) National legislation must be enacted to give effect to this right, and may provide for reasonable measures to alleviate the administrative and financial burden on the state.

Just administrative action

33.(1) Everyone has the right to administrative action that is lawful, reasonable and procedurally fair.

(2) Everyone whose rights have been adversely affected by administrative action has the right to be given written reasons.

(3) National legislation must be enacted to give effect to these rights, and must—
(a) provide for the review of administrative action by a court or, where appropriate, an independent and impartial tribunal;
(b) impose a duty on the state to give effect to the rights in subsections (1) and (2); and
(c) promote an efficient administration.

Access to courts

34. Everyone has the right to have any dispute that can be resolved by the application of law decided in a fair public hearing before a court or, where appropriate, another independent and impartial tribunal or forum.

Arrested, detained and accused persons

35.(1) Everyone who is arrested for allegedly committing an offence has the right—
(a) to remain silent;
(b) to be informed promptly—

(i) of the right to remain silent; and
(ii) of the consequences of not remaining silent;
(c) not to be compelled to make any confession or admission that could be used in evidence against that person;
(d) to be brought before a court as soon as reasonably possible, but not later than—
(i) 48 hours after the arrest; or
(ii) the end of the first court day after the expiry of the 48 hours, if the 48 hours expire outside ordinary court hours or on a day which is not an ordinary court day;
(e) at the first court appearance after being arrested, to be charged or to be informed of the reason for the detention to continue, or to be released; and
(f) to be released from detention if the interests of justice permit, subject to reasonable conditions.

(2) Everyone who is detained, including every sentenced prisoner, has the right—
(a) to be informed promptly of the reason for being detained;
(b) to choose, and to consult with, a legal practitioner, and to be informed of this right promptly;
(c) to have a legal practitioner assigned to the detained person by the state and at state expense, if substantial injustice would otherwise result, and to be informed of this right promptly;
(d) to challenge the lawfulness of the detention in person before a court and, if the detention is unlawful, to be released;
(e) to conditions of detention that are consistent with human dignity, including at least exercise and the provision, at state expense, of adequate accommodation, nutrition, reading material and medical treatment; and
(f) to communicate with, and be visited by, that person's—
(i) spouse or partner;
(ii) next of kin;
(iii) chosen religious counsellor; and
(iv) chosen medical practitioner.

(3) Every accused person has a right to a fair trial, which includes the right—
(a) to be informed of the charge with sufficient detail to answer it;
(b) to have adequate time and facilities to prepare a defence;
(c) to a public trial before an ordinary court;
(d) to have their trial begin and conclude without unreasonable delay;
(e) to be present when being tried;
(f) to choose, and be represented by, a legal practitioner, and to be informed of this right promptly;
(g) to have a legal practitioner assigned to the accused person by the state and at state expense, if substantial injustice would otherwise result, and to be informed of this right promptly;
(h) to be presumed innocent, to remain silent, and not to testify during the proceedings;
(i) to adduce and challenge evidence;
(j) not to be compelled to give self-incriminating evidence;
(k) to be tried in a language that the accused person understands or, if that is not practicable, to have the proceedings interpreted in that language;
(l) not to be convicted for an act or omission that was not an offence under either national or international law at the time it was committed or omitted;
(m) not to be tried for an offence in respect of an act or omission for which that person has previously been either acquitted or convicted;
(n) to the benefit of the least severe of the prescribed punishments if the prescribed punishment for the offence has been changed between the time that the offence was committed and the time of sentencing; and
(o) of appeal to, or review by, a higher court.

(4) Whenever this section requires information to be given to a person, that information must be given in a language that the person understands.

(5) Evidence obtained in a manner that violates any right in the Bill of Rights must be excluded if the admission of that evidence would render the trial unfair or otherwise be detrimental to the administration of justice.

Limitation of rights

36.(1) The rights in the Bill of Rights may be limited only in terms of law of general application to the extent that the limitation is reasonable and justifiable in an open and democratic society based on human dignity, equality and freedom, taking into account all relevant factors, including—

(a) the nature of the right;
(b) the importance of the purpose of the limitation;
(c) the nature and extent of the limitation;
(d) the relation between the limitation and its purpose; and
(e) less restrictive means to achieve the purpose.

(2) Except as provided in subsection (1) or in any other provision of the Constitution, no law may limit any right entrenched in the Bill of Rights.

States of emergency

37.(1) A state of emergency may be declared only in terms of an Act of Parliament, and only when—

(a) the life of the nation is threatened by war, invasion, general insurrection, disorder, natural disaster or other public emergency; and
(b) the declaration is necessary to restore peace and order.

(2) A declaration of a state of emergency, and any legislation enacted or other action taken in consequence of that declaration, may be effective only—

(a) prospectively; and
(b) for no more than 21 days from the date of the declaration, unless the National Assembly resolves to extend the declaration. The Assembly may extend a declaration of a state of emergency for no more than three months at a time. The first extension of the state of emergency must be by a resolution adopted with a supporting vote of a majority of the members of the Assembly. Any subsequent extension must be by a resolution adopted with a supporting vote of at least 60 per cent of the members of the Assembly. A resolution in terms of this paragraph may be adopted only following a public debate in the Assembly.

(3) Any competent court may decide on the validity of—

(a) a declaration of a state of emergency;
(b) any extension of a declaration of a state of emergency; or
(c) any legislation enacted, or other action taken, in consequence of a declaration of a state of emergency.

(4) Any legislation enacted in consequence of a declaration of a state of emergency may derogate from the Bill of Rights only to the extent that—

(a) the derogation is strictly required by the emergency; and
(b) the legislation—
  (i) is consistent with the Republic's obligations under international law applicable to states of emergency;
  (ii) conforms to subsection (5); and
  (iii) is published in the national Government Gazette as soon as reasonably possible after being enacted.

(5) No Act of Parliament that authorises a declaration of a state of emergency, and no legislation enacted or other action taken in consequence of a declaration, may permit or authorise—

(a) indemnifying the state, or any person, in respect of any unlawful act;
(b) any derogation from this section; or
(c) any derogation from a section mentioned in column 1 of the Table of Non-Derogable Rights, to the extent indicated opposite that section in column 3 of the Table.

Table of Non-Derogable Rights

1 *Section Number*	*2* *Section Title*	*3* *Extent to which the right is protected*
9	Equality	With respect to unfair discrimination solely on the grounds of race, colour, ethnic or social origin, sex, religion or language
10	Human dignity	Entirely
11	Life	Entirely
12	Freedom and security of the person	With respect to subsections (1)(d) and (e) and (2)(c)
13	Slavery, servitude and forced labour	With respect to slavery and servitude
28	Children	With respect to: — subsection (1)(d) and (e); — the rights in subparagraphs (i) and (ii) of subsection (1)(g); and subsection (1)(i) in respect of children of 15 years and younger
35	Arrested, detained and accused persons	With respect to: — subsections (1)(a), (b) and (c) and (2)(d); — the rights in paragraphs (a) to (o) of subsection (3), excluding paragraph (d) — subsection (4); and — subsection (5) with respect to the exclusion of evidence if the admission of that evidence would render the trial unfair.

(6) Whenever anyone is detained without trial in consequence of a derogation of rights resulting from a declaration of a state of emergency, the following conditions must be observed:

(a) An adult family member or friend of the detainee must be contacted as soon as reasonably possible, and informed that the person has been detained.

(b) A notice must be published in the national Government Gazette within five days of the person being detained, stating the detainee's name and place of detention and referring to the emergency measure in terms of which that person has been detained.

(c) The detainee must be allowed to choose, and be visited at any reasonable time by, a medical practitioner.

(d) The detainee must be allowed to choose, and be visited at any reasonable time by, a legal representative.

(e) A court must review the detention as soon as reasonably possible, but no later than 10 days after the date the person was detained, and the court must release the detainee unless it is necessary to continue the detention to restore peace and order.

(f) A detainee who is not released in terms of a review under paragraph (e), or who is not released in terms of a review under this paragraph, may apply to a court for a further review of the detention at any time after 10 days have passed since the previous review, and the court must release the detainee unless it is still necessary to continue the detention to restore peace and order.
(g) The detainee must be allowed to appear in person before any court considering the detention, to be represented by a legal practitioner at those hearings, and to make representations against continued detention.
(h) The state must present written reasons to the court to justify the continued detention of the detainee, and must give a copy of those reasons to the detainee at least two days before the court reviews the detention.

(7) If a court releases a detainee, that person may not be detained again on the same grounds unless the state first shows a court good cause for re-detaining that person.

(8) Subsections (6) and (7) do not apply to persons who are not South African citizens and who are detained in consequence of an international armed conflict. Instead, the state must comply with the standards binding on the Republic under international humanitarian law in respect of the detention of such persons.

Enforcement of rights

38. Anyone listed in this section has the right to approach a competent court, alleging that a right in the Bill of Rights has been infringed or threatened, and the court may grant appropriate relief, including a declaration of rights. The persons who may approach a court are—

(a) anyone acting in their own interest;
(b) anyone acting on behalf of another person who cannot act in their own name;
(c) anyone acting as a member of, or in the interest of, a group or class of persons;
(d) anyone acting in the public interest; and
(e) an association acting in the interest of its members.

Interpretation of Bill of Rights

39.(1) When interpreting the Bill of Rights, a court, tribunal or forum—

(a) must promote the values that underlie an open and democratic society based on human dignity, equality and freedom;
(b) must consider international law; and
(c) may consider foreign law.

(2) When interpreting any legislation, and when developing the common law or customary law, every court, tribunal or forum must promote the spirit, purport and objects of the Bill of Rights.

(3) The Bill of Rights does not deny the existence of any other rights or freedoms that are recognised or conferred by common law, customary law or legislation, to the extent that they are consistent with the Bill.

APPENDIX T

Constitution of United States of America: Bill of Rights and Thirteenth to Fifteenth Amendments

Amendment I[1]

Congress shall make no law respecting an establishment of religion, or prohibiting the free exercise thereof; or abridging the freedom of speech, or of the press; or the right of the people peaceably to assemble, and to petition the government for a redress of grievances.

Amendment II[2]

A well regulated militia, being necessary to the security of a free state, the right of the people to keep and bear arms, shall not be infringed.

Amendment III[3]

No soldier shall, in time of peace be quartered in any house, without the consent of the owner, nor in time of war, but in a manner to be prescribed by law.

Amendment IV[4]

The right of the people to be secure in their persons, houses, papers, and effects, against unreasonable searches and seizures, shall not be violated, and no warrants shall issue, but upon probable cause, supported by oath or affirmation, and particularly describing the place to be searched, and the persons or things to be seized.

Amendment V[5]

No person shall be held to answer for a capital, or otherwise infamous crime, unless on a presentment or indictment of a grand jury, except in cases arising in the land or naval forces, or in the militia, when in actual service in time of war or public danger; nor shall any person be subject for the same offense to be twice put in jeopardy of life or limb; nor shall be compelled in any criminal case to be a witness against himself, nor be deprived of life, liberty, or property, without due process of law; nor shall private property be taken for public use, without just compensation.

Amendment VI[6]

In all criminal prosecutions, the accused shall enjoy the right to a speedy and public trial, by an impartial jury of the state and district wherein the crime shall have been committed, which district shall have been previously ascertained by law, and to be informed of the nature and cause of the accusation; to be confronted with the witnesses against him; to have compulsory process for obtaining witnesses in his favor, and to have the assistance of counsel for his defense.

---

[1] 1791. [2] 1791. [3] 1791. [4] 1791. [5] 1791. [6] 1791.

Amendment VII[7]

In suits at common law, where the value in controversy shall exceed twenty dollars, the right of trial by jury shall be preserved, and no fact tried by a jury, shall be otherwise reexamined in any court of the United States, than according to the rules of the common law.

Amendment VIII[8]

Excessive bail shall not be required, nor excessive fines imposed, nor cruel and unusual punishments inflicted.

Amendment IX[9]

The enumeration in the Constitution, of certain rights, shall not be construed to deny or disparage others retained by the people.

Amendment X[10]

The powers not delegated to the United States by the Constitution, nor prohibited by it to the states, are reserved to the states respectively, or to the people.

Amendment XIII[11]

Section 1. Neither slavery nor involuntary servitude, except as a punishment for crime whereof the party shall have been duly convicted, shall exist within the United States, or any place subject to their jurisdiction.

Section 2. Congress shall have power to enforce this article by appropriate legislation.

Amendment XIV[12]

Section 1. All persons born or naturalized in the United States, and subject to the jurisdiction thereof, are citizens of the United States and of the state wherein they reside. No state shall make or enforce any law which shall abridge the privileges or immunities of citizens of the United States; nor shall any state deprive any person of life, liberty, or property, without due process of law; nor deny to any person within its jurisdiction the equal protection of the laws.

Section 2. Representatives shall be apportioned among the several states according to their respective numbers, counting the whole number of persons in each state, excluding Indians not taxed. But when the right to vote at any election for the choice of electors for President and Vice President of the United States, Representatives in Congress, the executive and judicial officers of a state, or the members of the legislature thereof, is denied to any of the male inhabitants of such state, being twenty-one years of age, and citizens of the United States, or in any way abridged, except for participation in rebellion, or other crime, the basis of representation therein shall be reduced in the proportion which the number of such male citizens shall bear to the whole number of male citizens twenty-one years of age in such state.

Section 3. No person shall be a Senator or Representative in Congress, or elector of President and Vice President, or hold any office, civil or military, under the United States, or under any state, who, having previously taken an oath, as a member of Congress, or as an officer of the United States, or as a member of any state legislature, or as an executive or judicial officer of any state, to support the Constitution of the United States, shall have engaged in insurrection or rebellion against the same, or given aid or comfort to the enemies thereof. But Congress may by a vote of two-thirds of each House, remove such disability.

Section 4. The validity of the public debt of the United States, authorized by law, including debts incurred for payment of pensions and bounties for services in suppressing insurrection or rebellion, shall not be questioned. But neither the United States nor any state shall assume or pay any debt or obligation incurred in aid of insurrection or rebellion against the United States, or any claim for the loss or emancipation of any slave; but all such debts, obligations and claims shall be held illegal and void.

[7] 1791. [8] 1791. [9] 1791. [10] 1791. [11] 1865. [12] 1868.

Section 5. The Congress shall have power to enforce, by appropriate legislation, the provisions of this article.

Amendment XV[13]

Section 1. The right of citizens of the United States to vote shall not be denied or abridged by the United States or by any state on account of race, color, or previous condition of servitude.

Section 2. The Congress shall have power to enforce this article by appropriate legislation.

[13] 1870.

APPENDIX U

Constitution of Zimbabwe: Declaration of Rights[1]

11 Fundamental rights and freedoms of the individual

Whereas every person in Zimbabwe is entitled to the fundamental rights and freedoms of the individual, that is to say, the right whatever his race, tribe, place of origin, political opinions, colour, creed or sex, but subject to respect for the rights and freedoms of others and for the public interest, to each and all of the following, namely—

(a) life, liberty, security of the person and the protection of the law;
(b) freedom of conscience, of expression and of assembly and association; and
(c) protection for the privacy of his home and other property and from the compulsory acquisition of property without compensation;

and whereas it is the duty of every person to respect and abide by the Constitution and the laws of Zimbabwe, the provisions of this Chapter shall have effect for the purpose of affording protection to those rights and freedoms subject to such limitations of that protection as are contained herein, being limitations designed to ensure that the enjoyment of the said rights and freedoms by any person does not prejudice the rights and freedoms of others or the public interest.

12 Protection of right to life

(1) No person shall be deprived of his life intentionally save in execution of the sentence of a court in respect of a criminal offence of which he has been convicted.

(2) A person shall not be regarded as having been deprived of his life in contravention of subsection (1) if he dies as the result of the use, to such extent and in such circumstances as are permitted by law, of such force as is reasonably justifiable in the circumstances of the case—

(a) for the defence of any person from violence or for the defence of property;
(b) in order to effect a lawful arrest or to prevent the escape of a person lawfully detained;
(c) for the purpose of suppressing a riot, insurrection or mutiny or of dispersing an unlawful gathering; or
(d) in order to prevent the commission by that person of a criminal offence;

or if he dies as the result of a lawful act of war.

(3) It shall be sufficient justification for the purposes of subsection (2) in any case to which that subsection applies if it is shown that the force used did not exceed that which might lawfully have been used in the circumstances of that case under the law in force immediately before the appointed day.

13 Protection of right to personal liberty

(1) No person shall be deprived of his personal liberty save as may be authorised by law in any of the cases specified in subsection (2).

(2) The cases referred to in subsection (1) are where a person is deprived of his personal liberty as may be authorised by law—

---

[1] Chapter III of the Constitution of Zimbabwe 1979 (The Zimbabwe Constitution Order 1979, SI 1979 1600, as amended).

(a) in consequence of his unfitness to plead to a criminal charge or in execution of the sentence or order of a court, whether in Zimbabwe or elsewhere, in respect of a criminal offence of which he has been convicted;

(b) in execution of the order of a court punishing him for contempt of that court or of another court or tribunal or in execution of the order of Parliament punishing him for a contempt;
[Paragraph as amended by section 26 of Act 31 of 1989]

(c) in execution of the order of a court made in order to secure the fulfillment of an obligation imposed on him by law;
[Paragraph as amended by section 4 of Act 30 of 1990]

(d) for the purpose of bringing him before a court in execution of the order of a court or an officer of a court or before Parliament in execution of the order of Parliament;
[Paragraph as amended by section 26 of Act 31 of 1989 and by section 9 of Act 15 of 1990]

(e) upon reasonable suspicion of his having committed, or being about to commit, a criminal offence;

(f) in execution of the order of a court or with the consent of his parent or guardian, for the purposes of his education or welfare during a period beginning before he attains the age of twenty-one years and ending not later than the date when he attains the age of twenty-three years;

(g) for the purpose of preventing the spread of an infectious or contagious disease;

(h) if he is, or is reasonably suspected to be, of unsound mind, addicted to drugs or alcohol, or a vagrant, for the purpose of his care, treatment or rehabilitation or the protection of the community; or

(i) for the purpose of preventing his unlawful entry into Zimbabwe or for the purpose of effecting his expulsion, extradition or other lawful removal from Zimbabwe or the taking of proceedings relating thereto.

(3) Any person who is arrested or detained shall be informed as soon as reasonably practicable, in a language that he understands, of the reasons for his arrest or detention and shall be permitted at his own expense to obtain and instruct without delay a legal representative of his own choice and hold communication with him.

(4) Any person who is arrested or detained—

(a) for the purpose of bringing him before a court in execution of the order of a court or an officer of a court; or

(b) upon reasonable suspicion of his having committed, or being about to commit, a criminal offence;

and who is not released, shall be brought without undue delay before a court; and if any person arrested or detained upon reasonable suspicion of his having committed or being about to commit a criminal offence is not tried within a reasonable time, then, without prejudice to any further proceedings that may be brought against him, he shall be released either unconditionally or upon reasonable conditions, including in particular such conditions as are reasonably necessary to ensure that he appears at a later date for trial or for proceedings preliminary to trial.

(5) Any person who is unlawfully arrested or detained by any other person shall be entitled to compensation therefor from that other person or from any person or authority on whose behalf or in the course of whose employment that other person was acting:

Provided that—

(a) any judicial officer acting in his judicial capacity reasonably and in good faith; or

(b) any other public officer, or person assisting such public officer, acting reasonably and in good faith and without culpable ignorance or negligence;

may be protected by law from liability for such compensation.

14 Protection from slavery and forced labour

(1) No person shall be held in slavery or servitude or required to perform forced labour.

(2) For the purposes of subsection (1) 'forced labour' does not include—

(a) any labour required in consequence of the sentence or order of a court;
(b) labour required of any person which is lawfully detained which, though not required in consequence of the sentence or order of a court—
 (i) is reasonably necessary in the interests of hygiene or for the maintenance of management of the place at which he is detained; or
 (ii) is reasonably required for the purposes referred to in section 13(2)(f) or (h);
(c) any labour required of a member of a disciplined force in pursuance of his duties as such or any labour required of any person by virtue of a written law in place of service as a member of such force;
(d) any labour required by way of parental discipline; or
(e) any labour required by virtue of a written law during a period of public emergency or in the event of any other emergency or disaster that threatens the life or well-being of the community, to the extent that the requiring of such labour is reasonably justifiable in the circumstances of any situation arising or existing during that period or as a result of that other emergency or disaster, for the purpose of dealing with that situation.

15 Protection from inhuman treatment

(1) No person shall be subjected to torture or to inhuman or degrading punishment or other such treatment.

(2) No treatment reasonably justifiable in the circumstances of the case to prevent the escape from custody of a person who has been lawfully detained shall be held to be in contravention of subsection (1) on the ground that it is degrading.

(3) No moderate corporal punishment inflicted—
(a) in appropriate circumstances upon a person under the age of eighteen years by his parent or guardian or by someone *in loco parentis* or in whom are vested any of the powers of his parent or guardian; or
(b) in execution of the judgment or order of a court, upon a male person under the age of eighteen years as a penalty for breach of any law;

shall be held to be in contravention of subsection (1) on the ground that it is inhuman or degrading.

[Subsection as inserted by section 5 of Act 30 of 1990]

(4) The execution of a person who has been sentenced to death by a competent court in respect of a criminal offence of which he has been convicted shall not be held to be in contravention of subsection (1) solely on the ground that the execution is carried out in the manner prescribed in section 315(2) of the Criminal Procedure and Evidence Act [*Chapter 59*] as that section existed on the 1st October, 1990.

[Subsection as inserted by section 5 of Act 30 of 1990. As at the 1st October, 1990, section 315(2) of the Criminal Procedure and Evidence Act [*Chapter 59 of 1974*] provided that 'where sentence of death is carried out, the person sentenced shall be hanged by the neck until he is dead'.]

(5) Delay in the execution of a sentence of death, imposed upon a person in respect of a criminal offence of which he has been convicted, shall not be held to be a contravention of subsection (1).

[Subsection as inserted by section 2 of Act 9 of 1993]

(6) A person upon whom any sentence has been imposed by a competent court, whether before, on or after the date of commencement of the Constitution of Zimbabwe Amendment (No. 13) Act, 1993, in respect of a criminal offence of which he has been convicted, shall not be entitled to a stay, alteration or remission or sentence on the ground that, since the sentence was imposed, there has been a contravention of subsection (1).

[Subsection as inserted by section 2 of Act 9 of 1993]

16 Protection from deprivation of property

(1) No property of any description or interest or right therein shall be compulsorily acquired except under the authority of a law that—

(a) requires—
  (i) in the case of land or any interest or right therein, that the acquisition is reasonably necessary for the utilisation of that or any other land—
    A. for settlement for agricultural or other purposes; or
    B. for purposes of land reorganisation, forestry, environmental conservation or the utilisation of wild life or other natural resources; or
    C. for the relocation of persons dispossessed in consequence of the utilisation of land for a purpose referred to in subparagraph A or B; or
  (ii) in the case of any property, including land, or any interest or right therein, that the acquisition is reasonably necessary in the interests of defence, public safety, public order, public morality, public health, town and country planning or the utilisation of that or any other property for a purpose beneficial to the public generally or to any section of the public; and

  [Paragraph as substituted by section 6 of Act 30 of 1990]

(b) requires the acquiring authority to give reasonable notice of the intention to acquire the property, interest or right to any person owning the property or having any other interest or right therein that would be affected by such acquisition; and

  [Paragraph as substituted by section 6 of Act 30 of 1990]

(c) subject to the provisions of subsection (2), requires the acquiring authority to pay fair compensation for the acquisition before or within a reasonable time after acquiring the property, interest or right; and

  [Paragraph as substituted by section 6 of Act 30 of 1990]

(d) requires the acquiring authority, if the acquisition is contested, to apply to the High Court or some other court for the prompt return of the property if the court does not confirm the acquisition, and to appeal to the Supreme Court; and

  [Paragraph as substituted by section 3 of Act 9 of 1993]

(e) except where the property concerned is land or any interest or right therein, enables any claimant for compensation to apply to the High Court or some other court for the determination of any question, relating to compensation and to appeal to the Supreme Court.

  [Paragraph as inserted by section 3 of Act 9 of 1993]

(2) A law referred to subsection (1) which provides for the compulsory acquisition of land or any interest or right therein may—

(a) specify the principles on which, and the manner in which, compensation for the acquisition of the land or interest or right therein is to be determined and paid;
(b) fix, in accordance with principles referred to in paragraph (a), the amount of compensation payable for the acquisition of the land or interest or right therein;
(c) fix the period within which compensation shall be paid for the acquisition of the land or interest or right therein;

and no such law shall be called into question by any court on the ground that the compensation provided by that law is not fair.

[Subsection as substituted by section 6 of Act 30 of 1990]

(3) Where any person, by virtue of a law, contract or scheme relating to the payment of pensions benefits, has a right, whether vested or contingent, to the payment of pensions benefits or any commutation thereof or a refund of contributions, with or without interest, payable in terms of such law, contract or scheme, any law which thereafter provides for the extinction of or a diminution in such a right shall be regarded for the purposes of subsection (1) as a law providing for the acquisition of a right in property.

(4) Nothing contained in or done under the authority of any law shall be held to be in contravention of subsection (1) to the extent that the law in question authorises the taking of possession of property compulsorily during a period of public emergency or in the event of any other emergency or disaster that

threatens the life or well-being of the community or where there is a situation that may lead to such emergency or disaster and makes provision that—

(a) requires the acquiring authority promptly to give reasonable notice of the taking of possession to any person owning or possessing the property;

(b) enables any such person to notify the acquiring authority in writing that he objects to the taking of possession;

(c) requires the acquiring authority to apply within thirty days of such notification to the High Court or some other court for a determination of its entitlement to take possession;
[Paragraph as amended by section 13 of Act 25 of 1981]

(d) requires the High Court or other court to order the acquiring authority to return the property unless it is satisfied that the taking of possession is reasonably justifiable, in the circumstances of any situation arising or existing during that period or as a result of that other emergency or disaster or that may lead to such emergency or disaster, for the purpose of dealing with that situation;
[Paragraph as amended by section 13 of Act 25 of 1981]

(e) requires—

(i) when possession is no longer reasonably justifiable as referred to in paragraph (d), wherever possible, the prompt return of the property in the condition in which it was at the time of the taking of possession; and

(ii) the payment within a reasonable time of fair compensation for the taking of possession and, where appropriate, for the failure to return the property in accordance with subparagraph (i) or for any damage to the property; and
[Subparagraph as amended by section 6 of Act 30 of 1990]

(f) enables any claimant for compensation to apply to the High Court or some other court for the prompt return of the property and for the determination of any question relating to compensation, and to appeal to the Supreme Court.
[Paragraph as amended by section 13 of Act 25 of 1981]

(5) Nothing contained in or done under the authority of any law shall be held to be in contravention of subsection (1) to the extent that the law in question imposes or authorises the imposition of restrictions or limitations, to the extent permitted by paragraph 2 of Schedule 6, on the remittability of any commutation of a pension.
[Subsection repealed as inserted by section 3 of Act 9 of 1993]

(6) [Subsection repealed by section 6 of Act 30 of 1990]

(7) Nothing contained in or done under the authority of any law shall be held to be in contravention of subsection (1) to the extent that the law in question makes provision for the acquisition of any property or any interest or right therein in any of the following cases—

(a) in satisfaction of any tax or rate;

(b) by way of penalty for breach of any law, including any law of a foreign country which, by or in terms of an Act of Parliament, is recognised or applied for any purpose in Zimbabwe, whether under civil process or after conviction of an offence, or forfeiture in consequence of a breach of the law or in pursuance of any order referred to in section 13(2)(b);
[Paragraph as amended by section 6 of Act 30 of 1990]

(c) upon the removal or attempted removal of the property in question out of or into Zimbabwe in contravention of any law;

(d) as an incident of a contract, including a lease or mortgage, which has been agreed between the parties to the contract, or of a title deed to land fixed at the time of the grant or transfer thereof or at any other time with the consent of the owner of the land;

(e) in execution of the judgment or order of a court in proceedings for the determination of civil rights or obligations;

(f) by reason of the property in question being in a dangerous state or prejudicial to the health or safety of human, animal or vegetable life or having been constructed or grown on any land in contravention of any law relating to the occupation or use of that land;

(g) in consequence of any law with respect to the limitation of actions, acquisitive prescription or derelict land;

(h) as a condition in connection with the granting of permission for the utilisation of that or other property in any particular manner;

(i) by way of the taking of a sample for the purposes of a law;

(j) where the property consists of an animal, upon its being found trespassing or straying;

(k) for so long only as may be necessary for the purpose of any examination, investigation, trial or inquiry;

(l) in the case of land, for so long only as may be necessary for the purpose of the carrying out thereon of—

(i) work for the purpose of the conservation of natural resources of any description; or

(ii) agricultural development or improvement which the owner or occupier of the land has been required, and has without reasonable or lawful excuse refused or failed, to carry out;

(m) in consequence of any law requiring copies of any book or other publication published in Zimbabwe to be lodged with the National Archives or a public library;

(n) for the purposes of, or in connection with, the prospecting for or exploitation of minerals, mineral oils, natural gases, precious metals or precious stones which are vested in the President on terms which provide for the respective interests of the persons affected;

(o) for the purposes of, or in connection with, the exploitation of underground water or public water which is vested in the President on terms which provide for the respective interests of the persons affected;

except so far as that provision or, as the case may be, the thing done under the authority thereof is shown not to be reasonably justifiable in a democratic society.

(8) Nothing contained in or done under the authority of any law shall be held to be in contravention of subsection (1) to the extent that the law in question makes provision for the acquisition of any property or any interest or right therein in any of the following cases—

(a) for the purpose of the administration, care of custody of any property of a deceased person or a person who is unable, by reason of any incapacity, to administer it himself, on behalf and for the benefit of the person entitled to the beneficial interest therein;

(b) by way of the vesting or administration of any property belonging to or used by or on behalf of an enemy or any organisation which is, in the interests of defence, public safety or public order, proscribed or declared by a written law to be an unlawful organisation;

(c) by way of the administration of moneys payable or owing to a person outside Zimbabwe or to the government of some other country where restrictions have been placed by law on the transfer of such moneys outside Zimbabwe;

(d) as an incident of—

(i) a composition in insolvency accepted or agreed to by a majority in number of creditors who have proved claims and by a number of creditors whose proved claims represent in value more than fifty *per centum* of the total value of proved claims; or

(ii) a deed of assignments entered into by a debtor with his creditors;

(e) by way of the acquisition of the shares, or a class of shares, in a body corporate on terms agreed to by the holders of not less than nine-tenths in value of those shares of that class thereof.

(9) Nothing in this section shall affect the making or operation of any law in so far as it provides for—

(a) the orderly marketing of any agricultural produce or mineral or any article or thing prepared for market or manufactured therefor in the common interests of the various persons otherwise entitled to dispose of that property or for the reasonable restriction of the use of any property in the interests of safeguarding the interests of others or the protection of lessees or other persons having rights in or over such property; or

(b) the taking of possession or acquisition in the public interest of any property or any interest or right therein where that property, interest or right is held by a body corporate established directly by law for a public purpose in which no moneys have been invested other than moneys provided from public funds.

(9a) Nothing in this section shall affect the making or operation of any Act of Parliament in so far as it provides for the extinction of any debt or other obligation gratuitously assumed by the State or any other person.

[Subsection as inserted by section 6 of Act 30 of 1990]

(10) In this section—

'**acquiring authority**' means the person or authority compulsorily taking possession of or acquiring the property or the interest of right therein;

'**agricultural purpose**' includes forestry, fruit-growing and animal husbandry, including the keeping of poultry, bees or fish;

'**land**' includes anything permanently attached to or growing on land;

[Definition as inserted by section 6 of Act 30 of 1990]

'**pensions benefits**' means any pension, annuity, gratuity or other like allowance—

(a) which is payable from the Consolidated Revenue Fund to any person;

(b) for any person in respect of his service with an employer or for any spouse, child or dependent of such person in respect of such service;

(c) for any person in respect of his ill-health or injury arising out of and in the course of his employment or for any spouse, child or dependant of such person upon the death of such person from such ill-health or injury;

(d) for any person upon his retirement on account of age or ill-health or other termination of service;

'**piece of land**' means a piece of land registered as a separate entity in the Deeds Registry.

17 Protection from arbitrary search or entry

(1) Except with his own consent or by way of parental discipline, no person shall be subjected to the search of his person or his property or the entry by others on his premises.

(2) Nothing contained in or done under the authority of any law shall be held to be in contravention of subsection (1) to the extent that the law in question makes provisions—

(a) in the interests of defence, public safety, public order, public morality, public health or town and country planning;

(b) without derogation from the generality of the provisions of paragraph (a), for the enforcement of the law in circumstances where there are reasonable grounds for believing that the search or entry is necessary for the prevention, investigation or detection of a criminal offence, for the seizure of any property which is the subject-matter of a criminal offence or evidence relating to a criminal offence, for the lawful arrest of a person or for the enforcement of any tax or rate;

(c) for the purposes of a law which provides for the taking of possession or acquisition of any property or interest or right therein and which is not in contravention of section 16;

(d) for the purpose of protecting the rights and freedoms of other persons;

(e) that authorises any local authority or any body corporate established directly by or under an Act of Parliament for a public purpose to enter on the premises of any person in order to inspect those premises or anything thereon for the purpose of any tax or rate or in order to carry out work connected with any property of that authority or body which is lawfully on those premises; or

(f) that authorises, for the purpose of enforcing the judgment or order of a court in any civil proceeding, the search of any person or property by order of a court or the entry upon any premises by such order;

except so far as that provision or, as the case may be, the thing done under the authority thereof is shown not to be reasonably justifiable in a democratic society.

(3) A law referred to in subsection (2) which makes provision of the search of the person of a woman shall require that such search shall, unless made by a medical practitioner, only be made by a woman and shall be conducted with strict regard to decency.

18 Provisions to secure protection of law

(1) Subject to the provisions of this Constitution, every person is entitled to the protection of the law. [Subsection as amended by section 3 of Act 4 of 1993]

(2) If any person is charged with a criminal offence, then, unless the charge is withdrawn, the case shall be afforded a fair hearing within a reasonable time by an independent and impartial court established by law.

(3) Every person who is charged with a criminal offence—

(a) shall be presumed to be innocent until he is proved or has pleaded guilty;

(b) shall be informed as soon as reasonably practicable, in a language that he understands and in detail, of the nature of the offence charged;

(c) shall be given adequate time and facilities for the preparation of his defence;

(d) shall be permitted to defend himself in person or, save in proceedings before a local court, at his own expense by a legal representative of his own choice;

(e) shall be afforded facilities to examine in person or, save in proceedings before a local court, by his legal representative the witnesses called by the prosecution before the court and to obtain the attendance and carry out the examination of witnesses to testify on his behalf before the court on the same conditions as those applying to witnesses called by the prosecution; and

(f) shall be permitted to have without payment the assistance of an interpreter if he cannot understand the language used at the trial of the charge;

and, except with his own consent, the trial shall not take place in his absence unless he so conducts himself as to render the continuance of the proceedings in his presence impracticable and the court has ordered him to be removed and the trial to proceed in his absence.

(4) When a person is tried for any criminal offence, the accused person or any person authorised by him in that behalf shall, if he so requires and subject to payment of such reasonable time after judgment a copy for the use of the accused person of any record of the proceedings made by or on behalf of the court.

(5) No person shall be held to be guilty of a criminal offence on account of any act or omission that did not, at the time it took place, constitute such an offence, and no penalty shall be imposed for any criminal offence that is severer in degree or description than the maximum penalty that might have been imposed for that offence at the time when it was committed.

(6) No person who shows that he has been tried by a competent court for a criminal offence upon a good indictment, summons or charge upon which a valid judgment could be entered and either convicted or acquitted shall again be tried for that offence or for any other criminal offence of which he could have been convicted at the trial for that offence, save—

(a) where a conviction and sentence of the High Court or of a court subordinate to the High Court are set aside on appeal or review on the ground that evidence was admitted which should not have been admitted or that evidence was rejected which should have been admitted or on the ground of any other irregularity or defect in the procedure;
[Paragraph as amended by section 3 of Act 4 of 1993]

(7) No person shall be tried for a criminal offence if he shows that he has been pardoned for that offence.

(8) No person who is tried for a criminal offence shall be compelled to give evidence at the trial.

(9) Subject to the provisions of this Constitution, every person is entitled to be afforded a fair hearing within a reasonable time by an independent and impartial court or other adjudicating authority established by law in the determination of the existence or extent of his civil rights or obligations.
[Subsection as amended by section 3 of Act 4 of 1993]

(10) Except in the case of a trial such as is referred to in subsection (14) or with the agreement of all the parties thereto, all proceedings of every court and proceedings for right or obligation before any other

adjudicating authority, including the announcement of the decision of the court or other authority, shall be held in public.

(11) Nothing in subsection (10) shall prevent—

(a) the court or other adjudicating authority from excluding from the proceedings, except the announcement of its decision, persons other than the parties thereto and their legal representatives to such extent as the court or other authority—

(i) may by law be empowered so to do and may consider necessary or expedient in circumstances where publicity would prejudice the interests of justice, or in interlocutory proceedings, or in the interests of justice of public morality, the welfare of persons under the age of twenty-one years or the protection of the private lives of persons concerned in the proceedings; or

(ii) may by law be empowered or required so to do in the interests of defence, public safety, public order or the economic interests of the State; or

(b) the court from excluding from proceedings preliminary to trial in respect of a criminal offence persons other than the accused person and his legal representative when so required by law, unless the accused person otherwise requests.

(12) Notwithstanding anything contained in subsection (4), (10) or (11), if in any proceedings before such court or other adjudicating authority as is referred to in subsection (2) or (9), including any proceedings by virtue of section 24, a certificate in writing is produced to the court or other authority signed by a Minister that it would not be in the public interest for any matter to be publicly disclosed, the court or other authority shall make arrangements for evidence relating to that matter to be heard *in camera* and shall take such other action as may be necessary or expedient to prevent the disclosure of that matter.

(13) Nothing contained in or done under the authority of any law shall be held to be in contravention of—

(a) subsection (2), (3)(e) or (9) to the extent that the law in question makes reasonable provision relating to the grounds of privilege or public policy on which evidence shall not be disclosed or witnesses are not competent or cannot be compelled to give evidence in any proceedings;

(b) subsection (3)(a) to the extent that the law in question imposes upon any person charged with a criminal offence the burden of proving particular facts;

(c) subsection (3)(e) to the extent that the law in question imposes reasonable conditions which must be satisfied if witnesses called to testify on behalf of an accused person are to be paid their expenses out of public funds;

(d) subsection (6) to the extent that the law in question authorises a court to try a member of a disciplined force for a criminal offence notwithstanding any trial and conviction or acquittal of that member under the appropriate disciplinary law, so, however, that any court so trying such a member and convicting him shall in sentencing him to any punishment take into account any punishment awarded him under that disciplinary law; or

(e) subsection (8) to the extent that the law in question authorises a court, where the person who is being tried refuses without just cause to answer any question put to him, to draw such inferences from that refusal as are proper and to treat that refusal, on the basis of such inferences, as evidence corroborating any other evidence given against that person.

(14) In the case of a person who is held in lawful detention, the provisions of subsection (2) shall not apply in relation to his trial for a criminal offence under the law regulating the discipline of persons held in such detention, save that the case of such person shall be afforded a fair hearing within a reasonable time, and the person or authority conducting the trial shall be regarded as a court for the purposes of this section.

(15) For the purposes of this section, a local court shall not be regarded as not being an independent and impartial court by reason of—

(a) the fact that a member of the court has an interest in the proceedings because of his position in the tribal society; or

(b) the traditional or customary tribal practices and procedures.

19 Protection of freedom of conscience

(1) Except with his own consent or by way of parental discipline, no person shall be hindered in the enjoyment of his freedom of conscience, that is to say, freedom of thought and of religion, freedom to change his religion or belief, and freedom, whether alone or in community with others, and whether in public or in private, to manifest and propagate his religion or belief through worship, teaching, practice and observance.

(2) Except with his own consent or, if he is a minor, the consent of his parent or guardian, no person attending any place of education shall be required to receive religious instruction or to take part in or attend any religious ceremony or observance if that instruction, ceremony or observances relates to a religion other than his own.

(3) No religious community shall be prevented from making provision for the giving by persons lawfully in Zimbabwe of religious instruction to persons of that community in the course of any education provided by that community, whether or not that community is in receipt of any subsidy, grant or other form of financial assistance from the State.

(4) No person shall be compelled to take any oath that is contrary to his religion or belief or to take any oath in a manner that is contrary to his religion or belief.

(5) Nothing contained in or done under the authority of any law shall be held to be in contravention of subsection (1) or (3) to the extent that the law in question makes provision—

- (a) in the interests of defence, public safety, public order, public morality or public health;
- (b) for the purpose of protecting the rights and freedoms of other persons, including the right to observe and practise any religion or belief without the unsolicited intervention of persons professing any other religion or belief; or
- (c) with respect to standards or qualifications to be required in relation to places of education, including any instruction not being religious instruction, given at such places;

except so far as that provision or, as the case may be, the thing done under the authority thereof is shown not to be reasonably justifiable in a democratic society.

(6) References in this section to a religion shall be construed as including references to a religious denomination and cognate expressions shall be construed accordingly.

20 Protection of freedom of expression

(1) Except with his own consent or by way of parental discipline, no person shall be hindered in the enjoyment of his freedom of expression, that is to say, freedom to hold opinions and to receive and impart ideas and information without interference, and freedom from interference with his correspondence.

(2) Nothing contained in or done under the authority of any law shall be held to be in contravention of subsection (1) to the extent that the law in question makes provision—

- (a) in the interests of defence, public safety, public order, the economic interests of the State, public morality or public health;
- (b) for the purpose of—
  - (i) protecting the reputations, rights and freedoms of other persons or the private lives of persons concerned in legal proceedings;
  - (ii) preventing the disclosure of information received in confidence;
  - (iii) maintaining the authority and independence of the courts or tribunals or Parliament; [Subparagraph as amended by section 26 of Act 31 of 1989]
  - (iv) regulating the technical administration, technical operation or general efficiency of telephony, telegraphy, posts, wireless broadcasting or television or creating or regulating any monopoly in these fields;
  - (v) in the case of correspondence, preventing the unlawful dispatch therewith of other matter; or
- (c) that imposes restrictions upon public officers;

except so far as that provision or, as the case may be, the thing done under the authority thereof is shown not to be reasonably justifiable in a democratic society.

(3) No religious denomination and no person or group of persons shall be prevented from establishing and maintaining schools, whether or not that denomination, person or group is in receipt of any subsidy, grant or other form of financial assistance from the State.

(4) Nothing contained in or done under the authority of any law shall be held to be in contravention of subsection (3) to the extent that the law in question makes provision—

(a) in the interests of defence, public safety, public order, public morality, public health or town and country planning; or

(b) for regulating such schools in the interests of persons receiving instruction therein;

except so far as that provision or, as the case may be, the thing done under the authority thereof is shown not to be reasonably justifiable in a democratic society.

(5) No person shall be prevented from sending to any school a child of whom that person is parent or guardian by reason only that the school is not a school established or maintained by the State.

(6) The provisions of subsection (1) shall not be held to confer on any person a right to exercise his freedom of expression in or on any road, street, lane, path, pavement, side-walk, thoroughfare or similar place which exists for the free passage of persons or vehicles.

21 Protection of freedom of assembly and association

(1) Except with his own consent or by way of parental discipline, no person shall be hindered in his freedom of assembly and association, that is to say, his right to assemble freely and associate with other persons and in particular to form or belong to political parties or trade unions or other associations for the protection of his interests.

(2) The freedom referred to in subsection (1) shall include the right not to be compelled to belong to an association.

(3) Nothing contained in or done under the authority of any law shall be held to be in contravention of subsection (1) to the extent that the law in question makes provision—

(a) in the interests of defence, public safety, public order, public morality or public health;

(b) for the purpose of protecting the rights or freedoms of other persons;

(c) for the registration of companies, partnerships, societies or other associations of persons, other than political parties, trade unions or employers' organisations; or

(d) that imposes restrictions upon public officers;

except so far as that provision of, as the case may be, the thing done under the authority thereof is shown not to be reasonably justifiable in a democratic society.

(4) The provisions of subsection (1) shall not be held to confer on any person a right to exercise his freedom of assembly or association in or on any road, street, lane, path, pavement, side-walk, thoroughfare or similar place which exists for the free passage of persons or vehicles.

22 Protection of freedom of movement

(1) No person shall be deprived of his freedom to movement, that is to say, the right to move freely throughout Zimbabwe, the right to reside in any part of Zimbabwe, the right to enter and leave Zimbabwe and immunity from expulsion from Zimbabwe.

(2) Any restriction on a person's freedom of movement that is involved in his lawful detention shall not be held to be in contravention of subsection (1).

(3) Nothing contained in or done under the authority of any law shall be held to be in contravention of subsection (1) to the extent that the law in question makes provision—

(a) for the imposition of restrictions on the freedom of movement of persons generally or any class of persons that are required in the interests of defence, public safety, public order, public morality or public health;

(b) for the imposition of restrictions on the acquisition or use of land or other property in Zimbabwe;

(c) for the imposition of restrictions by order of a court on the movement or residence within Zimbabwe of any person or on any person's right to leave Zimbabwe—

(i) in consequence of his having been found guilty of a criminal offence under the law of Zimbabwe or for the purpose of ensuring that he appears before a court for trial for such a criminal offence or for proceedings preliminary to trial;

(ii) for proceedings relating to his extradition or lawful removal from Zimbabwe; or

(iii) for the purpose of ensuring that he appears before a court as a witness for the purposes of any criminal proceedings;

(d) for the imposition of restriction on the movement or residence within Zimbabwe of persons who are neither citizens of Zimbabwe nor regarded by virtue of a written law as permanently resident in Zimbabwe or for excluding or expelling from Zimbabwe any person who is not a citizen of Zimbabwe;

(e) for the imposition of restrictions by order of a court on the right of any person to leave Zimbabwe that are required for the purpose of ensuring that he appears before a court or other adjudicating authority for the purposes of any civil proceedings; or

(f) for the imposition of restrictions on the residence within Communal Land of persons who are not tribespeople to the extent that such restrictions are reasonably required for the protection of the interests of tribespeople or their well-being;
[Paragraph as amended by section 23 of Act 23 of 1987]

except, in the case of any provision referred to in paragraph (a) to (e), so far as that provision or, as the case may be, the thing done under the authority thereof is shown not to be reasonably justifiable in a democratic society.

(4) The provisions of subsection (3)(a) shall not be construed as authorising a law to make provision, for preventing any person from leaving Zimbabwe or excluding or expelling from Zimbabwe any person who is a citizen of Zimbabwe.

23 Protection from discrimination on the grounds of race, etc.

(1) Subject to the provisions of this section—

(a) no law shall make any provision that is discriminatory either of itself or in its effect; and

(b) no person shall be treated in a discriminatory manner by any person acting by virtue of any written law or in the performance of the functions of any public office or any public authority.

(2) For the purposes of subsection (1), a law shall be regarded as making a provision that is discriminatory and a person shall be regarded as having been treated in a discriminatory manner if, as a result of that law or treatment, persons of a particular description by race, tribe, place of origin, political opinions, colour or creed are prejudiced—

(a) by being subjected to a condition, restriction or disability to which other persons of another such description are not made subject; or

(b) by the according to persons of another such description of a privilege or advantage which is not accorded to persons of the first-mentioned description;

and the imposition of that condition, restriction or disability or the according of that privilege or advantage is wholly or mainly attributable to the description by race, tribe, place of origin, political opinions, colour or creed of the persons concerned.

(3) Nothing contained in any law shall be held to be in contravention of subsection (1)(a) to the extent that the law in question relates to any of the following matters—

(a) adoption, marriage, divorce, burial, devolution of property on death or other matters of personal law;

(b) the application of African customary law in any case involving Africans or an African and one or more persons who are not Africans where such persons have consented to the application of African customary law in that case;

(c) restrictions on entry into or employment in Zimbabwe or on the enjoyment of services provided out of public funds in the case of persons who are neither citizens of Zimbabwe nor regarded by virtue of a written law as permanently resident in Zimbabwe;

(d) qualifications, not being qualifications specifically relating to race, tribe, place of origin, political opinions, colour or creed, for service as a public officer or as a member of a disciplined force or for service with any public authority or any body corporate established directly by or under an Act of Parliament for a public purpose;

(e) the appropriation of public revenues or other public funds; or

(f) the according to tribespeople to the exclusion of other persons of rights or privileges relating to Communal Land.

[Paragraph as amended by section 20 of Act 23 of 1987]

(4) The provisions of subsection (1)(b) shall not apply to—

(a) anything that is expressly or by necessary implication authorised to be done by section 75(2), 94(2) or 98(2), or by any provision of a law that is referred to in subsection (3); or

(b) the exercise of any discretion relating to the institution, conduct or discontinuance of civil or criminal proceedings in any court vested in any person by or under this Constitution or any other law.

24 Enforcement of protective provisions

(1) If any person alleges that the Declaration of Rights has been, is being or is likely to be contravened in relation to him (or, in the case of a person who is detained, if any other person alleges such a contravention in relation to the detained person), then, without prejudice to any other action with respect to the same matter which is lawfully available, that person (or that other person) may, subject to the provisions of subsection (3), apply to the Supreme Court for redress.

[Subsection as amended by section 9 of Act 15 of 1990]

(2) If in any proceedings in the High Court or in any court subordinate to the High Court any question arises as to the contravention of the Declaration of Rights, the person presiding in that court may, and if so requested by any party to the proceedings shall, refer the question to the Supreme Court unless, in his opinion, the raising of the question is merely frivolous or vexatious.

[Subsection as amended by section 9 of Act 15 of 1990]

(3) Where in any proceedings such as are mentioned in subsection (2) any such question as is therein mentioned is not referred to the Supreme Court, then, without prejudice to the right to raise that question on any appeal from the determination of the court in those proceedings, no application for the determination of that question shall lie to the Supreme Court under subsection (1).

[Subsection as amended by section 13 of Act 25 of 1981]

(4) The Supreme Court shall have original jurisdiction—

(a) to hear and determine any application made by any person pursuant to subsection (1) or to determine without a hearing any such application which, in its opinion, is merely frivolous or vexatious; and

(b) to determine any question arising in the case of any person which is referred to it pursuant to subsection (2);

and may make such orders, issue such writs and give such directions as it may consider appropriate for the purpose of enforcing or securing the enforcement of the Declaration of Rights:

Provided that the Supreme Court may decline to exercise its powers under this subsection if it is satisfied that adequate means of redress for the contravention alleged are or have been available to the person concerned under other provisions of this Constitution or under any other law.

[Subsection as amended by section 20 of Act 23 of 1987 and by section 9 of Act 15 of 1990]

(5) If in any proceedings it is alleged that anything contained in or done under the authority of any law is in contravention of section 16, 17, 19, 20, 21 or 22 and the court decides, as a result of hearing the parties, that the complainant has shown that the court should not accept that the provision of the

law concerned is reasonably justifiable in a democratic society on such of the grounds mentioned in section 16(7), 17(2), 19(5), 20(2) and (4), 21(3) or 22(3)(a) to (e), as the case may be, as are relied upon by the other party without proof to its satisfaction, it shall issue a rule *nisi* calling upon the responsible Minister to show cause why that provision should not be declared to be in contravention of the section concerned.

(6) If in any proceedings it falls to be determined whether any law is in contravention of the Declaration of Rights, the Attorney-General shall be entitled to be heard by the court on that question and if in any such proceedings any law is determined by that court to be in contravention of the Declaration of Rights, then, whether or not he has exercised his right to be heard in those proceedings, the Attorney-General shall have the like right with respect to an appeal from that determination as if he had been a party to the proceedings.

(7) Whether any law is held by a competent court to be in contravention of the Declaration of Rights, any person detained in custody under that law shall be entitled as of right to make an application to the Supreme Court for the purpose of questioning the validity of his further detention, notwithstanding that he may have previously appealed against his conviction or sentence or that any time prescribed for the lodging of such an appeal may have expired.

[Subsection as amended by section 9 of Act 15 of 1990]

(8) A written law may confer upon the Supreme Court powers additional to those conferred by this section for the purpose of enabling the Supreme Court more effectively to exercise the jurisdiction conferred upon it by this section.

[Subsection as amended by section 13 of Act 25 of 1981]

(9) A written law may make provision with respect to the practice and procedure—

(a) of the Supreme Court in relation to the jurisdiction and powers conferred upon it by or under this section; and

(b) of subordinate courts in relation to references to the Supreme Court under subsection (2);

including provision with respect to the time within which any application or reference shall or may be made or brought.

[Subsection as amended by section 13 of Act 25 of 1981]

25 Savings in the event of public emergencies

Notwithstanding the foregoing provisions of this Chapter, an Act of Parliament may in accordance with Schedule 2 derogate from certain provisions of the Declaration of Rights in respect of a period of public emergency or a period when a resolution under section 31J(6) is in effect.

[Section as amended by section 20 of Act 23 of 1987]

26 Interpretation and other savings

(1) In this Chapter, unless the context otherwise requires—

'**child**' includes a stepchild and a lawfully adopted child and 'parent' and cognate expressions shall be construed accordingly;

'**court**' means any court of law in Zimbabwe, including a tribal court, but does not, except for the purposes of section 12 or 14, include a court established by or under a disciplinary law;

'**legal representative**' means a legal practitioner who is lawfully in Zimbabwe;

[Definition as substituted by section 20 of Act 23 of 1987]

'**parental discipline**' includes school or other quasi-parental discipline.

(2) Subject to the provisions of subsection (3), nothing contained in or done under the authority of any written law shall be held to be in contravention of the Declaration of Rights to the extent that the law in question

(a) is a law with respect to which the requirements of section 52 were applicable and were complied with;

(b) [Paragraph repealed by section 20 of Act 23 of 1987]

(c) [Paragraph repealed by section 20 of Act 23 of 1987]
(d) [Paragraph repealed by section 20 of Act 23 of 1987]

(3) [Paragraph repealed by section 20 of Act 23 of 1987]

(4) For the purposes of this section, the reference—
(a) [Paragraph repealed by section 20 of Act 23 of 1987]
(b) in subsection (2) to a written law includes any instrument having the force of law.
[Paragraph repealed by section 20 of Act 23 of 1987]

(5) In relation to any person who is a member of a disciplined force of Zimbabwe, nothing contained in or done under the authority of the disciplinary law of that force shall be held to be in contravention of any of the provisions of the Declaration of Rights, other than sections 12, 14, 15, 16 and 23.

(6) In relation to any person who is a member of a disciplined force that is not a disciplined force of Zimbabwe and who is present in Zimbabwe under arrangement made between the Government and the government of some other country, or an international organisation, nothing contained in or done under the authority of the disciplinary law of that force shall be held to be in contravention of the Declaration of Rights.

(7) No measures taken in relation to a person who is a member of a disciplines force of a country with which Zimbabwe is at war or with which a state of hostilities exists and no law, to the extent that it authorises the taking of such measures, shall be held to be in contravention of the Declaration of Rights.

SELECT BIBLIOGRAPHY

Books and Reports

A Bill of Rights for New Zealand: A White Paper (Government Printer, 1985)

Abraham H and Perry B, *Freedom and the Court* (7th edn, Oxford University Press, 1998)

Alcock A, *The History of the International Labour Organisation* (Macmillan, 1971)

Allan T, *Constitutional Rights and the Common Law: Law, Liberty and Justice* (Clarendon Press, 1993)

—— *Law, Liberty and Justice: The Legal Foundation of British Constitutionalism* (Oxford University Press, 1993)

Allison, *A Continental Distinction in the Common Law: A Historical and Comparative Perspective on English Public Law* (Clarendon Press, 1996)

Alston P, Parker S and Seymour J, *Children, Rights and the Law* (Clarendon Press, 1992)

Amar A, *The Bill of Rights* (Yale University Press, 1998)

—— *The Constitution and Criminal Procedure: First Principles* (Yale University Press, 1997)

Aniteau C and Rich W, *Modern Constitutional Law* (2nd edn, West Group, 1997)

Anthony M, Bulmer M, Rees A and Smith A (eds), *Citizenship Today: The Contemporary Relevance of T H Marshall* (UCL Press, 1998)

Archbold, *Criminal Pleading, Practice and Evidence* (Sweet & Maxwell, 1999)

Arlidge, Eady and Smith on Contempt (2nd edn, Sweet & Maxwell, 1999)

Arts Council Working Party, *The Obscenity Laws* (Andre Deutsch Ltd, 1969)

Bailey S (ed), *Cross on Local Government Law* (9th edn, Sweet & Maxwell, 1996)

—— *Cross on Principles of Local Government Law* (2nd edn, Sweet & Maxwell, 1997)

Bailey S, Harris D and Jones B, *Civil Liberties: Cases and Materials* (4th edn, Butterworths, 1995)

Bainham A, *Children: The Modern Law* (2nd edn, Jordans, 1998)

Baker C (ed), *Human Rights Act 1998: A Practitioner's Guide* (Sweet & Maxwell, 1998)

Banton M, *International Action against Racial Discrimination* (Oxford University Press, 1996)

Barendt E, *Freedom of Speech* (Clarendon Press, 1985)

Barlow A *et al*, *Advising Gay and Lesbian Clients* (Butterworths, 1999)

Barry B, *The Liberal Theory of Justice* (Clarendon Press, 1973)

—— *Theories of Justice* (University of California Press, 1989)

Baskerville S, *Of Law and Limitations* (Fairleigh Dickenson, 1994)

Beatson J, Forsyth C and Hare I (eds), *The Human Rights Act and the Criminal Justice and Regulatory Process* (Hart Publishing, 1999)

Beddard R, *Human Rights and Europe* (3rd edn, Cambridge University Press)

Bennion F, *Statutory Interpretation* (3rd edn, Butterworths, 1997)

Berger R, *Government by Judiciary* (Harvard University Press, 1971)

Betten L and Grief N, *EU Law and Human Rights* (Longman, 1998)

—— *The Human Rights Act 1998: What it Means* (Kluwer Law, 1999)

Bill of Rights Compendium (Butterworths, South Africa, 1996)

Birkinshaw P, *Freedom of Information: The Law, the Practice and the Ideal* (2nd edn, Butterworths, 1996)

—— *Reforming the Secret State* (Hull University Press, 1990)

Black H L, *A Constitutional Faith* (Knopf, 1968)

Blackstone W, *Commentaries on the Laws of England* (1st edn, Oxford, 1765) (Facsimile Edition, University of Chicago Press, 1979)

Blackstone's Commentaries on the Laws of England, Kerr R (ed),(4th edn, John Murray, 1876)

Blackstone's Criminal Practice (Blackstone Press, 1999)

Blake N and Fransman L (eds), *Immigration, Nationality and Asylum Under the Human Rights Act 1998* (Butterworths, 1999)

Bork R, *The Tempting of America: the Political Seduction of the Law* (MacMillan, 1990)

Borrie and Lowe, *The Law of Contempt* (Lowe N and Sufrin B) (3rd edn, Butterworths, 1996)

Bradley A and Ewing K, *Constitutional Law* (12th edn, Longman, 1997)

Bradney A, *Religions, Rights and Laws* (Leicester University Press, 1993)

Brazier M, *Medicine, Patients and the Law* (Penguin Books, 1992)

Briggs A, *The History of Broadcasting in the UK, Vol I: The Birth of Broadcasting* (1961); *Vol II: The Golden Age of Wireless* (1965); *Vol IV: Sound and Vision* (Oxford University Press, 1979)

Bringing Rights Home: Labour's Plans to Incorporate the European Convention on Human Rights into United Kingdom Law (Labour Party, 1996)

Broadcasting in the 90s: Competition, Choice and Quality (1988), Cm 517 (White Paper)

Brown L and Kennedy T, *The Court of Justice of the European Communities* (Sweet & Maxwell, 1994)

Brownlie I (ed), *Basic Documents on Human Rights* (3rd edn, Oxford University Press, 1992)

—— *Principles of Public International Law* (5th edn, Oxford University Press, 1998)

—— *System of the Law of Nations: State Responsibility, Part I* (Clarendon Press, 1983)

Bulmer M and Rees A, *Citizenship Today: The Contemporary Relevance of T H Marshall* (UCLP 1996)

Butterworth's Discrimination Law Handbook (Butterworths, 2000)

Cardozo B, *The Nature of the Judicial Process* (Yale University Press, 1991)

Chaskalson M, *Constitutional Law of South Africa* (Juta, 1996)

Cheyney D, Dickson L, Fitzpatrick J and Uglow S, *Criminal Justice and the Human Rights Act 1998* (Jordans, 1999)

Clapham A, *Human Rights in the Private Sphere* (Clarendon Press, 1993)

Clayton R & Tomlinson H, *Civil Actions Against the Police* (3rd edn, Sweet & Maxwell, 2001)

—— *Judicial Review Procedure* (2nd edn, Wiley Chancery Law, 1997)

—— *Police Actions: A Practical Guide* (2nd edn, John Wiley & Sons, 1991)

Clayton R, Tomlinson H and Shukla V, *Human Rights Handbook* (Hart Publishing, 2000)

Clements L, *Community Care and the Law* (Legal Action Group, 1996)

Clements L, Mole N, Simmons A, *European Human Rights: Taking a Case Under the Convention* (2nd edn, Sweet & Maxwell, 1999)

Clerk & Lindsell on Torts (17th edn, Sweet & Maxwell, 1996)

Cohen M (ed), *Ronald Dworkin and Contemporary Jurisprudence* (Duckworth, 1984)

Constitution Unit, Human Rights Legislation (1996)

Cooper-Stephenson K, *Charter Damages Claims* (Carswell, 1990)

Coppel J, *The Human Rights Act 1998 – Enforcing the European Convention in the Domestic Courts* (Wiley Chancery Law, 1999)

Corker D and Young D, *Abuse of Process and Fairness in Criminal Proceedings* (Butterworths, 2000)

Corwin E, *The Constitution and What it Means Today* (14th edn, Princeton University Press, 1978)

Council of Europe, *Yearbook of the European Convention for the Prevention of Torture and Inhuman or Degrading Treatment or Punishment Volume 1 (1989-1992)* and *Volume 2 (1993)*

Cox A, *The Court and the Constitution* (Houghton Miffin, 1987)

Craig P, *Administrative Law* (3rd edn, Sweet & Maxwell, 1994)

Cranston M, *What are Human Rights?* (Bodley Head, 1973)

Craufurd Smith R, *Broadcasting Law and Fundamental Rights* (Clarendon Press, 1997)

Craven M, *The International Covenant on Economic, Social and Cultural Rights, Revised Edition* (Clarendon Press, 1998)

Cross R, *Statutory Interpretation* (3rd edn, Butterworths, 1995)

Daniels N, *Reading Rawls* (Stanford University Press, 1989)

Demerieux M, *Fundamental Rights in Commonwealth Carribbean Constitutions* (Faculty of Law Library, University of West Indies, 1992)

De Smith, Woolf and Jowell, *Judicial Review of Administrative Action* (5th edn, Sweet & Maxwell, 1995)

Devlin P, *The Judge* (Oxford University Press, 1979)

—— *Trial by Jury* (Stevens, 1966)

DFE Circular 10/94, Expulsions from School

Dicey A, *Introduction to the Study of The Law and the Constitution* (10th edn, Macmillan, 1965)

Donnelly J, *The Concept of Human Rights* (Croom Helm, 1985)

Drzemczewski A, *The European Convention in Domestic Law: A Comparative Study* (Oxford University Press, 1983)

Duncan and Neill on Defamation (2nd edn, Butterworths, 1983)

Dworkin R, *A Matter of Principle* (Clarendon Press, 1985)

—— *Freedom's Law* (Oxford University Press, 1996)

—— *Life's Dominion* (Harper Collins, 1993)

—— *Taking Rights Seriously* (Duckworth, 1978)

Eldergill A, *Mental Health Review Tribunals Law and Practice* (Sweet & Maxwell, 1997)

Ely J, *Democracy and Distrust* (Harvard University Press, 1980)

Emiliou N, *The Principle of Proportionality in European Law* (Kluwer, 1996)

Erskine May, *Parliamentary Practice* (Limon D and Mckay W, eds) (22nd edn, Butterworths, 1997)

Evans M and Morgan R, *Preventing Torture: A Study of the European Convention for the Prevention of Torture* (Oxford University Press, 1998)

Ewing K and Gearty C, *Freedom under Thatcher: Civil Liberties in Modern Britain* (Oxford University Press, 1990)

Faulks K, *Citizenship in Modern Britain* (Edinburgh University Press, 1998)
Fawcett J, *The Application of the European Convention on Human Rights* (Clarendon Press, 1987)
Feinberg J, *Offense to Others* (Oxford University Press, 1985)
Feldman D, *Civil Liberties and Human Rights in England and Wales* (Clarendon Press, 1993)
—— *The Law Relating to Entry, Seizure and Search* (Butterworths, 1986)
Fenwick H, *Civil Liberties* (2nd edn, Cavendish Publishing, 1998)
Finnis J, *Natural Law and Natural Rights* (Clarendon Press, 1980)
Fontana J, *The Law of Search and Seizure in Canada* (3rd edn, Butterworth-Heinemann, 1992)
Fordham M, *Judicial Review Handbook* (2nd edn, John Wiley, 1997)
Franks Committee, *Report on Section 2 of the Official Secrets Act 1911* (1972 Cmnd 5104)
Friel J and Hay D, *Special Educational Needs and the Law* (Sweet & Maxwell, 1996)

Galligan D, *Due Process and Fair Procedures* (Clarendon Press, 1996)
Gardiner J (ed), *Aspects of Incorporation of the European Convention into Domestic Law* (British Institute of International and Comparative Law, 1993)
Gatley on Libel and Slander (Milmo P and Rogers W, eds) (9th edn, Sweet & Maxwell, 1998)
George R P (ed), *Natural Law Theory* (Clarendon Press, 1992)
Ghandi P, *The Human Rights Committee and the Right of Individual Communication* (Dartmouth, 1998)
Gibbons T, *Regulating the Media* (2nd edn, Sweet & Maxwell, 1998)
Gomien D, Harris D and Zwaak L, *Law and Practice of the European Convention on Human Rights and the Social Charter* (Council of Europe Publishing, 1996)
Gordon R, *Judicial Review and Crown Office Practice* (Sweet & Maxwell, 1999)
Goudie J and Coppel J, *Local Authorities and the Human Rights Act 1998* (Butterworths, 1999)
Griffith J, *Coloured Immigrants in Britain* (Oxford University Press – Institute of Race Relations, 1961)
Griffith Jones D, *Law and Business of Sport* (Butterworths, 1997)
Griffiths J A G, *The Politics of the Judiciary* (5th edn, Fontana, 1997)
Grosz S, Beatson J and Duffy P, *Human Rights: The 1998 Act and the European Convention* (Sweet & Maxwell, 2000)
Guest S, *Ronald Dworkin* (2nd edn, Edinburgh University Press, 1992)
Guild E and Leisieur G, *The European Court of Justice on the European Convention on Human Rights* (Kluwer, 1998)
Gunther G, *Learned Hand the Man and the Judge* (Harvard University Press, 1994)
Gunther G, and Sullivan K, *Constitutional Law* (13th edn, Foundation Press, 1997)
Gurry F, *Breach of Confidence* (Oxford University Press, 1984)

Hale B, *From the Test Tube to the Coffin, Hamlyn Lectures* (Sweet & Maxwell, 1996)
Halsbury's Laws of England, Vol 8(2) 'Constitutional Law and Human Rights' (4th edn, Reissue, Butterworths, 1996)
Halsbury's Statutes (4th edn, Butterworths, 1994) Vol 12
Hamilton C, *Family, Law and Religion* (Sweet & Maxwell, 1995)
Hanks P, *Constitutional Law in Australia* (2nd edn, Butterworths, 1996)
Hare R M, *Moral Thinking: Its Levels, Methods and Point* (Clarendon Press, 1981)
Harper R, *Medical Treatment and the Law* (Family Law, 1999)

Harris B, *The Law and Practice of Disciplinary and Regulatory Proceedings* (2nd edn, Barry Rose, 1999)
Harris D and Joseph S (eds), *International Covenant on Civil and Political Rights and United Kingdom Law* (Clarendon Press, 1995)
Harris D, O'Boyle M and Warbrick C, *Law of the European Convention on Human Rights* (Butterworths, 1995)
Hart H L A, *Essays in Jurisprudence and Philosophy* (Clarendon Press, 1983)
—— *The Concept of Law* (2nd edn, Clarendon Press, 1994)
Hartley T, *The Foundations of European Community Law* (4th edn, Oxford University Press, 1998)
Harvey J H, *Industrial Relations and Employment Law* (Perrins B, Elias P and Napier B, eds) (Butterworths [looseleaf], 2000)
Hatchard J, *Individual Freedoms and State Security in the African Context: The Case of Zimbabwe* (James Currey, 1993)
Heuston R F U, *Essays in Constitutional Law* (Stevens, 1964)
Hill C, *Liberty against the Law* (Allen Lane, 1996)
Hogg P W, *Constitutional Law of Canada* (4th edn, Carswell, 1997)
Hohfeld W, *Fundamental Legal Conceptions as applied in Judicial Reasoning* (Yale University Press, 1919)
Hollins T, *Beyond Broadcasting to the Cable Age* (London BFI for The Broadcasting Research Unit, 1984)
Home Office Review of Human Rights Instruments (Amended), 26 August 1999
Horowitz M, Kingscote G and Nicholls M, *Rayden and Jackson on Divorce and Family Matters: The Human Rights Act 1998, A Special Bulletin for Family Lawyers* (Butterworths, 1999)
House of Commons, National Heritage Committee, Fourth Report on Privacy and Media Intrusion, March 1993, (1992-93) HC Papers 294
Hunt A, *Reading Dworking Critically* (Burg Publishers, 1992)
Hunt M, *Using Human Rights Law in the English Courts* (Hart Publishing, 1997)
Huscroft G and Rishworth P (eds), *Rights and Freedoms* (Brookers, 1995)
Hyams O, *Law of Education* (Sweet & Maxwell, 1998)

Inness J C, *Privacy, Intimacy and Isolation* (Oxford University Press, 1992)
Institute for Public Policy Research, A Human Rights Commission: the options (1997)
Institute of Public Policy Research, Labour's Plans to Incorporate the European Convention on Human Rights into UK Law: Response to the Consultation Paper (March 1997)
Interception of Communications in the United Kingdom, Cmnd 9438 (1985), Government White Paper
International Labour Organisation, *Protection of Workers' Personal Data: An ILO Code of Practice* (ILO, 1997)

Jackson D, *The United Kingdom Confronts the European Convention on Human Rights* (University of Florida Press, 1997)
Jacob F, *The European Convention on Human Rights* (1st edn, Oxford University Press, 1975)
Jacobs F and White R, *The European Convention on Human Rights* (2nd edn, Oxford University Press, 1996)

Jaconelli J, *Enacting a Bill of Rights* (Clarendon Press, 1980)
Jaswal N, *Role of the Supreme Court with Regard to the Life and Personal Liberty* (Ashish, 1990)
Jenks C W, *Orthodoxy and Innovation in the Law of Nations* (The Proceedings of the British Academy, Vol LVII, 1971)
Jennings I, *The Law and the Constitution* (5th edn, University of London Press, 1967)
Jennings Sir Ivor, *The Approach to Self Governance* (Cambridge University Press, 1958)
Justice, Human Rights Bill: Justice Briefing for the Second Reading in the House of Lords
—— *JUSTICE, Privacy and the Law* (Justice, 1970)
—— *Under Surveillance: Covert Policing and Human Rights Standards* (Justice, 1998)
Justice/All Souls Review of Administrative Law, Administrative Justice (Clarendon Press, 1988)
Justice Public Law Project, *A Matter of Public Interest, Reforming the Law and Practice on Interventions in Public Interest* Cases (Justice, 1996)

Kelly J M, *The Irish Constitution* (3rd edn, Butterworths, 1994)
Kemp Allen, Sir Carleton, *The Queen's Peace* (Stevens & Son, 1953)
Kempees P, *A Systematic Guide to the Case-Law of the European Court of Human Rights, Vols I-II* (1960-1994) and *Vol III* (1995–1996) (Nijhoff, 1996, 1998)
Kennedy I and Grubb A (eds), *Principles of Medical Law* (Oxford University Press, 1998)
Kenny, *Cases on Tort* (4th edn, 1926)
Kilkelly U, *The Child and the European Convention on Human Rights* (Ashgate, 1999)
Klug F, *Reinventing the Community: the Rights and Responsibilities Debate* (Charter 88, 1996)
Klug F, Starmer K and Weir S, *The Three Pillars of Liberty* (Routledge, 1996)
Kokott J, *The Burden of Proof in Comparative and International Human Rights Law* (Kluwer Law International, 1998)
Kulshreshtha S, *Fundamental Rights and the Supreme Court* (Rawat Publications, 1995)

Lasky H, *Liberty and the Modern State* (Penguin, 1948)
Lauterpacht H, *An International Bill of the Rights of Man* (Columbia University Press, 1945)
Law Commission, *A Criminal Code for England and Wales* (Law Com No 177, 1999)
—— *Bail and the Human Rights Act* (Consultation Paper No 157, 1999)
—— *Binding Over* (Law Com No 222, Cm 2439, 1994)
—— *Consent and Offences Against the Person* (Consultation Paper No 134, 1994)
—— *Criminal Law: Binding Over – The Issues,* Working Paper No 103 (HMSO, 1987)
—— *Criminal Law, Report on Criminal Libel* (Law Comm No 149, 1985)
—— *Evidence in Criminal Proceedings: Hearsay and Related Topics* (Law Com No 245) June 1997
—— *Grounds for Divorce* (Law Comm No 190, 1990)
—— *Offences Against Religion and Public Worship* (Law Comm No 145, 1985)
—— *Offences Relating to Interference with the Course of Justice* (Law Comm No 96, 1979)
—— *Report on Aggravated, Exemplary and Restitutionary Damages* (Law Com No 247)
Lawson and Schermers, *Leading Cases of the European Court of Human Rights* (Ars Aequi Libri, 1997)
Learned Hand, *The Bill of Rights* (Harvard University Press, 1958)
Leigh L, *Police Powers in England and Wales* (2nd edn, Butterworths, 1985)
Leill P, Coleman J and Poole K P, *The Law of Education* (9th edn, Butterworths, 1998)

Lesser H and Taylor-Gooby P, *Political Philosophy and Social Welfare* (RKP, 1980)
Lester Lord and Oliver D (eds), *Constitutional Law and Human Rights* (Butterworths, 1997)
Lester Lord and Pannick D, *Human Rights Law and Practice* (Butterworths, 1999)
Levenson H and Fairweather F, *Police Powers: A Practitioner's Guide* (3rd edn)
Levy L, *The Emergence of a Free Press* (Oxford University Press, 1985)
Lewis C, *Judicial Remedies in Public Law* (2nd edn, Sweet & Maxwell, 2000)
Liberty, *A People's Charter* (National Council for Civil Liberties, 1991)
—— *Getting It Right: Future Issues Under the Human Rights Act 1998* (Liberty, 1998)
—— *Manifesto for Human Rights* (National Council of Civil Liberties, 1997)
—— *Response to Labour's plans to incorporate the European Convention on Human Rights in UK law* (March 1997)
Lidstone K and Palmer C, *Bevan and Lidstone's: Investigation of Crime* (2nd edn, Butterworths, 1996)
Livingston S and Owen T, *Prison Law* (2nd edn, Oxford University Press, 1999)
Locke, *Two Treatises on Government* (Laslett P (ed)), (Cambridge University Press, 1960)
Longford Report: Pornography (Coronet, 1972)
Lord Chancellor's Consultation Paper, Infringement of Privacy (July 1993)
Loughlin M, *Public Law and Political Theory* (Clarendon Press, 1992)
Loveland I (ed), *Constitutional Law: A Critical Introduction* (Butterworths, 1996)
—— *Importing the First Amendment* (Hart Publishing, 1998)
Lyons D, *Forms and Limits of Utilitarianism* (Clarendon Press, 1965)

Macdonald I and Blake N, *Immigration Law and Practice in the United Kingdom* (4th edn, Butterworths, 1995)
MacIntyre A, *After Virtue* (Duckworth, 1981)
Madison J, Hamilton A and Jay J, *The Federalist Papers* (Penguin, 1987)
Mahajan V, *Constitutional Law of India* (7th edn, Easter Book, 1991)
Markesinis B (ed), *The Impact of the Human Rights Bill on English Law* (Oxford University Press, 1998)
Marshall G, *Constitutional Theory* (Oxford University Press, 1971)
Marshall T H, *Citizenship and Social Class* (Cambridge University Press, 1950)
Maxwell P, *Maxwell on the Interpretation of Statutes* (12th edn, Sweet & Maxwell, 1969)
McAuslan P, *The Ideologies of Planning* Law (Pergamon, 1980)
McCrudden C (ed), *Anti-Discrimination Law* (International Library of Essays in Law and Legal Theory, 1991)
McGoldrick D, *The Human Rights Committee* (Clarendon Press, 1995)
McGregor H, *McGregor on Damages* (16th edn, Sweet & Maxwell, 1997)
McManus J, *Education and the Courts* (Sweet & Maxwell, 1998)
Meiklejohn A, *Free Speech and its Relation to Self Government* (Harper & Sons, 1948)
Melden A, *Rights and Persons* (Blackwell, 1967)
Merrills J, *The Development of International Law by the European Court of Human Rights* (2nd edn, University of Manchester Press, 1995)
Michahelowski S and Woods L, *German Constitutional Law* (Dartmouth, 1999)
Mill J S, *On Liberty* (Cambridge University Press, 1982)

Ministry of Defence, *The Defence Advisory Notices, A Review of the D Notice System* (Ministry of Defence Open Government Document No 93/06)

Mithani A, *Directors' Disqualification* (Butterworths, 1998)

Mount F, *The British Constitution Now: Recovery or Decline?* (Charter 88, 1992)

—— *The Recovery of the Constitution* (Charter 88, 1992)

Negrine R (ed), *Cable Television and the Future of Broadcasting* (1985)

Neuwahl N and Rosas A, *The European Union and Human Rights* (Kluwer, 1995)

New South Wales Law Reform Commission, *Report No 75, Defamation* (October 1995)

Nolan M & Sedley S, *The Making and Remaking of the British Constitution* (Blackstone, 1997)

Nowak J and Rotunda R, *Constitutional Law* (5th edn, West Group, 1995)

Nozick R, *Anarchy State and Utopia* (Blackwell, 1974)

Olowofoyeku A, *Suing Judges: A Study of Judicial Immunity* (Clarendon Press, 1993)

Oppenheim, *International Law* (9th edn, Longman, 1992)

Outhwaite W and Wheeler M, *The Civil Practitioners Guide to the Human Rights Act 1998* (Old Bailey Press, 1999)

Palmer J and Palmer S, *Constitutional Rights of Prisoners* (6th edn, Anderson Publishing, 1999)

Paul J, *Reading Nozick* (Blackwell, 1981)

Pettiti, Decaux and Imbert, *La Convention Européene des Droits de L'Homme* (2nd edn, Economica, 1999)

Phipson on Evidence (20th edn, Sweet & Maxwell, 2000)

Protocol II to the European Convention on Human Rights and Explanatory Report May 1994 CH (94 5)

Quinton A M, *Utilitarian Ethics* (Duckworth, 1973)

Rawls J, *A Theory of Justice* (Clarendon Press, 1971)

Rayden and Jackson on Divorce and Family Matters (Booth M, Maple G, Biggs A, Wall N, eds) (17th edn, Butterworths, 1997)

Raz J, *The Morality of Freedom* (Clarendon Press, 1986)

Regan D, *Utilitarianism and Co-operation* (Clarendon Press, 1980)

Reid K, *A Practitioner's Guide to the European Convention of Human Rights* (Sweet & Maxwell, 1998)

Report of the Committee of Administrative Tribunals and Enquiries Cmnd 218 (1957) – The Franks Report

Report of the Committee of Experts on the Application of Conventions and Recommendations (1962)

Report of Committee of Privy Councillors, Cmnd 283 (1957), *'The Birkett Committee'*

Report of the Committee on Data Protection, Cmnd 7341 (1978)

Report of the Committee on Privacy, Cmnd 5012 (1972)

Report of the Committee on Privacy and Related Matters, Cmnd 1102 (1990)

Report of the Select Committee on a Bill of Rights, HL, paper 176

Review of Press Self-Regulation, Cmnd 2315 (1993)

Review of Public Order, Cmnd 9510

Rights Brought Home: The Human Rights Bill White Paper, Cm 3782 (1997)
Roach K, *Constitutional Remedies in Canada* (Canada Law Book, 1999)
Robertson A and Merrills J, *Human Rights in Europe: A Study of the European Convention on Human Rights* (Manchester University Press, 1993)
—— *Human Rights in the World* (4th edn, Manchester University Press, 1996)
Robertson G, *Crimes Against Humanity* (Allen Lane, 1999)
—— *Freedom the Individual and the Law* (7th edn, Penguin, 1993)
Robertson G and Nicol A, *Media Law* (3rd edn, Penguin Books, 1992)
Robilliard F, *Religion and the Law: Religious Liberty in Modern English Law* (Manchester University Press, 1984)
Rodley N, *The Treatment of Prisoners under International Law* (2nd edn, Oxford University Press, 1999)
Rolph C H, *Books in the Dock* (Andre Deutsch, 1969)
Royal Commission on Criminal Procedure (1981), Cmnd 8092
Russell R and Muther J, *History of the United Nations Charter: the Role of the United States 1940–45* (Brookings Institution, 1958)

Salmon J, *Jurisprudence* (10th edn, Stevens)
Sands P, Mackenzie R and Shany Y (eds), *Manual on International Courts and Tribunals* (Butterworths, 2000)
Scarman Sir Leslie, *English Law: The New Dimension* (Stevens, 1974)
Schabas W, *International Human Rights Law and the Canadian Charter* (Carswell, 1991)
—— *The Abolition of the Death Penalty in International Law* (2nd edn, Cambridge University Press, 1997)
Schauer F, *Free Speech: A Philosophical Enquiry* (Cambridge University Press, 1982)
Scheffler S, ed, *Consequentialism and its Critics* (Oxford University Press, 1988)
Schoeman F, *Privacy and Social Freedom* (Cambridge University Press, 1992)
Schwarze J, *European Administrative Law* (Sweet & Maxwell, 1992)
Seervai H M, *Constitutional Law of India* (4th edn, N M Tripathi Ltd, 1991)
Select Committee of Delegated Powers and Deregulation of the House of Lords, Sixth Report 5 November 1997
Sen A and Williams B (eds), *Utilitarianism and Beyond* (Cambridge University Press, 1982)
Sendall B, *Independent Television in Britain; Origin and Foundations 1946–62* (Macmillan, 1982)
Sermet L, *The European Convention on Human Rights and Property Rights* (Council of Europe, 1998)
Sharvananda S, *Fundamental Rights in Sri Lanka* (Arnold's International Printing House Private Ltd, 1993)
Shelton D, *Remedies in International Human Rights Law* (Oxford University Press, 1999)
Sieghart P, *The International Law of Human Rights* (Clarendon Press, 1983)
Simons Lord, *Report of the Joint Parliamentary Committee on Indian Constitutional Reform* (HL 6 and HL 5 1933/34)
Singh M P, *German Administrative Law: A Common Lawyer's View* (Springer-Verlag, 1985)
Singh R, *The Future of Human Rights in the United Kingdom* (Hart Publishing, 1998)
Skyrme T, *History of the Justices of the Peace* (Barry Rose, 1994)

Smart J J C and Williams B, *Utilitarianism: For and Against* (Cambridge University Press, 1973)
Smith J and Hogan B, *Criminal Law* (9th edn, Butterworths, 1999)
Society of Conservative Lawyers, *Another Bill of Rights?*
—— *The Pollution of the Mind; New Proposals to Control Public Indecency and Obscenity* (1972)
Spencer S and Bynoe I, *A Human Rights Commission: The Options for Britain and Northern Ireland* (Institute for Public Policy Research, 1998)
Starmer K, *European Human Rights Law* (Legal Action Group, 1999)
Street H, *Freedom, the Individual and the Law* (Penguin, 1963)
Stuart D, *Charter Justice in Canadian Criminal Law* (Carswell, 1991)
Supperstone M and O'Dempsey D, *Supperstone and O'Dempsey on Immigration and Asylum* (4th edn, Sweet & Maxwell, 1996)
Supperstone M, *Brownlie's Law of Public Order and National Security* (2nd edn, Butterworths, 1981)
Sutton D, Kendall J and Gill J, *Russell on Arbitration* (21st edn, Sweet & Maxwell, 1997)
Swindells H, Neaves A, Kushner M and Skilbeck R, *Family Law and the Human Rights Act 1998* (Family Law, 1999)

Taggart M (ed), *The Province of Administrative Law* (Hart Publishing, 1997)
Tamopolsky W S, *The Canadian Bill of Rights* (2nd edn, McClelland and Stewart, 1975)
Toulson R and Phipps C, *Confidentiality* (Sweet & Maxwell, 1996)
Tribe L, *American Constitutional Law* (3rd edn, Freedom Press, 2000)
—— *Constitutional Choices* (Harvard University Press, 1985)
Tuck R, *Natural Rights Theories: Their Origin and Development* (Cambridge University Press, 1979)

van Beuren G, *The International Law on the Rights of the Child* (Nijhoff, 1995)
van Dijk P and van Hoof G, *Theory and Practice of the European Convention on Human Rights* (3rd edn, Kluwer, 1998)
Vilbert F, *Constitutional Reform in the United Kingdom – An Incremental Agenda* (Institute of Economic Affairs, 1990)

Wacks R, *Human Rights in Hong Kong* (Oxford University Press, 1992)
—— *Privacy and Press Freedom* (Blackstone, 1995)
—— *The Protection of Privacy* (Sweet & Maxwell, 1980)
Wade H W R and Forsyth C, *Administrative Law* (7th edn, Clarendon Press, 1994)
Wadham J and Mountfield H, *Blackstone's Guide to the Human Rights Act 1998* (Blackstone Press, 1999)
Wallace R, *International Human Rights Law: Text and Materials* (Sweet & Maxwell, 1997)
Watson A, *Legal Transplants in Comparative Law* (2nd edn, University of Georgia Press, 1993)
Wedderburn W, *The Worker and the Law* (3rd edn, Penguin, 1986)
Wells H G, *H G Wells on the Rights of Man* (Penguin Press, 1940)
Westin A, *Privacy and Freedom* (Atheneum, 1967)
Wickramaratne J, *Fundamental Rights in Sri Lanka* (Navrang, 1996)
Williams G, *Human Rights Under the Australian Constitution* (Oxford University Press, 1999)
Wintemute R, *Sexual Orientation and Human Rights* (Clarendon Press, 1995)

Wolff R, Robert Nozick: *Property Justice and the Minimal State* (Polity, 1991)
—— *Understanding Rawls* (Princetown University Press, 1977)
Woolf Lord, *Access to Justice* (The Stationery Office, 1996)

Yourow H, *The Margin of Appreciation in the Dynamics of European Human Rights Jurisprudence* (Kluwer, 1996)

Zander M, *A Bill of Rights?* (4th edn, Sweet & Maxwell, 1997)
—— *The Police and Criminal Evidence Act 1984* (3rd edn, Sweet & Maxwell, 1995)
Zuckerman A, *The Principles of Criminal Evidence* (Clarendon Press, 1989)

Articles, Essays and Lectures

Alder J, 'Housing and the Human Rights Act 1998' [1999] HLJ 67
—— 'Obsolescence and Renewal: Judicial Review in the Private Sector' in Leyland P and Woods T (eds) *Administrative Law Facing the Future: Old Constraints and New Horizons* (Blackstone, 1997)
Alexander L, 'Cutting the Gordian Knot: State Action and Self-help Repossession' 2 Hastings Const LQ 893
Allan T, 'Fairness, Equality, Rationality' in Forsyth C and Hare I (eds), *The Golden Metwand and the Crooked Cord* (Clarendon Press, 1998)
—— 'Commonwealth Constitutions and the Right Not to be Deprived of Property' (1993) 42 ICLQ 523
—— 'The Limits of Parliamentary Sovereignty' [1985] PL 614
Allen F, 'Remembering Shelley v Kraemer: of Public and Private Worlds' [1989] 67 Wash U LQ 709
Alpa G, 'Protection of Privacy in Italian Law' in Markesinis B (ed), *Protecting Privacy* (Oxford University Press, 1999)
Amos M, 'Damages for breach of the Human Rights Act 1998' [1999] EHRLR 178
Anderson D, 'Compensation for Interference with Property' [1999] EHRLR 543
—— 'The Failure of American Privacy Law' in Markesinis B (ed), *Protecting Privacy* (Oxford University Press, 1999)
Andrews J, 'Compensation for Nationalisation in the UK' (1986) 12 ELR 65
—— 'Leasehold Enfranchisement and the Public Interest in the UK' (1986) II ELR 366
Ashworth A, 'Article 6 and the Fairness of Trials' [1999] Crim LR 261
—— 'The Impact on Criminal Justice' in Markesenis B (ed), *The Impact of the Human Rights Bill in English Law* (Oxford University Press, 1998)
Ashworth A and Blake M, 'The Presumption of Innocence in English Criminal Law' [1996] Crim LR 306
Auld Lord Justice, 'Investigations and Surveillance' in Beatson J, Forsyth C and Hare I (eds), *The Human Rights Act and the Criminal Justice and Regulatory Process* (Hart Publishing, 1999)
Austin R, 'The Data Protection Act 1984: The Public Law Implications' [1984] PL 618
Ayliffe J and Dew R, 'The Development of the Common Law and Equity. An Example: The Presumption of Advancement' in *Wilberforce Chambers, The Essential Human Rights Act 1998* (Wilberforce Chambers, 2000)

Bakan J, 'Constitutional Arguments: Interpretation and Legitimacy in Canadian Constitutional Thought' (1989) 27 Osgoode Hall LJ 123

Bala N and Redfearn J D, 'Family Law and the "Liberty Interest": Section 7 of the Canadian Charter of Rights' (1983) 15 Ottawa LR 274

Balkan J, 'Pornography, Law and Moral Theory' [1985] Ottawa LR 1

Bamforth N, 'Parliamentary Sovereignty and the Human Rights Act 1998' [1998] PL 572

—— 'The Application of the Human Rights Act 1998 to Public Authorities and Public Bodies' (1999) 58 CLJ 159

—— 'The Scope of Judicial Review: Still Uncertain' [1993] PL 239

Barendt E, 'Libel and Freedom of Expression in English Law' [1993] PL 449

—— 'Privacy as a Constitutional Right and Value' in Markesinis B (ed), *Protecting Privacy* (Oxford University Press, 1999)

—— 'The Importance of United States Free Speech Jurisprudence' in Loveland I (ed), *A Special Relationship* (Clarendon Press, 1995)

Barnes M, 'Planning and Compensation' and 'Public Authorities and Land Compensation' in *Wilberforce Chambers, 'The Essential Human Rights Act 1998* (Wilberforce Chambers, 2000)

Barnum D G, 'Freedom of Assembly and the Hostile Audience in Anglo-American Law' (1981) *29* American J of Comparative L *59*

Barnum D, Sullivan J and Sunkin M, 'Constitutional and Cultural Underpinning of Political Freedom in Britain and the United States' (1992) 12 OJLS 362

Baylis C, 'Justice Done and Justice Seen to be Done – The Public Administration of Justice [1991] 21 Victoria University of Wellington LR 177

Beatson J, 'Prematurity and Ripeness for Review' in Forsyth C and Hare I (eds), *The Golden Metwand and the Crooked Cord* (Clarendon Press, 1998)

Beatty D, 'The Canadian Charter of Rights: Lessons and Laments' (1997) 60 LQR 481

Beloff M, 'Pitch, Pool, Rink ... Court? Judicial Review in the Sporting World' [1989] PL 95

—— 'Natural Justice – (The Audi Alteram Partem Rule) and Fairness', in Supperstone M and Goudie J, *Judicial Review* (2nd edn, Butterworths, 1997)

—— 'Time, Time's On My Side, Yes It Is' in Forsyth C and Hare I (eds), *The Golden Metwand and the Crooked Cord* (Clarendon Press, 1998)

—— 'What Does It all Mean? Interpreting the Human Rights Act 1998' in Betten L (ed), *The Human Rights Act 1998: What It Means* (Nijhoff, 1999)

Beloff M and Mountfield H, 'Unconventional Behaviour? Judicial uses of the European Convention in England and Wales' [1996] EHRLR 467

Bennion F, 'A Human Rights Act Provision Now in Force' (1999) 163 JP 164

—— 'What Interpretation "Possible" Under Section 3(1) of the Human Rights Act 1998' [2000] PL 77

Berlin I, 'Two Concepts of Liberty' in Hardy H and Hausheer R (eds), *Isaiah Berlin The Proper Study of Mankind* (Chatto & Windus, 1997)

Bernhardt R, 'The Convention and Domestic Law' in Macdonald R St J, Matscher and Petzold (eds), *The European System for the Protection of Human Rights* (Nijhoff, 1993)

Best R, 'Freedom of Speech in Parliament: Constitutional Safeguard or Sword of Oppression?' (1994) 24 VUWLR 91

Beyleveld D, 'The Concept of Human Rights and the Incorporation of the ECHR' [1995] PL 577

Bezanson R P, 'Libel Law and the Realities of Litigation: Setting the Record Straight' (1985) 71 Iowa L Rev 226

Bikle H W, 'Judicial Determination of Questions of Fact Affecting the Constitutional Validity of Legislative Action' (1924) 37 Harv LR 6

Bindman G, 'When Will Europe Act Against Racism?' [1996] EHRLR 143

Bingham Lord, 'Should there be a Law to Protect Rights of Personal Privacy?' [1996] EHRLR 450

—— 'The European Convention on Human Rights: Time to Incorporate' (1993) 109 LQR 390 and in Gordon R and Wilmot-Smith R (eds), *Human Rights in the United Kingdom* (Clarendon Press, 1996)

—— 'The Way We Live Now: Human Rights in the New Millenium' [1998] I Web JCL I 1-056

Bingham Sir Thomas, 'Should Public Law Remedies be Discretionary?' [1991] PL 64

—— 'The European Convention on Human Rights: Time to Incorporate' (1993) 109 LQR 390

Birtles W, 'The Common Law Power of the Police to Control Public Meetings' (1973) 36 MLR 587

Bix B and Tomkins A, 'Unconventional use of the Convention' [1992] MLR 721

Black H L, 'Bill of Rights' (1960) 35 New York University LR 865

Black H, 'The Supreme Court, 1966 Term-Foreword: State Action, Equal Protection and California's Proposition' 81 Harv LR 69

Black J, 'Constitutionalising Self-Regulation' (1996) 59 MLR 24

Black-Branch J, 'Entrenching Human Rights under Constitutional Law: the Canadian Charter of Rights and Freedoms' [1998] EHRLR 312

Blackburn R, 'Current topic: a Human Rights Committee for the UK Parliament—the options' [1998] EHRLR 534

Blake N, 'Judicial Review of Discretion in Human Rights Cases' [1997] EHRLR 391

—— 'Opinion for Justice on the International Principles Governing Detention of Asylum Seekers', 27 May 1998

Blom-Cooper L and Gelber C, 'The Privy Council and the Death Penalty in the Caribbean: A Study in Constitutional Change' [1998] EHRLR 386

Bowers J and Lewis J, 'Whistleblowing: Freedom of Expression in the Workplace' [1996] EHRLR 637

Boyle A, 'Freedom of Expression as a Public Interest in English Law' [1992] PL 574

Boyron S, 'General Principles of Law and national courts: apply a jus commune' [1998] 23 ELR 171

Bradley A W, 'Scope for Review: the Convention Right to Education and the Human Rights Act 1998' [1999] EHRLR 395

—— 'The Sovereignty of Parliament—in Perpetuity?' in Jowell J and Oliver D (eds), *The Changing Constitution* (3rd edn, Clarendon Press, 1994)

Bratza N and O'Boyle M, 'Opinion: The Legacy of the Commission to the New Court Under the Eleventh Protocol' [1997] EHRLR 211

Brennan W J, 'The Supreme Court and the Meiklejohn Interpretation of the First Amendment' (1965) 79 Harv LR I

Bringing Rights Home: Labour's Plans to Incorporate the European Convention in UK Law [1997] EHRLR 71

Brown Sir Simon, 'Habeas Corpus—A New Chapter' [2000] PL 31

Browne-Wilkinson Lord, 'The Infitration of a Bill of Rights' [1992] PL 397
—— 'The impact on judicial reasoning' in Markesinis B (ed), *The Impact of the Human Rights Bill on English Law* (Clarendon Press, 1998)
Buchanan G S, 'A Conceptual History of the State Action Doctrine: The Search for Governmental Responsibility' [1997] 34 Houston LR 333
Butler A, 'Constitutional Rights in Private Litigation: A Critique and Comparative Analysis' (1993) 22 Anglo-American LR
—— 'Regulatory Offences and the Bill of Rights' in Huscroft G and Rishworth P, *Rights and Freedoms* (Brookers, 1995)
—— 'Same Sex Marriage and Freedom from Discrimination in New Zealand' [1998] PL 396
—— 'The Bill of Rights debate: why the New Zealand Bill of Rights Act 1990 is a Bad Model for Britain' (1997) 17 OJLS 323 1-081
Buxton Sir Richard, 'The Human Rights Act and Private Law' (2000) 116 LQR 48
—— 'The Convention and the English Law of Evidence' in Beatson J, Forsyth C and Hare I, *The Human Rights Act and the Criminal Justice and Regulatory Process* (Hart Publishing, 1999)
Byrnes A, 'And Some Have Bills of Rights Thrust Upon Them: The Experience of Hong Kong's Bill of Rights' in Alston P, *Promoting Human Rights Through Bills of Rights* (Oxford University Press, 1999)

Cameron I, 'The Swedish Experience of the European Convention on Human Rights since Incorporation' (1999) 48 ICLQ 20
Cameron J, 'Abstract Principle v Contextual Conceptions of Harm: A Comment on *R v Butler*' (1992) 37 McGill LJ 1135
Campbell E, 'Taxation and Human Rights' in *Wilberforce Chambers, The Essential Human Rights Act 1998* (Wilberforce Chambers, 2000)
Cane P, 'Standing up for the Public' [1995] PL 276 3-085
—— 'Standing Representation and the Environment' in Loveland I (ed), *A Special Relationship: American Influences on Public Law in the UK* (Oxford University Press, 1995)
Carnwath Sir Robert, 'The Reasonable Limits of Local Authority Power' [1996] PL 244
Carter J, 'Employment and Labour Relations Law' in Baker C (ed), *Human Rights Act 1998: A Practitioner's Guide* (Sweet & Maxwell, 1998)
—— 'Immigration and Asylum', in Baker C (ed), *The Human Rights Act 1998: A Practitioner's Guide* (Sweet & Maxwell, 1998)
Cassesse A, 'Can the Notion of Inhuman and Degrading Treatment Be Applied To Socio-Economic Conditions?' (1991) 1 EJIL IYI
—— 'The International Criminal Tribunal for the Former Yugoslavia and Human Rights' [1997] EHRLR 329
Cavalluzzo P, 'Freedom of Association—Its Effect Upon Collective Bargaining and Trade unions' [1998] Queen's LJ 267
Chaskalson M, 'The Problem with Property: Thoughts on the Constitutional Protection of Property in the United States and the Commonwealth' (1993) 9 SAJHR 1449
Chayes A, 'The Role of the Judge in Public Law Litigation' (1976) 89 Harv LR 1281
Childs M, 'Constitutional Review and Underinclusive Legislation' [1998] PL 647
Christian T and Ewing K, 'Labouring Under the Canadian Constitution' [1998] 17 ILJ 73

Churchill R and Young J, 'Compliance with Judgments of the European Court of Human Rights and Decisions of the Committee of Ministers: The Experience of the United Kingdom 1975-1987' [1991] British Yearbook of International Law
Clapham A, 'The Privatisation of Human Rights' [1996] EHRLR 20
Clayton G, 'Reclaiming Public Ground: The Right to Peaceful Assembly' [2000] 63 MLR 252
Clayton G and Pitt G, 'Dress Codes and Freedom of Expression' [1997] EHRLR 54
Clayton R, 'Life After *Pepper v Hart*' [1996] JR 77
Coffin F, 'The Frontier of Remedies: A Call for Exploration' (1979) 67 Cal LR 983
Cole K, 'Federal and State "State Action": the Undercritical Embrace of a Hypercritical Doctrine' (1990) 29 Georgia Law Rev 224
Coleman F and McMurtrie S, 'Too Hot to Handle' [1993] NLJ 10
Colvin E, 'Section Seven of the Canadian Charter of Rights and Freedoms' (1989) 68 Canadian Bar Review 560
Colvin M, 'Surveillance and the Human Rights Act 1998' in Beatson J, Forsyth C and Hare I (eds), *The Human Rights Act and the Criminal Justice and Regulatory Process* (Hart Publishing, 1999)
Commentary of the International Law Commission on the Final Draft Articles of the Vienna Convention YBLIC (1996), ii 172
Condorelli L, '*Premier Protocole Additionnel: Article 1*' in Pettiti, Decaux and Imbert (eds), *La Convention Européene des droits de l'homme* (2nd edn, Economica, 1999)
Cooke Lord, 'Mechanisms for Entrenchment and Protection of a Bill of Rights: the New Zealand Experience' [1997] EHRLR 490
—— 'The British Embracement of Human Rights' [1999] EHRLR 243
—— 'A Sketch from the Blue Train. Non-discrimination and Freedom of Expression: The New Zealand Contribution' (1994) NZLJ 10
Cooke Sir Robin, 'Fundamentals' (1998) NZLR 158
Cooper-Stephenson K, 'Tort Theory for the Charter Damages Remedy' (1988) 52 Sak L Rev I
Corder H, 'South Africa's Transitional Constitution: Its Design and Implementation' [1996] PL 291
Corner T, 'Planning, Environment and the European Convention on Human Rights' [1998] JPL 301
Craig J and Nolte N, 'Privacy and Free Speech in Germany and Canada; Lessons for an English Privacy Tort' [1998] EHRLR 162
Craig P, 'Formal and Substantive Conceptions of the Rule of Law' [1997] PL 467
—— 'Prerogative, Precedent and Power' in Forsyth C and Hare I (eds), *The Golden Metwand and the Crooked Cord* (Clarendon Press, 1998)
—— 'Sovereignty of the United Kingdom Parliament after Factortame' [1991] Yearbook of European Law 221
—— 'Ultra Vires and the Foundations of Judicial Review' (1998) 58 CLJ 63
Cretney S M, 'The Codification of Family Law' (1981) 44 MLR I
Cumper P, 'School Worship: Praying for Guidance' [1998] EHRLR 45
Cunningham A, 'ECHR, Customary Law the Constitution' (1994) 43 ICLQ 537

Daintith T, 'Disobeying a constable: a fresh look at *Duncan v Jones*' [1966] PL 248
Davies O, 'Habeas Corpus or Judicial Review?' [1997] JR II

—— 'Self-Incrimination, Fair Trials and the Pursuit of Corporate and Financial Wrongdoing' in Markesinis, B ed, *The Impact of the Human Rights Bill on English Law* (Oxford University Press, 1991)

—— 'The Fruit of the Poisoned Tree—Entrapment and the Human Rights Act 1998' (1999) 163 JP 84

Davis H, 'Constitutional Reform and the Right to Free and Fair Elections' [1999] EHRLR 411

Davis K C, 'An Approach to Problems of Evidence in the Administrative process' (1942) 55 Harv LR 364

de Burca G, 'Fundamental Rights and the Reach of EC Law' (1993) 13 OJLS 283

—— 'The Principle of Proportionality and its Application in EC Law' (1993) 13 YEL 105

de la Mare T, 'The Human Rights Act 1998: The Impact on Judicial Review' [1999] JR 32

de Smith S, 'Fundamental Rights in the New Commonwealth' (1961) 10 ICLQ 83

Dennis I, 'Duress, Murder and Criminal Responsibility' [1980] 96 LQR 208

—— 'Instrumental Protection, Human Right or Functional Necessity? Re-assessing the Privilege Against Self-incrimination' (1995) 52 CLJ 342

Devlin Lord, 'The Law and Lawmakers' (1976) 39 MLR I

Dienes C, 'The Trashing of the Public Forum: Problems in First Amendment Analysis' (1986) Gev Wash LR 109

Dike C, 'The Case Against Parliamentary Sovereignty' [1976] PL 283

Dixon D, Coleman C and Bottomley K, 'PACE in Practice' (1991) 141 NLJ 1586

Dixon Sir Owen, 'The Common Law as an Ultimate Constitutional Foundation' (1957) 31 ALJ 240

Donson F, 'Civil Liberties and Judicial Review: Can the Common Law Really Protect Rights?' in Leyland P and Woods T, *Administrative Law Facing the Future: Old Constraints and New Horizons* (Blackstone, 1997)

Doody M, 'Freedom of the Press, the Canadian Charter of Rights and Freedoms, and a New Category of Qualified Privilege' (1983) 61 Canadian Bar Review 126

Doyle J and Wells B, 'How Far Can the Common Law Go Towards Protecting Human Rights?' in Alston P (ed) *Promoting Human Rights Through Bills of Rights* (Oxford University Press, 1999)

Drabble R, 'Sex Discrimination in United Kingdom Social Security Law: The Impact of the European Union' [1997] EHRLR 242

Drzemczewski A and Wooldridge F, 'The Closed Shop Case in Strasbourg' (1982) 31 ICLQ 396

Duffy P, 'A Case for Equality' [1998] EHRLR 134

—— 'The Protection of Privacy, Family Life & Other Rights Under Act 8 of the ECHR' 3 YEL 2 201

Duffy P and Hunt M, 'Goodbye Entick v Carrington: the Security Service Act 1996' [1997] EHRLR II

Dyzenhaus D, 'Regulating Free Speech' (1991) 23:2 Ottawa L Rev 289

Eady D, 'A Statutory Right to Privacy' [1996] EHRLR 243

Eagles I, 'Disclosure of Material Obtained on Discovery' (1984) 47 MLR 284

Edwards R, 'Generosity and the Human Rights Act: The Right Interpretation' [1999] PL 400

Eekelaar J, 'The Death of Parliamentary Sovereignty—A Comment' (1997) 113 LQR 185

—— 'The Eclipse of Parental Rights' (1986) 102 LQR 4

Eissen M, 'The Principle of Proportionality in the Case Law of the Court' in MacDonald R St J, Matscher F and Petzold H (eds), *The European System for the Protection of Human Rights* (Nijhoff, 1993)

Elliott M, 'Lightfoot: Tracing the Perimeter of Constitutional Rights' [1998] JR 217

—— 'The Demise of Parliamentary Sovereignty: The Implications for Justifying Judicial Review' (1999) 115 LQR 119

—— 'The Ultra Vires Doctrine in a Constitutional Setting: Still the Central Problem in Administrative Law' [1999] 59 CLJ 129

Emmerson B, 'This Year's Model—The Options for Incorporation' [1997] EHRLR 313

England G, 'Some Thoughts on Constitutionalizing the Right to Strike' [1988] Queen's LJ 168

Epstein R A, 'Was *New York Times v Sullivan* Wrong?' (1986) 53 U Chi LR 782

Etherington B, 'Freedom of Association and Compulsory Union Dues' [1987] 19:1 Ottawa LR I

—— '*Lavigne v OPSEU*: Moving Toward or Away from a Freedom to No Associate?' (1991) 23 Ottawa LR 533

Ewing K, 'Freedom of Association and the Employment Act 1999' [1999] ILJ 283

—— 'New Constitutional Constraints in Australia' [1993] PL 256

—— 'Social Rights and Constitutional Law' [1999] PL 104 1-016, 2

—— 'The Human Rights Act and Parliamentary Democracy' (1999) 62 MLR 79

Ewing K and Gearty C, 'Rocky Foundations for Labour's New Rights' [1997] EHRLR 146

Explanatory Report to Protocol No 11 to the European Convention on Human Rights (1994) 17 EHRR 501

Fairley D, 'D Notices, Official Secrets and the Law' (1990) 10 OJLS 430

Farber D and Nowak J, 'The Misleading Nature of Public Forum Analysis: Content and Context in First Amendment Analysis' (1984) 70 Va LR 1219

Farran, 'The UK Before the European Court of Human Rights' (Blackstone Press, 1996)

Feldman D, 'Precedent and the European Court of Human Rights' in *Law Commission, Bail and the Human Rights Act* (Consultation Paper No 157, The Stationery Office, 1999)

—— 'Proportionality and the Human Rights Act 1998' in Ellis E (ed), *The Principles of Proportionality in the Laws of Europe* (Hart Publishing, 1999)

—— 'Remedies for Violation of Convention Rights Under the Human Rights Act' [1998] EHRLR 691

—— 'Secrecy, Dignity or Autonomy? Views of Privacy as a Social Value' (1994) 47 CLP 41

—— 'The Developing Scope of Article 8 of the European Convention on Human Rights' [1997] EHRLR 265

—— 'The Human Rights Act 1998 and Constitutional Principles' [1999] LS 165

—— 'The King's Peace, the Royal Prerogative and Public Order: the Roots and Early Development of Binding Over Powers' [1998] CLJ 101

Fenwick H, 'The Right to Protest, the Human Rights Act and the Margin of Appreciation' [1999] 62 MLR 491

Finkin M, 'Employee Privacy, American Values and the Law' 1996-1997 72 Chicago-Kent LR 222

Fisher W, 'The Development of Modern American Legal Theory and the Judicial Interpretation of the Bill of Rights' in Lacey M and Haakonssen (eds), *A Culture of Rights* (Cambridge University Press, 1991)

Fitzmaurice G, 'The Law & Procedure of the International Court of Justice 1951-4: Treaty Interpretation and Other Treaty Points' 33 BYIL 223
Forde M, 'The "Closed Shop" Case' (1982) II ILJ 1
Fordham M, 'Interim Relief and the Cross Undertaking' [1997] JR 136
—— 'What is "Anxious Scrutiny"?' [1996] JR 81
Forsyth C, 'Of Fig Leaves and Fairy Tales: the Ultra Vires Doctrine, the Sovereignty of Parliament and Judicial Review' (1995) 55 CLJ 122
—— 'The Scope of Judicial Review: "Public Duty" Not "Public Source"' [1987] PL 356
Fortin J, 'Rights Brought Home for Children' [1999] 62 MLR 350
Frazer T, 'Appropriation of Personality—A New Tort?' (1983) 99 LQR 281
Fredman S, 'Bringing Rights Home' (1998) 114 LQR 538
—— 'Council of Civil Servants v Minister for Civil Service' (1985) 14 ILJ 42
—— 'Equality Issues' in Markesinis B (ed), *The Impact of the Human Rights Bill on English Law* (Oxford University Press, 1998)
Fredman S and Morris G, 'Public or Private: State Employees and Judicial Review' (1991) 107 LQR 298
Freedland M, 'Government by Contract and Public Law' [1994] PL 86
Freeman F, 'Death, Dying and the Human Rights Act 1998' [1999] CLP 218
Freeman J, 'Justifying Exclusion: A Feminist Analysis of the Conflict between Equality and Association Rights' (1989) 47:2 UTFLR 269

Gearty C, 'Freedom of Assembly' in McCrudden and Chambers (eds), *Individual Rights and the Law in Britain* (Oxford University Press, 1994)
Ghai Y, 'Sentinels of Liberty or Sheep in Woolf's Clothing? Judicial Politics and the Hong Kong Bill of Rights' (1997) 60 MLR 459
Ghandi S and James J, 'The English Law of Blasphemy and the European Convention on Human Rights' [1998] EHRLR 430
Giffin N, 'Judicial Supervision of Human Rights: Practice and Procedure', Administrative Law Bar Association Seminar, 5 February 2000
Gilmour J, 'Witholding and Withdrawing Life, Support from Adults at Common Law' (1993) 31 Osgoode Hall LJ 473
Gledhill K, 'Standing, Capacity and Unincorporated Associations' [1996] JR 67
Goldberg A and Derschowitz A, 'Declaring the Death Penalty Unconstitutional' (1970) 83 Harv LR 1773
Goodhart A, 'The Shaw Case: The Law of Public Morals' (1961) 77 LQR 560
Gordon R, 'Editorial Review' [1999] COD I
—— 'Why We Need a Constitutional Court' in Gordon R and Wilmot-Smith R (eds), *Human Rights in the United Kingdom* (Oxford University Press, 1996)
Goriely T, 'The Development of Criminal Legal Aid in England and Wales' in Young R and Wall D (eds), *Access to Criminal Justice: Legal Aid, Lawyers and the Defence of Liberty* (Blackstone, 1996)
Goudie J, 'Interest and Favour' in Supperstone M and Goudie J, *Judicial Review* (2nd edn, Butterworths, 1997) 11-66
Gray K and Gray S, 'Civil Rights, Civil Wrongs and Quasi-Public Places' [1999] EHRLR 46
Grief N, 'Convention Rights and the Environment' in Betten L (ed), *The Human Rights Act 1998: What it Means* (Kluwer, 1999)

—— 'The Domestic Impact of the European Convention on Human Rights as Mediated through Community Law' [1991] PL 555
Green N, 'Proportionality and the Supremacy of Parliament in the UK' in Ellis E (ed), *The Principle of Proportionality in the Laws of Europe* (Hart Publishing, 1998)
Grosz S, 'Procedural issues under the Human Rights Act', Lecture 28 May 1998
Grosz S, McNulty A and Duffy P, 'Pre-Trial Detention in Western Europe' (1979) 23 International Commission of Jurists Review 35
Guidelines on the Use of Equipment in Police Surveillance Operations, 19 December 1984, Dep NS 1579

Hall Williams J, 'The Ladies Directory and Criminal Conspiracy. The Judge as Custos Morum' (1961) 24 MLR 626 11-147
Halpin A, 'Hohfeld's Conceptions: From Eight to Two' (1985) 44 CLJ 435
Handford 'Moral Damage in Germany' (1978) 27 ICLQ 849
Harlow C, 'Back to Basics: Reinventing Administrative Law' [1997] PL 245
Harmer L, 'The Right to Strike: Charter Implications and Interpretations' (1998) Vol 47:2 UTFLR 420
Harper T, 'Defence of Literature and the Arts Society' (1978) NLJ 423
Harris D, 'Recent Cases on Pre-Trial Detention and Delay in Criminal Proceedings in the European Court of Human Rights' (1970) 44 BYIL 87
Harrison R E, 'Mass Media and the Criminal Process: Public Service or Public Circus?' (1992) NZLJ 271
Hart H L A, 'Are there any natural rights?', in Quinton A (ed), *Political Philosophy* (Oxford University Press, 1967)
Havers P, 'The Impact of the Convention on Medical Law in *JUSTICE, The Human Rights Act and Common Law*, Seminar, 25 September 1998
Havers P and Thomas O, 'Bias Post-Pinochet and Under the ECHR' [1999] JR III
Hazell R, 'Reinventing the Constitution: can the State survive?' [1999] PL 84
Henderson A, 'Brandeis Briefs and the Proof of Legislative Facts in Proceedings Under the Human Rights Act 1998' [1998] PL 563
Hendy J, 'The Human Rights Act, Article II, and the Right to Strike' [1999] EHRLR 582
Henkin L, '*Shelley v Kraemer*: Notes for a Revised Opinion' 110 Pa L R 473
Hepple B, 'The Impact on Labour Law' in Markesinis B (ed), *The Impact of the Human Rights Bill on English Law* (Oxford University Press, 1998)
Higginbotham A, 'Race, Sex, Education and Missouri Jurisprudence: *Shelley v Kraemer* in Historical Perspective' (1989) 67 Wash Univ LQ 673
Higgins R, 'Policy Considerations and the International Judicial Process' (1968) 17 ICLQ 58
—— 'The Taking of Property by the State: Recent Developments in International Law' (1982) 176 Recueil des Cours 259
—— Foreword to Harris D and Joseph S (eds), *The ICCPR in UK Law* (Clarendon Press, 1995)
Hill K, 'Freedom of the Media and the Criminal Law' (1992) NZLJ 278
Hoffman Lord, 'A Sense of Proportion', in Andenas M and Jacobs (eds), *European Community Law in the English Courts* (Clarendon Press, 1998)
—— 'The influence of the European principle of proportionality' in Ellis E (ed), *The Principle of Proportionality in the Laws of Europe* (Hart Publishing, 1999)

Hogg P W, 'Interpreting the Charter of Rights: Generosity and Justification' (1990) 28 Osgoode Hall LJ 817

Hooper Sir Anthony, 'The Impact of the Human Rights Act on Judicial Decision Making' [1998] EHRLR 676

Hope J, 'A Constitutional Right to a Fair Trial? Implications for the Reform of the Australian Criminal Justice System' (1996) 24 Federal LR 173

Horowitz M, 'The Misleading Search for State Action under the Fourteenth Amendment' 30 S Cal R 208

Howell J, 'Delay and Planning Judicial Review: 6 Weeks or Out?' [1999] JR 9

Hunt M, 'The "Horizontal Effect" of the Human Rights Act' [1998] PL 423

Hunter C and Dymond A, 'Housing Law' in Baker C (ed), *The Human Rights Act 1998: A Practitioner's Guide* (Sweet & Maxwell, 1998)

Irvine Lord, 'Activism and Restraint: human rights and the interpretative process' [1999] EHRLR 350

—— 'Constitutional Reform and a Bill of Rights' [1997] EHRLR 483

—— 'Judges and Decision-Makers: The Theory and Practice of Wednesbury Review' [1996] PL 591

—— 'Keynote address' in Beatson J, Forsythe C and Hare I (ed), *Constitutional Reform in the United Kingdom: Practice and Principles* (Hart Publishing, 1998)

—— 'Response to Sir John Laws' [1996] PL 636

—— 'The Legal System and Law Reform Under Labour' in Bean D (ed), *Law Reform for All* (Blackstone, 1996)

—— 'The Development of Human Rights in Britain Under an Incorporated Convention on Human Rights' [1998] PL 221

Ison T, 'A Constitutional Bill or Bills—The Canadian Experience' (1997) 60 MLR

Jacobs F, 'Recent Developments in the Principle of Proportionality in EC Law', in Ellis E (ed), *The Principle of Proportionality in the Laws of Europe* (Hart Publishing, 1999)

—— 'The Right to a Fair Trial in European Law' [1999] EHRLR 141

James R and Longley D, 'Judicial Review and Tragic Choices' [1995] PL 367

Jayawickrama N, 'The Bill of Rights' in Wacks R (ed), *Human Rights in Hong Kong* (Oxford University Press, 1992)

Jones T H, 'The Devaluation of Human Rights Under the European Convention' [1995] PL 430

Jones, 'Human Rights: Rights of Relatives of Victims—Views of the Human Rights Committee in the Quinteros Communication' (1984) 25 Harv I LJ 470

Joseph P, 'New Zealand's Bill of Rights Experience' in Alston P (ed), *Promoting Human Rights Through Bills of Rights: Comparative Perspectives* (Oxford University Press, 1999)

Jowell J, 'Is Equality a Constitutional Principle?' (1994) 7 CLP I

—— 'Of Vires and Vacuums: The Constitutional Context of Judicial Review' [1999] PL 448

—— 'The Rule of Law Today', in Jowell J and Oliver D, *The Changing Constitution* (Clarendon Press, 1994)

Jowell J and Lester A, 'Beyond Wednesbury: Substantive Principles of Administrative Law' [1987] PL 368

Judge D, 'Capital Punishment: Burke and Dicey Meet the European Convention on Human Rights' [1999] PL 6

Kahn-Freund O, 'The European Social Charter' in Jacobs F (ed), *European Law and the Individual*

Karsten I, 'Atypical Families and the Human Rights Act: The Rights of Unmarried Fathers, Same Sex Couples and Transsexuals' [1999] EHRLR 195

Kennett G, 'Individual Rights, the High Court and the Constitution' (1995) 19 Mel U L Rev No 3

Kentridge J, 'Equality' in Chaskalson M, *Constitutional Law of South Africa* (Juta, 1996)

Kentridge S, 'Lessons from South Africa' in Markesinis B (ed), *The Impact of the Human Rights Bill on English Law* (Oxford University Press, 1999)

—— 'Parliamentary Supremacy and the Judiciary under a Bill of Rights: some lessons from the Commonwealth' [1997] PL 96

—— 'The Incorporation of the European Convention on Human Rights' in Beatson J, Forsyth C and Hare I (eds), *Constitutional Reform in the United Kingdom: Practice and Principles* (Hart Publishing, 1998)

Kerrigan K, 'Unlocking the Human Rights Floodgates' [2000] Crim LR 71

Kidd, 'Disciplinary Proceedings and the Right to a Fair Trial Under the European Convention on Human Rights' (1987) 36 ICLQ 856

Kirby M, 'Lord Cooke and Fundamental Rights' in Rishworth R (ed), *The Struggle for Simplicity in the Law* (Butterworths, 1997)

Kitson T, 'The European Convention on Human Rights and Local Plans' [1998] JPL 321

Klerk Y and de Jonge E, 'The Netherlands' in Gearty C A (ed), *European Civil Liberties and the European Convention on Human Rights* (Kluwer, 1997)

Klug F, 'The Human Rights Act, *Pepper v Hart* and all that' [1999] PL 246

Klug F and Starmer K, 'Incorporation through the backdoor' [1997] PL 223

Klug F and Wadham K, 'The "Democratic Entrenchment" of a Bill of Rights: Liberty's proposals' [1993] PL 579

Kolinsky D, 'Advisory Declarations: Recent Developments' [1999] JR 231

Kramer M J, 'Rights without Trimmings', in Kramer M J, Simmonds NE & Steiner H, *A Debate Over Rights* (Clarendon Press, 1998)

Lavender N, 'The Problem of the Margin of Appreciation' [1997] EHRLR 380

Laws Sir John, 'Illegality: the problem of jurisdiction' in Supperstone M and Goudie J (eds), *Judicial Review* (2nd edn, Butterworths, 1997)

—— 'Is the High Court the Guardian of Fundamental Constitutional Rights?' [1993] PL 59

—— 'Judicial Remedies and the Constitution' (1994) 57 MLR 213

—— 'Law and Democracy' [1995] PL 72

—— 'Meiklejohn, The First Amendment and Free Speech in English Law' in Loveland I (ed), *Importing the First Amendment* (Hart Publishing, 1998)

—— 'Overview' in Beatson J, Forsythe C and Hare I, *The Human Rights Act and the Criminal Justice and Regulatory Process* (Hart Publishing, 1999)

—— 'The Constitution: Morals and Rights' [1996] PL 623

—— 'The Ghost in the Machine: Principle in Public Law' [1989] PL 27

—— 'The Limitation of Human Rights' [1998] PL 254
—— 'Wednesbury' in Forsyth C and Hare I (eds), *The Golden Metwand and the Crooked Cord* (Clarendon Press, 1998)
Lee E, 'The Declaration of Philidelphia: Restrospect and Prospect' (1994) 133 Int Lab Review 467
Lee H, 'The Australian High Court and Implied Fundamental Guarantees' [1993] PL 606
Lee S, 'Comment' [1985] PL 632
Leigh I and Lustgarten L, 'Horizontal Rights, the Human Rights Act and Privacy: Lessons from the Commonwealth' (1999) 48 ICLQ 57
—— 'Making Rights Real: the Courts, Remedies and the Human Rights Act; (1999) 58 CLJ 509
—— 'Spycatcher in Strasbourg' [1992] PL 200
Leigh L, 'Of Free Speech and Individual Reputation' in Loveland I (ed), *Importing the First Amendment* (Hart Publishing, 1998)
Leiper R, 'What is a "Good Reason" for Extending Time' [1996] JR 212
Lerner N, 'Religious Human Rights Under the United Nations' in van der Veyer J and Witte J (eds), *Religious Human Rights in the Global Perspective: Legal Perspectives* (Nijhoff, 1996)
Lester A, 'A Bill of Rights for England' (Charter 88, 1991) 1-047
—— 'Freedom of Expression' in St John Macdonald R St J, Matscher F and Petzold H (eds), *The European System for the Protection of Human Rights* (Kluwer, 1993)
—— 'Fundamental Rights: the United Kingdom Isolated' [1984] PL 47
—— 'Government Compliance with International Human Rights Law: a new year's legitimate expectation' [1996] PL 187
—— 'Impact of European Human Rights Law' [1996] JR 21 2-012
—— '*Pepper v Hart* Revisited' (1994) 15 Statute LR 10
—— 'Taking Human Rights Seriously' in Gordon R and Willmot-Smith R (eds), *Human Rights in the United Kingdom* (Oxford University Press, 1996)
—— 'The Art of the Possible—Interpreting Statutes Under the Human Rights Act' [1998] EHRLR 520 4-06
—— The Crisis Facing Human Rights in Europe; Does the British Government Really Care? (Charter 88, 1993)
—— 'The Impact of the Human Rights Act on Public Law' in Beatson J, Forsyth C and Hare I (eds), *Constitutional Reform in the United Kingdom: Practice and Principles* (Hart Publishing, 1998)
—— 'The Mouse that Roared: The Human Rights Bill 1995' [1995] PL 198 1-049 1-064
—— 'UK Acceptance of the Strasbourg Jurisdiction: What Really Went On in Whitehall in 1965' [1998] PL 237
—— 'Universality versus Subsidiarity: A Reply' [1998] EHRLR 73
Lester A and Pannick D, A Joint Opinion: Independent Schools and the European Convention on Human Rights (ISIS, 1982)
Leval P N, 'The No-Money, No-Fault Libel Suit: Keeping Sullivan in its Proper Place' (1988) 101 Harv LR 1287
Lewin K, 'The Significance of Constitutional Rights for Private Law; Theory and Practice in West Germany' (1968) 17 ICQR 572

Lewis-Anthony S, 'Case Law of Article 11 of the European Convention on Human Rights' in 'Freedom of Association', Reykjavik Seminar Proceedings, 3HA *Yearbook of the European Convention on Human Rights* (Nijhoff, 1993)

Liddy J, 'The Concept of Family Life Under the ECHR' [1998] EHRLR 15

Lightman G and Bowers J, 'Incorporation of the ECHR and its Impact on Employment Law' [1998] EHRLR 560

Linden T, 'Bodies Which are Bound by the Human Rights Act (1)' Lecture 6 November 1998 *The Human Rights Act and Public Law* (Justice)

Lister R, 'Welfare Rights and the Constitution' in Barnett A, Ellis C and Hirst P (eds) *Debating the Constitution* (Polity, 1993)

Livingstone S, 'Article 14 and the Prevention of Discrimination in the European Convention on Human Rights' [1997] EHRLR 25

Loveland I, '*Sullivan v The New York Times* Goes Down Under' [1996] PL 126

—— 'Privacy and Political Speech: A Agenda for the "Constitutionalisation" of the Law of Libel' in Birks P (ed), *Privacy and Loyalty* (Clarendon Press, 1997)

—— 'The Criminalisation of Racial Violence' in Loveland I (ed), *A Special Relationship* (Clarendon Press, 1995)

Low T, 'Financial Services: Parliamentary Anatomy of Human Rights' in *Wilberforce Chambers, The Essential Human Rights Act 1998* (Wilberforce Chambers, 2000)

Luba J, 'Acting on Rights—The Housing Implications of the Human Rights Act', Lecture, September 1999

Lyell Sir Nicholas, 'Whither Strasbourg? Why Britain Should Think Long and Hard before incorporating the European Convention on Human Rights' [1997] EHRLR 132

MacDonald R St J, 'The Margin of Appreciation' in Macdonald R St J, Matscher F and Petzold H (eds), *The European System for the Protection of Human Rights* (Kluwer, 1983)

Mackay Lord, 'Parliament and the Judges—A Constitutional Challenge', Lecture to the Citizenship Foundation 8 July, 1996

Madott D, 'Libel Law, Fiction, and the Charter' (1983) Vol 21:4 Osgoode Hall LJ 74

Mahoney P, 'Judicial Activism and Judicial Self-Restraint in the Court: Two Sides of the Same Coin' [1990] HRLJ 57

—— 'Marvellous Riches of Diversity or Invidious Cultural Relativism' 19 HRLJ 1

—— 'Universality versus Subsidiarity in the Strasbourg Case Law on Free Speech: Explaining Some Recent Judgments; [1997] EHRLR 364

—— 'Vindicating Rights: Excluding Evidence Obtained in Violation of the Bill of Rights' in Huscroft G and Rishworth P (eds), *Rights and Freedoms* (Brooker's, 1995)

Marcus G, 'Interpreting the Charter on Fundamental Rights' (1994) 10 SAJHR 92

Mariott J and Nichol D, 'The Human Rights Act, Representative Standing and the Victim Culture' [1998] EHRLR 730

Markesinis B, 'Privacy, Freedom of Expression and the Horizontal Effect of the Human Rights Bill: Lessons from Germany' (1999) 115 LQR 47

Markus K and Westgate M, 'Pre-emptive Costs Orders' [1998] JR 76

Marriott J and Nicholl D, 'The Human Rights Act, Representative Standing and the Victim Culture' [1998] EHRLR 730

Marshall G, 'Patriating Rights—Without Reservations' in Beatson J, Forsyth C and Hare I (eds), *Constitutional Reform in the United Kingdom: Practice and Procedure* (Hart Publishing, 1998)
Marston G, 'The United Kingdom's Part in the Preparation of the European Convention on Human Rights' (1993) 43 ICLQ 819
Martens S, 'Incorporating the European Convention: The Role of the Judiciary' [1998] EHRLR 5
McBride J, 'The Right to Property' (1996) 21 EL Rev Checklist No 1 40
—— 'Proportionality and the European Convention on Human Rights' in Ellis E (ed), *The Principle of Proportionality in the Laws of Europe* (Hart Publishing, 1999)
McCarthy R, 'The Human Rights Act and Social Services Functions', Lecture 10 May 1999
McCormick N, 'Rights in Legislation' in Hacker P and Raz J, *Law Morality and Society* (Clarendon Press 1977)
McCoy T, 'Current State Action theories, the Jackson Nexus Requirement and Employee Discharge by Semi-Public and State Aided Institutions' 31 Vand L Rev 785
McCrudden C, 'The Impact of Freedom of Speech' in Markesinis B (ed), *The Impact of the Human Rights Bill on English Law* (Oxford University Press, 1998)
McDonald M, 'Towards a Constitutional Analysis of non-Media Qualified Privilege' (1989) II DULJ (ns) 94
McDowell M, 'The Principle of Open Justice in a Civil Context' [1995] NZLR 214
McGoldrick D, 'The United Nations Convention on the Rights of the Child' (1991) 5 IJLF 132
McHarg A, 'Reconciling Human Rights and the Public Interest: Conceptual problems and Doctrinal Uncertainty in the Jurisprudence of the European Court of Human Rights' [1999] 62 MLR 671.
Meiklejohn A, 'The First Amendment is an Absolute' [1961] Sup Ct Rev 245
Michael J, 'Privacy' in Markesinis B (ed), *The Impact of the Human Rights Bill on English Law* (Oxford University Press, 1998)
Miles J, 'Standing Under the Human Rights Act 1998; Theories of Rights Enforcement and the Nature of Public Law Adjudication' [2000] 59 CLJ 133
Mills S, 'The International Labour Organisation, the United Kingdom and Freedom of Association: An Annual Cycle of Condemnation' [1997] EHRLR 35
Montgomery J, 'Children as Property' (1988) 51 MLR 323
Milton J, 'Areopagitica: A Speech for Licensed Printing' in *Prose Writings* (Everyman, 1958)
Moon G, 'The Draft Discrimination Protocol to the European Convention on Human Rights: A Progress Report' [2000] EHRLR 49
Moon R, '*R v Butler*: The Limits of the Supreme Court's Feminist Re-Interpretation of Section 163' (1993) 25:2 Ottawa LR 361
Morris G, 'Political Activities of Public Servants and Freedom of Expression' in Loveland I (ed), *Importing the First Amendment* (Hart Publishing, 1998)
—— 'The European Convention on Human Rights and Employment: To Which Acts Does it Apply?' [1999] EHRLR 498
—— 'The Human Rights Act and the Public/Private Divide in Employment Law' (1998) 27 ILJ 293
Morrison C C, 'The Margin of Appreciation in European Human Rights Law' (1970) 6 HRJ 263
Mowbray A, 'The European Court of Human Rights' Approach to Just Satisfaction [1997] PL 647

Mullally S, 'Equality Guarantees in Irish Constitutional Law—The Myth of Constitutionalism and the "Neutral" State' in T Murphy and P Twomey (eds), *Ireland's Evolving Constitution* (Hart Publishing, 1998)

Munday R, 'Inferences from Silence and European Human Rights Law' [1996] Crim LR 370

Murdoch J, 'Safeguarding the Liberty of the Person: Recent Strasbourg Jurisprudence' (1993) 42 ICLQ 494

Naismith S, 'Photographs, Privacy and Freedom of Expression' [1996] EHRLR 150

Nardell G, 'Collateral Thinking: The Human Rights Act and Public Law Defences' [1999] EHRLR 296

Neenan C, 'Reviewing Prerogative Powers: Roskill's List Revisited' [1998] JR 36

Neill B, 'Privacy: A Challenge for the Next Century' in Markesinis B (ed), *Protecting Privacy* (Oxford University Press, 1999)

Neuchatel Colloquy: Merger of the European Commission and European Court of Human Rights: Second Seminar on International Law and European Law at the University of Neuchatel 14-15 March 1986 (1987) HRLJ 8

Newbold A, 'The Crime/Fraud Exception to Legal Professional Privilege' (1990) 53 MLR 472

Nicol A and Rogers H, 'Contempt of Court, Reporting Restrictions and Disclosure of Sources' in *Yearbook of Copyright and Media Law*, Volume IV 1999 (Oxford University Press, 1999)

Nicolson and Reid, 'Arrest for Breach of the Peace and the European Convention on Human Rights' [1996] Crim LR 764

Nowicki M, 'Prevention and Remedy: New Standards for Domestic Protection of Rights' (1998/9) 12 Interights Bulletin 175

O'Donnell T, 'The Margin of Appreciation Doctrine: Standards in the Jurisprudence of the Court' (1982) 4 HRQ 474

O'Leary S, 'Accession by the European Community to the European Convention on Human Rights—The Opinion of the ECJ' [1996] EHRLR 362

Oliver D, 'Is the Ultra Vires rule the basis of judicial review' [1987] PL 543

Olowofoyeku A, 'State Liability for the Exercise of Judicial Power' [1998] PL 444

Opsahl T, 'The Right to Life' in MacDonald R St J, Matscher F and Petzold H (eds), *The European System for the Protection of Human Rights* (Dordrecht, Nijhoff, 1993)

Optican S, 'Rolling Back s 21 of the Bill of Rights' [1997] NZLJ 42

Osborne C, 'Does the End Justify the Means? Retrospectivity, Article 7 and the Marital Rape Exemption' [1996] EHRLR 406

O'Sullivan D, 'The Allocation of Scarce Resources and the Right to Life Under the European Convention on Human Rights' [1998] PL 389

Owen T, 'Prisoners and Fundamental Rights' [1997] JR 81

Owen R, 'Impact of European Convention on Human Rights on Medical Negligence and Personal Injury Litigation' in *JUSTICE, The Human Rights Act and Common Law*, Seminar, 25 September 1998

Palmer E, 'Limitation Periods in Cases of Sexual Abuse: A response Under the European Convention' [1996] EHRLR III

Pannick D, 'Judicial Review of Sporting Bodies' [1997] JR 150

—— 'Principles of interpretation of Convention Rights Under the Human Rights Act and Discretionary Areas of Judgment' [1998] PL 545

—— 'Religious Feelings and the European Court' [1995] PL 7

Peacock J and Fitzpatrick F, 'Tax Law' in Baker C (ed), *The Human Rights Act 1998: A Practitioner's Guide* (Sweet & Maxwell, 1998)

Peck S, 'An Analytical Framework for the Application of the Charter' (1987) 25 Osgoode Hall LJ 1

Penner R, 'The Canadian experience with the Charter of Rights: are there lessons for the United Kingdom?' [1996] PL 104

Petter A, 'Canada's Charter Flight: Soaring Backwards into the Future' (1989) 16 Journal of Law and Society 151

Petter A and Monahan P, 'Developments in Constitutional Theory: The decision in Dolphin Delivery', in Devlin R F (ed), *Constitutional Interpretation* (Edmond Montgomery, 1991)

Petzold H, 'The Convention and the Principle of Subsidiarity' in McDonald R St J, Matscher F and Petzold H (eds), *The European System for the Protection of Human Rights* (Nijhoff, 1993)

Phillips M J, 'The Inevitable Incoherence of Modern State Action Doctrine' [1984] St Louis ULJ 683

Phillips S, 'The Court v the Executive: Old Battles on New Battlegrounds?' [1996] EHRLR 45

Phillipson G, 'The Human Rights Act, "Horizontal Effect" and the Common Law: a Bang or a Whimper?' (1999) 62 MLR 824

Picard E, 'The Right to Privacy in French Law' in Markesinis B (ed), *Protecting Privacy* (Oxford University Press, 1999)

Pilkington, 'Damages as a Remedy for the Infringement of the Canadian Charter of Rights and Freedoms' (1984) 62 Canadian Bar Review 517

Plant R, 'Citizenship Rights and Welfare' in Coote A (ed), *The Welfare of Citizens* (Rivers Oram, 1992)

Plucknett T, 'Dr Bonham's Case and Judicial Review' (1926) 40 Harv L Rev 35

Pollard D, 'Judicial Review of the Prerogative Power in the United Kingdom and France in Leyland P and Woods T, *Administrative Law Facing the Future: Old Constraints and New Horizons* (Blackstone Press, 1997)

Poulter S, 'Towards Legislative Reform of the Blasphemy and Racial Hatred Laws' [1991] PL 371

Prosser W, 'Privacy' (1960) 48 Calif Review 383

Quint P, 'Free Speech and Private Law in German Constitutional Theory' (1989) 48 Maryland LR 247

Raggi R, 'An Independent Right to Freedom of Association' (1977) 12 Harv CR-CLL R I

Ramraj V, 'Keegstra, Butler and Positive Liberty: A Glimmer of Hope for the Faithful', Vol 51:2 University of Toronto Faculty of Law Review 304

Raz J, 'Professor Dworkin's Theory of Rights' 26 Political Studies 123

Reich C, 'The New Property' (1964) 73 Yale LJ 733

Reiner R and Leigh L, 'Police Powers' in McCrudden and Chambers (eds), *Individual Rights and the Law in Britain* (Oxford University Press, 1994)

Renouf S, '"One More Battle to Fight": Trade Union Rights and Freedom of Association in Canada' [1989] Vol 27:2 ALR 226

Richards Sir Stephen, 'The Impact of Article 6 of the ECHR on Judicial Review' [1999] JR 106

Rishworth P, 'Coming Conflicts Over Freedom of Religion' in Huscroft G and Rishworth P (eds), *Rights and Freedoms* (Brookers, 1995)

—— 'Reflections on the Bill of Rights After *Quilter v Attorney-General*' [1998] NZLR 683

Rishworth R, 'Lord Cooke and the Bill of Rights' in Rishworth R (ed), *The Struggle for Simplicity in the Law* (Butterworths, 1997)

Roberts P, 'Taking the Burden of Proof Seriously' [1995] Crim LR 783

Ryan A, 'The British, the Americans and Rights' in Lacey and the Haakonssen, *A Culture of Rights* (Cambridge University Press, 1991)

Ryssdal R, 'The Coming of Age of the European Convention on Human Rights' (1996) 1 EHRLR 18

Salgado R, 'Protection of Nationals' Rights to Property under the European Convention on Human Rights: *Lithgow v United Kingdom*' 27 Virginia Journal of International Law 865

Sands P, 'Human Rights, Environment and the Lopez-Ostra Case' [1996] EHRLR 597

Sartorius R, 'Hart's Concept of Law', in Summers R (ed), *More Essays in Legal Philosophy* (1971)

Schermers H G, 'Adaptation of the 11th Protocol to the European Convention on Human Rights' (1995) 20 ELR 559

—— 'International Protection of the Right to Property' in Matscher and Petzold (eds), *Protecting Human Rights—the European Dimension: Essays in Honour of G H Wiarde* (Koln, 1990)

Schiemann K, 'Interventions in Public Interest Cases' [1996] PL 240

Schneider R, 'State Action—Making Sense out of Chaos—an Historical Approach' 37 U Fla L R 737

Schwartz H, 'The Short Happy Life and the Tragic Death of the New Zealand Bill of Rights Act' [1998] NZLR 259

Schwarzchild M, 'Value Pluralism and the Constitution: in Defense of the State Action Doctrine' (1988) 5 Supreme Court 129

Schwelb E, 'The Protection of the Right of Property of Nationals Under the First Protocol to the European Convention on Human Rights' *(1964)* 13 American Journal of Comparative Law 518

Sedley Sir Stephen, 'Human Rights: A Twenty-First Century Agenda' [1995] PL 386

—— 'Law and Public Life' in Nolan M and Sedley S (eds), *The Making and Remaking of the British Constitution* (Blackstone, 1997)

—— 'The Sounds of Silence: Constitutional Law Without a Constitution' (1994) 110 LQR 270

—— 'Public Power and Private Power' in *Freedom Law and Justice* (Sweet & Maxwell, 1999)

—— 'The Common Law and the Constitution' in Nolan Lord and Sedley Sir Stephen, *The Making and Remaking of the British Constitution* (Blackstone, 1997)

—— 'The Crown In Its Own Courts', in Forsyth C and Hare I, *The Golden Metwand and the Crooked Cord* (Clarendon Press)

—— 'The First Amendment: A Case for Import Controls?' in Loveland I (ed), *Importing the First Amendment* (Hart Publishing, 1998)

Sharpe S, 'Article 6 and the Disclosure of Evidence in Criminal Trials' [1999] Crim LR 273
Shaw A and Butler A, 'Arbitrary Arrest and Detention Under the New Zealand Bill of Rights' [1993] NZLJ 139
Sherlock A, 'Deportation of Aliens and Article 8 ECHR' (1998) 23 ELR Checklist No 1, HR 62
Singh R, 'Privacy and the Media After the Human Rights Act' [1998] EHRLR 712
Singh S, Hunt M and Demetriou M, 'Is There a Role for the "Margin of Appreciation" in National Law After the Human Rights Act' [1999] EHRLR 15
Sloljar S, 'A Re-examination of Privacy' (1984) 4 LS 67
Smallbone D, 'Recent Suggestions of an Implied "Bill of Rights" in the Constitution Considered as Part of a General Trend of Constitutional Interpretation' (1993) 22 FLR 254
Smillie J, 'The Allure of "Rights Talk"' (1994) 8:2 Otago LR 188
Smith A T H, 'Judicial Law-Making in the Criminal Law' (1984) 100 LQR 46
—— 'The Human Rights Act and the Criminal Lawyer: The Constitutional Context [1999] Crim LR 231
—— 'The Public Order Act 1986 Part I: The New Offences' [1987] Crim LR 156
Smyth M, 'The United Kingdom's Incorporation of the European Convention and its Implications for Business' [1998] EHRLR 273
Starmer K, 'Reviewing the Margin of Appreciation in the Dynamics of the European Human Rights Jurisprudence' [1998] EHLRR 357
Stavros S, 'Freedom of Religion and Claims for Exemption from Generally Applicable, Neutral Laws: Lessons from Across the Pond?' [1997] EHRLR 607
Steiner E, 'France' in Gearty C A (ed), *European Civil Liberties and the European Convention on Human Rights* (Kluwer, 1997)
Stevens J and Feldman D, 'Broadcasting Advertisements by Bodies with Political Objects, Judicial Review and the Influence of Charities Law' [1997] PL 615
Steyn K, 'Consistency—A Principle of Public Law' [1997] JR 22
—— 'Incorporation and Devolution—a few reflections on the challenging scene' [1998] EHRLR 153
—— 'The Role of the Bar, the Judge and the Jury' [1999] PL 51
Steyn K and Wolfe D, 'Judicial Review and the Human Rights Act: Some Practical Considerations' [1999] EHRLR 614
Stoll H, 'General Rights to Personality in German Law' in Markesinis B (ed), *Protecting Privacy* (Oxford University Press, 1999)
Stone R, 'Exclusion of Evidence Under Section 78 of the Police and Criminal Evidence Act: Practice and Principles' [1995] 3 Web JCLI
Storey N, 'Implications of the ECHR in the Immigration and Asylum Context' [1998] EHRLR 452
Stoykewych R, 'Street Legal: Constitutional Protection of Public Demonstration in Canada' (1985) 43 UTFLR 43
Straw J and Boateny P, 'Bringing Rights Home: Labour's Plans to Incorporate the European Convention on Human Rights into UK Law' [1997] EHRLR 71
Strickland H C, 'The State Action Doctrine and the Rehnquist Court' (1991) 18 Hastings Const LQ 577
Supperstone M and Coppel J, 'Judicial Review after the Human Rights Act' [1999] EHRLR 301

Swede R 'One Territory—Three Systems? the Hong Kong Bill of Rights' [1995] 44 ICLQ 360
Sze Ping-fat, 'Freedom of the Press' (1996) 16 Lit 291
—— 'Freedom of the Press Revisited' (1997) 17 Lit 50

Taggart M, 'Tugging on Superman's Cape: Lessons from the Experience with the New Zealand Bill of Rights' [1998] PL 266
Tarnopolsky W S, 'Just Deserts or Cruel and Unusual Treatment or Punishment? Where Do We Look for Guidance?' (1978) 10 Ottawa LR I
Thomas D, 'Incorporating the European Convention on Human Rights: its Impact on Sentencing Law' in Beatson J, Forsyth C and Hare I (eds), *The Human Rights Act and the Criminal Justice and Regulatory Process* (Hart Publishing, 1999)
Thorne S, 'Dr Bonham's Case' (1938) LQR 543
Thorold O, 'Implications of the Convention for UK Mental Health Legislation' [1996] EHRLR 619
Tierney S, 'Press Freedom and Public Interest: The Developing Jurisprudence of the European Court of Human Rights' [1998] EHRLR 419
Tomuschat C, 'Freedom of Association' in MacDonald R, Matscher F and Petzold H (eds), *The European System for the Protection of Human Rights* (Nijhoff, 1993)
Toube D, 'Requiring Reasons at Common Law' [1997] JR 68
Treacey V, 'Prisoners' Rights Lost in Semantics' (1989) 28 Howard J of Criminal Law 27
Trechsel S, 'The Right to Liberty and Security of the Person—Article 5 of the European Convention on Human Rights in the Strasbourg Case Law' (1980) 1 HRLJ 88
Tribe L, 'The Puzzling Persistence of Process-Based Constitutional Theory' (1980) 89 Yale LJ 1063
—— 'Refocusing the State Action Inquiry' in Constitutional Choices (Harvard University Press, 1985)
Tridimas T, 'Proportionality in Community Law: Searching for the Appropriate Standard of Scrutiny' in Ellis E (ed), *The Principle of Proportionality in the Laws of Europe* (Hart Publishing, 1999)
Tushnet M, '*Shelley v Kraemer* and Theories of Equality' 33 New York School of Law R 383 5-056

Van Alstyne W and Karst K, 'State Action' 14 Stan LR 3
Van Bueren G, 'Education: Whose Right is it Anyway?' in Heffernan L (ed), *Human Rights: A European Perspective* (Round Hall Press, 1994)
—— 'The UN Convention on the Rights of the Child' (1991) 3 JCL 63
van Dijk P, 'Access to the Court' in MacDonald R St J, Matscher F and Petzold H (eds), *The European System for the Protection of Human Rights* (Kluwer, 1983)
van Gervin W, 'The Effect of Proportionality on Actions of Member States of the European Community: National Viewpoints from Continental Europe' in Ellis E (ed), *The Principle of Proportionality in the Laws of Europe* (Hart Publishing, 1999)
Vermeulen, 'Scope and Limits of Conscientious Objections' in *Proceedings of the Council of Europe: Seminar on Freedom of Conscience* (Council of Europe Press, 1992)
Vickers L, 'Whistleblowing in the Public Sector and the ECHR' [1997] PL 594
Vogt E, 'Dupond Reconsidered: or the "Search for the Constitution and the Truth of Things Generally"' (1982) Charter Edition, UBCLR 141

Voss E, 'Germany' in Gearty C A (ed), *European Civil Liberties and the European Convention on Human Rights* (Kluwer, 1997)

Wacks R, 'The Poverty of "Privacy"' (1980) 96 LQR 73
Wade Sir William, 'Habeas Corpus and Judicial Review' (1997) 113 LQR 55
—— 'Horizons of Horizontality' (2000) 116 LQR 217
—— 'Human Rights and the Judiciary' [1998] EHRLR 520
—— 'Sovereignty and the European Communities' (1972) 88 LQR I
—— 'Supremacy: Revolution or Evolution' (1996) 112 LQR 568 1-074
—— 'The basis of legal sovereignty' [1955] CLJ 172
—— 'The United Kingdom's Bill of Rights' in Beatson J, Forsyth C and Hare I (eds), *Constitutional Reform in the United Kingdom: Practice and Principles* (Hart Publishing, 1998)
—— 'What has happened to the Sovereignty of Parliament' (1991) 107 LQR I
Wadham J, 'A Bill of Rights' in Bean D (ed), *Law Reform for All* (Blackstone, 1996)
—— 'The Intelligence Services Act 1994' (1994) 57 MLR 916
—— 'Why Incorporation of the European Convention on Human Rights is Not Enough' in Gordon R and Wilmott-Smith R, *Human Rights in the United Kingdom* (Oxford University Press, 1996)
Walkate J, 'The Right of Everyone to Change His Religion or Belief' (1983) 2 Neth Int L R 146
Walker C P, 'Prisoners in Parliament—Another View' [1982] PL 389
Walker P, 'Unreasonableness and Proportionality' in Supperstone M and Goudie J (eds), *Judicial Review* (2nd edn, Butterworths, 1997)
Walker Sir Robert, 'Impact of European Standards on the Right to a Fair Trial in Civil Proceedings in English Domestic Law' [1999] EHRLR 4
Wallington P, 'Discretionary Powers—the Limits of Legality' in Supperstone M and Goudie J (eds), *Judicial Review* (2nd edn, Butterworths, 1997)
Walsh B, 'The United Nations Convention on the Rights of the Child: a British View' (1991) 5 IJLF 170
Warbrick C, 'The Structure of Article 8' [1998] EHRLR 32
Warner J P, 'The Relationship between European Community Law and the National Laws of member States' (1977) 93 LQR 349
Warren S and Brandeis L, 'The Right to Privacy' (1890) 4 Harv LR 193
Watson J, 'Badmouthing the Bench: Is There a Clear and Present Danger? To What?' (1992) 56 Saskatchewan L Rev 113
Watt B, 'The Legal Protection of HIV and Health Care Workers and the Human Rights Jurisprudence of the European Court of Justice' [1998] EHRLR 301
Weber J, 'The King's Peace: A Comparative Study' (1989) 10 J of Legal History 135
Weiler J H H and Lockhart N H S, 'Taking Rights Seriously: the European Court and its Fundamental Rights Jurisprudence' (1995) 32 CMLR 51
Weir T, 'Downhill—All the Way' [1999] 1 FLR 193
Weschler H, 'Towards Neutral Principles of Constitutional Law' 73 Harv L Rev I
White R, 'Social Security' in Baker C (ed), *The Human Rights Act 1998: A Practitioner's Guide* (Sweet & Maxwell, 1998)
Whitman, 'Constitutional Torts' (1980) 79 Mich LR 5
Widdows K, 'The Denounciation of International Labour Conventions' (1994) 33 ICLQ 1052

Wildhaber L, 'Right to Education and Parental Rights' in Macdonald R St J, Matscher F and Petzold H (eds), *The European System for the Protection of Human Rights* (Nijhoff, 1993)
Williams G, 'Preventive Justice and the Rule of Law' (1953) 16 MLR 417
Wintemute R, 'Lesbian and Gay Britons, the Two Europes and the Bill of Rights Debate' [1997] EHRLR 466
—— 'Recognising New Kinds of Direct Sex Discrimination: Transsexualism, Sexual Orientation and Dress Codes' (1997) 60 MLR 334
Winterton G, 'Extra-Constitutional Notions in Australian Constitutional Law' [1986] 16 FLR 223
—— 'The British Grundnorm: Parliamentary Sovereignty Re-examined' (1976) 92 LQR 591
Wong W, 'The Sunday Times Case: Freedom of Expression vs English Contempt of Court Laws in the Court' 17 New York University Journal of International Law and Politics 35
Woolf Lord, 'Droit Public—English Style' [1995] PL 57

Young R, 'The Merits of Legal Aid in the Magistrates' Court' [1993] Crim LR 336
—— 'Will Widgery Do?: Court Clerks, Discretion and the Determination of Legal Aid' in Young R and Wall D (eds), *Access to Criminal Justice: Legal Aid, Lawyers and the Defence of Liberty* (Blackstone Press, 1996)

Zines L, 'A judicially created bill of rights' (1994) 16 Syd LR 166